P9-CKE-894

ISAIAH BERLIN

Michael Ignatieff was born in Toronto, educated at the University of Toronto, and gained a doctorate in history at Harvard. He was senior research fellow at King's College, Cambridge, for several years and has held visiting posts in France, the USA and Canada. His books range from *The Needs of Strangers*, an essay on the philosophy of human needs, to a family memoir, *The Russian Album*, and two novels, including *Scar Tissue* which was shortlisted for the Booker Prize. In 1993, he wrote and presented the prize-winning television series, *Blood and Belonging,* and in early 1998 published his study of morality in modern conflict, *The Warrior's Honor*. His most recent book is *The Virtual War: Kosovo and Beyond*. He lives in London.

ALSO BY MICHAEL IGNATIEFF

Fiction

Asya

Scar Tissue

Non-Fiction

A Just Measure of Pain

The Needs of Strangers

The Russian Album

Blood and Belonging: Journeys into the New Nationalism

The Warrior's Honour: Ethnic War and the Modern Conscience

The Virtual War: Kosovo and Beyond

'A beautifully organised biography. Not only does it underline the importance of Berlin's contribution to contemporary thought...it also highlights his humanity, and his prodigious capacity as a conversationalist'
Independent

'Michael Ignatieff's life of Berlin is elegant and vivid...this is a brilliant profile...Those of us who owe so much to Berlin, now owe to Ignatieff the possibility that others will start to understand our debt'
Scotsman

'An admirable biography of an intellectual life... handled with intelligence and understanding'
Sunday Telegraph

'A witty, sensitive, self-effacing life of Isaiah Berlin'
Miranda Seymour, *Independent*

'A fine biography of the most remarkable intellectual of his generation'
Literary Review

'An intelligent and sympathetic biography'
Independent on Sunday

'Ignatieff has composed a brilliant *sinfonia eroica* out of the myriad themes of Berlin's life'
Daily Telegraph

'A sterling biography of one of the intellectual touchstones of this century...What a mind, what a life, what a book!
Canada Post

Isaiah Berlin, by Steve Pyke, 14 June 1990

Michael Ignatieff

ISAIAH BERLIN

A Life

V

VINTAGE

Published by Vintage 2000

2 4 6 8 10 9 7 5 3 1

Copyright © Michael Ignatieff 1998

The right of Michael Ignatieff to be identified as the author of this work has been asserted by him in accordance with the Copyright, Designs and Patents Act, 1988

This book is sold subject to the condition that it shall not by way of trade or otherwise, be lent, resold, hired out, or otherwise circulated without the publisher's prior consent in any form of binding or cover other than that in which it is published and without a similar condition including this condition being imposed on the subsequent purchaser

First published in Great Britain by
Chatto & Windus in 1998

Vintage
Random House, 20 Vauxhall Bridge Road,
London SW1V 2SA

Random House Australia (Pty) Limited
20 Alfred Street, Milsons Point, Sydney
New South Wales 2061, Australia

Random House New Zealand Limited
18 Poland Road, Glenfield, Auckland 10,
New Zealand

Random House (Pty) Limited
Endulini, 5A Jubilee Road, Parktown 2193,
South Africa

The Random House Group Limited Reg. No. 954009
www.randomhouse.co.uk

A CIP catalogue record for this book
is available from the British Library

ISBN 0 09 957731 3

Papers used by Random House are natural, recyclable products made from wood grown in sustainable forests. The manufacturing processes conform to the environmental regulations of the country of origin

Printed and bound in Great Britain by
Cox & Wyman Limited, Reading, Berkshire

i

For S. Z.

Contents

Illustrations

1

Albany

Albany is set back behind a small carriage yard off Piccadilly, opposite Hatchards bookshop and Fortnum & Mason's. It was established in the late eighteenth century as a residence for gentlemen with estates in the country who wished to have a *pied-à-terre* in town. In the long lobby leading to the garden there is a bust of Byron, who lived there in 1816, and plaques to other Victorian worthies, Lord Melbourne, Lord Chancellor Eldon and Viscount Palmerston. All the male English institutions – the public schools, the Oxford and Cambridge colleges, the London clubs, the Inns of Court – have a family resemblance, and the Albany belongs to that family. The corridor is high, cold and austere; the mosaic tiles gleam underfoot; and there are burnished boards high on the walls, listing the secretaries of the management committee, running continuously back to 1799.

His rooms lie at the end of the covered wooden walkway that extends the length of the garden. Framed between sashed curtains, gentlemen can be seen taking tea in their drawing rooms. All of his life has been spent in places just like this, in the walled gardens and high-windowed rooms of English institutional privilege.

He answers the bell himself and allows himself to be kissed, in the Russian fashion, once on each cheek and once for good measure. It is a declaration of our common Russian ancestry, the formal beginning and ending to all our meetings. He always wears the same sober, dark-

I

coloured suit, with a buttoned waistcoat and cuffed trousers. The tailoring is conservative, the worsted of the best quality. His black lace-up shoes are well polished and fissured with tiny cracks of age. He usually wears one particular tie with a pattern of Penny Black stamps. Dangling from his waistcoat pocket, at the end of a chain, is a lorgnette-like pair of pearl magnifiers, which he places on top of his glasses in order to read small print.

He leads me into a cosy room with a view of the walkway and a fine set of eighteenth-century French etchings on the walls. Embossed invitations line the mantelpiece. He slowly settles down into the battered, white easy chair next to the fire. The phone is at his elbow and it rings often. When it does, the same sequence of gestures ensues. He mutters, 'With pleasure, with pleasure, now let me see', cups the receiver between neck and shoulder, retrieves his diary from his waistcoat pocket, pushes his glasses above his eyebrows, places his pince-nez on the bridge of his nose, fingers the diary pages, ponders, then says, 'Wednesday at 3 p.m.', scribbles, re-pockets his diary, puts down the phone, blinks and says, 'Now where were we?' His social network stretches from Jerusalem to Washington, from his generation to my own; the web encompasses academe, publishing, politics and the arts, and a good part of his life now is spent keeping up with its intrigues, dramas, fallings-out and comings back together.

In front of him on the coffee table are spread a cluster of tins containing salted almonds and a type of Finnish crispbread, which he spirits along to dinner parties in his suit pockets. On the bookcase nearest his chair rises a ziggurat of chocolate bars. He is an inveterate nibbler, popping nuts and chocolate into his mouth as he talks, leaning forward in his chair to forage in the tins with his right hand. The left arm usually remains curled in, close to his body.

Next to the tins is a newly published book, often from a former student ('I never read anything any more,' he sighs), a plump manuscript of his, revised by his editor Henry Hardy and awaiting his reaction ('I can't bear to read *myself*, let alone anybody else'). But each morning he avidly peruses *The Times*. The faces stare up from its obituary pages – the wife of a Law Lord, a professor of physics, and once a woman he loved.[1] He lingered over her face: 'Wildly untruthful she was. Wildly. But desirable to the last degree.' He shakes his head. 'All I seem to do at my age is attend funerals.' In teasing mode, I report that in Paris they say, '*Mais Berlin est mort, n'est-ce pas?*' 'Perhaps I am,' he says with a small smile.

In the pictures of him in the 1930s – walking in Magdalen Gardens, standing in a slanting beam of light in All Souls' quad – he is a plump, small-shouldered figure in a three-piece suit, with curly black hair and dark eyes behind thick glasses, his right hand cupping his left arm at the elbow. He half-turns away from the camera or strikes a mock-solemn pose. His oldest friends say he has changed little. 'A baby elephant, always the same baby elephant,' Stephen Spender said to me.[2] In the earliest pictures of him taken by a Riga society photographer in 1910, even at the age of one, his eyes are striking – large, dark, playful, intelligent, already amused. He has kept the certainties he began with, as the loved only child of a prosperous Jewish merchant's family. The same gaze still meets the world eighty-seven years later.

His voice is astonishingly rapid and, for the uninitiated, nearly incomprehensible. Joseph Brodsky once said that his English was just like his Russian, only faster, 'courting the speed of light'.[3] He seems to bubble and rattle like a samovar on the boil. Virginia Woolf, who first met him at a dinner in New College in November 1933, said that he looked like a swarthy Portuguese Jew and talked with the vivacity and assurance of a young Maynard Keynes.[4] The genealogy of his vocal mannerisms is the story of how all the layers of his identity settled into his voice. In the earliest tapes of his lectures, the voice is a Russian impersonation of strangulated Oxford upper-class diction, all tight lips and clipped vowel sounds, unconsciously borrowed from the beau ideal of the 1930s, his lifelong friend and rival, Maurice Bowra. Old friends, like George Weidenfeld, also hear some of David Cecil in the melodic gabbling, the helter-skelter pace. It is ironic that the voice which two generations of British radio listeners took to be the voice of the Oxford intellect should actually have been a Riga Jew's unconscious impersonation of his English contemporaries. Over time, it went from being an impersonation to being the man himself. Now, in the last quarter of his life, Russian recidivism has occurred. Old Slavic and Jewish sonorities have re-asserted themselves and the delivery has slowed from a gabble to a confidential murmur.

The voice is the despair of typists and stenographers: there seems nothing to cling to, no pauses, no paragraphing, no full stops. Yet after a time one learns that the murmur has an arcane precision all its own. There are sentences always; paragraphs always. Even if the subordinate clauses open up a parenthesis that seems to last for ever, they do close, eventually, in a completed thought. Each sentence carries clarity along its spine with qualification entwined around it. The order is melodic, intuitive and associational rather than logical. This darting, leaping style of speaking is a style of thinking: he outlines a proposition and anticipates objections and qualifications as he speaks, so that both proposition and qualification are spun out in one and the same sentence simultaneously. Since he dictates all of his written work, the way he writes and the way he talks are identical: ornate, elaborate, old-fashioned, yet incisive and clear. Judging from school compositions, he was writing and talking like this when he was eleven.

Inarticulate intelligences have to struggle across the gulf between word and thought; with him, word and thought lead each other on unstoppably. He suspects his own facility and thinks that inarticulate intelligence may be deeper and more authentic, but his facility is one secret of his serenity. Words come at his bidding and they form into sentences and paragraphs as quickly as he can bring them on. Since the Romantics, the life of the mind has been associated with solitude, anguish and inner division. With him, it has been synonymous with wit, irony and pleasure.

To love thinking, as he does, you must be quick, but you must also be sociable. He hates thinking alone and regards it as a monstrosity. With him, thinking is indistinguishable from talking, from striking sparks, from bantering, parrying and playing. His talk is famous, not only because it is quick and acute, but because it implies that thought is a joint sortie into the unknown. What people remember about his conversation is not what he said – he is no wit and no epigrams have attached themselves to his name – but the experience of having been drawn into the salon of his mind. This is why his conversation is never a performance. It is not his way of putting on a show; it is his way of being in company.

He will tell you that he is 'intolerably ugly'. Certainly it is a noble rather than a handsome face, but age has thinned him down, greying the hair around his balding head, exposing the eyebrows, the expressive nose and the strong cheek and jaw-lines. When he is not pursing his lips into a frown or a mock expression of disapproval, they have a fine, full shape.

He looks now as if he was always supposed to look like this, as if his whole life was leading him towards this appearance of rabbinical wisdom. But it is an ironic result, since he is by conviction and temperament as unrabbinical as it is possible for an old Jew to be.

Ageing has been a gentle gradient so far, but it is getting steeper. He has the small-shouldered stoop of an old man. His hearing is less good than it used to be: he finds it hard to follow the ebb and flow of talk around the long, baize-covered table where the fellows gather for All Souls' elections; and he finds large dinner parties a trial; but concerts give him and his wife, Aline, as much pleasure as ever. Every performance is inventoried in his mind in a receding series, stretching back to the Salzburg of the 1930s, to the Queen's Hall, to auditoria long demolished and performers – Kempf, Schnabel, Solomon, Lipatti – long departed.

Being renowned for acuteness of mind means that his friends watch him – and he watches himself – for any signs of falling off. As far as he is concerned, falling off is occurring daily. 'I can't remember a thing,' he will say, and then, just to confound his fears, he will set about ('Wait, wait, here it comes') retrieving the name of a conductor in a Salzburg festival programme in August 1932. His memory is freakish, so unusually fine-grained as to seem scarcely human, and so effortlessly in command of his past that he gives the impression of having accumulated everything and lost nothing.

He always claims that he does not find himself in the least interesting. This is artful and disingenuous, since many of his best stories are about himself, but it is true that he seems self-contained rather than self-absorbed. He does listen to other human beings and appears to hear what they say, though it is a curious and not especially warm form of listening, more like a pause between his own talk. He is often criticised by activist friends for being more interested in inner experience than in public commitment. But that is the man: more curious about the varieties of human self-deception than *realpolitik*.

His only noticeable form of narcissism is hypochondria. He likes being mildly, curably ill. He loves doctors, regimes, nursing homes; he will take to his bed at the slightest provocation. Students remember him conducting tutorials from his bed, the covers scattered with books, papers, cups of tea and biscuits. On the night table of the small single bed where he sleeps now, next to his wife's room, there is a platoon of pill bottles, ointments, boxes, tumblers of water. He will tell you he is faring badly, but the truth is that he has benefited from an almost complete dispensation from the ills of the flesh. His good fortune, in this and almost every other respect, is maddening. To the degree that luck is a real category shaping lives, he is one of the luckiest men alive.

The thought of writing his memoirs fills him with dismay. 'Never,' he says and then shudders with comic finality. Besides, he fears his own candour and does not want it to find its way into print. But if he wasn't going to write his own life, then who, said his friends, would capture some of his talk before it was lost? That was how this book began in September 1987. I was not a former student or surrogate son: he seems to have been born without a paternal instinct. I was simply there, initially, to interview him. I taped his talk, hour after hour, like a servant taking buckets to a fountain. When he agreed to a biography, after we had worked together for several years, it was his decision that it be published posthumously, and that he should not read a word of it. 'Après moi le déluge,' he said.

The afternoons at Albany continued for a decade. Beneath the continuous low murmur of his voice, the tape recorder on the low coffee table also picked up the click of almonds in their tins and registered the chimes of the French clock on the mantelpiece as it sounded the hours. One question from me would set him talking for an hour as he roved back and forward, telling and re-telling the old stories, sweeping across decades, past famous faces, pausing over obscure people for the simple pleasure of proving to himself that they had not been forgotten. The ambition was to enfold all his experience – literally every last letter and bus-ticket, every remembered joke and remark – into a crisp, economical story which, once elaborated, polished and given its punch-line, could then be filed away in the labyrinthine archive of his mind, safe from the ruin of time. It was a virtuoso display of a great intelligence doing battle with loss.

I heard the same stories many times, as if repetition proved that he had mastered his life, penetrated its darkest corners and dispelled its silences. It became obvious why he never wrote an autobiography: his stories had done the trick. They both saved the past and saved him from introspection.

His candour about his past, like the candour about his illnesses, was very Russian. He told me everything, but only when I learned to ask the right questions. He let me read his letters, and they turned out to be as spontaneous as his talk. He was prodigal with words and time. To an obscure graduate student in Oregon he would expound his distinction between two concepts of liberty with the same gusto that he devoted to sharing gossip with Arthur Schlesinger Jr. In this endless flow of verbal facility, it seemed as if he genuinely believed that he could be personal with almost anyone.

He was candid about sex; more than candid about his friends; candid about his failings. He liked to say that his success – professorships, a knighthood, the Order of Merit – depended upon a systematic over-estimation of his abilities. 'Long may this continue,' he always said.

Self-denigration came naturally, but it was also a pre-emptive strike against criticism. 'I am an intellectual taxi; people flag me down and give me destinations and off I go' was all he would ever offer, when pressed to say what his intellectual agenda had been. Yet this was wrong. Many of his essays were demanded of him by chance and circumstances, but he accepted only the assignments that fitted his own itinerary. There is no doubt that there was an itinerary and, when he had completed it, the result was a unique and coherent body of work. To use the distinction he made famous, the range of his work may make him seem like a fox, who knows many things; in reality, he was a hedgehog, who knew one big thing. One purpose of this book is to elaborate what this one big thing was.

To know one big thing he had to master all the strands within himself. He took three conflicting identities, Russian, Jewish and English, and braided them together into a character at one with itself. He might have suppressed any element of what he was. In the duress of exile, many do survive by suppressing some part of who they are. But he suppressed nothing, allowed all the claims within to be answered, and in so doing forged a liberal temperament that may be as important a legacy as his work.

It is often said that his equanimity, together with his liberalism, are the products of privilege. He has had a lucky and privileged life – parents who adored him, an exile that did not scar him, election to All Souls at twenty-three, marriage to a gifted, supportive and wealthy woman – these have enabled him to make manifest what is often frustrated in others. But make it manifest he did, when others might have thrown their advantages away. There is in his temperament some impalpable source of health and well-being. He is well in his skin, at home in the world, at ease even with the advancing prospect of his own death. This cool, even cold serenity seems mysterious, unapproachable, unavailable to me; and in all our afternoons together, it is this that I most wish to understand. To be an intellectual is often to be unhappy: his happiness is an achievement worth seeking to explain.

'Do you wish you could live for ever?' he once asked me. His mother lived until she was ninety-four. I told him the idea filled me with horror. He heard me out, then said, 'All of my friends think the same. But I do not. I wish it would continue indefinitely. Why not?' Albert Einstein met him once and remarked afterwards that he seemed like 'a kind of spectator in God's big but mostly not very attractive theater'.[5] He has never tired of life's theatre and he imagines himself watching its lighted stage for ever.

At the end of our afternoons, he often accompanies me out. I help him into his coat, while he fits his lame left arm in first, then throws the coat over the right with a heave of his shoulders. He plumps a brown fedora onto his head, places his umbrella on his right arm and leads the way out into the glare and noise of Piccadilly. He walks slowly on the backs of his heels, his feet pointing out, precisely, very upright, his head turning this way and that to take in every detail of the unfolding scene. 'Look,' he will say of a bright-haired Amazon with a backpack striding past us. 'She must be a Norwegian. Terrifyingly blonde.' He pauses and inspects rain-gear in Cordings men's shop, staring down at thick corduroy plus-fours, in yellow and green, and other garments of the country gentry, with friendly curiosity. He passes the entrance to the Meridien Hotel, and surveys an American businessman, whose otherwise expressionless, late-twentieth-century face is distinguished by an elaborate brown moustache, which wings away from his cheeks. As the man passes out of earshot, Isaiah cups his hand over his mouth in an elaborate stage-whisper. 'Amazing moustache,' he says, then adds, as if to himself, 'Life is inexhaustible.'

At Piccadilly Circus we part, he towards the Athenaeum Club in Pall Mall, to take tea with a Russian scholar wanting to hear about his night with Anna Akhmatova. In front of the stand selling sex magazines, London policemen's helmets in plastic and piles of the *Evening Standard*, I embrace him; he stands back, bows ironically, briskly turns and is gone, ducking between two taxis, pointing his umbrella into the thick of the traffic to make it stop, whistling soundlessly to himself.

2

Riga, 1909–15

His memory of his birthplace was framed by two sphinxes, standing guard at the entrance to the Albertstrasse apartment, reclining plaster figures with paws, breasts and a pharaoh's head-dress. They are still there – mossy with damp and chipped with age – guarding the entrance to the Art Nouveau apartment block where he was born, on the fourth floor, on 6 June 1909.[1] In his parents' bed, in all likelihood, with a German doctor and nurse in attendance, his father pacing up and down the parquet outside, chloroform oozing beneath the door.

He may have been lucky to survive. After many hours of labour, the German doctor delivering the child, – 'Do you want his name? It was Hach' – placed forceps on the infant's left arm, and yanked him into the world so violently that the ligaments were permanently damaged.

Isaiah was not the first-born. His mother had had a stillbirth in 1907 and been told she would never be able to have children again. His parents greeted his arrival with the astonishment reserved for miracles. These facts – the stillborn sister, the longed-for realisation of his parents' wishes, the injury at birth, an only child – are vitally important, though interpreting their significance is not easy. He himself never liked interpreting them at all. But there is a story in the Bible that might be taken as an oblique fable about his own beginnings. It is the story of Hannah, the barren woman who goes to the temple to pray for a son, and who is so distraught that the high priest takes her for mad: 'And she was in bitterness of soul, and prayed unto the Lord, and wept sore.' In her desperation, Hannah promised that if God would grant her a son, she would give him into His service. Her faith – her primitive, intense desire for a child – was eventually rewarded. She and her husband Elkanah had a child, who grew up to become the prophet Samuel.[2] Isaiah's mother, Mussa Marie Berlin, was intensely moved by these verses and by the promise of hope that they contained, for they spoke so directly to her own desperation: having lost one child, having been told she would never give birth again. She was at the relatively advanced age of twenty-nine when her deliverance came. It is easy to see why, whenever Berlin himself brought to mind the desperate faith of Hannah, his eyes would fill with tears.

Tears came easily when watching a film or when quoting the Gettysburg Address, but for all that, he paid close attention to his own emotional truth. Towards his mother's memory, he maintained something like awe at her strength of character, mixed with irritation at the tidal force of her claim upon him. Towards Riga he maintained something close to indifference. Too far back perhaps, or too Latvian. There was little nostalgia in him and, despite being an exile, no obvious sense of loss. Nursery rhymes and popular songs from his childhood came back at his bidding and he sang them cheerfully in a musical whisper. But there wasn't much that he seemed to grieve for. The past did not make painful claims.

The first six years of his life were spent in the apartment on the Albertstrasse. His Latvian governess would take him out on leading strings, between the sphinxes, down the street to the public garden, grandly called the Esplanade, where Crimean veterans sunned themselves and re-lived Inkerman and Sevastopol. Riga was then the capital of Livonia, a province of the Tsarist empire. The Russian imperial presence consisted of a garrison, a detachment of cavalry, an Orthodox cathedral of recent construction, a small administration of clerks and copyists presided over by a governor with a staff, retinue and carriage. The Russians had done little to alter Riga's older identity as a Hanseatic trading town, with German as the language of culture and commerce. There was a Bourse, largely controlled by German-speaking merchants, and a Corinthian *Deutsche Oper*. Young Wagner had been *chef d'orchestre* in Riga in the 1850s and Bruno Walter had begun his conducting career there in 1900. In the Riga of 1909, Russian was the language of administration, but the number of Russians in the city was small, and the languages one would have heard in the streets, besides German, would have been Latvian and Yiddish.

At the top of the social pyramid of Tsarist Riga were the Baltic barons, Russian-speaking Germans – the Korffs and Benckendorfs, Keyserlings and Budbergs – family dynasties built on service to Peter the Great and to succeeding Tsars. They owned the great estates of the region and the grand houses of the town. Beneath them came the German merchants of the Bourse and the foreign timber traders. Next came the Jewish Merchants and the Jewish professional classes; beneath them came the Jewish artisans who lived in the Red Dvina ghetto. At the bottom were the Latvians: recently urbanised country people, with a peasant culture. They represented the majority, yet were disenfranchised in their own land. In Riga, they were domestic servants, labourers and governesses.

Albertstrasse was in new Riga, across the river from the cobbled streets of the Hanseatic old town, in a development of Art Nouveau apartment houses in the Paris style. Sergei Eisenstein's father – a converted Riga Jew – had designed some of these blocks, and Eisenstein himself spent his early years in Riga.[3] There were Jewish schools in the new Riga district, but it was not an especially, or even exclusively, Jewish neighbourhood.

Riga lay outside the Pale of Settlement, the area of the Western and Polish provinces of the Russian empire where Jews had been confined by statute since the partitions of Poland at the end of the eighteenth century.[4] As long as they stayed put, Riga Jews were exempt from the humiliating restrictions of Tsarist rule: the laws forbidding them to own land; to enter certain trades; to change their names to Christian ones; the laws banning them from the *Gymnasium* and the universities.[5]

Even when they travelled out of Riga none of the Pale restrictions applied to the Berlin family. Isaiah's father was a Merchant of the First Guild, a small élite, given honorary citizenship in the empire and exempted from the laws that applied to lesser Jews. They were free to travel and trade throughout the empire. While the sawmills and timber yards of Mendel Berlin's business were located in the Jewish ghetto and employed ghetto workers, for the child born in the building between the sphinxes the ghetto remained *terra incognita*.

In Berlin's papers there is a manuscript, eighty-six pages long, written in a spidery hand in an accountant's duplicate book, dated March 1946.[6] It is his father's call to his son to renew the connection to the family's Riga past, to the Berlins, Volschonoks and Schneersons, the rabbis, scholars and merchant princes of Jewish Russia. I asked whether Isaiah was aware of his father's memoir – he had no recollection of it whatsoever.

In photographs, Mendel Berlin appears as a small, plump, dapper man in well-tailored three-piece suits, with a tightly clipped moustache and thinning hair. In his son's recollections, he came across as a gentle, intelligent, timid man ruled by his emotional and domineering wife; a businessman who dealt in Riga timber before the revolution and afterwards in pigs' bristles. The loves of his life were not Talmud or the Psalms, but his wife, his successful son, light French comedies and the operettas of Franz Lehár.

While this suggests that Mendel was an assimilated European businessman who happened to be a Jew, his memoir created a different picture. It evoked the piety and yearning of the Pale city of Vitebsk in Tsarist Poland, where he was born in 1883; he told how his grandfather – a vague, otherworldly rabbi – used to devote all his waking hours to the study of holy books. Mendel remembered how, when he walked home from Hebrew school at night, he would detour around the local Polish Catholic church lest his clothes brush the walls by accident. He recalled the numbing lessons in the Hebrew school; the sting of the rabbi's correction when he forgot his Hebrew letters; the long, black silk caftan and embroidered skullcap he wore in synagogue; the mournful blast of the ram's horn. All of this brought the traditional Jewish world closer to Mendel's beginnings than his son had led me to believe.

At my urging, Isaiah read his father's memoir. All very unreliable, he said sternly, as if marking a deficient undergraduate essay. 'Pure sentimental return to roots,' he insisted. 'He worked up all this Jewish feeling in old age.' In 1946, when Mendel composed the memoir, he was sixty-three, nearing the end of his professional life; he had been in exile in London for twenty-five years; the Soviet conquest of Latvia meant that he would never see Riga again; the Holocaust had turned his past to dust. It was hardly surprising that the roots he had sunk in England should suddenly have seemed insubstantial and that he should have attempted to salvage what he could of his deeper allegiances.

His son would have none of this. 'He broke away from it. He was totally emancipated, didn't eat kosher, never went to synagogue.' When I pointed out that his father taxed him gently in the memoir for not knowing his Talmud, Isaiah shot back, 'He didn't, either.'

Jewishness may be a central fact about Berlin, but he fashioned the kind of Jew he was and resented his father's desire to define these claims on his behalf. By the time of their son's birth, the Berlins had ascended to a world far removed from the pieties of Vitebsk. The distance was linguistic as well as social. In his own childhood, Berlin's father had spoken Yiddish, but he never spoke it to his son. In Albertstrasse, the first language was Russian, the second German.

The historian Lewis Namier once compared Eastern European Jewry to a block of ice, which started to thaw when the rays of European enlightenment began to shine upon it. As the block melted, the streams of Jewish life – Zionist, *bundist*, secular and religious – then flowed into the river of bourgeois culture.[7] The Berlins, Volschonoks and Schneersons of Riga were swept along in these currents of Jewish assimilation.

Berlin's mother was a Volschonok and she grew up in an observant household in the Riga ghetto, but not even her Orthodox father was able to prevent her from receiving a European education and developing European yearnings to train as a singer – yearnings which, not fulfilling herself, she poured into her son. Berlin's father may have received a traditional Jewish education in the Hebrew schools of Vitebsk, but as a teenager he moved to Riga, entered the *Gymnasium* and secured the secular German education of his time. Then he was taken into his great-uncle's timber concern where the languages of business were German and Russian. Soon he was travelling to Paris, London, Berlin.

Isaiah claimed that to be secular and sceptical, as he was, required no break with the family past. Yet consider these details from his father's memoir: how, in 1904, travelling on the night-train from Paris to Menton, Mendel and his uncle put on their prayer shawls and performed their devotions while the Gentiles slept. Or this: once a year Mendel Berlin journeyed to Lubavich, a small village in the Smolensk *gubernia* of western Russia, to consult the rabbi on business matters and seek his blessing. It seems odd: a figure in a business suit queuing outside a country synagogue alongside poor folk in need of comfort and advice.

The oracle in question was no ordinary rabbi.[8] He was the leader of one of the most important sects of Hassidic Jews in Eastern Europe, known as Lubavich, after the small *shtetl* town in eastern Poland where the sect's religious leader came to live. Established in the 1780s by Rabbi Schneur Zalman Schneerson, the Lubavicher were among the most mystical and devout of the Hassidic sects. The Hassidim sought renewal of an old, institutionalised faith through singing, dancing and other forms of direct and joyous communion with God. The Lubavicher and other Hassidim were fiercely resisted within traditional Jewish Orthodoxy for their focus on an individual's personal relationship with God and his fellow man rather than on the intricacies of Jewish law, and for the extraordinary power and greatness attributed to their leaders.

Isaiah's adoptive paternal great-grandmother was a Schneerson, a lineal descendant of the sect's founder. From birth, therefore, he belonged to Hassidism's royal family. In the annual pilgrimage to Lubavich, a Berlin would have been received with honour. Mendel Berlin's memoir took obvious pride in these Hassidic forebears. The son was more sceptical. Origins, he always said, are a fact, full stop, but nothing to be proud of. To take pride was to surrender to the dubious determinism of the blood. Mendel used to attribute his son's memory and scholarly achievements to his rabbinical ancestors. Berlin thought this was absurd. As for the modern Lubavich Hassidim – with their three-quarter-length black frock-coats, wide-brimmed hats, beards and ringlets – he regarded them as alarming fanatics. Any mention of the Lubavich Hassidim, locked in violent conflict with the black population of Brooklyn, or giving their support to an intransigent struggle with the Palestinians over Hebron – would cause his face to tighten into a rare and uncharacteristic expression of dislike. Yet Rabbi Schneerson, their religious leader, was a cousin.

The name, Isaiah, was given him by his parents as a mark of respect to his adoptive great-grandfather. This man, a grand merchant prince and a member of the Lubavich sect, was born in Vitebsk but moved to Riga as a young man in order to escape the Pale restrictions on Jewish business. He married Chayetta Schneerson, one of the daughters of the Zemach Zadek, then the leader of the Lubavich. Marriage into the royal Lubavich line gave Isaiah senior access to formidable networks of business and economic intelligence. Like any oracle, the rabbi was both the recipient and dispenser of useful confidential information. Isaiah Berlin senior, or

Schaie as he was known, was thus a complex mixture of ancient piety and modern capitalist acumen. He set up in business supplying railroad ties and pit-props for German and Russian industry. By the 1890s he owned 75,000 acres of forest land in a broad swathe on either side of the River Dvina, stretching back into the Pale lands around Andreapol. In these forests, Jewish timber cutters felled the pines, assembled them into rafts and poled them down the Dvina to the port of Riga, where Schaie Berlin's sawmills in the Riga ghetto turned them into lumber for shipment to St Petersburg, Hamburg and London. By the turn of the century his sawmills and forests employed several hundred workers, most of them Jews.[9]

Before Schaie Berlin's time, Baltic Germans controlled the export trade. Jews generally lacked the languages and culture necessary for success in foreign commerce. It was this most pious Hassid who made the breakthrough, by taking Isaiah's father into the business and making him his chief negotiator in the European trade. Since he had no children of his own, he brought the fifteen-year-old Mendel, who was actually his great-nephew, from Vitebsk and enrolled him in the German *Gymnasium*. When he showed promise, Schaie took him into the business, adopted Mendel's father, Dov Behr Zuckerman, as his son and Mendel as his grandson, and they changed their names to Berlin.

By the turn of the century Schaie's timber business was so substantial that he had been made a Merchant of the First Guild and granted honorary citizenship of the Russian empire to be passed on to his heirs. Every morning the Russian governor would send a messenger to enquire after his well-being, and in the afternoon Berlin's beadle was despatched from the sawmill, to reciprocate. The old merchant rose early, toured his mills in a coach and pair, visited the exchange to gossip with his Gentile colleagues, lunched, napped in his flat above the mills, and then descended to the office in the afternoon, to write letters and tell stories to his entourage. Evenings were spent in restaurants and clubs. He was soon wealthy enough to afford a royal progress through the spas and resorts of Europe every winter and spring, accompanied by rabbis, kosher butchers, accountants and by Mendel, then in his early twenties. In Menton, the old man dined and drank and enjoyed himself, on holiday from self-denial. Mendel passed the time reading Russian literature forbidden in the empire – Tolstoy's banned works and the leaflets of the Russian social democrats – while the old man's wife, Chayetta, languished upstairs in a vast drawing room, singing quietly in a minor key.

Schaie spent Passover in Bad Homburg, dining in the local kosher restaurant, then talking business in the cafés and pump-rooms with Gentile businessmen, in a mixture of Yiddish and German. He attended synagogue in Frankfurt, where the Jews were so ostentatiously pious, Mendel noticed, that, not wishing to infringe the prohibition against labour on the Sabbath, they employed a Gentile at the entrance to open and shut their umbrellas. Back in Riga, all Schaie's employees had to attend his private synagogue on the Sabbath, and the master's beadle would also appear at Albertstrasse, bidding the family to its devotions. He was a hard paternalist of the old school.

Under the old man's eye, Mendel rose to become the head of Schaie's export business. He also began courting Mussa Marie Volschonok, his first cousin, daughter of a strict Hassid, Isaac Solomon Volschonok, also employed in the Berlin timber business. Mussa Marie was a diminutive, dark-haired, plump woman whose defining features were inexhaustible vitality, a fine singing voice and a passionate, clinging temperament. While still a teenager, Mendel came courting, sometimes staying the night at her house and sleeping on a pair of chairs in the downstairs salon. She turned down his first proposal of marriage – to Mendel's 'consternation, horror and also shame'. When, several months later, she changed her mind and accepted him at last, he felt certain, as he sadly confessed in his memoir, 'that mother accepted me only after calculating that she has after all to get married and she might do worse than accepting me'. He knew he was timid and not good-looking, but he had prospects – as Schaie Berlin's heir – and he evidently doted on her.

The wedding took place in Riga on 13 March 1906. She was twenty-six, he was twenty-three. With marriage, a new apartment in Albertstrasse and additional income as an insurance agent for a London company, Mendel entered the happiest period of his life. But he also began to resent his adoptive grandfather's tyrannies. The old man thought nothing of summoning his grandson by telegram in the middle of the night to German spa towns simply to translate a business letter. Now that Mendel had a family, he disliked being at Schaie's beck and call. But his period of servitude was coming to an end. In 1908 the old man died, at the age of sixty-seven, leaving Mendel the business, which he promptly sold, to start a new timber partnership of his own.

When Isaiah was born the next year – and named after the departed patriarch – he came into the world at the highest point of his family's fortunes. Mendel quickly became head of the Riga association of timber merchants and built up his volume of business with the London timber market.

The young Isaiah was smothered by his doting parents and never lost a taste for being spoiled. All his life he loved regression in all its cosiest forms, taking to his bed whenever possible, preferably in small, warmly heated rooms. At the same time, he did not believe that he was, as he put it, 'mother-fixated'. If anything, it was he who dominated them both. There is something of the young domestic tyrant in the early photographs. Isaiah's volubility, the non-stop talking, might have had its beginnings in being a preternaturally bright and bubbling only child, sure that no one – certainly no younger sister or older brother – would interrupt his monologues.

In his memory, he dominated the scene around him. He was taken to see Chayetta Berlin, widow of Schaie, the founding father, some time in 1912. The room was an overheated, dimly lit salon, immaculate, gleaming and sad, at the end of which, in an armchair, sat a yellowed old lady, in flounced Victorian widow's weeds with a kerchief on her head. His parents ushered him forward and bade him kiss her hand. She was the matriarch of the clan, and he the namesake of her dead husband. But there was something repugnant about the wrinkled old face, the darkness, the yellowed flesh. Isaiah refused. The shame of the parents was great, his victory complete. When they took their leave, the matriarch's hand had still not been kissed. He never saw her again.

In another early memory, he also played the infant tyrant. In 1912 his father's sister, Evgenia, married Isaac Landoberg, a dashing adventurer, one-time boxer, gallery owner and man about town. Isaiah, aged three, was taken to the wedding reception, in a white silk suit. A dance band is playing: the couples swirl around him. He is placed on a table – exhibited to aunts and uncles, chucked under the chin, made a spectacle of. Someone is holding him up; the dancers whirl around him, the music grows louder and louder. Suddenly he is shouting, in infantile fury, 'Ich *hasse diese Scheissemusik! Ich hasse diese Scheissemusik!'* He stamps his foot at the shit music, and the adult world stops dancing.

Apart from these grand occasions, the Berlins lived quietly. They took family holidays at the Baltic resorts and winter cures at the German spas, but the general impression of their life in the Albertstrasse flat is of a family turned in upon the child at its centre. In a letter written to the psychiatrist Anthony Storr, in 1978, Berlin himself pondered why it was that, having 'received a full measure of parental love at all times', he should have been plagued, all his life, with the feeling that his achievements were of 'very little or of no value'.[10] Certainly this works as a warning against deducing the adult from the child; yet the self-doubt of which he speaks – however real it sometimes was – was also part of a carefully cultivated strategy of self-deprecation, intended to deflect and disarm criticism. Beneath this exterior, there was a quiet and unshakeable sense of self-worth. It cannot be irrelevant that he began life in front of an audience of two worshipping, over-awed parents.

3

Petrograd, 1916–20

The certainties of Riga were short-lived. In July 1914 the Austrian Archduke was assassinated in Sarajevo. Isaiah was just five. The Russian and German empires mobilised against each other, and Riga Jewry was caught in between. Their language was German, their citizenship Russian. As the Russian forces were driven back, the Russian high command, believing the Jews were giving aid and comfort to the enemy, ordered them all deported behind the front lines. The Jews of Riga escaped deportation only by bribing the Governor General. Most refugees from the Pale fled eastwards, but some went north to Riga. Isaiah, now six, was out in the street with his governess when they came upon two old refugees from the *shtetl*, one a man, the other a woman, begging in the street. Isaiah had a biscuit in his hand and held it out to the old man, only to see it snatched away by the woman. 'He only eats once a day,' she said, devouring the biscuit before Isaiah's frightened gaze.

By May 1915 the Baltic was under German naval blockade and the timber trade was at a standstill. Mendel had managed to re-orient the business away from export to supplying the Russian railroads, but still a large portion of his timber was sitting in local yards. When a fire wiped out his stock, Mendel accused the German owner of the yard of setting it deliberately; the German retaliated by denouncing Berlin to the police, for setting it to claim the insurance. By then imperial Russia was in full retreat along the eastern front and the German armies were within twenty-five miles of the city.

This was the context – a nasty dispute, tinged with anti-Semitic implications and the growing threat of German invasion – that led Mendel, in the summer of 1915, to despatch his wife and son by train to Andreapol, a small company town upriver on the Dvina, an hour or so from Riga, where the family's timber concessions were concentrated. Mendel himself went to Petrograd to secure compensation for his fire loss, in an atmosphere, so he hoped, 'less poisonous' than that of Riga.[1]

Andreapol, a logging town of about 1,000 inhabitants deep in the forests around Pskov, was full of pious, practising Jews who worked as loggers, cutters, sawmill workers and timber stackers. But there was also a traditional Russian landowner, dying of tuberculosis, in a big house surrounded by a park; and Russian officers on leave from nearby regiments used to serenade young ladies with balalaikas or read them sentimental verse. One such officer read to Isaiah's mother by the auburn light of an oil lamp. In both Isaiah's and his mother's memory, Andreapol became a sepia print of old Russia in its dying hours. Displacement to this new world was neither strange nor threatening: Andreapol was effectively owned by the Berlin timber firm, and everyone deferred to the young princeling.

In the Hebrew school, sitting on plank benches with timber-cutters' children, Isaiah received his first formal religious instruction. It was also his first experience of schooling, and to the end of his life he could still remember the words of a song he learned with the other children, about the stove in the corner that kept a poor family warm. From an old rabbi, he learned the letters of the Hebrew alphabet. The rabbi too was never forgotten. Once he paused and said, 'Dear children, when you get older, you will realise how in every one of these letters there is Jewish blood and Jewish tears.' When Berlin told me this story, eighty years later, in the downstairs sitting room of his home in Oxford, Headington House, for a split second his composure deserted him and he stared out across the garden. Then he looked back at me, equanimity restored, and said, 'That is the history of the Jews.'

In 1916 Mendel Berlin moved the family from Andreapol to Petrograd, where he now worked for the Russian government supplying timber for the railway system. Several members of the Berlin family were already in Petrograd: Uncle Isaac and Aunt Evgenia Landoberg, Yitzhak and Ida Samunov. The young child found Uncle Isaac irresistibly romantic, because by then he was caught up in the socialist movement and came back to their flat with tales of revolvers, searches and derring-do. Aunt Ida, his mother's sister, was a tender and highly intelligent soul, tiny in stature and warm in disposition, even more so – Berlin eventually believed – than his mother.

From the family's arrival in Petrograd in 1916 until their departure for England in 1921, Isaiah did not attend school. He educated himself in the library of the family's rented flat on Vassilievsky Island in the north of the city. The apartment was above a small ceramics factory, and multicoloured fragments of ceramic mosaic littered the inner courtyard. There were maids and tutors, but few children to play with. Solitude allowed Isaiah's precocity to flourish. He swears he read *War and Peace* and *Anna Karenina* at the age of ten. He loved the former, but could not make head or tail of the latter.

Isaiah's Hebrew lessons continued, together with instruction in the Talmud. At the time, it all seemed an exercise in boredom. 'I mean, it was all like this: some story about two men seizing a garment and tearing it between them. To whom does it belong? That sort of question I did not find fascinating.' These were the Jewish tradition's elementary lessons in the ambiguities of human justice, and if the child found them tiresome, the adult never forgot them.

More fascinating were Jules Verne's *Twenty Thousand Leagues under the Sea*, Mayne Reid's cowboy adventures and Alexandre Dumas' *Three Musketeers* – all in Russian translations. Late in his life, when asked what he had wanted to be when he was a child, Berlin said that he used to dream of being a scientist in a Jules Verne novel, undersea, watching the world of nature through a porthole. It is a fantasy of omniscient distance – exploring the depths, yet remaining immune from their dangers.

This childhood reading remained vivid to him throughout his life. In August 1956, when he visited the Lenin Library in Moscow, closely followed by the KGB, he signed out a number of Russian books and spent the morning reading them. When Isaiah left, the agent assigned to shadow him discovered that they were only dog-eared original editions of two German adventure stories for children, translated into Russian.

Besides what he gleaned from reading, there were the scraps of knowledge tossed to him at his parents' dinner table by his aunts and uncles. He remembered Uncle Isaac teaching him who Garibaldi and his Red Shirts were; he recalled how his progressive Aunt Evgenia solemnly set out to demolish certain Hebrew myths about Mordecai and Esther. Unlike the retiring Mendel and Marie, Isaac and Evgenia were swept up in the rising tide of Petrograd politics in autumn 1916, but apart from the stories they brought back from the streets, the drastic events outside – the slow dissolution of a regime, the ongoing collapse of the imperial army – made no impression on a seven-year-old. The first political tremor he registered at all was the portentous black type of the newspaper headlines announcing Rasputin's murder in late autumn of that year.

A whole regime was crumbling around him, and of course he had not the slightest inkling of it. He went for walks with his Jewish governess on the Nevsky Prospekt. He would gaze in the shop windows, at the toy stores with their English train sets and German stuffed bears, at the confectioneries, where his attention would be riveted by a certain type of chocolate bar, whose name – *Khvorost* – and whose shape, like tree boughs piled on top of each other, he never forgot.

In the winter of 1916–17 his parents took him to hear the Russian bass Fyodor Chaliapin singing the title role in *Boris Godunov* at the Marinsky Theatre. What he liked best was the moment when Boris sees the ghost of Dimitry: Chaliapin fell to his knees, crawled under the table and drew the tablecloth over his head. Isaiah's lifelong love of opera began here, with Boris, and with the spectacle of an adult reduced to animal terror, all seen in the safe frame of a theatre. Soon, of course, there was to be real fear in adults' eyes, and none of it in the magic frame of suspended disbelief.

He was kept inside on the bright winter's day in late February 1917 when the crowds began surging through Vassily Ostrov towards the centre of the city. The family went to the windows to watch the large plywood banners inscribed with such slogans as 'Land and Liberty!', 'All Power to the Duma', 'Down with the Tsar', 'Down with War', floating above the caps and kerchiefs of the crowd. When the first cordon of troops marched towards them in formation, the crowd did not give way. The military line wavered, broke and then the crowd and army mingled together, tossing caps in the air, singing the *Marseillaise* in Russian, making common cause and setting off together across the Neva bridges for Winter Palace Square. He was seven and a half when he saw this – the first euphoric morning of the February Revolution. His parents – like most liberal Jews – seemed to share the popular excitement, though Mendel and Marie were not the kind of people to throw on a coat, rush downstairs and join the crowd.

When it seemed safe to go out in the streets, Isaiah and his governess went for a stroll near their home. Isaiah was bending down to examine a battered Russian translation of Jules Verne, on sale from a bookseller who had laid out his wares on the snowy sidewalk, when the roadway suddenly filled with a small group of men, perhaps fifteen in all, sweeping past with a frightened person in their clutches. Afterwards, Isaiah learned that the man was a *Pharaon*, one of the municipal policemen who were the last people in uniform to remain loyal to the old regime. He had been spotted on the roof of a nearby building and had been dragged down into the street. All the seven-year-old had time to see was a man with a white face twisting and turning as he was borne away. The child could not know where they were taking him, but even then it seemed clear that he would not escape with his life. However brief the scene, it made an indelible impression. Much later, in the 1930s when contemporaries were intoxicated with revolutionary Marxism, the memory of 1917 continued to work within Berlin, strengthening his horror of physical violence and his suspicion of political experiment, and deepening his lifelong preference for all the temporising compromises that keep a political order safely this side of terror.

Initially, the *Pharaon* were among the only victims of revolution, and at first Berlin's parents were swept along by the excitement. They avidly followed the proclamations of the Provisional Government, the speeches in the Duma by Miliukov, Gutchkov and Rodzianko. But the liberals in whom the Berlins placed their trust still wanted to wage war. Miliukov renewed the Russian imperial claim on the Dardanelles, drastically misreading the war-weariness of the capless deserters who milled about the Petrograd streets. By the spring of 1917, demonstrators were already chanting, 'Down with the capitalist Ministers. Down with Miliukov-Dardanellski.' By midsummer, the liberals' hour had passed; order in the streets was visibly disintegrating and power was ebbing from the Duma towards the Petrograd Soviet and to a small band of Maximalists, as the Bolsheviks were then known.

To escape the heat and the increasing tension and violence in the city, mother and son spent the summer in a *dacha* at Staraya Russa. There were fancy-dress parties, tombolas, and afternoons in the park listening to an Italian orchestra playing at a band stand. The Italians had left their sheet music behind in Italy. Each afternoon they announced first a Venetian, then a Finnish, then an Italian march. Isaiah gradually realised that it was the same tune, played over and over.

His circle of friends at Staraya Russa included Leonard Schapiro, who was later to become Professor of Russian History at the London School of Economics. The two little boys, one seven and the other eight, would sit on the *dacha* veranda or wander through the parks of the resort, talking earnestly about the art of Alexander Benois, Leon Bakst and other Russian painters of the time. Schapiro showed Berlin coloured postcards of their work and even modelled a plaster bust of the dying French revolutionary hero, Marat.[2] These summer conversations – of a scarcely credible precocity – laid down the earliest layer of cultural and artistic references that were to astonish his English contemporaries later on.

When the family returned to Petrograd in the autumn of 1917, Isaiah noticed, as they drove home in a taxi, that the walls of the city were plastered with posters for elections to the new constituent assembly. Already young men were tearing down the posters of other parties and putting up ones emblazoned with the hammer and sickle.

While Marie and Isaiah had been away, Mendel had been shuttling back and forth between his timber concessions in Andreapol and the little office he maintained at the apartment in Vassily Ostrov. Despite the worsening situation, Mendel's business with the Windon-Rybinsk Railways – supplying them with sleepers and construction wood – continued to prosper. In May, George Payne, an English timber trader, had arrived in Petrograd, seeking to import Baltic and Scandinavian plywood in return for English textiles. When Payne's exchange deal fell through, Mendel bought the plywood consignment from him, then shipped it from Archangel to London, where he made a healthy profit, lodged in sterling in a London bank. One morning, later in the summer, he returned to find his office ransacked, business papers gone and a calling card from a sinister-sounding outfit calling itself the Counter-Espionage Office. This was a remnant of the Tsarist apparatus of war-time intelligence and, when he showed up at their office, Mendel was asked to explain his dealings with foreigners. Although he was released without charge, the incident was enough to upset a timid man. He burned all his papers relating to trade with England and decided to move the family from Vassily Ostrov, where he felt under suspicion as a bourgeois from his proletarian neighbours, to what he supposed was a safer and more elegant address, 16 Angliisky Prospekt, near the Neva embankment in the city proper.

The rooms in Angliisky Prospekt faded from Isaiah's memory, though not the artisans' shops in the basements below, especially a tinker who repaired samovars, under a laboriously misspelled sign: SHAMOVAR. At the bottom of the street were a small cinema, which showed war newsreels, and a soup kitchen, which fed a steadily lengthening queue of the destitute.

Destitution never visited the Berlins. In Angliisky Prospekt, their neighbours included Rimsky-Korsakov's son-in-law, a Jewish cellist; a Caucasian princess; and an assistant minister of Finnish affairs, whose daughter became Isaiah's playmate. This small circle underwent together the convulsion that began in late October 1917.

They first knew that something was happening when the lifts in the apartment stopped working. Then the trams ceased to operate. Then newspapers disappeared from the streets. As the Bolsheviks suppressed the opposition newspapers, they kept re-surfacing – for a time at least – under new names. Thus a liberal paper called *Day* was closed down in October, only to re-appear days later as *Evening*, then as *Night*, then as *Midnight*, making a final appearance as *Dead of Night*, until finally silenced for good.[3] At first, the family must have laughed over this, but there was no laughter when a group of men with armbands and rifles appeared at the front door. The tenants were ordered to form a house committee for the purpose of democratic administration of the apartment block. The secretary of the committee was to be the stoker Koshkin, whom few of the tenants had ever noticed before, because he lived in the basement and kept the boilers filled with coal. Koshkin now began giving the orders, dressed in a colonel's striped trousers in place of his old, coal-grimed overalls. Princess Emeretinsky and Rimsky-Korsakov's daughter were made to stoke the stoves, remove refuse and sweep the yard. But somehow – a tip perhaps – the Berlins were exempted from these reversals of fortune. They were also protected by their maid, a peasant woman of strong Tsarist convictions, who would answer the door when search parties began marauding and would send them away. The family jewellery, hidden under the snow on the balcony, was never seized.

For a few weeks, fear about where the revolution might be headed gave way to euphoria at the Balfour Declaration, which promised the Jews a national home in Palestine. For more than a decade Chaim Weizmann, the Zionist leader, had been pressing the British Government for such a declaration. Now, in late 1917, with British troops poised to drive the troops of the Ottoman Empire from Palestine, the British Foreign Secretary, Arthur Balfour, despatched a letter to Baron Rothschild, declaring that the government viewed with 'favour the establishment of a national home for the Jewish people', provided – in words that were to become notorious – 'that nothing shall be done which may prejudice the civil and religious rights of existing non-Jewish communities in Palestine'. The declaration was announced on 9 November 1917, just after the Bolshevik Revolution, and Isaiah remembered his family's excitement about this place called Palestine and the blue, white and gold flags that he and other children were given to wave at a meeting in a synagogue basement.

Mendel was always a sceptic about Palestine, but Marie's Zionism was bred in the bone. Two of her sisters, Ida (who married Yitzhak Samunov) and Evgenia (who married Isaac Landoberg), were eventually to make their lives anew in Palestine. But though the whole Berlin clan greeted the Balfour Declaration with rejoicing, for the moment, at least, Evgenia and Isaac cast their lot with the revolution. In 1917 Landoberg was not a Bolshevik but a member of their rivals to the left, the Socialist Revolutionaries. He stormed around Petrograd with a huge pistol in his belt, which so frightened Isaiah's mother that she dropped it into a full kitchen basin to render it harmless.[4]

Mendel and Marie were more cautious. They kept their heads down and tried to see which way the revolution would turn. Initially, their livelihood was not touched by it. When the Bolsheviks nationalised the railways, Mendel Berlin was hired as a state contractor to provide timber from the Andreapol forests. As a state employee, he was provided with a travel pass on the railways, documents exempting him from searches and arrests, food and clothing coupons and a pistol, which he hoped he would never have to fire.

The family spent the summer of 1918 in a rented *dacha* among the royal parks and gardens of Pavlovsk, a resort town south of Petrograd. At the band stand, Isaiah heard a symphony by César Franck. He sat with his friend Schapiro in the arbours of the palace park. He read *Quo Vadis*. As far as he could remember, the revolution meant nothing. By then Lenin had sued for peace and taken Russia out of the war. To a child, everything was as it should be. Certainly men in leather jackets with guns could be seen strolling in the parks, impressing the girls. They were recruits to Lenin's secret police, the Cheka, but to a child's eyes, they seemed like exciting gangsters. By the autumn and winter of 1918–19, however, when the family returned to Petrograd, even Isaiah realised that something menacing had begun to happen. The house committee in Angliisky Prospekt ordered everyone to vacate their extra rooms in order to conserve heat. Isaiah slept with his mother, while his father slept next door in his study-office. For the next two and a half years their life was reduced to the compass of these two rooms, in an atmosphere of searches, privation and fear that forced them to turn ever more in upon themselves. The bond between mother and son grew even closer. Thanks to his state food coupons, Mendel would get the occasional bag of white flour and smuggle it home under his fur coat, past the police checkpoints. The flour was baked into a white loaf, exclusively reserved – so Mendel remembered – for their son. Through the lean years of Lenin's war communism, Isaiah was so well fed that when he queued for food at a local food shop, a woman behind him was heard to sneer that he was too plump to need food at all.

In the cramped rooms on Angliisky Prospekt he gave himself over to reading. There were vellum-bound editions of Tolstoy, Turgenev, Zhukovsky (the tutor of Pushkin), Pushkin himself, translations of Heine and Goethe and, above all, that treasure-house of Russian-Jewish learning, the *Jewish Encyclopaedia*. The encyclopaedia itself had been run as a kind of welfare-for-work scheme – by the philanthropist Baron Gunzburg – for threadbare Jewish writers.[5] As Isaiah pored over its entries, the lore and history of Judaism, as expressed by the best minds of the Russian nineteenth-century Jewish intelligentsia, settled in his mind.

They were summering in a *pension* in Pavlovsk in 1919 when the Cheka ransacked the villa. The squad was searching for jewellery, but Mendel managed to keep it hidden in the flowerpots on the veranda. He had been interrogated before, but this search was the last straw. It was not just the privation of Lenin's regime that he loathed but, in Mendel's words, 'the feeling of being imprisoned, no contact with the outside world, the spying all round, the sudden arrests and the feeling of absolute helplessness against the whim of any hooligan parading as a Bolshevik'.

Having decided on exile, the family considered the options. Palestine was rejected: it was too far away; the Jewish community numbered only 50,000; and they knew no one there. They did consider the German capital, because it was cheap and by then full of Russians. They also considered Paris, but the Dreyfus affair gave them fears that the French would be anti-Semitic. Unsurprisingly, they settled on Riga. Latvia was now an independent republic and the Soviet regime was prepared to let bona fide Latvians emigrate there. Moreover, Mendel seems to have thought that he could resume his work in the Riga timber trade.

Though the decision to leave was taken in the summer of 1919, it was not until October 1920 that the formalities were finally completed. The family left everything behind at Angliisky Prospekt, taking only the permitted 3,000 Romanov roubles per person and some jewellery sewn into the lining of their son's overcoat. Such was his relief at departing that the only thing Isaiah missed as they closed the door on the flat was the stately *Jewish Encyclopaedia* and the standard editions of the Russian classics left on the shelves.

The Berlins left Petrograd on 5 October 1920. The timing of their departure may have been set by the fortunes of the fighting between the Red Army and the Poles in western Russia. In August 1920, the Reds were at the gates of Warsaw. By October, the Polish counter-attack had forced the Russians to accept an armistice, signed at Riga on 6 October. The journey – only 300 miles as the crow flies – took ten days. They stopped for more than twenty-four hours, Mendel remembered, in Pskov station. At other smaller stations they would barter salt and candles for bread and eggs from the peasants on the platform. 'You can imagine the comfort of it,' Mendel remembered dryly, 'there being no washing or sanitary arrangements in the [train] and having to wait for the next stop, sometimes for hours, to satisfy one's physical needs.'[6]

At the Latvian-Soviet border, the Latvians on board – policemen and firemen mostly – cheered and were soon allowed to proceed to Riga, while Jews and other foreigners were taken off the train. To Mendel's intense indignation, they spent a night in cold, unheated barracks before being sent to a Russian bath for delousing. He was told that they would have to remain there for a week. A border official, who recognised the Berlin name, hinted that he could get them on the next train, for a consideration. 'Although frightened of possible provocation, I felt so dejected and degraded,' Mendel recalled, that he paid the bribe, and the next night they set off for Riga in a crowded third-class carriage.[7]

On the night train to Riga, Isaiah was dozing in the compartment when some Latvians sat down and began a vigorously anti-Semitic conversation, obviously assuming that the frightened family opposite were Russian Jews who would not understand what they were saying. Marie Berlin, who had fluent Latvian, listened and then observed tartly that, while there were a great many things wrong with the Soviet Union, anti-Semitism was not one of them. When the Latvian military control came through the train, the Latvians accused Marie of being a communist spy. At Riga station, police boarded the train and led Marie away, while Isaiah and Mendel looked on in horror. At this point another Latvian, who had been seated in the compartment, informed Mendel that he was a member of the Latvian secret service. He was prepared to release Marie, in return for a consideration. Mendel paid him his bribe, and the family was allowed to leave. But a case was drawn up against her, and throughout the autumn of 1920, the Berlins kept receiving legal papers informing Marie that she was due to answer charges.

The incident on the train not only revealed the intransigent Jewish consciousness in Isaiah's mother; it also laid bare his own identity. As he later recalled to me, 'We were Jews ... We were not Russian. We were not Letts. We were something else. We had to have a home. There was no point living in a perpetual *qui vive*. Above all there was no point denying it, concealing it. To do so was undignified and unsuccessful. That's where it comes from ... From her.' Mendel was a more pliable figure. 'If assimilation had been possible, he would have been happy to assimilate. She never.'

They reached Riga on 15 October 1920 and went to stay, not at Albertstrasse, which they no longer owned, but nearby with a relative. Having had to bribe two sets of officials on the way, Mendel's wallet was empty. He cabled London, and fortunately the bank cabled back to say that he still had access to the sizeable profits from his plywood deals – more than £10,000 – lodged in his account. At first Mendel re-established himself in the timber trade. Their family connections to Riga remained: both Mendel's and Marie's fathers, bearded patriarchs, were still living there, together with brothers and sisters and a raft of young cousins. These were reasons enough to stay, but the incident on the train and Marie's continuing difficulties with the authorities helped to convince the Berlins that they should leave. Mendel set about securing visas for England. Besides his timber connections there, he wanted to give Isaiah the advantages of a British public-school education. He was, as his son remembered, a confirmed 'Anglo-maniac'. Mendel belonged to that generation of Russian liberals whose very definition of what it was to be civilised was English: bicycles meant Raleigh; sugar meant Tate and Lyle; steamships meant Cunard; education meant the British public school; and in a post-Versailles world of Mussolinis, Lenins and Pilsudskis, decent, dull and incorruptible public authority meant King George V.

While Mendel busied himself with the formalities of departure, Isaiah continued to be tutored at home by a German professor who dinned Latin and German into him and made him read Goethe. This exposure to German *Kultur* was not especially successful. All his life, Berlin's German remained imperfect, and as for the German professor, he judged his eleven-year-old pupil to be superficial. The judgement lodged in Isaiah's mind for life. 'There is a certain truth in it. Dr Kupfer was not wrong.'

In January 1921 Mendel went ahead to England to prepare their way and to send back tickets and visas. In February Isaiah and his mother said goodbye to their relatives and left Riga by train for Ostend. When the ferry docked at Dover, his father was waiting on the other end of the gangplank, and Isaiah, in his Russian gaiters, overcoat and fur cap, rushed down the gangplank into his arms. Mendel had champagne waiting for his wife in the reserved compartment of the train that took them to London, but when he offered Marie a glass, she said he had been much too extravagant. Isaiah listened to them squabble quietly while the train sped towards London in the dark.

Their destination turned out to be a part of south London where there was not a single Russian and very few Jews. Mendel's partner from the plywood deal of 1916, George Alexander Payne, had informed him that the English did not live in towns. So it was that on 3 February 1921, Isaiah spent his first night in England in a spacious rented bungalow in St James' Road in Surbiton, a southern suburb of London. Next morning he had his first meal in England, a resolutely non-kosher plate of bacon and eggs. After breakfast, Isaiah got up, went over to the piano in the salon and, with one hand, picked out 'God Save the King'.[8]

4

London, 1921–8

At the end of his first day at Arundel House School in Surbiton, Isaiah came home in tears – so his mother remembered – unable to understand a word the teachers or boys were saying. There had been English lessons in Petrograd, but evidently they were not enough. When asked in later life what English he actually possessed on arrival in exile, he liked to sing in a high, whispered voice, 'It von't be a stylish marridze. I can't afford a carridze. But you'll look sveet upon ze seat of a bicycle built for two.' Apart from 'Daisy, Daisy', Isaiah had command of scarcely seventy-five words. He had never been to school in Petrograd and now he stood there with row upon row of English schoolboys gazing at him. To make things worse, it was January, halfway through the school year. In the circumstances, tears were unsurprising.

A local lady who had been a nanny in Russia tutored him in English, and Isaiah memorised interminable lists of vocabulary and went on disconsolate expeditions with her to a local zoo. During their first year in England, the family changed addresses three times: St James Road, Surbiton; 8 Berrylands Road, Surbiton; Effingham Road, Long Ditton, Surrey. He had no memory of these phantom lodgings.

The loneliness of a child exiled into a foreign tongue is easy to imagine. English schoolboy lore – football teams, cartoon characters, dirty songs and jokes, snobberies and cruelties – was beyond his ken, while all the impressive things he knew seemed worthless or an embarrassment.

The marks of exile remained faint but visible throughout his life: abstractly, in his respect for the need to belong; politically, in his Zionism; morally, in his fascination with the marginal, excluded or enraged figures of nineteenth-century history. But personally? In a slight touchiness, a hyper-sensitivity to small slights, to any gesture that treated him as an outsider.

In other ways, exile was an entirely positive experience. Vladimir Nabokov, who arrived in England at about the same time, wrote in *Speak, Memory* that exile provided the 'syncopal kick' that propelled him out of childhood, out of that easy familiarity with his surroundings which, had it continued, might have prevented him from becoming a writer. Dispossession became the condition of his art.[1]

In Berlin's case, exile consolidated detachment. Being a foreigner, he could watch, but he could not play. Because language was acquired, it could not be taken for granted. He had to make it his own. Isaiah always emphasised how rapidly the assimilation occurred: within six months he had a part in *Babes in the Wood* – you cannot get more English than that – as 'second murderer'. His one and only line was: 'I'm a comin', I'm a comin'.' By the end of his first year he was calling money 'chink', and pronouncing 'say' as 'sigh', like the other boys. And when some child called him a 'dirty Jew' – no, he corrected himself, 'a dirty German' (this was 1921) – other boys beat his aggressor up. The Surbiton boys who stood up for him on that playground became part of his folklore of English fair play. But the incident also says something about the uncanny ability of a plump, unprepossessing Jewish child in a Gentile school, a bookish boy with a foreign accent and a limp left arm, to win people over.

He ought to have looked back on his talent for assimilation with pleasure. Instead, eagerness to please figured at the top of his list of vices. He always worried that a Jew should not be so emollient and accommodating. It was a central moral dilemma in his life to reconcile a sense of dignity with this eagerness to fit in. Ingratiation, he maintained, was the characteristically Jewish sin, always hoping, against the evidence, that one would 'pass'. Paradoxically, of course, this extreme sensitivity to the dilemmas of assimilation made him uniquely successful at it. He became a master at fitting in, at the price of lingering self-dislike.

One of the paradoxes of his temperament was to wish that he had been one of life's noble intransigents – those who did not bend, but made others submit to their will. Look at my heroes, he used to say. Not one of them was a nice, grass-eating, accommodating liberal. They were all hard, difficult, 'impossible' characters – Toscanini, Churchill, Weizmann – men whose vices he excused because they did not include a fatal eagerness to please.

A child from Petrograd, who two summers before had been discussing the art of Bakst and the music of Franck in the parks of Pavlovsk, was now immersed in the suburban world of the English lower middle classes. Most of his schoolmates were the sons of tradesmen and self-employed small businessmen. Isaiah's family was probably wealthier than theirs. His mother had a maid to help her with the housework; there was private tuition for his English and, briefly, a piano teacher, until it became apparent that his damaged left arm prevented all hope of progress on the keyboard.

Exile, which is generally a *glissade* of social decline, was a smooth and straight road for the Berlins. Being a Riga timber merchant with long-established ties to London, Mendel could pick up his life where he had left it. The Midland Bank still held Mendel's profits from his war-time plywood contracts and, with this money, he set himself up in Bishopsgate, London EC1, and gave his firm the loyal name of 'The British and Overseas Trading Company', importing building timber from Latvia. Within months of arrival, the family was attending a smart West End synagogue. Soon Mendel had befriended an eminent QC in the City and was seeking his advice about which London public school to send his son to. When his wife broke her ankle, Mendel secured the services, not of any doctor, but of the Queen's personal physician, a man whom Isaiah remembered as a 'real old-fashioned bedside-manner charlatan'.

Adopted countries do not necessarily return an exile's devotion. The Berlins had some lucky early encounters with their adopted home. For several weeks, while his mother was away recovering from her broken ankle, Isaiah took all his meals at school, with the headmaster and his wife, returning to the house in Surbiton only to sleep. He learned English table-manners and added hugely to his vocabulary. England became synonymous in his mind with the decency of this kindly headmaster and his wife.

All his life, he attributed to Englishness nearly all the propositional content of his liberalism: 'that decent respect for others and the toleration of dissent is better than pride and a sense of national mission; that liberty may be incompatible with, and better than, too much efficiency; that pluralism and untidiness are, to those who value freedom, better than the rigorous imposition of all-embracing systems, no matter how rational and disinterested, better than the rule of majorities against which there is no appeal'. All of this, he insisted, was 'deeply and uniquely English'.[2]

Actually, his liberalism included some very un-English stuff: Alexander Herzen, Benjamin Constant, Giuseppe Mazzini, among others, and the English elements were refracted through rose-tinted glasses. It is an exile's prerogative to love an adopted home with an absence of irony that is impossible for a native. Isaiah more or less accepted everything the English liked to believe about themselves: that they were practical, untidy, eccentric, fair-minded, empirical, common-sensical and that ubiquitous word, decent. His was a version of Englishness frozen in the moment when he first encountered it in the 1920s: the England of Kipling, King George, G.K. Chesterton, the gold standard, empire and victory. The long slide into imperial decline and self-doubt lay decades ahead. Narrow-minded provincialism, philistinism and insularity played no part in his idea of England. If the English took to him, it was because he offered them back their most self-approving myths.

What about the Riga and Petrograd he had left behind? Longing, nostalgia? He was always peremptory on the subject of longings: 'None. New Life. I began afresh.'

His first surviving composition, dating from 1922 when he was twelve, suggests otherwise. It was a gripping tale, in Mayne Reid dime-store-novel style, of the murder of Uritzky, an early Soviet commissar and head of the Petrograd Cheka. Uritzky was fanaticism incarnate: 'he possesed a clever but also cruel look and all his countenence bore an expression of a phanatic. he signed death verdicts without moving his eyebrow. his leading motto in life was "The purpose justifies the WAYS." '[3]

In the story, Uritzky is murdered by a son avenging his father's death at the hands of the Cheka. Isaiah's father was to recall that it took a year after they had safely established themselves in Surbiton before he could hear a car draw up outside in the street without parting the lace curtains to take an apprehensive look.[4] Some of these emotions worked themselves into his son's composition. Both the language, which retained Russian constructions, and the subject suggest that Berlin remained imaginatively in Petrograd for some time after he had begun a new life in Surbiton.

In January 1922 the family moved into the Royal Palace Hotel, Kensington, while a newly purchased house in Holland Park was readied for them. Isaiah was preparing for common-entrance examinations to the London public schools at a crammer in Quebec Street, behind Marble Arch. Upstairs, a Mr Crouch poured in the classics; downstairs, a Mr Bird administered the mathematics. One day Isaiah told 'a great big bold gratuitous lie'. He set off from the hotel, telling his parents he was going to Quebec Street. Instead, he walked up and down Kensington High Street, looking in the shop windows, until it was time to go home. He returned to find that his father had rung the school and discovered that he had not showed up that day. All his life Isaiah remembered his father's dressing-down, and even more Mendel's tearful, uncomprehending disillusion. Though it passed, it left the child aware of just how deeply his parents idealised their only son.[5]

In autumn 1922 they moved into a three-storey terraced house, in Upper Addison Gardens, Holland Park. Every evening, throughout the 1920s, Mendel would return from work in Bishopsgate on the London Underground, dine quietly with his wife and son, then sit in the easy chair in the front room, reading his newspaper, while upstairs Isaiah swotted at his homework. Mendel rarely dined out, because he did not like the rough conviviality of the London timber trade; he would rather spend the evening with his wife, although, as Isaiah began to understand, he bored her. 'It was obvious. She picked quarrels with him of an obvious and unnecessary kind.' He liked a little mild extravagance from time to time, whereas she liked to pinch pennies. He did not like arguments and discussions; she thrived on them. She read the latest fiction, Knut Hamsun, D.H. Lawrence, a *bien pensant* Austrian feminist named Baroness Zutner, and thirsted for intellectual stimulation; he did not. 'If you put a book in his hand, he read it.' Otherwise, he preferred the operettas of Offenbach. He had a clear, bright, clerical mind and would have made, his son believed, a better civil servant than a businessman. He lacked the daring and dynamism for big business gambles. In later life, him could not help feeling sorry for him. 'He never lived his life. And if you haven't lived your life, what have you had?'

She, on the other hand, did live her life – through her son. In all his recollections there was never a note of disparagement or pity towards *her*; rather a kind of awe at the force of her love, the size of her frustration and vitality. 'She resented being married to him. Felt he was dull, depended on her. She wanted to be loved, she wanted to be lifted, nothing ever happened, so all her love was turned on me.' She nagged and smothered him. She couldn't stand him sitting about: she wanted activity, interest, life and vitality. He should be doing something. And when she brought him breakfast in bed ('Yes, I was spoiled'), she would ask him, 'What is the plan for the day?' and he would fume, 'There is no plan, none whatever!'

She was maddening, but she was bursting with energy. She kept the house spotless, went about warbling arias from Italian *bel canto*, used to reminisce about a man she loved and couldn't marry, fussed over her son and, through sixty five years, lived vicariously through him. This did not mean that he confided in her. When I suggested this, he seemed amused by the very idea. 'I never told anybody my troubles. I never had many troubles to tell and, not having them to tell, they evaporated.' If this sounds like a defence of the uses of repression, he was quick to admit it was.

Mother and son may never have had a confessional relationship, but she had an enduring impact on his best instincts. She was an immensely shrewd judge of people. It was from her that he learned to value character more than intelligence, vitality more than sophistication, and moral substance more than verbal quickness.

In photographs she is a small, round, plump woman, with large, dark, expressive eyes, who stands slightly apart from her husband, keeping her distance from the camera, a wary, intelligent and ironic expression on her face. In the photographs, there are English gardens in the background, but she does not seem quite at home in them. Isaiah used to say that she took to exile in England like an indomitable refugee, like 'someone sitting on her bags in Ellis Island with fourteen children'. She was a natural Zionist, always convinced – though she did not visit Palestine until after the Second World War – that her people would never be completely at home in England. After they moved to Hollycroft Avenue, Hampstead, in 1928, she became chairwoman of the Brondesbury Zionist society, which she dominated totally.

All her life she sent her son motherly communications on small sheets of thin blue paper, in a large, decisive, rolling hand, her English functioning like a fisherman's net, on which were snagged an exotic linguistic catch of Hebrew, German and Russian phrases. German was used to show off her *Kultur*; and Hebrew to display her supply of biblical saws. Her English was flavoured with Russian constructions and heavily accented, but it was forceful and fluent. The language of the home was mostly English, though now and then when she lost her temper she would burst into Russian. Both she and her son knew that they could be ruder to each other in Russian. When he went too far, she would shout, 'Talk in English.'

When they first arrived in England, the Berlins seemed to have discarded even some of their Jewishness. There had been that non-kosher breakfast of bacon and eggs on arrival. But this lapse was brief. Marie went to the butcher's to buy some meat in the early months of their stay in Surbiton and noticed a small gentleman with a white beard, sitting in the corner. When she asked Mr Hearnshaw, the butcher, who this might be, he replied that Mr Fogelnest came from Reading every week to prepare the food for the two Jewish families in Surbiton. She went up to Mr Fogelnest and discovered that he was indeed a kosher butcher. They talked, discussed the Jewish community in Reading and Surbiton, and suddenly she burst into tears. She returned home with Mr Fogelnest's preparations and for the rest of her life maintained a kosher table. There was also a Passover Seder every year and fasting on Yom Kippur. Mendel was easy-going about religious matters; she never.

By 1923 the Berlins had taken their place in Jewish London; and with English Jews, not Russian ones. They had moved out of the *émigré* ghetto for good. Their place was sufficiently secure that when Mendel applied for British Citizenship, three of his Gentile friends in the timber trade signed their names beneath his application.[6]

But acceptance was never entirely complete. Isaiah had won admission to Westminster, one of London's élite private schools. On a school visit, he had seen all the boys, wearing top hats and Eton jackets, filing in to worship in Westminster Abbey. He was looking foward to his first term at the school, but Mr Crouch, his tutor, happened to remark that, with a name like Isaiah, life might be a trifle difficult at Westminster. Had he considered changing his name to James or Robert? Isaiah came home to tell his parents he did not want to go to Westminister after all.

St Paul's School on Hammersmith Road was a venerable Christian establishment, established in 1509, but it did not exclude Jews or maintain a Jewish quota. Later the governors did fix such quota – at 15 per cent – and when Berlin discovered this, he resigned from the Old Paulines.[7] In 1922 there were something like seventy Jewish boys out of a total of 500. Leonard Schapiro, with whom Isaiah had played in the park in Pavlovsk in 1919, and whose family had emigrated at the same time as the Berlins, was at St Paul's. In June 1922 Isaiah sat the scholarship exam. To everyone's surprise, he failed. A place, yes; but no scholarship.

In the autumn of 1922 he set off along Holland Park Road, across Addison Bridge, down to Hammersmith, dressed in the grey flannels, blazer and cap of St Paul's junior school. St Paul's was a grammar school for ambitious middle- and lower-middle-class boys. At first, Isaiah still felt foreign and ill at ease. He lacked the cultural hinterland that other English boys could take for granted. But within a year his talents for assimilation had borne fruit. He worked hard, played cricket and football badly, felt that he was reasonably popular and never thought of himself as the owlish, studious type. His oft-stated view that he never stood out at St Paul's is not entirely confirmed by the school records. He was top of his form twice and took a vocal part in the debating society. His mother kept his report cards, and in these his masters sound impressed but not overwhelmed: 'he is sometimes inclined to write about ultimates, instead of addressing himself to the question in hand'.[8]

Arthur Calder-Marshall, also at St Paul's, remembered being astonished by the way Berlin talked. 'It was like playing an instrument – not in pursuit of truth or beauty or of anything except sheer pleasure – like a fountain.'[9] In the school corridors, lined with plaster busts of Plato, Socrates and Cicero, and flanked with lockers overflowing with sports kit, satchels and overshoes, Isaiah would stroll along talking non-stop. It was not his loquacity that was exotic to the English, but the idea that talking was an end in itself.

In a schoolboy review of a London stage performance of *The Cherry Orchard* of the late 1920s, Isaiah was already writing with airy adolescent fluency, arguing that any English production was bound to miss the Russian spirit of the play. In a tart comment written at the bottom of the essay, his St Paul's teacher noted the 'hint of superiority' in his review 'which even if you possess . . . you should hide'.[10]

While some of his Jewish schoolmates remembered themselves clinging to their Jewish identity, in the face of Canon Colet's and Cardinal Manning's portraits staring down from the examination hall, Isaiah insisted that he was entirely at home in an Anglo-Catholic institution and just as close to Gentiles like Calder-Marshall as he was to his Jewish friends. St Paul's was merely the first of a chain of English institutions where there would be chapels, Christian prayers, Anglican grace at the beginning and end of meals. In all of them Isaiah would feel more or less at home, keeping silent while those around him mumbled their ancestral responses.[11]

In mid-adolescence, with Leonard Schapiro, Isaiah made visits to certain poor west London synagogues – not the smart one where he had his bar mitzvah, but Hassidic ones in the Portobello Road, where the faithful rocked back and forth in prayer. For a time Hassidic ritual exerted a certain spell, though how much was the nostalgic lure of the past, and how much authentic spiritual stirrings, it is hard to determine. Quite early on, it seems, Isaiah was a religious sceptic. In a letter written in 1989 he suggested that his scepticism was of long standing:

I wish I could lay claim to having similar religious feelings or experiences – ever since I persuaded myself that a personal God – an old man with a beard – the Ancient of Days – or anyway some kind of individual conceivable in human terms – was unlikely to exist, I have never known the meaning of the word God; and I cannot even claim to be an atheist or an agnostic – I am somewhat like a tone-deaf person in relation to music – I realise that others are deeply inspired by it, and I respect that, and I have great sympathy for religious ceremonies and works and poetry: but God?[12]

Before he entered Oxford, before he had read a line of Hume, he was already a Humean sceptic. And so he remained, all his life, despite keeping the major Jewish festivals, Passover and Yom Kippur. He saw no contradiction in any of this. He always believed that these observances had nothing to do with belief; they were declarations of Jewish allegiance rather than affirmations of a creed. Towards the creed, he maintained an attitude of respectful but unflinching doubt.

It was always assumed he would go to Oxford. There was never any question of joining his father in business. Isaiah was mystified by balance sheets and book-keeping and, on the few occasions he went to lunch with his father's hearty, red-faced business associates, could not understand their jokes. In the spring of 1927 he sat the examination for Balliol. Not only did he not win a scholarship, he did not even win a place. His memory always inventoried such setbacks. As he remembered it, his classics were not up to standard and his oral examination, the *viva*, was hopeless. Weeks later he sat the examination for Corpus Christi College and, to everyone's gratification, won an entrance scholarship in classics.

With his future decided, he could now begin to look up from his desk and let his curiosity range more freely. Because St Paul's was a London school, with access to the concert halls, theatres and lecture rooms of the capital, Paulines had a reputation, in Oxford at least, of arriving as undergraduates in an over-sophisticated frame of mind, rotten before they were ripe.

There is a whiff of over-ripe precocity in the teenage Isaiah: voluble, outwardly confident, devouring books of every sort: Aldous Huxley, Anatole France, Dickens, Thackeray, Austen ('who bored me stiff'), Chesterton's essays; the poetry of Eliot and Carl Sandburg. He was impressed by the gloomy sweep of Oswald Spengler's *Decline of the West* and Gilbert Murray's essays on the Greeks. Perhaps the paramount influence on his later style was Macaulay, whom he first read at the age of fourteen. The rolling periods of his mature prose are Macaulayian, long sentences that gather momentum like a great stone rolling downhill, accumulating subordinate clauses as they accelerate. While some of his reading – Joyce, Eliot, and so on – was in the new modern idiom, his real passion was for the formal grandeur of Victorian prose.

As these English influences began to mould his speech and his habits of thought, Isaiah might have shed Riga and Petrograd as well, had it not been for a crucial friendship that began when he was an adolescent. Schmuel Rachmilievitch was a Russian Jew, born in Riga and exiled in

London, where he worked unhappily as a legal adviser in the timber business. But ideas were his passion: he was an authentic example of the pre-revolutionary Russian intellectual. Educated in various German universities before the war, he had been a Menshevik social democrat before the revolution and used to sit, so he told Isaiah, straddling the logs in the timber yards of Riga, trying to raise the consciousness of Jewish timber workers. After the revolution, he escaped Russia via the Black Sea and Constantinople. In London there was no real place for such a rare social type. He had enormous learning but no degree and was too exotic and undisciplined a creature to find a home in the backwaters of English academic life. So he lodged with a Riga family, the Shalits, got up a smattering of English commercial law in order to pay his way, and lived for Saturday when he could spend the day reading in the British Museum. Evenings he spent in the concert halls of London, glaring down at the conductor, so Isaiah remembered, muttering disapproval so volubly that it was a wonder the orchestra could play at all.

He was thirty and Isaiah was fifteen when they met at the Shalits and began a friendship that lasted thirty years. Rachmilievitch was a pure amateur, passionate, ingenious, voluble, slightly mad and obviously inspiring for a schoolboy. Isaiah's first exposure to Kant came, not at Oxford, but from Rachmilievitch's *précis* of the lectures he had attended on Kant's moral philosophy at Heidelberg. He spoke English with a strong Yiddish accent, and when he was in full flow he was unstoppable. 'Vait a moment, vait a moment, I vill answer,' he would say if Isaiah attempted to get a word in edgeways. 'Now Kant says,' and then he would be off, at furious speed, jumping to Husserl, to Schopenhauer, and back again. If anyone first turned Isaiah towards philosophy, it was Rachmilievitch. This strange, excitable man never wrote down a single one of his theories, took Isaiah under his wing only to watch the bright pupil fly farther than he could ever have imagined, and ensured that Isaiah's intellectual centre of gravity always remained Russian. Obscure Russian writers of the previous century tumbled out of Rachmilievitch; references to this or that vanished or forgotten controversy in the history of Russian socialism tripped off his tongue; and, little by little, Isaiah absorbed it all. A decade later, when he came to write the acknowledgements for his first book, a biography of Karl Marx, the unknown name of S. Rachmilievitch figured besides Oxford lights like A.J. Ayer and Stuart Hampshire.[13]

Rachmilievitch was an inspiration, but in his failure to find a place in English society and his brilliant chatter, which vanished like smoke, he was also a warning. He was what Isaiah might well have become, had there not been an as yet unseen element of self-discipline to mould the chatter into consequential thought; had there not been the beckoning opportunities of Oxford to give Berlin the belonging that Rachmilievitch never achieved.

Rachmilievitch's friendship provided Isaiah with an enviable intellectual grounding, but in other ways he remained a backward and timid adolescent. He remembered going to dances in Bayswater where, instead of dancing, he would make himself unpopular with the hostesses by gathering the boys around him and telling them stories. At one of these dances he met Betty Spiro, a shy, ascetic and very intelligent girl, a year younger than he, from the girls' school at St Paul's. She hated dancing as much as Isaiah did, so they sat in the corner and talked about books. She was a 'pensive, slightly melancholy girl with the most beautiful manners', whose nerve endings seemed very close to her skin.[14]

These tentative ventures into the world of dances, parties and early courting left Isaiah convinced that he had no place in it. In a letter written to Aunt Ida Samunov in Jerusalem, just before going up to Oxford in the summer of 1928, he mentions the forthcoming engagement of some family friends, and then adds, 'anyhow, I, who am vowed to eternal celibacy, am very glad. Which, from me, is enough.'[15] He continued to believe this until well past forty.

His parting success at St Paul's was to be awarded the Truro Prize for an essay on the theme of freedom. His lifelong hostility towards determinism is here given its first expression.[16] The eighteen-year-old positioned himself between the determinists ('be they Russian communists, American industrialists or Italian fascists [who] work to achieve an essentially collectivist state') and the German idealists, who seek to escape the evidence of a deterministic world by means of flight into an inner realm of freedom. The essay defends the real freedom of inner experience from the determinists, and the real freedom of external action in the outer world from the idealists. Perhaps the note in the essay that strikes a genuinely autobiographical chord is his defence of convention:

Convention does not in itself imply slavery; it is largely that instinctive law that arises out of men's fear of anarchy, which is as far removed from freedom as tyranny itself. In this function convention is often a safeguard of inner liberty, creating as it does a broad external disciplinary equality which leaves room for complete inner non-conformity. It hurts no man to conform if he knows that conformity is only a kind of manners, a sort of universal etiquette.

The defence of convention was to occupy a large place in his later thought. From St Paul's onward, he lived inside conventional, rule-ordered institutions, rich in lore and custom, absurd perhaps, but absurdly convincing as well.

The essay can be forced to divulge the later, more mature self, but only at the cost of losing the contours of the self who actually wrote it: an eighteen-year-old brimming with quotations half-understood, references half-grasped, ideas half-formed, generalisations that sweep too high above the ground. As his dull but not unperceptive school masters at St Paul's said, there was promise there, but it needed discipline. Enemies of promise lay in wait in Oxford and nothing was less inevitable than that promise should be so startlingly fulfilled.

5

Oxford, 1928–32

He went up to Oxford in the autumn of 1928, a plump young man with crinkly black hair and animated dark eyes, bushy eyebrows and thick glasses. He wore a dark three-piece suit like his father and in photographs cradled his left arm. His mother worried about him – he was bookish; didn't dance; didn't circulate – but she needn't have done. Oxford was a liberation. He was getting away from his parents and launching himself into the big world.

The college that had chosen him, Corpus, was a small, almost exclusively Gentile establishment, which produced clergymen and dons, specialised in the classics and set its face against all manifestations of the twentieth century. There were no typewriters in the college office: the President wrote every piece of correspondence out in his own copperplate hand. The tutors did not approve of the new syllabus of philosophy, politics and economics, introduced in 1920, and undergraduates of Corpus were not supposed to read these subjects.[1]

A generation of glamorous undergraduates – Cyril Connolly, Harold Acton, Brian Howard, Evelyn Waugh – was just graduating as Berlin arrived. He remembered hearing Harold Acton reading *Sea and Sardinia* by D.H. Lawrence in a 'very oily, buttery voice' and recoiling at the homo-erotic affectation of it all. Homosexuality was not just a sexual disposition in the 1920s: it was also a style of revolt against the dunderheaded anti-intellectualism of the public schools. Looking back,

Berlin remembered an extravagant Latin American, the self-styled Queen of Peru, who gave loud parties in a house that the college proctors used to raid, and where it was reputed indecencies went on. There was another languid aesthete named Frank Curtis, whose father was reputed to be a colonel in the Guards and who insisted on being called François Capel. If asked what college he went to, he drawled, 'My dear, I simply can't remember.' The likes of Capel read *transition*, a surrealist journal published in Paris, and went around Oxford's streets carrying lavatory chains with which to defend themselves from the hearties, bluff public-school boys in rugby shirts who drank beer and liked to attack 'pansies'.

The university Berlin entered in 1928 – almost exclusively male, middle-class, devoted to the teaching of the classics – no longer exists, any more than the horse-drawn cabs that still met the trains at Oxford station. It was an Oxford ruled by the male public-school ethos, by class privilege, by an ideal of civilised gentility, which faced its first inquisition by conscience in the 1930s. The aesthetes, he remembers, were killed 'stone dead' by the financial crisis of 1931: their fathers no longer had the money to pay for their clothes and their subscriptions to French magazines; and, with the onset of the Depression, they woke to the reality that they would have to buckle down to jobs upon graduation.

His mother need not have worried: he was soon the centre of a circle of friends, who came to include John Hilton, Bernard Spencer, Martin Cooper and Stephen Spender. In his first three years, he lived in the college annexe in Magpie Lane. The rooms were heated with coal fires; there was no running water. A college servant – the scout – woke the young men up every morning, bearing a ewer of hot water for washing and shaving. The toilets were a cold run across the quad. Mornings began with prayers in chapel – or a bleary-eyed roll-call, usually taken in pyjamas, in the dining hall for those, like Isaiah, who did not attend prayers. Lunch was bread and cheese, fetched from the dining hall and taken in one's room. Dinner was in hall; scholars like Isaiah had to wear a gown, and one of the classics scholars had to pronounce a long Latin grace. He learned it by heart and remembered his anxiety that, as a Jew, he might be asked to recite it in public. He never was.

He had won a scholarship to read classics and modern history, but the college's tutor took one look at his classics and said they would never do. He was to read Pass Mods, a preparatory course in classics, for two terms, and then begin Greats, a seven-term course in ancient history and philosophy, both ancient and modern. The classics formed yet another geological stratum of his learning, just as the cadences of Cicero and Seneca were to become one of the sources of his rhetoric. But he was not a strong classics scholar; classicists had neat, tidy minds. His was neither.

Berlin liked to contradict the image others had of him as a high flyer. The accent of memory was upon hard work late at night: Xenophon, Herodotus, Seneca, Plautus and earnest screeds read aloud every week to his somnolent and uninspired classics tutor. His essays on most subjects were 'much too long', the tutor grumbled. Whenever he indulged in a purple passage, the dour Dr Grundy was there to write a deflating 'Oh?' in the margin.

Some deflation of schoolboy hubris was to his benefit. 'I did discover I was nothing like as good as some people. I didn't mind. I'm under-ambitious. No wish to shine.' This humble self-portrait is disingenuous. Stephen Spender, his contemporary, met him after his first year and remembered that already Isaiah was a 'famous undergraduate'. Famous for what? 'For talking.'[2] His rooms in Corpus became a 'place of resort' for talk and gossip. One friend, Bernard Spencer, was a poet, an aesthete whom the heartier members of college attacked one night, shaving off half his whiskers; Martin Cooper had musical tastes; Spender was reading English. The talk in Isaiah's rooms was about concerts, plays, poems and novels, not the Wall Street crash, the German elections or the fate of the Labour government. There were parties organised on the principle that the food should reflect the character of the person invited. The black-tempered Humphry House was served a black meal, black pudding, burned toast, black coffee, black olives; the budding poet Stephen Spender was served alphabet soup.

By the end of his second year, in 1930, Berlin inherited the editorship of *Oxford Outlook*, an undergraduate magazine, from his old school friend, Arthur Calder-Marshall. *Outlook* had an arch, high-brow tone; it took its intellectual cues from the fashionable London magazines, like *London Mercury* and *Criterion*. A certain affectation of worldly knowledge and sophistication was the ruling style and Isaiah's early contributions borrowed this idiom. Editing *Outlook* brought him into contact with all of the brightest undergraduates of his generation.[3]

Few memories of undergraduate roistering remain. He did recall once having drunk a few too many punches at a party, staggering up the High Street, weaving to and fro, tipping his hat to the ladies and apologising for his deportment. Stephen Spender remembered an undergraduate party where Isaiah stood at a window with a bowl in his hand, chucking cherries at passers-by. But these were exceptional. Another contemporary, Diana Hubback, recalled that he 'seemed completely adult at a time when his youthful friends were only just emerging from adolescence'.[4] He did seem astonishingly cosmopolitan. Sceptics wondered when he found time actually to acquire his erudition. Shiela Grant Duff, who met Berlin in early 1931, used to wonder whether he actually read the books he cited so effortlessly. Perhaps he 'sat in the middle of the room and imbibed' them.[5] He was in fact a dipper, with an extraordinarily acute sense, from a few pages, of whether a book was worth reading, and he sometimes claimed familiarity with work he hardly knew at all. A lifelong dislike of Freud, for example, was based on only casual acquaintance with what Freud had actually written. A selective intelligence coupled with a prodigious memory enabled him to amass the breadth of reference that amazed his friends. But he was never an orderly worker: his work rooms were a cosy chaos, cluttered with books and papers, gramophone records, unanswered letters and half-drunk cups of tea. He liked reading at night – preferably in bed – and lay there, browsing and scribbling at a furious rate, until two, sometimes three in the morning, and then sleeping through breakfast and early tutorials.

The person who taught him intellectual self-discipline was a modest Scotsman, Frank Hardie, his philosophy tutor at Corpus. Beginning in Isaiah's second year, Hardie set to work, patiently forcing his brilliant pupil to drive some paths through the jungle in his mind. Every week Hardie would listen to Isaiah's undergraduate essay read aloud and then pick it apart, cutting through the purple passages, the flights of fancy, gently exposing contradictions and inconsistency in a soft, precise Scots accent. Hardie's dissection was sobering but the effect was inspirational. Remembering these sessions sixty years later, Berlin would become animated, punctuating his words by smacking the palm of his right hand over the top of his left: 'Obscurity [smack] and pretentiousness [smack] and sentences which doubled over themselves [smack] he wrung right out of me [smack], from then until this moment [smack].'

Hardie became the single most important intellectual influence upon

Berlin's undergraduate life: orienting him towards the British empiricism that became his intellectual morality. It was remarkable that someone so undisciplined and intuitive should have realised how much he needed what this mild, retiring Scotsman had to teach him. But this was to prove a lifetime pattern: seeing in others what he lacked himself, and having the shrewdness and self-confidence to go in search of it.

Oxford philosophy had only just entered the twentieth century: its leading philosophers were still rebutting the Bradleian idealism of the preceding century. As for Russell, Wittgenstein, and the revolution germinating in nearby Cambridge, Oxford philosophy tutors of the late 1920s and early 1930s took little notice. G. E. Moore's *Principia Ethica* – which did so much to define the ethical ambience of the Bloomsbury Group – was not on any syllabus, though Isaiah found his way to it on his own, some time in 1930, and was impressed by its expositional clarity, its pure moral tone and the comforting implication that goodness might be as clear, distinct and intuitively apprehensible as primary colours. He must also have been impressed by the way in which intellectual scepticism could go hand-in-hand with social conservatism. Moore wrote, 'on any view commonly taken, it seems certain that the preservation of civilised society, which these rules are necessary to effect, is necessary for the existence, in any great degree, of anything which may be held to be good in itself'.[6] The function of philosophy was to defend 'civilised society' by purifying its talk about itself, clarifying its moral rules and thereby strengthening the commitment of its 'young men' to its values. The possibility that values – far from being objectively discernible like colours – might be both contestable and incommensurable was not on anyone's horizon.

From Moore, Isaiah then found his way to Russell, but not from Russell to Wittgenstein. Berlin did not become aware of Wittgenstein until a dashing young undergraduate, Freddie Ayer – wearing, so Isaiah remembered, a very smart dinner jacket and a carnation in his buttonhole – gave a paper on the *Tractatus* to a gathering of philosophy dons at Christ Church in the spring of 1932.

In the summer of 1931, Berlin made a friendship with the most notorious and celebrated young don of his day, then regarded as 'mad, bad, and dangerous to know'. This was Maurice Bowra, a small, stocky, belligerent-looking classicist, built like a bulldog, who was then Dean of

Wadham College and the centre of a circle of the brightest young dons and undergraduates in Oxford.[7]

Oxford is an institution devoted to the seduction of the young, and Bowra was its most assiduous seducer. Cyril Connolly remembered how Bowra collected him and then introduced him around a room: 'This is Connolly. Coming man. [Pause]. Hasn't come yet.' Isaiah first came to Bowra's attention through his friend Martin Cooper, who, hearing that Bowra was looking for someone to check his translation of a poem by the Russian poet Alexander Blok, put the two of them together. The first meeting was not auspicious. Isaiah read the first two lines:

> A tempest from the sea ...
> A siren sitting on apple branches ...

A siren? Isaiah asked to see the original. The Russian word actually meant a winged mythological creature, possibly a fire-bird. Bowra looked the word up in the dictionary. 'Barn-owl,' it says here, he reported gruffly. Since this would never do, he pencilled 'Turtle dove' into the proof and sent it off, obviously miffed that this precocious undergraduate had found his Russian wanting. Still, in parting, he told Isaiah to visit him again. Soon Isaiah was in the inner circle. Bowra proved to be a decisive influence: barrel-shaped, vain, red-faced, voluble, always to be found at parties, 'roaring in a voice with the carrying power of the Last Trump', he showed that vitality and appetite for life need not be squeezed out of donnish existence. In the 1930s Bowra liked to portray himself as the leader of the 'immoral front', all those communists, homosexuals and non-conformists who stood for pleasure, conviction and sincerity against the dull, fastidious mandarins of the Oxford senior common rooms. He was also a celebrated wit, sought out and feared in turn for the sharpness of his tongue. As Isaiah recalled, 'the words came in short sharp bursts of precisely aimed, concentrated fire as image, pun, metaphor, parody, seemed spontaneously to generate one another in a succession of marvellously imaginative patterns, sometimes rising to high, wildly comical fantasy'. Here, in other words, was a Paganini of talk, a virtuoso of that apparently wild, yet disciplined free association that was to become Isaiah's own speciality.[8] Berlin's very diction – the rapid-fire gabble – came from Bowra.

When Isaiah later said that meeting Maurice had been a 'liberation', he meant that Bowra had given him the confidence to be himself, to let the talk flow, to let the exuberance bubble over. Bowra helped him to refuse the buttoned-up donnish persona on offer in the common rooms of his time. For a cautious, moralizing young undergraduate there seemed something delightful about a young don who, when asked about the conscience, thundered that it 'was a loud thing which struck twelve and said don't'.[9]

Bowra licensed Isaiah's talk; showed him that a public persona could be built around such brilliant garrulousness; made him realise that he didn't have to repress this part of himself in order to succeed.[10] But he also provided a sustaining audience for Isaiah's interest in things Russian, helping to keep the door open to the Russian past in an Oxford where, without him, it might have been slowly shut.[11]

When Berlin met Bowra in 1931, Oxford undergraduate life was turning away from the aesthetic towards the political. Hitler's successes in the German elections, the British flight from sterling and the abandonment of the gold standard, the formation of the National Government and the riots of the unemployed pressed in upon the largely privileged undergraduates of the day and turned all conversation towards the darkening political environment. As Berlin reported in a letter in September 1931, 'Politics has become so interesting that even I have begun to follow them with some avidity.'[12] Suddenly, communism was fashionable and the Soviet Union a beacon of hope to those who felt there was something rotten about the liberal civility which Isaiah so much admired.

Stephen Spender did most to bring home the realities of European politics to Berlin and his circle. Spender left Oxford in 1931 and travelled in Germany. His letters back made it impossible for Isaiah to ignore what was happening as Hitler edged closer to power:

I cannot exaggerate the seriousness of the political situation in Germany. It looks as if the whole system . . . will break down and that, in December, after another general election, all people of Jewish extraction will be shot, all foreigners will be turned out of the country and all the poor boys will be shipped off to Heligoland or somewhere to break stones.[13]

Spender's political acumen and sexual candour drew them together. As Spender was to put it in his memoir of the 1930s, *World Within World*, 'Isaiah had an interest in other people's lives which was strengthened by the conviction that he himself was detached from the passions which moved them.'[14] Isaiah lived his erotic life through the female undergraduates who came to confess their troubles, and through adventurers like Stephen who were exploring both sides of their erotic nature. Spender remembered walking through the streets of Salzburg on an August evening in 1931, together with Isaiah, when he saw a boy he fancied and went off with him.[15] Isaiah was not especially shocked, though Spender himself looked back on it as an episode of exhibitionism. Later, when they went on a walking holiday in the Lake District and were taken, by some, to be a pair of homosexual lovers, Isaiah was amused rather than dismayed. The advantage of vicariousness, of course, is that you do not risk a mistake; you can watch other people making them for you.

By early 1932 Spender had witnessed the Blackshirts smashing Jewish shop windows and had felt the atmosphere of intimidation and fear spreading throughout Germany. In a letter written to Isaiah, the challenge to his mandarin detachment was explicit:

I didn't mean that rawness and violence were better in themselves than Oxford. What I do mean is that if our world is a world of violence, of rawness, then [when] one leaves Oxford one is bound to have to deal with it, so it is best to accept the real conditions of contemporary life as soon as possible. One has got to put up with them for better or worse, and the only hope of changing them is in facing them, not in living in a dream of the old world. But I am tired of saying what is so obvious to me. The point is that if philosophy withdraws to the seclusion of Oxford and is studied by people who see nothing outside of Oxford, it will create a remote idealistic world which is quite as cloistered as the Church ever was, but which provides a trap for people with brains, which the Church no longer does (*pace* T.S. Eliot).[16]

As a Jew, foreigner and outsider, Berlin felt he was not cut out for taking public stands. But he regarded Stephen's politics with a vicarious respect. He could not fail to see that any genuine defence of the 'civilised life' had to understand how cloistered Oxford's version of civilisation actually was. It was Stephen who provided this rude check with reality and made it impossible for Isaiah to withdraw into academic detachment. He found Spender's personal imbroglios comic and absurd, his poetry and plays sentimental and 'larmoyant'; and he couldn't understand why Stephen briefly joined the communist party in 1936. But he respected the deep appetite for life in Spender's engagement with his times, and felt there was a Russian kind of seriousness in Spender's sense of political commitment.

Spender's lifelong friend and rival, Wystan Auden, treated Spender like a schoolmaster; Berlin treated him like an equal. If Isaiah talked 'in a monologue where sometimes all the words seemed joined together into one huge word', he also knew how to *listen*. As his friends noticed this capacity for listening, for empathy with their predicaments, he began, even in his twenties, to acquire a reputation for being wise, for having some mysterious gift of sound human judgement.

In Spender's company, in the summer of 1930, Berlin made his first visit to Salzburg. These visits, which continued until the Anschluss in 1938 and then resumed after the war, had a central importance in Isaiah's life. He never forgot the feeling of physical excitement that took hold of him when he settled into his bunk in the third-class sleeper bound for Salzburg. Founded in 1920 by the impresario Max Reinhardt and the poet Hugo von Hofmannsthal, the Salzburg Festival devoted itself to the music of Mozart and Beethoven just as Bayreuth consecrated itself to Wagner.[17] Reinhardt was Jewish; Hofmannsthal from a Jewish family that had converted to Catholicism – Salzburg, in political terms, was an anti-Bayreuth. When Toscanini refused to play the *Giovinezza*, the fascist hymn, and was assaulted by fascist thugs in Milan in the 1920s, and when he refused to play at Bayreuth, he became a hero to anti-fascists throughout Europe. In Salzburg in 1935 he gave the famous performance of Beethoven's *Fidelio*, where – as both Spender and Berlin remembered – the prisoners' chorus, as the men cast off their chains and rose up into the light, seemed to give voice to that 'humanistic piety' that was everywhere under attack in the Europe of the 1930s. As long as he lived, Berlin never forgot that performance: moral conviction and musical expression fused in a moment of awesome feeling.

Thanks to Toscanini, Berlin and Spender thought of Salzburg as the cultural home of the European cosmopolitan opposition to Nazi aesthetics. But the town itself was hardly free of fascist manifestations: the town paper was notably anti-Semitic, and Isaiah had his only direct encounter with fascists in the town's cafés and restaurants. Drunken, red-faced men in *Lederhosen*, white socks and Nazi armbands used to bang the tables for service and mutter darkly about the swarthy cosmopolitans at the other tables. Berlin's mother became so worried about her son's summer ventures that she actually begged him not to go, and he agreed, only to sneak off anyway.

The fascist presence in Salzburg could not have been over-bearing, because life in the small town – staying in a cheap *Gasthof*, getting up late, breakfasting in cafés, going to noon-time concerts, reading or walking in the afternoons, attending concerts in the evening – became his definition of heaven. In the first summer, besides Spender, he was accompanied by Walter Ettinghausen, a friend from St Paul's, and a diminutive ex-Marlborough schoolboy, Michael Corley, son of a prosperous blanket manufacturer. Spender was always puzzled by Corley, who behaved as if he were Isaiah's page, loving, devoted, and yet quizzical and amused by his mild hypochondria. When Isaiah came down with a cold and was confined to bed in his *Gasthof*, in August 1930, Spender asked Corley when Isaiah would recover, and Corley drolly replied, 'Isaiah never recovers.'[18]

The trips to Salzburg were much more than holidays, and Berlin's increasing devotion to music much more than a hobby. Music had always been important in his life. His mother went about the house warbling in a sugary but pure soprano; at St Paul's he frequented the Queen's Hall and the Wigmore Hall and, by nineteen, had heard most of the classical piano repertoire of Beethoven and Schubert. At Oxford be became a music critic for *Oxford Outlook*. While he never learned to play an instrument properly or even to read a score, he loved music with real passion, and his musical loves – for Bach, Mozart, Beethoven, Schubert, but also for lighter figures like Rossini and Donizetti – offer some clue to the essentially ordered, contented and serene interior life he came to live. He loved the classical nineteenth-century repertoire – piano especially – because it expressed a commitment, at once aesthetic and ethical, to the world of dignity and clear light. He respected Wagner but disapproved of his violence and sexual passion. He recoiled not only from the intensity of the feeling, or even the force of the eroticism, but from what he took to be Wagner's insincerity. In a letter to Spender in 1935, he argued that Wagner was one of those artists incapable of feeling emotion directly. He had to ask himself, 'What is erotic passion?'; 'What is jealousy?' and then set out to construct a musical paraphrase of emotions he was incapable of feeling at first hand.[19] Whereas Verdi touched the heart more directly, because he felt the emotions without the need for paraphrase. True or not, this distinction between types of artists was also an indirect exploration of his own anxieties. He wondered whether he was capable of feeling emotions directly and thought he was worrying too much about the impression he was making on others. Early on, he identified this kind of self-consciousness as an obstacle both to art and inner contentment.

In and through music, he learned emotional pitch, learned to distinguish between true and false feeling. He always had a vivid sense of the difficulty of knowing what one feels and expressing these emotions without sentimentality. This is why his love of music was both aesthetic and ethical. For it was in the concert hall that he grasped the nature of emotional authenticity.

Musical and moral qualities were never entirely distinct in his mind. It was for both moral and musical reasons that Toscanini became Berlin's abiding artistic hero: the Toscanini who demanded a personal apology from Mussolini, for his treatment at the hands of fascist thugs, was inseparable from the implacable disciplinarian who could take an orchestra through three bars countless times in search of a fugitive perfection that only he could hear. There was something 'fiery and implacable, something un-English' that captivated Isaiah about Toscanini's conducting. The word he came to use for this quality was from the Italian: *terribilità*, and all his life he loved art that possessed this sense of fierce and implacable necessity.

There is a strong analogy between what Berlin learned from Toscanini and what he was to learn from Bertrand Russell: that artists and thinkers of greatness have a core idea, which, however complex the adumbration and defences of it may be, is always simple. Once found, it unlocked the nature of a work.[20] Berlin's work as an interpreter of intellectual figures of the past was much influenced by the conductors he admired. His interpretation always sought to reveal a thinker's essential melodic line. He also admired Toscanini's artistic modesty, his respect for composers' intentions. 'When he said the least good composer is higher than the best conductor, he meant it.' Berlin too always presented his own insights as if they were merely adumbrating the melodic lines of intellectual composers greater than himself.

Another figure in Salzburg was Sheila (Sigle) Lynd, the vivacious daughter of an Irish journalist, Robert Lynd, and the poet Sylvia Dryhurst. The Lynd sisters, Sheila and Maire (also known as B.J. [Baby Junior]), had a Pre-Raphaelite, Celtic beauty and were also fiercely intelligent and left-wing. During the summer of 1931 Isaiah became seriously attracted to Sheila, and in the concert halls and cafés there blossomed a repressed kind of romance. 'Nothing happened,' Isaiah remembered flatly. 'We never kissed. Never touched. Very inhibited.' It was the first time he had ventured into the deep waters and he quickly withdrew. Sheila soon moved on to more physically demonstrative partners, but the two remained close friends, even after Sheila plunged into active communist politics.

His return from his stirring but troubling encounter with Sheila Lynd brought Isaiah to the first fork in the road of his career. In his examinations, he had gained a first-class degree in Greats, together with the John Locke Prize in philosophy. Now he had to decide what to do next. Following in his father's footsteps was out of the question. He was tempted to continue at Oxford for another year and take PPE (Philosophy, Politics and Economics). But there was also the possibility of going into law. In the autumn of 1931 he briefly considered a career at the Bar, but concluded that the law was too dull for words. There was also the possibility of journalism. The President of Corpus had informed him that the editor of *The Manchester Guardian*, C.P. Scott, a Corpus man himself, was looking for a sound classics scholar, interested in foreign affairs and gifted with 'an easy knack of writing'. The President advised Isaiah to give up his fourth year at Oxford, since 'so good an opening into public life' rarely occurred, and certainly not in the pit of the Depression. C.P. Scott invited him for an interview. Scott was a nationally known figure, a white-bearded, blue-eyed patriarch among British editors, who inspired a certain measure of fear. He did not waste words. 'Do you write with facility?' he asked Isaiah. When Berlin confessed that he did not, Scott sized him up and said, 'Then you're no good to me.' The interview was concluded. The job went instead to Isaiah's friend, Goronwy Rees.[21]

As C.P. Scott had decided the matter, Isaiah returned to Oxford for the academic year of 1931, to read PPE, then a relatively new subject, regarded suspiciously by many dons, who dismissed it as 'girls' greats' – that is, an easy alternative to classics, suitable for young women. Berlin concentrated on philosophy with Frank Hardie and became a regular attender of the undergraduate philosophy club, the Jowett Society, where he gained a reputation for sceptical demolition of other people's positions, rather than for advancing arguments of his own. He also attended a course of lectures given by R.G. Collingwood. The subject was the philosophy of history, and Collingwood stood alone among Oxford philosophers in his insistently historical approach to philosophical problems. If there was any single source in Oxford for Berlin's later interest in the philosophy of history, in philosophical pioneers like the eighteenth-century Neapolitan Giambattista Vico, and in his evolving conviction that thinking historically was the best way to do philosophy, it was Collingwood. The two never became close – Collingwood gently rebuffing one of Berlin's invitations to join a seminar – but the influence was important.

As for the politics parts of the PPE syllabus, there were no politics tutors in Corpus, and so Berlin was grandly told to read *The Times'* editorials to make up the deficiency. Nor was there any political philosophy to speak of. The domains of philosophy that Isaiah was to make his own – the philosophy of history and the theory of liberty – formed no part of his undergraduate syllabus. Indeed, later, when he set out on these paths, there was almost no one in Oxford he could follow or with whom he could share his interests.

For economics, he went to a tutor at Queen's but he disliked the discipline. It was also his first exposure to the social sciences and, while he was a dutiful student, he found them tedious. Capitalism was never to figure among his objects of study or interest. This disdain for the social sciences, coupled with an active suspicion about their scientific pretensions, became a fixed feature of his intellectual orientation. In the summer of 1932 he sat his final examinations and was awarded a first-class degree.[22]

Richard Crossman, a newly appointed fellow at New College, then persuaded the college's Warden, H.A.L. Fisher, that New College needed another philosophy tutor. With artful mendacity he contrived to imply that Berlin had received three offers from other colleges. No college had, in fact, made any offer of any kind. But with recommendations from Frank Hardie and the evidence of a strong first, Berlin was given a post as tutor in philosophy in New College as of October 1932. There was no application, no interview. Berlin had published nothing other than some music and book reviews in an Oxford undergraduate magazine; he was only months from passing his own undergraduate finals; he had never taught before; and now he was embarked upon the life of an Oxford don.

The passage from an undergraduate to a don's life proved a highly disagreeable shock. The senior common room at New College was mortally dull. 'Everyone talked about automobiles and by-passes.' Jasper Ridley, a brilliant philosophy undergraduate at Balliol, put his head round the door of the New College senior common room, took one look and whispered, 'Who *are* these gargoyles?' Now Isaiah was one of the gargoyles. The realisation made him miserable. The first time he dined at high table he was so utterly mute that Crossman hissed at him across the table, 'Be bright, Berlin, be bright. If you aren't, they won't take to you, you know.' He could talk to Crossman, but found him a brash, aggressive bully, with a vein of cynicism running through his talk. 'He was a left-wing Nazi. He was anti-capitalist, hated the civil service, respectability, conventional values, of a decent honest dreary kind. What he wanted was young men singing songs, students linking arms, torchlit parades. There was a strong fascist streak in him. He wanted power, hated liberalism, mildness, kindness, amiability . . .'

Berlin liked talking philosophy to undergraduates, but he had little sense of having found a vocation. Indeed, while he was always a dutiful don, he was never to enjoy teaching very much. He was uncomfortable with the parental aspects. Father–son, father–daughter relations were never his line. What seems to have depressed him most was that he had to become 'responsible'.

Interestingly, the best friend he made at New College was its Warden, the liberal grandee and former Cabinet minister, H.A.L. Fisher. Fisher's indiscretions about his college colleagues were legendary. 'Before the war,' he used to say, 'this college was a splendid place – Gilbert Murray and so on. What do I find now? One enormous mausoleum.' Isaiah's sentiments exactly. He and Fisher began to lunch alone in the Warden's lodgings and then took walks together, much to the annoyance of more senior colleagues, who could not see what there was to be said for this bespectacled Jew with a quick tongue. Fisher was the first grandee Berlin had ever met, the first one with that lordly sense of the ways of the world which, far from repelling Isaiah, seemed positively alluring. Fisher once came out of a meeting with the college fellows and remarked to Isaiah, 'I have just treated them to an immense quantity of Victorian gush: I think it worked.' Berlin had found Crossman's cynicism repellent. Fisher's had a grandeur and wit that made it appealing.

He soon became friends, not only with Fisher, but with his wife – a grand woman in her own right, whose scathing frankness Isaiah much enjoyed – and with their daughter, Mary. She was then an undergraduate reading classics, pretty, fair-haired, blue-eyed, earnest and utterly devoted. Also living in the Warden's lodgings was Maire (B.J.) Lynd, sister of Sheila, Isaiah's romantic entanglement in Salzburg. Soon, Isaiah was dining in the lodge with these two charming and well-born young women, who were to become friends for life.

Apart from the Fishers, Isaiah's existence as a don was miserable. Within weeks, an escape beckoned. In October 1932, at Frank Hardie's urging, he sat the exam for a prize fellowship at All Souls. The college represented the very Parnassus of English academic life, an ancient and wealthy establishment that did no teaching whatsoever, took in no undergraduates or graduates, and had a reputation for electing the brightest fellows in England. Once elected, a fellow entered a version of academic heaven, researching, teaching, even following a career in London, with all his needs taken care of and no bothersome intrusions from the world outside to distract or annoy. Berlin barely knew what the college was, and he had no idea what he would do if he managed to get in. He sat the exams in the hall of All Souls during three days in late October 1932. He had barely any memory of the ordeal: there were three papers, one on general subjects, one on philosophy and one on economics. The most daunting part of the ordeal was being called out in front of the fellows and being asked, first to read a passage in German, then to translate it by sight. Isaiah stumbled in the middle of his translation, and heard the Warden of All Souls, a venerable ex-Viceroy of India, Lord Chelmsford, intone, 'Go on', which made him stumble all the more. As he left the room, blushing with embarrassment, he heard Chelmsford mutter, 'At least we don't have to have that one.' As Isaiah was to learn later, another fellow, the Bishop of Gloucester, objected to the very idea of electing a Jew to a fellowship.

On 4 November 1932 Berlin's friend Goronwy Rees – a fellow since the previous year – came up to him in the High Street and told him he had been elected. Isaiah was dumbfounded. The thing seemed impossible: the first Jew ever elected to All Souls, and only the third Jew ever elected as a fellow of an Oxford college. As soon as the news was announced, *The Jewish Chronicle* ran the story, and so the whole Jewish community knew of his success. The Chief Rabbi wrote him a letter of congratulations and the grandest Jewish figure of them all, Baron Rothschild, invited him to spend a weekend at Waddesdon, his palatial country house. At once, in one fell swoop, at the age of twenty-three, Berlin had been plucked from donnish obscurity and elected to what was then the most select club in English life, a college where Cabinet ministers, editors of *The Times* and the leading intellectual figures of his day mingled on equal terms. Crossman was furious: the hack who was to take over his humdrum teaching while he charmed the lecture hall with his brilliant lectures on Plato had stolen a march on him. Small wonder that Isaiah was elated: he moved out of New College and into his rooms at All Souls within days; 'talked for two days and nights without stopping'; then fell ill for two months from sheer nervous release.

6

All Souls

Two of his friends stood a music stand in the corridor outside his new rooms at All Souls, propped a mortar board and a gown on top of it and placed this academic scarecrow in front of Berlin's door, with a 'Don't Enter!' sign around its neck. For a week he allowed himself to collapse. Then he left college to convalesce, first under his mother's care at Hollycroft Avenue and then in a hotel in Amalfi, where he amused himself by communicating with the waiters in Latin.

When he returned to All Souls in January 1933, he had mastered the emotions that overwhelmed him on election. He settled into his rooms overlooking the great quad and the Radcliffe Camera and began to enjoy himself. He was to be at All Souls until 1938, when he took up a fellowship teaching philosophy at New College, and he always looked on those six years at All Souls in the 1930s as the happiest of his life. All Souls provided the setting in which all his characteristics could flourish: his need for company; his appetite for talk; his love of gossip; his fascination with the lives of others. An all-male institution also provided an escape from the burden of having an erotic life of his own.[1]

He enjoyed being a rare bird. No one so exotic was to join the college until John Plamenatz, a Montenegrin, was elected in 1936. Plamenatz once admitted to Berlin, in expectation of fellow-feeling, that whenever he was in a room with a pair of Englishmen he always felt alone, because of the silent complicity that passed between them.[2] Berlin never felt the same way, nor did he identify particularly with foreigners or fellow-Jews. Two of his closest friends in the college, the philosophers John Austin and Stuart Hampshire, were caricaturally English in their indirection, self-containment and reserve.[3]

All Souls provided the young Berlin with an experience of almost complete belonging. It had an aristocratic aura, yet it was sufficiently meritocratic not to engender feelings of shame. A Welsh schoolmaster's son, like Goronwy Rees, and a Riga timber merchant's son, like Isaiah, could both find themselves at dinner beside Robert Brand, the prominent City banker; Sir John Simon, the Foreign Secretary; or Geoffrey Dawson, editor of *The Times*. All Souls built its walls high against outsiders; once inside, it treated fellows as equals. The London fellows who journeyed up for the weekend enjoyed it precisely because it allowed them the illusion of becoming young men with ideas once again. Inside this bastion of privilege, there was something approaching a democracy of the intellect.

Being a fellow of All Souls also gave Isaiah entry to the upper reaches of Anglo-Jewish society: to weekends with the Rothschilds; to the Sieffs' dinners in Park Lane. These were Jews so grand that they were unsnubbable. The Rothschilds were also so wealthy that on one occasion when Berlin complained about the length of the journey back to Oxford, after a weekend with Victor Rothschild in Cambridge, he was flown home in a light plane.[4]

To criticise Berlin for being too easily seduced by high society, for becoming too worldly, is to miss an essential point about his character: he rejoiced in worldliness, in having some grasp of the inner workings of the world of power and influence, in knowing the gossip, in understanding what low motives actually did make the world turn. 'Worldliness', in his lexicon, became nearly synonymous with having that 'sense of reality' which most intellectuals and dons conspicuously lacked.

He never became a college man like his friend John Sparrow, then a London barrister and later Warden; or like A.L. Rowse, the Cornish-born Shakespearean scholar for whom he conceived a lifelong (and fully reciprocated) detestation.[5] He never let All Souls define his personality and his loyalties to the same degree, and it is doubtful that his feeling for the college was ever as strong after the war as it was in the 1930s. Yet he always felt a deep attachment to the 'little platoon' of college society and its ritualised male intimacy: the nightly dinners, where formal attire was always worn; the after-dinner conversations in the panelled common room, decorated with drawings and paintings of former fellows; the electors' committees, where annual admissions to the magic circle were decided.

He belonged to the college, with all the special attachment that a foreigner feels towards native institutions that adopt him, yet he retained enough distance to see how unreal Oxford must seem to an outsider. Writing in 1937, he described Oxford as 'a tight, self-contained system with a private and sometimes unreal and perverse system of symbols and values, usually out of relation with the outer world'.[6] Yet he was never ironical about the sense of belonging that it gave him. In a letter to Stephen Spender in Germany, written in 1935, he confessed that while Stephen might want to roam, he himself hated to be uprooted: 'consequently I passionately defend all small societies, fixed disciplines etc. which merely rationalises my love of the womb I expect (a womb with a view, a womb of one's own etc.)'.[7]

His rooms were soon a place of resort: the Rhodes Scholar from Germany, Adam von Trott, dropped by to borrow gramophone records and talk about Hegel; the English scholar Humphry House discussed literature and came away thinking that Isaiah knew less about Wordsworth, Dickens and the English tradition than he should have done. Maurice Bowra visited and bellowed cheerfully. Goronwy Rees, now a young journalist in London, would return at weekends, with gossip of politics and his love life.

Everyone called him Shaya, his family nickname. He never discarded the remains of this period, the notes and messages from friends, the doggerel obscenities of Maurice Bowra, scrawled on the backs of envelopes or torn out of notebooks and slipped under his door. A bevy of bright young undergraduate women came for tutorials; stayed to park their dogs, to borrow books and records; and eventually to take him into their confidence. H.A.L. Fisher's daughter, Mary, Maire Lynd, Diana Hubback, Shiela Grant Duff, Rachel Walker and Jenifer Fischer Williams all dropped by to confide in him. He was emotionally involved with them all, and they with him, as the beautiful young parishioners of some witty, glamorous, but sexless village priest. Like the village priest, he took confessions, but as a confessor he soon acquired a reputation as a gossip. This became so much a part of his public persona that it made its way into print in Wystan Auden and Louis MacNeice's *Letters from Iceland*, published in 1937. In one poem, a mock-will in which MacNeice distributed gifts and personal relics among his Oxford friends, he gave Isaiah 'a saucer of milk'.[8] The implication – that he had a touch of feline malice – was true enough to make him burn with indignation and shame.

Other friends of the 1930s remembered Berlin as less feline than priggish. He disapproved, for example, of couples holding hands in public. His disapproval towards overt homosexuality seems to have soured his first encounters with Auden, whom he found cold and arrogant, while Auden came away believing (according to Stephen Spender) that Berlin was one of those 'life-hating' Jews with an aversion to physical contact.[9] Sally Graves, a beautiful and much pursued friend, reproved him languidly: 'What some people don't seem to realise, is that people have *appetites*.'[10] He *was* afraid of appetite. He thought himself impossibly ugly – fat, oily, white-skinned and deformed – and he made a point of telling people so. As a result, he was thought so immune to mortal temptation that parents trusted him as a chaperone for their daughters on holidays to Ireland and Austria throughout the 1930s.

The first such expedition came in the summer of 1933, when he and Mary Fisher, Maire Lynd and Christopher Cox, a young don at New College, motored through southern Ireland, where they paid a call on Elizabeth Bowen at her house, Bowen's Court, County Cork. He found the novelist sitting in front of the house, preparing gooseberries for a dessert. Bowen invited them all to stay, and from that visit dated one of his strongest friendships. They were an unlikely pair: she a Protestant Anglo-Irish *grande dame*, tough, conservative in politics, sexually experienced, highly intelligent, but with no particular interest in abstract ideas; he an abstinent, agnostic, timid, left-wing Jew, with no particular taste for her work.[11] Yet he loved her tough shrewdness and aristocratic *élan*, while she seems to have fallen under the spell of his torrential verbal quickness and sense of humour. She became one of his closest confidantes in the 1930s; and the letters he wrote her were among his best.

It was to Elizabeth Bowen that he wrote in November 1933, after he met Virginia Woolf at dinner at the Fishers' in New College Lodge. Woolf had the fine-boned beauty he was to find attractive in women and he was fascinated by her way of speaking. Warden Fisher asked her whether she liked walking, and she replied that she did, because she liked coming upon goats. 'They look so ecclesiastical,' she said. After dinner, Isaiah retired into a corner with the Magdalen don C.S. Lewis. They talked unctuously about 'God, Shakespeare and the charade of life', until Isaiah overheard Virginia, nearby, mention Elizabeth Bowen.[12] He stepped forward and said that she was in America. A halting conversation then ensued about literature, before she turned away to talk to other guests. While Isaiah felt he had been rewarded with a few moments in the Elysian Fields, Mrs Woolf's reaction was considerably more caustic:

> I should think there were one hundred promising undergraduates in after dinner; and I shook hands with all, and tried to think what to say, but oh dear what a farce! One might as well go to a school treat and hand out penny buns. There was the great Isaiah Berlin, a Portuguese Jew by the look of him, Oxford's leading light; a communist, I think, a fire-eater – but at Herbert's [Fisher] everyone minces and mouths and you wouldn't guess to talk to them that they had a spark.[13]

He was to see Virginia Woolf several times after that, at Ben Nicolson's flat, where she sat on the floor with friends ranged around her and told a droll story about the time her dress caught fire and she had stood by the grate entirely unaware that she was ablaze. He could see that Virginia was a terrible snob; but he liked her aristocratic hauteur, quoting with relish the remark of Elizabeth Bowen's cook, that you could tell Virginia was a lady 'by the go of her'. Berlin reported that whenever he met her, he felt a trembling before and a tingling for days afterwards. Certainly she could be flirtatious. A postcard inviting him to dinner ended beguilingly, 'If you knock on my little grey door, I shall open it.'

He dined with Virginia and Leonard Woolf in Tavistock Square in 1938 and Virginia grew fond of him, remarking in a letter to her sister that his brilliantly quick repartee reminded her of the young Maynard Keynes. She liked his quickness but still looked on him as a 'violent Jew', although her anti-Semitism, which could become obscene and uncontrolled when she was mad, did not seem to stop either of them from becoming friends. Isaiah had already received an invitation to dine with her in London, during a visit home from Washington in 1941, when he received news of her suicide.[14]

He was always fascinated by celebrity, by character, by larger-than-life figures, and the Oxford of the 1930s provided a steady supply. William Butler Yeats came to tea at Maurice Bowra's in 1934, dressed in green and talking in what Isaiah thought was a bogus, grand poetic manner. Miguel de Unamuno, the Spanish existentialist, gave a lecture in 1935, maintaining with world-weary eloquence, as Berlin reported to Spender, that Europeans were 'too oppressed by our history to be able to act, too debilitated by the burden of the knowledge of the past to do anything but hesitate; perhaps Rousseau was right, we needed a new barbarism etc. in order to get rid of our burdens'.[15] Isaiah thought this was rubbish. He was more impressed by Gertrude Stein, who gave a loud, colloquial and brilliant lecture on American literature in the same year. He particularly enjoyed her brusque manner with hecklers ('You sit down, my boy, you don't want to know what I mean, you just want me to use your language. Well, I won't. I don't create for a public, only for myself, etc.'). One of the phrases she let slip in that lecture stayed in his mind: '*Must* things have something to do with everything?'[16]

For most of the 1930s he was a spectator, observing the entanglements of his friends, keeping a distance from his own emotions. In a letter to Elizabeth Bowen he defended 'the intellectuals, the sensitives, the observers, the persons who discuss' from the charge that they were 'cripples', able to see life from every angle but unable actually to live it. He cited Tolstoy as a triumphant example of an observer who nevertheless managed to plunge into life, to commit himself, to give himself wholly and 'lose nothing irrecoverable'.[17] The letter to Bowen is as close to a credo as anything he was to write in the 1930s. The question was whether he would live by it; whether he would take the plunge into the kind of emotional turmoil he was usually content to watch enveloping others.

One of the silent undergraduate witnesses of his evening at New College with Virginia Woolf was a twenty-year-old philosophy undergraduate, Rachel Walker. 'Tips' – as she was known – was the beautiful and intense daughter of a London barrister, who had died when she was eighteen. A picture of her that has survived shows her atop a chestnut mare in full riding gear, sharp-featured, impossibly English and elegant, her hair in a bun. Rachel lived in conditions of increasing acrimony with her widowed mother at The Mill House in Burford, outside Oxford.[18] She came to Berlin's rooms at All Souls for tutorials in philosophy and, by the summer of 1934, when she graduated, was writing him letters of growing intimacy. Isaiah's side of their correspondence does not survive, but it is obvious that he returned her affection, because she was soon thanking him effusively for the present of a toy dog, which she said she would take with her prayer book to Mass. When she died, she went on, 'I shall order a glass dome to be placed above it among my relics.'[19] After graduating from Oxford, she went to Paris to study with a French logician. From Paris, she sent 'darling, darling Shaya' letters of increasing passion. He seems to have replied, urging discretion and caution, which she wanted to hurl to the winds. In late August 1935 she returned to England. She stayed at Mill House, cut lavender with her widowed mother and felt miserable, except when she and Isaiah went to concerts together. She certainly came down to London and met his parents at Hollycroft Avenue, and though they were bound to be unhappy that she was not Jewish, they said nothing.

By September 1935 Rachel was back in Paris and had invited Berlin to visit, hoping that they could go to lectures on logic together or hear Paul Valéry lecturing at the Collège de France. By now her letters, as passionate and tender as ever, sounded a new note of strange, highly strung exultation.[20] In October 1935 Isaiah flew over to Paris to see her. Mary Fisher, who was also in Paris, and who was Tips' closest friend, was slightly alarmed by her exalted state, and by her 'extremely improbable and Machiavellian idea' of Isaiah.[21] So was Madame Parodi, the woman with whom both Mary and Tips were staying. As Isaiah arrived, she observed to Mary: '*J'ai l'impression que Mr Berlin est maître de la situation, non?*' He was not. The difference in age between them was small: he was twenty-six, she twenty-one; and he had reached one of those moments where cleverness and a way with words were not enough. As he ruefully confessed to a friend, he was no longer 'the observer and Figaro of situations' but 'an active agent', forced at last to declare himself.[22]

He and Rachel went for a walk at the Paris zoo and while he gazed gloomily at the caged animals, she proposed marriage. A letter to Elizabeth Bowen records what ensued:

Our meeting in the Zoo opposite the Python was exciting and tormenting in the extreme. Your remark about the seriousness and literalness of inter-racial conversation is absolutely true. I was conscious of talking with no effort throughout, entirely unaware of any effect my words had (a very unfamiliar sensation) and also of talking the most dreadful and unintelligible elaborate nonsense throughout. We went on aiming at each other, missing mostly with desperate gravity. Dear me. I can't possibly marry her. She thinks I can. We should be miserable at once. The last scene in which I forced myself to be sensible and pedestrian and analyse the situation calmly and declare that I must stop, was awful beyond words.[23]

This apparently was the end: he flew back to England, while she went to stay with a friend in Vienna. He told Bowen that he was going to stay away from impressionable young women, take strolls with Maurice Bowra, and return to the sexless life of a scholarly don. Elizabeth replied with tough, sisterly advice: 'As far as Miss Walker is concerned I do feel (and it's not entirely heartless to say so, because it includes myself) that women don't really mind being upset – I mean being disturbed – as much as men do.' She added, 'Don't now overdo the austerity.'[24]

As for Tips, there was desolation, and much worse, to follow. Deeply hurt, she left for Vienna and never saw Isaiah again. Within about a year Isaiah heard that she had returned to live with her mother in Burford. There she became seriously depressed and subject to violent rages. She wrote Isaiah a vituperative letter to which he did not reply.[25] After attacking her mother, she was hospitalised in a hospital in Northampton and, with various interludes, was to remain hospitalised for the rest of her life, enduring electro-convulsive therapy and finally a lobotomy, which left her in a semi-vegetative condition. She lived until 1992. None of those who were closest to her – neither Tips' sister, nor Mary Fisher – ever held Isaiah responsible for what happened.[26] But a burden of responsibility remained, and he accepted it. Certainly the story and its denouement had important effects on his own development. Tips was his first serious emotional encounter: it was to be nearly ten years before he allowed himself another.

In the winter of 1933 the Warden of New College, H.A.L. Fisher, approached him to write the volume of the Home University Library on

Karl Marx. It was a flattering offer, yet Isaiah knew next to nothing about the subject. The interesting question is why he did not turn it down. Others had: Sidney and Beatrice Webb, Frank Pakenham, later Lord Longford, and Harold Laski.[27] Isaiah himself held Marx's theories in the distaste to be expected of any refugee from the Russian Revolution. Why he should have accepted takes some explaining. By early 1933 the Depression had thrown Oxford into ferment and Marxism was attracting the brightest undergraduates. Isaiah himself attended meetings of the Pink Lunch Club, which brought together all of Oxford's donnish left-wingers – Crossman, Cole, Austin, Hampshire. In 1933, too, the Soviet Union was still astonishing the world. English opinion, by and large, did not know that the peasants of the Ukraine were dying in their millions, as forced collectivisation drove them off their land. It did not know that poets like Osip Mandelstam were being arrested and deported for writing a poem denouncing Stalin. Oxford undergraduates on the left looked eastwards for an alternative to slump and depression at home. Isaiah himself was immune to this enthusiasm: his own two years in Lenin's Russia, waiting for the Cheka to knock, had inoculated him against Marxism for ever. But he could feel the fascination all around him: his friend J.L. Austin went to Moscow in 1935 and came back impressed by the sober asceticism of a revolution in progress. Christopher Hill, then reading in the Lenin Library in Moscow, sent Berlin books on Marx.[28] His own father went to Russia in 1935 for his timber business and came back awed by the pace at which a backward society was rushing to join the industrial world. In London film societies, Isaiah watched the great classics of Soviet cinema: Eisenstein's *Potemkin*, Pudovkin's *Mother*, Vertov's *Man with a Camera*. He did not react like Nabokov's Pnin, sitting in the dark, weeping despite himself, but he could not help feeling a certain grudging respect for revolutionary sincerity. That it was in the service of delusion he certainly knew then; that it was responsible for terror and extermination he was not to know until later.

To write about Marx, therefore, was to join the swim of the major ideological current of his age and to take the measure of the challenge that it represented to his own inchoate liberal allegiances. What fascinated him was Marx's loathing for the very civilisation he himself admired. This set a pattern that was to last for the rest of his life: he defended his own commitments by writing about those who were its sworn enemies. So an ironic, self-mocking, uncommitted bourgeois decided, in the spring of 1933, to spend five years in the company of a fiercely dogmatic ideologue, who had despised everything Berlin stood for. It was certainly a bracing experience, but it was also a lonely one. For all the political interest in Marxism, there was no one in Oxford who worked on the history of Marxism as an intellectual speciality. In a wider sense, the study of the history of ideas – let alone socialist ones – barely existed at Oxford. Berlin's originality cannot be appreciated unless this is understood. From the beginning of his serious intellectual life, he worked alone. And work he did. He burrowed into MEGA, the massive collected works of Marx and Engels, published in German until Hitler's accession and then continued in Moscow. Having fluent Russian gave him a route to Marx barred to most other English scholars, with the exception of E.H. Carr. Russian sources, especially Plekhanov, on the precursors of Marx led him to the Enlightenment thinkers; and from there forward to the nineteenth-century socialists. The reading he did between 1933 and 1938 provided Berlin with the intellectual capital on which he was to depend for the rest of his life.

It was at this moment, while idly browsing in the stacks of the London Library, that he discovered Alexander Herzen, the aristocratic exile and foe of Tsarism, whose memoirs became one of his favourite books.[29] It is easy to see why he identified with Herzen: an aristocratic renegade who managed to reconcile genuine commitment with freedom from sectarian dogmatism. Herzen was both a kindred spirit – a generous, thoughtful, comic and morally serious man of letters – and a moral challenge: someone who showed the courage and political commitment that Isaiah himself knew he lacked.

In the end, however, it was not Herzen but Turgenev, the supreme liberal artist, who became a lifelong mirror. Berlin confessed to Shiela Grant Duff that, after reading Turgenev's *On the Eve*, he felt as if his inner nature had been found out, especially 'his callow and wordy idealism'.[30] The Russian writer embodied the liberal's 'negative capability', his capacity to act and make commitments despite an empathy that enabled him to see the other side of any coin. Turgenev helped Isaiah keep his liberal balance while delving ever deeper into the fierce hatreds and passions of Marx's world view. By 1935, he was beginning to write the Marx biography but, as he wrote to a friend, he found it torture.[31] He found it difficult to settle, words wouldn't come and then, when they did, in a torrent, he would discover that they were irrelevant to the subject.

While he struggled with Marx, Berlin debated his relation to political commitment. He admired committed friends – like the Lynd sisters, who were active communist party members by the mid-1930s, or Stephen Spender, who had thrown himself into anti-fascist activity and was to go to Spain to work for the republican radio service. But he had a strong sense that politics led people to make fools of themselves. When Shiela Grant Duff told him that the sight of the hunger-marchers tramping through Oxford made her ashamed to be living in the ivory tower, Isaiah replied tartly that she was succumbing to 'Tolstoyan sentimentalism'.[32]

Avoiding all commitments was tempting, but it was not an option. All Souls was one of the gathering places for the leading appeasers in the 1930s: John Simon, Lord Halifax, Geoffrey Dawson; these men believed that Hitler could not be stopped; and that a Nazi state stood as a buffer against communist expansion in Europe. Isaiah aligned himself with the young left-wing dons, Austin, Hampshire and others, who challenged these assumptions. He was one of those who cornered Simon, the Foreign Secretary, in the smoking room of All Souls after dinner in the autumn of 1935 and demanded that he impose oil sanctions on Italy for its invasion of Abyssinia. 'And what then?' Sir John replied coolly. 'Let Italy fall to the communists?'[33]

Like most of his friends on the left, Berlin supported the republican side in Spain. As he told Shiela Grant Duff, the Spanish cause was the litmus test which told you, infallibly, where your friends stood politically. But he added that it was about the only political issue that *was* clear-cut: 'on all other issues (e.g. Palestine) no clear proposition can be uttered which is not in some degree unjust to someone'.[34]

Like most of his friends, he was on the King's side over the abdication in 1936, believing that, 'in his awful and vulgar way', Edward VIII had stood for 'the Weimar republic, libertarianism, being allowed to be spontaneous, [and] say what one wished'.[35] The victory of Baldwin and the Church, in forcing his abdication, had ushered in a new era of grey conformity. Berlin sided with the left, with what his friend Maurice Bowra called the 'immoral front'. But his politics always had a disengaged and mocking side. During the famous Oxford by-election of 1938, when Quintin Hogg, a colleague at All Souls, ran for Parliament on a straight pro-appeasement, pro-Munich ticket against A.D. Lindsay, the Master of Balliol, Berlin found the whole business more funny than serious. Seeing a car parked in the High Street outside All Souls with 'A Vote for Hogg is a Vote for Hitler' on its bumper, and seeing another car nearby with a 'Vote for Hogg' on its bumper, he transferred the latter sign to the first car. He watched the car drive away with the syllogism completed: 'A Vote for Hogg is a Vote for Hitler. Vote for Hogg.'

Not everyone took such a playful view of Munich and its aftermath. One of his Oxford friends, Moore Crosthwaite, resigned from the British Embassy in Berlin in disgust.[36] Shiela Grant Duff, by then in Prague, wrote a furious pamphlet excoriating Chamberlain's betrayal of Czechoslovakia.[37] His friend, J.L. Austin, went to heckle at Hogg's meetings, and the election – which Hogg won – divided the town into bitter camps. Isaiah remained detached from the proceedings.

Some of his friends, like Shiela Grant Duff and Adam von Trott, thought him too detached and introspective; every one of Isaiah's melancholies had its own anatomy, Shiela joked; he lacked public spirit. Instead of the 'placid continuity' of Isaiah's life in his 'ivory tower', she told von Trott, she wanted a life of commitment and danger.[38]

Berlin's relationship with von Trott was to force him to make his first genuine stand of principle. He first met von Trott when he was a Rhodes Scholar reading PPE at Balliol. At the time, the tall, aristocratic German was turning over in his mind whether to try to remain in Oxford and take up philosophy or return to Germany and embark on a public career. His father had been a Minister of Education in a Wilhelmine administration. Adam formed part of a circle of left-wing, moneyed and good-looking undergraduates who included Peggy Garnett, Douglas Jay, Shiela Grant Duff, Diana Hubback and David Astor.[39]

Berlin and von Trott were soon walking together, through Christ Church Meadows or around Addison's Walk at Magdalen, talking philosophy – the extremely tall, thin von Trott, and the smaller, plumper, bespectacled figure at his side, striding between the limes, the one earnest and long-winded, the other deflating, ironic, comical and sharp. As Berlin remembered, 'whenever von Trott got into difficulty with something, he would say, "At this point I fall back on Hegel," like an acrobat falling safely backwards into a net. He believed in Hegel all right, but he wouldn't say what Hegel had said. It was meant to say, you are being too pedantic, too exact, there is a larger way of thinking about this than you people in Oxford can conceive.'[40]

Von Trott considered sitting the All Souls fellowship exam, but when he got a second-class degree, he decided to return to Germany. He left Oxford in the summer of 1933 to return to work in the prosecutor's office in provincial Hesse. He told Isaiah and other friends that his country was 'very sick', leaving them with the implication that it needed him. In January 1934 *The Manchester Guardian* carried a report on discrimination against the Jews in the German courts. Von Trott wrote a letter to the paper declaring that, from his experience, no such discrimination was practised in the court. While some of Trott's English friends argued that the letter served as cover to protect him from suspicion by the Nazi authorities, as he was already beginning to work against the regime, Isaiah was simply outraged. The facts of Nazi persecution were too obvious to be denied.[41] When he pointed this out, von Trott's defenders in Oxford accused him of betrayal. Besides, they implied that he took the position he did simply because he was a Jew. It took five months before Berlin could bring himself to write directly to Adam in Kassel:

> Forgive me for my very long silence ... The M.G. [*Manchester Guardian*] incident led to a very small explosion on my part, I admit, both because I thought it in itself harmful, not in keeping with your character and beliefs, and more particularly because of the idiotic defences of you put up in a spirit of uncritical loyalty by all your other friends ... I felt irritation that all my arguments were taken only as evidence of personal treachery and not estimated *an sich*.[42]

The explosion was not in fact 'very small': it was a parting of the ways. Isaiah's indignation was, as he put it, a fact about him. Such was Isaiah's standing in von Trott's eyes, both as a Jew and a friend, that von Trott tried assiduously to regain his favour throughout the 1930s. In his letters, Adam sadly and ironically invoked the vanishing cultural solidarity of Europe and said he wished he could read Isaiah's ongoing study of Marx.[43] They saw each other in late 1936 and again in March 1937, when Adam came to Oxford to seek the help of the Rhodes Trust in funding a trip to

China and Japan. On his return from China, he sought Isaiah's approval for returning to Germany and taking up a teaching post:

I can see you shake your head: but what is the alternative? All clear out and surrender? I know you wouldn't agree to that either. Anyway I am sure you will not lightly withdraw your friendship and confidence and of that I am rather proud.[44]

In the summer of 1939 von Trott visited England again, stayed with the Astors at Cliveden, met Halifax and other leading British politicians and dined at All Souls as guest of the Warden. There he met Berlin again and they argued until 3 a.m. in Isaiah's rooms. Von Trott said to him that, unless England and France stood up to Hitler, war would come and Hitler might win it. Isaiah asked what he thought should be done: 'Germany must be surrounded and stopped. This must be done very soon. German expansion must not occur.'

Even after this, Berlin remained dubious about his German friend's real attitude to the Nazis. Von Trott told English friends, for example, that Hitler's coming to power was a Hegelian watershed in European history and, for his own privileged class, a necessary chastisement.[45] Isaiah's suspicions of von Trott were perhaps influenced by the fact that, in this period, Oxford was visited by a number of Germans, sent by the regime to influence British opinion in a pro-appeasement direction. He remembered one particularly clumsy member of the German aristocracy who, in the common room of All Souls, happened to say that he thought German territorial demands in Europe were as reasonable as British imperial claims overseas. This remark, delivered into the stillness of the common room, was suddenly interrupted by a guttural growl from a man whom Isaiah had never seen before, seated in one of the window recesses. '*Wir Juden und die anderen Farbigen denken anders*' ('We Jews and the other coloured peoples think otherwise'), the stranger growled, and stalked out. This was Isaiah's first encounter with the Polish-born historian and devoted Zionist, Lewis Namier.[46]

Even when von Trott committed himself to plotting against the Hitler regime, it was not clear to Isaiah whether he did so because he opposed it morally, or because he feared Hitler's defeat would destroy Germany and ruin his own chances of becoming a major political figure. Berlin shared these doubts with his friends, particularly Maurice Bowra, and they were to have serious consequences. After the war began in 1939, while America was still neutral, von Trott visited Washington and met Felix Frankfurter, by then a Supreme Court Justice and a confidant of Roosevelt, in an attempt to persuade influential Americans to stay out of a war with the Germans – in the hope that given time, the domestic opposition, led by men like von Trott, would overthrow Hitler. Berlin had already given von Trott letters of introduction to Frankfurter on an earlier visit to Washington. But, on this occasion, Bowra wrote to Frankfurter casting doubt on von Trott's reliability. The Bowra letter, intercepted by the British postal censors, ended up in British intelligence files. When, in 1943, von Trott, by now committed to the assassination of Hitler, tried to make contact with the British secret service, the British refused a meeting. Afterwards von Trott's English friends, chiefly David Astor, blamed Bowra for compromising him with British intelligence; they believed therefore that Bowra bore some responsibility for von Trott's arrest and execution, after the failed von Stauffenberg plot of July 1944. Indirectly, Astor also blamed Berlin.

While Bowra publicly repented his lack of trust in von Trott, Isaiah remained adamant.[47] Much later, long after von Trott's heroic and terrible death at the hands of Nazi torturers in 1944, Berlin still refused to join the general consecration of him as a hero. In a letter to Shiela Grant Duff, written in 1956, he said that he had no wish to denounce the myth of the 'pure-hearted democrat and man of rigid principle', but in reality he had been 'an ambitious, fascinating, self-romanticising, personally delightful and politically ambivalent figure with a passion for very high-level intrigue'.[48] The von Trott story reveals the tenacity with which he resisted a sentimental undertow in others, his ruthlessness in judgement and the role of Jewishness in defining his ultimate commitments.

7

The Brethren, 1934–40

In the summer of 1934, after his 'little explosion' towards von Trott, Berlin paid his first visit to Palestine. He had been a Zionist since childhood: this was his first chance to see the Promised Land, ruled since 1918 as a League of Nations mandated territory by the British Colonial Office. Without realising it, he had chosen an auspicious moment to make his pilgrimage. In 1929 the first Arab riots against the Jewish presence in Palestine had taken place; in 1936, a full-scale Arab revolt both against the British Mandate and against Jewish immigration was to explode.[1] The summer he happened to choose belonged to the calm before the storm. After he left, the storm began in earnest, with Palestinian Arabs and Jews fighting each other and the British, rendering the territory ungovernable in the process and forcing the British to evacuate in 1948.

First he stopped over in Salzburg to hear Toscanini, then travelled to Venice, where he met up with his All Souls colleague, John Foster. They took ship together for Alexandria and Cairo. Much to Foster's surprise, when the train carrying them through the Sinai desert crossed the frontier into Palestine and a Jewish conductor in a uniform asked for their ticket, tears came into Berlin's eyes.[2] It was the first time he had ever seen a Jewish official in authority anywhere.

But his ironical composure returned when they reached Tel Aviv. He was both appalled and enthralled by the manic energy of the place: cars honking, policemen shouting at the traffic in both Hebrew and Yiddish, and wildly incongruous sights like a caravan of camels, 'led by a little Polish Jew in a black bowler hat making suitable Arab noises to the camels'.[3] But just when he thought he had landed in some exotic Oriental bazaar, he would catch sight of a group of intellectuals wandering up the street, discussing Hebrew etymologies, and feel that this was a city after his own heart.

The first wave of German refugees from Nazi Germany – more than 40,000 in 1934 alone – had begun to arrive, and their presence gave the town the feverish atmosphere of the Klondike gold-rush. The Germans were all over the place, 'swarming about with little portfolios under their arms doing business everywhere, in cafés, in buses, in bathing huts, in the sea, everywhere save their offices'.[4] They were often comically ill at ease in their new Mediterranean homeland. As Berlin wrote his parents, their first instinct on arriving in Tel Aviv was to buy a bus timetable – a *Fahrplan*: 'they come at 10.00 am to the place, no bus. They ask whether there will be a bus soon, the Jew in charge says no, no bus, no hope of bus. The German Jew begins, "*aber im Fahrplan . . .*"'[5]

But he himself was just as nonplussed to discover that he actually belonged to this noisy, vital Levantine family:

> As for the Jews they are most odd and fascinating, and I felt equally uneasy with them and away from them, like relations one hasn't seen for 30 years or something, to whom one knows one is, even feels, related, but whom one doesn't really know, and is afraid of, and has to treat on an oddly familiar footing, tho' knowing nothing about them, and even afraid of them.[6]

During his month in Palestine, he lived two lives: one with the British officials like John Foster and Thomas Hodgkin, a left-wing Oxford friend then working for the High Commissioner; the other with his Jewish friends and relations.[7] By day, he would watch synchronised motor-cycle riding displays at the British sports day at Nablus or drink in the bar of the King David with tired British officials out of a Somerset Maugham novel, who grumbled about the uppity Jews while their drinks were refilled by Nubian servants in *djellabahs*; in the evening, he went back to Aunt Ida and Uncle Yitzhak Samunov's to hear them denounce the imperial machinations of the British. Englishness and Jewishness came into conflict within him, and his letters home record the division. Aunt Ida, he confided to his mother, was a little too full of stories about 'British atrocities' for his taste; while most British officials were too pro-Arab.[8]

He journeyed about, sometimes in Foster's company, sometimes on his own; one day visiting a mosque in Damascus or the sea front in Beirut; sleeping under the stars in Jerash on a Roman gravestone, which engraved its inscription into his back through the folds of his Loden overcoat; then journeying up to a *kibbutz* where he met a memorable old Russian socialist revolutionary woman who, when he offered to pay for her meal, said in a leathery voice that there was such a thing as being over-mean and over-generous; and being over-generous was also a sin. He was insatiably curious, dashing up to the university to meet a historian of Zionism, making his first acquaintance with Gershom Scholem, the great Hebrew scholar; journeying to Amman to meet with fiercely anti-Zionist Palestinians. As he remarked to his parents, he would have gladly seen the Palestinian leader, the Grand Mufti himself, if the Mufti had been in the habit of meeting Jews.[9]

Yet instead of becoming more Zionist, he continued to see Palestine through English eyes and through the filter of some very English metaphors. He viewed Palestine as an English public school. The High Commissioner was the headmaster; the Colonial Office was the Board of Governors; the school itself was divided into the Arab house and the Jewish house. Most of the masters liked the Arab house, because its pupils were 'gay, affectionate, high spirited and tough, occasionally liable to break out and have a rag and break the skulls of a few Jews or an Englishman perhaps . . .' The Jewish house, Berlin said, was full of able and rich boys, 'who were allowed too much pocket money by their parents, rude, conceited, ugly, ostentatious, suspected of swapping stamps unfairly with the other boys, always saying they know better, liable to work too hard and not to play games with the rest'. To appropriate public-school metaphors like this was to use terms that moved uneasily between irony and self-dislike. Jewish energy is described as pushiness; cleverness becomes arrogance; exuberance turns into vulgarity; affection is seen as sentimentality. He never entirely ceased seeing his own people through the eyes of their detractors.[10]

On the whole, he fought the sentimental undertow of identification with Palestine all his life. He was a Zionist – but already he was troubled by the Zionist myth of Palestine as a land without people given to a people without land. There *was* a people on the land and a reckoning with their claims was inevitable. In letters he argued that Jews should work harder to integrate Arabs within the Palestinian economy. At the same time, he thought that British attempts to appease the Arabs were responsible for the radicalisation of Zionism and the emergence of groups prepared to use violence, both against the British and against the Arabs. He could see that the Arabs preferred to be governed badly by their own people rather than be well governed by the Jews, and that 'in fifteen years' time the Arab nationalists will be sincere, incorruptible, utterly brutal fascists. It is then that the real fun will begin.'[11]

Indeed, as he left Palestine and took ship for Italy, he had an anticipation of the 'fun' itself. While dining in the kosher section of the ship's restaurant, he met a handsome, poetic young man named Abraham Stern travelling to Italy to take up a scholarship in classics at the University of Florence offered by Mussolini's government. When they got talking, Isaiah asked him what Stern thought of the recent British move to create a legislative council in Palestine. We shall fight that, Stern said. Why? Because it would give the Arabs representation in proportion to their demographic superiority. But, Isaiah countered, the council was merely advisory. It does not matter, Stern replied. 'We will fight and fight, and if blood has to be shed ...'[12] He shrugged expressively. This was the man who went on to found the Lech'i, the most radical of the Jewish underground groups fighting to end British rule in Palestine. Both in what he wrote home, and in whom he chanced to meet on his return, Isaiah saw the future coming and was already defining his liberal Zionism in response.

He returned from Palestine to continue his research for the Marx biography, but the only person he could really talk to was Rachmilievitch. Here was someone who seemed on first-name terms with Isaiah's subject: the visionary, if apocalyptic, German and Russian exiles who peopled Marx's milieu in the Paris cafés and tenements of the 1840s. On Saturdays Berlin journeyed to London to meet up with Rachmilievitch in the British Museum Reading Room, deep in his own secretive, never-to-be-published researches. Over dinner or after concerts in the Queen's

Hall, they brought to life the controversies of the Central European agitators and intellectuals whom Rachmilievitch so resembled.

In intellectual terms Isaiah led a double life: the first with Rachmilievitch – rambling, historical, saturated in Russian, German and Jewish references, conducted in three languages at once; the second with his Oxford philosophy colleagues – precise, Anglo-Saxon, procedural and rationalistic. Election to All Souls had given him entry into a magic circle of brilliant philosophy dons. The most precocious of these was a thin, rakish, half-Jewish philosopher, A.J. Ayer, universally known as Freddie.[13] They ought to have been close – and they maintained a wary, competitive friendship for fifty years – but everything they had in common actually divided them. There was the matter of Jewishness. Berlin was never especially close to English Jews, and in any event both men lived their Jewishness very differently. For Ayer, Jewishness was an atavistic inheritance that a rational mind should discard, whereas for Berlin it was an identity which could be questioned but never discarded or transcended. The same difference coloured their religious outlook. Both were convinced Humean sceptics, but the young Ayer regarded religion with disdain, while Berlin kept the basic Jewish festivals – Passover and Yom Kippur – and always treated religious belief with ironical respect. Finally, while both belonged to Bowra's 'immoral front', the free-thinking Oxford left of the 1930s, Ayer was much more experimental in his personal life than Berlin. He had married a highly intelligent and stylish woman while still an undergraduate, and had already begun the series of affairs and erotic imbroglios that were to distinguish his private life thereafter. Thanks largely to Ayer's love-life, Isaiah primly regarded him as an artful dodger – clever, amusing but amoral. Their lifelong competition began with the All Souls election of 1932: he was chosen, while Freddie was not. After failing to win a place at All Souls, Ayer spent the winter of 1932–3 in Vienna, attending the philosophical seminars of the key figures of the Vienna circle, Moritz Schlick, Rudolf Carnap, Otto Neurath and Friedrich Waismann. During his four months in Vienna, Ayer wrote Isaiah important letters spelling out what he was learning: namely, that the key question of philosophy was 'what is one doing when one makes a theory'.[14] In the Vienna circle, a strictly empiricist doctrine of verification became the test of how to make adequate theories. If propositions could not be verified empirically or tested logically, they were nonsensical. This consigned most of the metaphysical questions of philosophy – what is the purpose of life? what is the nature of good? – to the rubbish bin. Logical positivism, as the Vienna circle doctrine came to be known, desired, in Bernard Williams's words, to turn philosophy into the humble 'obituarist of metaphysics' and 'secretary to science'.[15]

Ayer was intoxicated by these doctrines: he was an iconoclast by temperament, and the Vienna ideas applied the axe to the philosophy he had been taught. In a letter from Vienna to Isaiah, he conveyed his sense of intellectual excitement:

> Philosophy is grammar. Where you would talk about laws, they talk about rules of grammar. All philosophical questions are purely linguistical. And all linguistical questions are resolved by considering how the symbol under consideration is in fact used ... Altogether a set of men after my own heart.[16]

After returning to Oxford and becoming a tutor at Christ Church, Ayer became a brilliant populariser of the doctrines of the Vienna School in general and Wittgenstein in particular. Wittgenstein, by then in Cambridge, had never been a formal member of the Vienna circle and, while there were parts of his *Tractatus*, published in 1921, that seemed the fullest expression of the school's doctrines, there were other parts, particularly at the end, that the circle rejected as metaphysical and semi-religious speculation.[17] Until Ayer's efforts, Wittgenstein had been more present as a mythic figure than as a philosophic influence. People talked about him at dinner tables; but few had read him. At a dinner in 1934, at the home of Felix Frankfurter, who was spending a year away from the Harvard Law School as Eastman Professor at Oxford, there was a dispute between Isaiah, Freddie Ayer, Guy Burgess (over from Trinity College, Cambridge) and the lawyer Sylvester Gates as to whether Wittgenstein's dictum 'Whereof one cannot speak, thereof one must be silent' occurred once or twice in the *Tractatus*. Ayer and Berlin said it was once; Gates said it was twice. Bets were taken, and a taxi was despatched to Freddie's rooms to procure a copy of the sacred text. It revealed that Wittgenstein had in fact pronounced the sentence twice: once in the preface, once in the conclusion. Both Ayer and Berlin paid up. Berlin did read the

Tractatus, but the only phrase that seemed to have long-lasting resonance with him was Wittgenstein's famous remark 'Death is not an event in life.'[18]

When Ayer completed his brilliant exposition of Vienna school doctrine in *Language, Truth and Logic,* he sent the manuscript to Berlin and thought highly enough of his suggestions to thank him in the acknowledgements to the first edition published in 1936.[19] With the ruthlessness of youth, Ayer set out to demolish English philosophy using the dynamite provided by the Vienna School. Philosophy should be the analysis of either empirical or logical statements: if a proposition was neither, it was nonsensical. As for the content of ethics or moral philosophy, they were either statements of fact or expressions of emotional states. As Stuart Hampshire, then a young All Souls philosopher, later recalled, ethics seemed to 'have very little rational content of any kind'.[20]

Since logical positivism was 'consciously anti-clerical' – attacking the metaphysical basis of the teaching of the Church and the establishment – it had a left-wing and progressive aura. Freddie Ayer stood for Westminster city council on a Labour ticket and lived a bohemian life in a flat in Foubert's Place, amid the jazz clubs of London's Soho. Logical positivism was of a piece with this life: it associated reason with progressive politics, sexual freedom and anti-clerical, anti-authoritarian views on all questions.

There was much in this that excited Isaiah. In a review, written for T.S. Eliot's *Criterion,* in 1937, he described logical positivism as 'one of the most striking intellectual phenomena of the present time'.[21] He particularly approved of its attack on what he called 'the vaporous clouds of nonsense' in German philosophy, not that he had read any in his Oxford syllabus. Logical positivism seemed to promise that philosophy could be something more than misty conversation: it could generate results, it could make progress. Logical positivism, in Stuart Hampshire's words, seemed to leave behind the 'amateurishness' and 'provincialism' of the philosophy Oxford undergraduates had been taught in the late 1920s and early 1930s.

Ayer's main intellectual competitor was a tall, bespectacled and thin-haired philosopher, J.L. Austin, once memorably described as an inscrutable crane.[22] He had been elected to All Souls the year after

Isaiah. He too was drawn to the intellectual rigour promised by logical positivism, and until he began to develop his own mode of ordinary language analysis after the war, his disputes with Ayer were more in the nature of a competition for intellectual leadership than a fundamental difference of view. Austin was to become a central authority in Isaiah's life: so much so that visitors to Berlin's rooms after the war remembered seeing on his mantelpiece a metal sign that he had obviously acquired from an Oxford garage. It read simply: 'Austin'.[23] Austin and Berlin took to one another immediately, although the pairing was unlikely: a meticulously precise, emotionally reserved Englishman with the manner of a Chancery lawyer and a voluble Russian Jew with incredibly rapid diction and an intuitive mind of equal speed. They were soon inseparable, spending mornings, when they weren't teaching, in their rooms at All Souls or striding around Addison's Walk at Magdalen College, deep in conversation. Austin endeared himself to Isaiah for life by whispering *sotto voce*, 'They all *talk* about determinism and *say* they believe in it. I've never met a determinist in my life, I mean a man who really did believe in it, as you and I believe that men are mortal. Have you?'[24] This remark – aimed at Ayer – defined their mutual commitment to the idea that free agency was inseparable from the very definition of behaviour as human; in the very intelligibility of the language of purposes, intentions and valuations.

It was Isaiah's idea to broaden his *tête-à-tête* with Austin to include other young philosophers. One morning in 1935, while browsing in Blackwell's bookshop, he came upon *Mind and the World Order*, a work on the philosophy of knowledge by the Harvard pragmatist C.I. Lewis. Finding it an interesting and articulate statement of a pragmatic empiricism, he suggested to Austin that they give a class together on the book. Berlin was in for a surprise. Austin suddenly turned Grand Inquisitor when they were paired as teachers before a crowd of philosophical undergraduates. 'If there are three vermilion patches on this piece of paper, how many vermilions are there?' he asked. Berlin said there was one. 'I say there are three,' said Austin, and then proceeded – in 'slow, formidable and relentless' style – to demolish Berlin's position, leaving Isaiah looking, so observers remembered, distinctly unhappy.[25]

It was a sign of his intellectual maturity that, instead of fleeing Austin, Isaiah continued to seek him out. He went on to play an essential function as philosophical go-between, mediating between the logical positivism of Ayer and the emerging sceptical language philosophy of Austin. Isaiah conceived the idea of regular philosophical discussion, involving the two of them. Between the spring of 1937 and the summer of 1939, the 'brethren' met on Thursday evenings after dinner in Isaiah's rooms at All Souls. The magic circle was small: Ayer, Berlin, Hampshire, Austin, Donald MacNabb, A.D. Woozley and Donald MacKinnon. R.G. Collingwood was invited but declined.

The brethren's chief topics of discussion were theories of perception, personal identity and the possibility of knowing of other minds. The philosophical atmosphere of the room was full of the technical jargon of the Vienna circle: Isaiah kept trying, so Hampshire remembered, to dispel the obfuscatory cloud by arguing that they should discuss plain and evident examples. To anyone outside the circle, the discussions might have seemed Martian. They debated, for example, whether one could tell if one person's headache was worse than another person's. If everything we know about the world comes to us through our senses, how do we know anything about the contents of other minds? Strict empiricism seemed to entrap each perceiver in a solipsistic world of his own perceptions. Likewise, if everything we knew about the world comes to us through our senses, into what constituent blocks are our sense data divided? Suppose, Austin would say, you are looking at a visual field of seven black stripes and seven yellow stripes. Should one say that it consisted of fourteen discrete units of sense data, or one tiger's skin?

They read Kafka's *Metamorphosis* together and considered Gregor Samsa's predicament, because it seemed to tell them something about the relationship between personal identity and the persistence of memory. Was Samsa a man with the body of a cockroach or a cockroach with the memories and consciousness of a man? 'Neither,' Austin would declare. 'In such cases we should not know what to say. This is when we say, "words fail us".'[26]

Words rarely failed. The evenings were noisy: one of their number likened the debates to hunting with a pack of hounds. On one occasion, Ayer shouted at Austin that he was a greyhound who didn't want to run himself; just bite the other dogs. There was truth in this: Ayer at least had the Vienna doctrines to defend; at this period, Austin did not have a position of his own so much as an infinitely painstaking talent for demolishing other people's. Austin had it in him to strike fear in others. 'Would you mind saying that again?' he would enquire with a lethal stare. If you repeated it, he would intone, in a thin voice, 'It seems to me that what you have just said is complete nonsense.' The meetings were duels of will as much as of intellect and they left real wounds. This was no polite shadow-fencing,' Isaiah later remembered, 'but war to the death – my death, that is.' What they were fighting about was the very status, purpose and nature of their discipline: whether philosophy should try to be a science; which questions were relevant and answerable, which ones were not; how progress in philosophy could be achieved. Such duelling might well have destroyed Berlin's self-confidence for ever. It certainly showed him his limits as a philosopher, yet he was not damaged by the discovery. As he said later, 'I knew I wasn't first rate, but I was good enough. I was quite respected. I wasn't despised. I was one of the brethren.'[27]

Austin characteristically worried that the discussions would be too casual, too slapdash, unless rigorously ordered. He wrote to Isaiah saying that 'philosophical discussions are usually nugatory and unedifying through lack of strict rules of procedure'.[28] He then set out four pages of procedural suggestions, which would have been excessive in the House of Commons and were lunatic when applied to a body of seven people. None of Austin's suggestions was adopted. Isaiah managed to keep Austin's procedural mania in check.

Outsiders resented the circle. One philosopher came down from Leeds to read a paper in February 1938, and when he returned he despatched a scathing letter, observing that the Oxford philosophers published little and talked far too much.[29] As even Isaiah was to admit later. 'We were excessively self-centred. We thought no one had anything to teach us. We were the only people we were trying to please, and when we persuaded someone in the circle that something was true, this satisfied us completely, too completely.'[30] And yet sharing an initiate's language and experiencing the vertigo of insight taught Isaiah what true intellectual happiness was.

While he blossomed intellectually inside the circle, he became increasingly sceptical about logical positivism. He was among the first to see that there could be meaningful statements that did not fit either of

Ayer's categories. Hypothetical conditionals – if a horse named Charlemagne had entered the race, it would have won – were meaningful, but by definition could not be verified empirically. There were also conceptual truths – pink is closer to red than it is to black – which were meaningful, but whose truth, Berlin argued, was neither a matter of fact nor a deduction of logic. Ayer kept rebuilding the wall against such exceptions, insisting that colour relations, for example, were a matter of fact. But Berlin came to believe that these examples vitiated logical positivism's central claim that all meaningful statements were either deductive or empirical.

A similar puzzle emerged on the subject of the knowability of other minds. If someone said he had a headache, how could you actually verify that this was true? Verificationism seemed to open up a solipsistic world in which each individual might be persuaded of the truth of his senses, yet be unable to verify the correspondence between another person's use of language and the sense data to which his language was referring. This too seemed another breach in the wall. Berlin's paper of 1939, 'Verification', raised all of these objections and went on to argue that 'verifiability depends on intelligibility and not vice versa'. There were statements which were intelligible but which could not be verified. And this logical positivism could not explain. His papers were among the most penetrating critiques that logical positivism received before the war.[31]

He was good enough: the problem was that this kind of philosophy – with its scientistic bias, its lack of interest in ethical, historical and political questions – began to seem like a cul-de-sac. By the time one of his last articles in the analytical style, 'Logical Translation', was published in 1950, scepticism towards logical positivism was shading into sarcasm. The article is an attack on the reductive consequences of searching for 'incorrigible propositions'. The search for such arid islands of certainty was a waste of time. The more precise one's language became, the less it could actually say:

To say anything significantly about the world we must bring in something other than immediate experience (whatever 'immediate' may mean), namely the past and the future, and absent objects and other persons, and unrealised possibilities and general and hypothetical judgements, and so forth. And if these, because we cannot certify them as certain, are cut away, in the end literally nothing will be left. We cannot speak without incurring some risk, at least in theory; the only way of being absolutely safe is to say absolutely nothing.[32]

In reaction to logical positivism, his own cast of mind became ever more historical. He had a strong sense, as Bernard Williams has put it, that 'no abstract or analytical point exists out of all connection with historical, personal thought: that every thought belongs, not just somewhere, but to someone and is at home in a context of other thoughts, a context which is not purely formally prescribed'.[33] This habit of mind made Berlin increasingly impatient with the disembodied character of philosophical discussion and directed him – not away from philosophy – but towards a philosophy grounded in the history of ideas. The Marx biography, begun as a dutiful exercise without much sense of where it might lead, gradually opened up a wider universe in which Isaiah felt he genuinely belonged, in the history of ideas. It was the Marx project that rescued him from what was, at least for him, the dead-end of philosophy at Oxford.

If the narrowly philosophical period of his life was brief, it is worth asking what residue it left in his mature work. He always insisted on the cleansing properties of analytical philosophy. 'It got rid of a lot of clouds of Hegelianism which were no good ... it was a great rejuvenating force.'[34] But he was utterly unconvinced by logical positivism's redefinition of philosophy as the handmaiden of science. Philosophy's native province, he later wrote, was the 'permanent or semi-permanent categories in terms of which experience is conceived and classified'.[35] As 'permanent or semi-permanent' suggests, the subject matter of philosophy was historical. It was an unavoidable characteristic of such models and categories of thought that they changed over time. For Ayer and the positivists, the historicity of human thought was an incidental or uninteresting feature. For Berlin, it raised the central problem of philosophy itself: whether the idea of continuous, stable human values could be reconciled with the manifest historical variation in the way these values were expressed across time, across cultures and between individuals within cultures. The emphasis on values, moreover, returned ethics and political philosophy to centre stage.[36]

As Isaiah's doubts about academic philosophy grew, some of the Young

Turks believed that he was ducking the difficult analytical questions for pleasant excursions into more congenial nineteenth-century terrain. This objection was put in its sharpest form by Stuart Hampshire, a brilliant, tall and handsome Balliol undergraduate, elected as a fellow of All Souls in 1936. As Hampshire's own intellectual confidence increased, and as he fell ever more deeply under the spell of logical positivism, so his impatience grew with what he called Isaiah's 'period talking'. In a scathing letter, written in 1937, Hampshire took his friend to task for writing too vaguely 'about generalised states of mind, the spirit of this and that Zeitgeist'.[37] It was all very 'unpositivistic and unrealistic', and his history of ideas was being undermined by recourse to vague Hegelian-styled generalities.

Hampshire's letter remains the most effective methodological critique of Isaiah's work; it also defined the curiously tense character of their relationship as friends: Hampshire, the younger man, taking upon himself the role of intellectual and political conscience for his older, less precise, more wide-ranging friend. In the acknowledgements of Berlin's book on Marx, Hampshire is thanked, along with Ayer and Rachmilievitch, for his comments; but it is not clear to what degree Isaiah ever changed his views or approach as a result of Hampshire's often critical advice. He went his own way. Most of the essential questions that were to occupy his later life were not even suggested by Oxford analytical philosophy. They were seeded in Berlin's mind as a result of the apparently casual or contingent process by which a good mind picks up hints or phrases in the thoughts of others and makes of these a life's work. Two basic predispositions – that values might be incompatible; and that human beings were not infinitely malleable – took root very early. Already, in a letter to Elizabeth Bowen, written in November 1933, we find Berlin noticing that the philosopher Malebranche had observed that since the moral ends which human beings commonly pursued were in conflict with each other, the very idea of creating a perfect society was incoherent. This seminal idea had also cropped up elsewhere. Hadn't Kant said, he wrote to Bowen, that 'out of the crooked timber of humanity no straight thing was ever made'?[38] These were the chance encounters with ideas – not the fevered discussions with Ayer and Austin – that generated his later thought; and it was in his solitary reading, not in his reactions to criticism from Hampshire, that his mature thought slowly took shape.

Characteristically, Berlin never let Hampshire's criticisms dampen their friendship. Before his election to All Souls, Hampshire had shared rooms in Beaumont Street with two other undergraduates, and together they had run a high-brow discussion group called the Florentine Club, to which fashionable dons like Maurice Bowra and Isaiah had been invited. T.S. Eliot had come to one of these gatherings in Beaumont Street in 1934, and Isaiah had surprised the company by talking knowledgeably with Eliot about the German poet Wilhelm Busch, whose work Isaiah, in his mysterious way, was the only person in Oxford to have read. Berlin made Hampshire feel 'caricaturally English' and provincial by comparison, yet instead of being put off by Isaiah's European learning and ceaseless talk, he was strongly drawn to him. After a picnic lunch in the summer of 1936, at which Isaiah gobbled black olives and seemed, to Hampshire's amusement, to ignore the English countryside altogether, they became close friends.[39] Hampshire's elusive discretion and shy uprightness led Isaiah to nickname his friend 'the gazelle'.

In the summer of 1937 Hampshire and Berlin travelled through Ireland together. They were rowed out to the Blasket Islands in a coracle, sat beside peat fires and listened to the islanders singing, then contributed a quavering rendition of the All Souls song to the evening's festivities. They continued on their journey on Irish country buses, during which, Hampshire remembered, Isaiah amused himself by reading Flaubert's *Bouvard et Pécuchet* in Russian. They visited Bowen's Court in late July, with the writer Rosamond Lehmann and Goronwy Rees, and watched as Goronwy, with the verve of a matador, transferred his affections from Bowen to Lehmann – the episode that Bowen took as the bitter kernel of her most famous novel, *The Death of the Heart*.[40]

In the summer of 1938 Berlin finally delivered a manuscript on Marx to the publishers, only to be told that he had to cut it by 25,000 words. He shut himself up in a hotel in Beaulieu-sur-Mer, then at Hollycroft Avenue, which – as he candidly said – was perfect, because it was the only place where he was allowed to be bad-tempered at meals. Then at the end of the summer he went to Bowen's Court, where Elizabeth Bowen locked him into his bedroom every morning until lunchtime. He emerged with a manuscript squeezed down to the requisite size.[41]

In late September 1938 he took the overnight train and ferry from Ireland back to London, and shared a berth with an Irish horse-dealer, who leaped out onto the platform when the train stopped on the line and bought a newspaper with banner headlines proclaiming Chamberlain's deal with Hitler at Munich. The horse-dealer exclaimed 'The war is off!' and went back to sleep. War did seem entirely unreal. On Berlin's return, Oxford seemed beatific in the late, Indian-summer light.[42]

That autumn he paid a visit to the most famous refugee from Nazi Europe, Sigmund Freud. Freud's wife was a relative of a family friend, Oscar Phillip.[43] Through this intermediary, Isaiah arranged to call at Maresfield Gardens one Friday afternoon in October 1938. Freud himself answered the door-bell and ushered Berlin into the famous study with the Egyptian and Greek statuettes and figurines already displayed on every free space of the desk, cabinets and bookcases. When Freud asked Berlin what he did, and Isaiah replied in German that he attempted to teach philosophy, Freud replied sardonically, 'Then you must think me a charlatan.' This was close to the mark, but Berlin protested. 'Dr Freud, how can you think such a thing?' Freud then pointed to a figurine on the mantelpiece. 'Can you guess where it comes from?' When Berlin said he had no idea, Freud replied, 'It comes from Megara. I see you are not pretentious.' Then he explained that he had reached London thanks to the intercession of Princess Marie Bonaparte and asked whether Isaiah was familiar with other members of the Greek royal family. When Isaiah said he wasn't, Freud replied, 'I see you are not a snob.'

This part of the interrogation completed, Freud began musing aloud about whether he might set up his practice in Oxford. Berlin said there was bound to be a lot of demand for Dr Freud's services in a place like Oxford, and in his mind's eye he imagined the discreet, burnished brass plaque on an Oxford doorway reading, 'Dr Freud, 2pm–4pm', and a queue of neurotics stretching back for a mile.

Then Freud's wife, a gentle woman in her seventies, came in, with an amusing and ironical look on her face. She said, 'You know my cousin Oscar. He is an observant Jew?' Berlin said he was. She went on, 'Every Jewish woman wants to light the Sabbath candles on Friday night, but this monster,' and here she pointed at her husband, 'forbids it. Says it is a superstition.' Freud nodded with mock-gravity and said, 'Religion is superstition.' This was obviously a joke sewn into the very fabric of their marriage.

After this, the Freuds, their grandson Lucian and Berlin took tea in the garden, in an atmosphere which, Berlin remembered, was pure Vienna, circa 1912. The old man was in the penultimate stages of cancer of the jaw, but he gave no sign of pain, discomfort or complaint. When tea was over, Berlin departed, feeling that he had spent an hour in the company not of a genius, but of an old Jewish doctor, clever, malicious and wise.

Of greater consequence to Isaiah's later life was his meeting in early 1939 with another patriarch, the leader of the Zionist movement, Chaim Weizmann. They met in the palatial Park Lane apartment of Mrs Israel Sieff, at a meeting of the Friends of the Hebrew University of Jerusalem. Herbert Samuel, High Commissioner of Palestine, addressed the group and Isaiah was asked to give a brief speech of thanks to the hostess, Mrs Sieff. He was a young don, unused to such grand settings and, as he rose to speak, had to fight the impulse to say that the most important thing about Mrs Sieff was that she was 'very, very rich'. After avoiding this embarrassment, he was presented to Weizmann who, on discovering that Isaiah spoke Russian, invited him to tea at the Dorchester Hotel. Weizmann, he immediately thought, *was* a kind of genius, at least in his dealings with human beings, 'a great flirt' with 'a very velvety, extremely seductive voice'. Cosy he was not, but jolly, cynical, funny and not at all kind. He loved telling the story of how in 1915 he was stopped in a Moscow street by a policeman, who asked him what he was doing in the city. When Weizmann replied that he was working for the Jews, the policeman said, in a confidential whisper, 'Watch out, they'll kill you.' Weizmann would then add with a comic growl, 'He was right, of course. They *will* kill me.' This sardonic and ironic relationship to Jewishness drew Berlin to him immediately.[44]

They met at a low ebb in Zionist fortunes. The Peel Commission Report on the future of Palestine, commissioned after the Arab uprising of 1936, had recommended partition, which Weizmann's Jewish Agency accepted but the Arabs rejected out of hand. A conference in London in February and March 1939 failed to resolve the deadlock. Then, in May 1939, the British Government published a White Paper proposing the establishment, over the next decade, of a unitary Palestinian state in which Arabs and Jews would share authority. For a five-year period, 75,000 Jewish immigrants would be allowed; after 1943, further immigration would be banned. Both Arabs and Jews angrily rejected the White Paper.[45] Jews were particularly outraged by the ban on further emigration, despite the obvious evidence that Hitler had placed all of European Jewry in mortal peril. Weizmann and Berlin discussed the available options for the Jewish Agency, with Weizmann pessimistically concluding that if he ever lived to see the Promised Land, it would probably be in a British concentration camp.

With the declaration of war in September 1939, Isaiah – like all his Oxford colleagues – volunteered for war work. Immediately he was given a small, but galling reminder of his foreignness. He was offered the humble post of letter censor, but when it was discovered that he was born in Latvia, the offer was withdrawn.[46] While Freddie Ayer, Stuart Hampshire and John Austin went off to war, as young officers, Berlin had to remain disconsolately in Oxford, gathering with the wives of departed dons in the town hall to assemble gas masks and roll bandages.[47]

His *Marx* appeared at the outbreak of war in the Home University Library series. It was mildly praised in the *Times Literary Supplement*, and the major figures at Oxford – G.D.H. Cole, Master Lindsay of Balliol – all approved of it, though Lindsay did say that Berlin had neglected to emphasise the 'Hebrew prophet' side of Marx.[48] Berlin thought this ridiculous, as if a figure should be regarded as a Hebrew prophet simply because he was Jewish and wore a long beard. Left-wing reviews were more hostile, though the *Daily Worker* did grant that the work was superior to the usual reactionary trash put out by the bourgeoisie. High praise indeed![49]

The book has gone through four editions and is still in print. Its defects are obvious enough: Berlin never mastered Marx's economic theory in *Das Kapital*. Yet he took pride in getting inside the head of an antipathetic figure, and in a larger sense, the sojourn with Marx had a profound influence on his later thought. It gave him a lifelong target, for he genuinely loathed Marxian ideas of historical determinism and was to argue that they served as the chief ideological excuse for Stalin's crimes. At the same time, he was influenced by the Marxian sense that ideas and values were historical, and that the values of social groups in class struggle were incompatible.[50] Marxism accentuated his tendency to look historically at the values that liberals of his generation took as eternal verities.

For the duration of the phoney war, through the winter of 1940, Berlin remained gloomily teaching at Oxford. Outwardly the place remained the same. Bowra still told the same old jokes; David Cecil still ran in and out of Isaiah's rooms, gabbling with a voice like a crate of hens being carried across a field. While a certain sang-froid was maintained in the senior common rooms, Oxford was rife with rumours that the government in Whitehall was about to be evacuated there. Once the invasion of France began, Isaiah began to have very real fears for his own safety. As he wrote to Felix Frankfurter:

> I am not a soldier and can't be one and am in certain respects highly exposed, if only because I am a Jew and have written on Marx; I shd do my best not to be caught: if I could induce some institution in the USA to invite me, I would. But cold-blooded flight is monstrous.[51]

On 12 June 1940, as the Germans broke through the French lines and Paris lay open before their advance, Berlin went to deliver a paper on 'Other Minds' to the Moral Sciences Club in Cambridge. In Oxford, the imminent fall of France was on everyone's mind. In Cambridge, the otherworldiness of the dons was unreal.

All of the Cambridge philosophers turned out – Braithwaite, Broad, Ewing, Moore, Wisdom and a sixth figure, small and handsome of feature, who appeared surrounded with acolytes in tweed jackets and white open-necked shirts identical to his own. This was Ludwig Wittgenstein. Berlin delivered his paper on the problem of how one could have knowledge of others' inner mental states. It was, he remembered, 'terribly boring'. After a few initial questions, Wittgenstein became impatient and took over the discussion. Berlin remembered him saying, 'No, no, that is not the way to go about it at all. Let me. Don't let's talk philosophy. Let's talk business with each other. Ordinary business. In ordinary circs, I say to you, "You see a clock. The minute hand and the hour hand are both nailed to the clock face to certain ciphers. The whole face goes round, but the time remains the same." No? That is solipsism.'[52]

It was idiotic, Wittgenstein was saying, to claim that time had stopped simply because the hands of the clock remained motionless. Time changed whatever the clocks, whatever the sense data happened to record. This was a vintage demolition of Ayer's type of verificationism. No one else spoke. 'Broad sat there like a boiled lobster looking angry.

G.E. Moore, old and decrepit, looked open-mouthed.' Isaiah parried as best he could and the acolytes hung on every word and dared not interrupt. After an hour, Wittgenstein rose to his feet, his acolytes rose with him, and he leaned over the table and shook Isaiah's hands. 'Very interesting discussion. Thank you.' With that, he walked out. Other participants crowded around and said how rare it was to be complimented in this way. But Berlin was not fooled. Wittgenstein hadn't been much impressed with the paper or with Isaiah's arguments afterwards. But he did seem to think that Berlin had been honest and sincere, not trying to show off, as Freddie Ayer might have done. Wittgenstein's judgement was Berlin's own, and their encounter marked the symbolic, if not the actual, end of Isaiah's active philosophical career.

Out of the blue, in mid-June 1940, Guy Burgess appeared in Berlin's rooms at All Souls and suggested that they go to Russia together. Isaiah had known Burgess since early 1934, when they met at the Rothschilds' in Cambridge in company with Anthony Blunt. He immediately liked Burgess: he seemed an amusing, energetic, vulgar but irrepressible Trinity undergraduate. They kept in touch throughout the 1930s. It was an attraction of opposites: the fastidious, rather repressed don and the dishevelled, homosexual adventurer.[53] Isaiah watched with some fascination as Burgess navigated his way into a job at Conservative Central Office; then onto a City newsletter offering investors advice; then into writing speeches for a Conservative MP; then into working for Radio Luxembourg. All the while he revelled in the London low-life, and the tales of his escapades afforded Isaiah much vicarious enjoyment. Burgess would suddenly descend on Oxford from London and ring up from The Mitre, the hotel up the High Street from All Souls, proposing to visit, some transient male friend in tow. Isaiah would order Burgess to leave his friend at The Mitre, break out the whisky, and he and Burgess would talk into the small hours, never about politics but mostly about books, cinema and music. Berlin had no inkling of Burgess' deeper and darker involvements. Some time in 1938, however, Isaiah heard that Burgess had joined Britannia Youth, a neo-fascist group that used to send British schoolboys to Nazi rallies in Germany. Hearing this, Isaiah broke off all contact with him.

In June 1940 a sober and business-like Burgess arrived in Oxford. He explained away his temporary sojourn with the neo-fascists. 'I'm terribly unstable, it just came over me. Everything in England was so dreary. I thought at least the Nazis knew where they were going. Anyway I don't expect you to forgive me.'[54] But Isaiah did. Burgess then announced that he was bound for Russia on a mission for MI5. He had proposed to his mentor and protector, Harold Nicolson, then in a senior position at the Ministry of Information, that Isaiah – since he had fluent Russian – be appointed as a press officer at the British Embassy in Moscow. Isaiah, still smarting from being turned down for war-work as a foreigner, increasingly frightened that the Germans might overrun Britain and desperate to do something of credit in the war, leaped at the chance. On several occasions during the 1930s he had said how much he wanted to go to Russia. Now he had his opportunity. Burgess rapidly arranged visits to Gladwyn Jebb at the Foreign Office and Nicolson at the Ministry of Information. Both seemed to encourage the idea of a joint mission to Moscow. A visa to Russia would be required, but that could be procured on the way. Of the available routes to Russia, the easiest went through the west-coast ports of America to Vladivostok. In July 1940, in company with Guy Burgess, Isaiah set off by boat for Montreal, bound – so he thought – for Moscow.[55]

8

Isaiah's War: New York, 1940–1

The SS *Antonia* left Liverpool on 9 July 1940, crowded with child evacuees. They swarmed over the ship, 'behind, on, in, above, below every piece of furniture and rigging'.[1] Burgess and Berlin had separate cabins in first class, far above the mothers and guardians on the lower decks. Guy said nothing about his mission and Isaiah was left to wonder what it might be.

To reassure his parents, he wrote them that the journey was 'uneventful'; actually it was slow and nerve-racking. The ship zigzagged through the convoy lanes, with the escort destroyers dropping depth-charges to keep German submarines at bay. The crossing took ten days and Isaiah had more than enough time to wonder whether he had made the right decision. The job – press attaché in Moscow – seemed dubious: who could seriously suppose that he would have any success planting pro-British stories in *Pravda* at the height of the Hitler–Stalin pact?

On 20 July they disembarked at Quebec and made their way to New York. Within days, Burgess mysteriously announced that he was being recalled.[2] All Isaiah knew was that Burgess had been to see Michael Straight, a wealthy American contemporary from his days at Cambridge. He had no idea that Straight and Burgess were communists and that at least one of them was an active Soviet agent. In retrospect, it is clear that Burgess had used his connections with Harold Nicolson at the Ministry of Information to arrange a visit to Moscow, courtesy of His Majesty's

Government, with the innocuous Berlin to serve as cover. Once the journey was under way, either Moscow or London changed its mind, probably the latter. Isaiah later believed that someone in British Intelligence, perhaps Victor Rothschild, decided that Burgess was too unreliable – on personal rather than political grounds – to be trusted and had him recalled.[3] On his return, Burgess was dismissed from intelligence and fetched up in the BBC. Of all this Isaiah had not the slightest inkling. All he knew was that he was now left high and dry.

It does seem extraordinary that he should have thrown up his teaching job, crossed the North Atlantic in the middle of a war and set off for Moscow, without visas or official letters of accreditation, in the company of a man known to be both unorthodox and unstable. It never occurred to Berlin that Burgess might not be all he claimed to be, putting down the haste with which the trip had been set up and the suddenness with which it collapsed to the chaos of war-time. After Burgess returned to London on 30 July, Isaiah insisted that he would continue to Moscow as instructed. He went to see his old friend Felix Frankfurter, now a justice of the United States Supreme Court, at his summer house in Heath, Massachusetts. There he met the liberal theologian Reinhold Niebuhr, whose Zionist convictions, liberal opinions and personal charm won Isaiah over immediately. Not having explicit accreditation from the British Embassy in Moscow, Isaiah was unsure whether he had Ambassador Stafford Cripps' authorisation to proceed. Niebuhr said that he was an old friend of Cripps and would write to him immediately.[4]

Berlin went on to Washington to stay with his friend from All Souls, John Foster, who was legal counsellor at the British Embassy. He addressed a second request, through Foreign Office channels, for permission to continue to Moscow. He also went to the Soviet Embassy in Washington to secure a visa. The Russian Ambassador invited Isaiah to lunch. They engaged in steely banter in Russian. Why, Isaiah wanted to know, had the Soviets just occupied his birthplace, Riga, and snuffed out the independence of the Baltic republics? 'New Deal for Latvia, New Deal for Estonia, New Deal for Lithuania,' the ambassador replied, with an ingratiating smile, before authorising the visa.[5]

The fact that the Soviets cleared the way for his visit made it all the more humiliating when, several weeks later, Stafford Cripps replied that Niebuhr's letter was the first notification he had had of Berlin's mission.

He could see no useful function for Berlin in Moscow and, besides, would find it inconvenient to have on his staff someone of Latvian origin. An equally chilly note from Fitzroy Maclean of the Foreign Office arrived, saying that His Majesty had no desire to employ Mr Berlin in any capacity.[6]

There were not many times when depression and self-pity took hold of Isaiah, but this was one of them. He took refuge in a friend's suite in the Shoreham Hotel in New York throughout August 1940, unable to do anything in the dog-day heat, except read Dickens and feel pathetically Dickensian himself, 'like a comic litigant ground by the law courts into farcical squalor'.[7] He stared down at the ant-like figures streaming up the avenues far below and felt morbidly insignificant and worthless. The New York papers were full of the Battle of Britain and the first bombing of London. His mother had moved into his rooms at New College. His father joined her on the weekends but continued to work in the City even as the bombs fell. Compounding Isaiah's anxiety were rumours of imminent Nazi invasion. He now feared being marooned in New York while his ageing parents were despatched to a concentration camp.

He had set off in July, imagining that he was going to make 'a dashing contribution' to the war effort.[8] Now the bombs were falling on London and he was in shameful safety in New York, doing nothing, at the taxpayers' expense. This mood of self-castigation was not lifted by an evening spent with the most notorious escapee from England, Wystan Auden. The meeting was not a success: Isaiah had never approved of Auden's decision to leave England and now, having left himself, felt his own guilt even more keenly.[9]

When Berlin laid out his woes in a letter to Harold Nicolson at the Ministry of Information, Nicolson airily replied that he had never had much faith in the Moscow venture anyway. As for returning to England, he advised Isaiah to stay put in New York and 'not to indulge in the sentimentality of bomb dodging among the mouldering cloisters of Oxford'.[10]

Nor were his spirits lifted by his exposure to the 'great big glaring sunlit extrovert over-articulated scene' of America. In a letter to his father, he admitted that Americans were 'open, vigorous, $2\times2=4$ sort of people, who want yes or no for an answer', but he longed for the company of people with a European 'nuance'. To his Oxford friend Mary Fisher he confessed that he was miserably homesick for the complex and mysterious social mazes of Oxbridge: there were no mazes in America, nothing but flat, clear vistas. Conversations with Americans were equally disappointing: 'a total lack of salt, pepper, mustard'.[11]

Despite these disdainful first impressions, he was already meeting Americans who were to become friends for life. At John Foster's he met a young journalist, Joe Alsop, who had the twin attractions of being a relative of the President and a loquacious observer of war-time Washington. Through Frankfurter, Isaiah was introduced to several key figures in Roosevelt's Washington, particularly Ben Cohen, a lawyer with a lugubrious drawl from South Bend, Indiana, who had drafted much of the key legislation of the New Deal.[12]

Though Berlin hardly knew the United States at all, and what he had seen he had mostly disliked, he managed to impress British officials with his grasp of the American scene. He sat in the Georgetown garden of his friend Foster one muggy July night, barely forty-eight hours after his arrival, and kept up such a steady stream of commentary on American politics that his friends decided to put him to use. John Wheeler-Bennett and Aubrey Morgan, who were trying to set up an effective propaganda team to get America into the war, immediately went to Lord Lothian, the British Ambassador, to see if Isaiah could be given a job.[13] Lothian had a word with the embassy press attaché, who proposed that, as a test of his suitability, Isaiah make a study of the Associated Press reporting of British morale during the Battle of Britain. Meanwhile, Weizmann was urging Berlin to accept a job with the Jewish Agency, but he diplomatically declined the Chief's embrace. Instead, throughout September, as the Battle of Britain reached its climax, Isaiah went every day to the British library in the Rockefeller Center on New York's Fifth Avenue and read the AP coverage of the British war effort, which he thought, by and large, was 'defeatist and panic-stricken'.[14] Isaiah reported to this effect and the embassy was sufficiently pleased to offer him a permanent job with the British Press Service in New York. But instead of taking it up immediately, Berlin decided he must first return to Britain.[15] His friends in America had not reckoned on Isaiah's anxiety, redoubled by being Jewish, at being thought a coward, hiding in America while England was in danger. In early October he flew back by sea-plane with the British Ambassador, Lord Lothian, who was returning to London for consultations. As the plane refuelled in the Azores, the ambassador looked about him at the bare vistas and remarked dryly, 'Very unlike Broadway, isn't it?' They then flew on to Lisbon, where Isaiah spent several days in the Estoril Palace Hotel, crowded with Jewish refugees seeking visas and transport to America, before he found a flight home. An air-raid was under way as his sea-plane landed in Bristol harbour and, as the anti-aircraft batteries chattered around him, he was stirred by a virtuous sense of returning to the thick of battle. 'It was what I had come for.' He immediately took a train to Oxford, was reunited with his mother and father and resumed teaching. He also saw Burgess again and, none the wiser, accompanied him to lunch with Harold Nicolson at the Ministry of Information.[16]

A month into term, a letter arrived from the Ministry of Information ordering Berlin to return immediately to New York. Having reassured his parents, arranged his leave from New College, and having proved that he wasn't running away from the Blitz, Isaiah now returned to New York with a clear conscience. Yet when he departed in January 1941, he was miserably apprehensive. He was leaving behind his parents and the familiar world of Oxford; he worried that he might fail in his new career as an official. As he set off for New York, he wrote to Maire Lynd with uncharacteristic self-pity, 'I really cannot describe the blackness of my misery. To be lost at the age of 31 is most humiliating.'[17] In fact, America was to be the making of him.

His job was to get America into the war.[18] He was to be a propagandist, working with trade unions, black organisations and Jewish groups. He lived in mid-town Manhattan hotels and went to work every morning at the British Information Services on the forty-fourth floor of a building in the Rockefeller Center. There he went through piles of American press clippings ranged in shoe-boxes. From these he put together a weekly report for the Ministry of Information on the state of American public opinion. In the early months of 1941 the isolationists were in the ascendant and the prospects of getting America into the war seemed remote.

The information service was, as he recalled, 'gay, raffish, ineffective and full of old friends, essentially nice to visit but not impressive' – in other words, a world away from the 'efficient grimness' of the Foreign Office.[19] Daphne Straight, an earl's daughter who had taken refuge in

New York and worked in the office with him, remembered Berlin as a voluble, slightly mad professor – pockets overflowing with sweets, handkerchiefs, press cuttings, lapels dusted with cigarette ash – but he was far from ineffectual.[20] He worked long hours and soon assembled an extremely useful network of American contacts.

The work pitched him into a world for which Oxford life offered little preparation: lobbying editors, meeting influential businessmen, rabbis and politicians, shepherding delegations of British trade unionists into meetings with American union bosses. He soon found common ground with the leaders of the New York garment workers' union, David Dubinsky and Sid Hillman, who turned out to be firmly pro-British. Other unions – especially John L. Lewis's American coal miners – were more hostile. They didn't take kindly to the British Information Service's attempts to draw American working men into an imperialist war; and they were resistant to British-inspired campaigns to get unions to defer strike action until the war's end. Other unions were suspicious of British attempts to influence their internal elections in a pro-British direction. But he began to love America. He sent his friends excited descriptions of his adventures in this alien world. From the CIO convention in Detroit, in November 1941, where he had accompanied 'some hefty specimens' from the British trade union movement, as well as the less than hefty Deputy Prime Minister, Clement Attlee, he described how 'all the German-born delegates from Milwaukee and Wisconsin and Minnesota bought thumbs up badges of British War Relief offered to them by a very homely Jew who later took me to a kosher restaurant'.[21] A lunatic world, he said, but one he was making his own.

While the British campaign against American neutrality became more effective during the course of 1941, it stood little chance, by itself, of turning the tide of opinion.[22] Berlin came to believe that Roosevelt wanted to win the war without actually having to fight it. In this he judged American opinion correctly. While Americans were more favourable towards the Allied cause at the end of 1941 than at the beginning, 80 per cent of the public was still opposed to the despatch of American troops and remained so until Pearl Harbor and the German declaration of war.[23]

Berlin's work may have changed little, but it certainly changed him. He took to it with avidity: attracted by America's vitality and amused by its vulgarity. He discovered in himself a journalist's ear for gossip and intrigue; and gave himself entirely to becoming his government's eyes and ears in the New World. The experience also subtly altered his deeper intellectual outlook. Practical experience was teaching him that judgement and character could be a good deal more important than mere intelligence. The people he admired most were those who saw the world plainly. The quotation from Bishop Butler, with which he began his introduction to *Karl Marx*, was canonical for Isaiah: 'Things and actions are what they are, and the consequences of them will be what they will be: why then should we desire to be deceived?' But in pre-war Oxford, he was too young and untried for his realism to be much more than an attitude. It was in America, in daily contact with politicians, trade union leaders, congressmen, journalists and fellow-lobbyists, that realism became a fact of his character. There he learned how the business of life was done; how deals were made, how illusions were created and used, how opinion could be moulded and shifted. It was in America that he had his first encounters with genuine celebrity. Greta Garbo met him through a mutual friend, Raimund von Hofmannsthal and after staring at him for what seemed a heart-stoppingly long period of time, observed in a smoky voice, "You have beautiful eyes."

Others were less susceptible. At first, he sometimes made a comic impression. Harold Ross, famed editor of the *New Yorker*, took him to lunch at the Algonquin Hotel, listened to Isaiah and at the end of lunch drawled, 'Young man, I can't understand a word you say, but if you write anything, I'll print it.' This became a pattern in America: he became famous by being misunderstood. The arch patois that was natural to the common rooms of Oxford was – for the New York and Washington of 1941 – inconceivably exotic. He began to attract a reputation for being a vivid character and lively company: hard to understand, perhaps, but full of ironical curiosity towards American life. Americans loved to hear their country described in his rapid-fire semi-Martian vernacular.

His work with the trade unions was interesting, but barriers of class, experience and education prevented him from becoming anything more than a visiting anthropologist in their midst. Work with Jewish organisations was a very different matter. The British White Paper of 1939, banning further Jewish immigration and so envisaging Jews as a permanent minority within a Palestinian state had disillusioned American Jewish opinion. Keeping American Jewry sympathetic to the British cause was not easy.

In Palestine, Jewish underground groups, with the exception of the Stern gang, ceased their campaigns against the British, and the British Special Operations Executive began training Jewish underground fighters as guerrillas in preparation for the expected invasion of Palestine by Rommel's Afrika Korps, then advancing towards Cairo.[24] The Jewish Agency demanded that, in addition to these guerrilla forces, a Jewish army be created for the defence of Palestine. If there were Czech, Polish and Free French units in the Allied forces, why shouldn't Jews fight as Jews for the Allied cause? Berlin had to defend the official line that a Jewish army was unnecessary, because Jews could always enlist as individuals in the British armed forces; and harmful, because a Jewish fighting force would alienate the Arabs, and might one day be turned against the British themselves. The former of these reasons could be stated publicly. The latter was not for public consumption. For the first time, Isaiah had to learn to say one thing and believe another.

On his arrival, the New York office despatched him to meet Rabbi Stephen Wise, President Roosevelt's chief fixer in New York Jewish politics and the most influential Jewish leader of his day. Isaiah told his parents that Wise was 'erratic, noisy, unreliable', but also had 'imagination, courage and a golden heart'. Next, Felix Frankfurter provided Berlin with an introduction to the Governor of New York, Herbert Lehmann, whom he found to be like a 'little brown bear, swinging his legs from his chair'.[25] But the figure who made the greatest impression was Supreme Court Justice Louis Brandeis, whom Berlin approached with reverence as a 'saint and gentleman, a kind of Jewish Lord Balfour'. By then Brandeis was within months of his death and he was a shrunken shell inside his black judicial robes. But he still radiated formidable moral and intellectual authority. He told Isaiah that most American Jews supported Zionism, but they wouldn't emigrate and they wouldn't contribute large sums of money to the Zionist cause. He was also sceptical about the real political influence of the Jewish lobby: he said American Catholics were better organised. When Isaiah asked him why American Jews were not more forthright in supporting the Allied cause in Europe, Brandeis exclaimed, 'Because they're just so ignorant! I can't tell you how ignorant they are.'[26]

These meetings offered Isaiah a kaleidoscope of available American Jewish identities: he was drawn to Wise because of his vitality, and to Brandeis because of his nobility. The people he couldn't bear were the apologetic American Jews: Edward Warburg, spoiled scion of the prominent banking family; Arthur Krock and Walter Lippmann, the two most famous columnists of their day, who both gave the impression of writhing inwardly at the very fact of being Jews; or Arthur Hays Sulzberger, publisher of the *New York Times*, who took Isaiah aside and said, 'Mr Berlin, don't you believe that if the word Jew was banned from the public press for fifty years, it would have a strongly positive influence?'[27] Lewis Namier had once memorably denounced such Jews as 'trembling amateur gentiles'. Isaiah soon made friends with a brilliant Russian expert in the State Department, Charles Bohlen, and together they coined the acronym OTAG (Order of Trembling Amateur Gentiles).[28]

The 'trembling amateur gentiles' set Berlin's hero, Chaim Weizmann, in enhanced relief. In his dignity and authority he resembled Brandeis: by sheer force of personality he had forced the British Government and the American administration to treat him as a Head of State in waiting. Yet he was more human than Brandeis, more amusing, more cosily Russian. Weizmann came to the States in April 1941, at the behest of the British Government, to drum up Jewish support for the Allied cause and to raise money for the Jewish Agency. Weizmann was 'an irresistible political seducer' and Isaiah quickly succumbed. He was never blind to Weizmann's vanity and ruthlessness, but he enormously admired his tenacious moderation and his 'sense of reality'. In America Isaiah became an intimate friend, dining with the Weizmanns alone, then taking Vera Weizmann to the cinema afterwards, while Chaim remained in his hotel suite, making phone calls to his web of allies, confidants and informants. Berlin sent his parents a comic account of Weizmann's *modus operandi* with rich American donors:

> Very funny when he talks on the telephone to somebody unknown, smiles sweetly, says, 'How are you Mr Heineman, yes, of course, we must meet soon, it will be *very* nice to see you, we must arrange . . .'

then turns to me, while the other talks and whispers loudly 'money' then turns back, 'It would be delightful to see you, how is your daughter etc.?' I ask 'Is he rich?' W. answers, 'vehrry. A terrible fellow. But very rich.'[29]

As a Zionist, Isaiah believed the White Paper ban on immigration to Palestine was an abomination. As a British official, he was required to defend it. His friendship with Weizmann was bound to put his loyalties to the test. Berlin managed this balancing act by formally reporting his conversations with Weizmann, while keeping back a certain amount of internal Zionist in-fighting and rumour. Weizmann, for his part, used Isaiah as one of his many conduits to Whitehall, but took care not to disclose sensitive information that Berlin would feel obliged to report to his superiors. Both trod delicately, but for Isaiah a conflict of loyalties was inevitable.[30]

At the beginning, his chief role was to smooth relations between Weizmann and Supreme Court Justice Felix Frankfurter, who had influence with Roosevelt on the Palestine issue. Frankfurter and Weizmann both had their vanities, and Isaiah was able to serve as a buffer whenever they did not want to communicate directly. He also maintained ties with Weizmann's *bête noire* and rival for the Zionist leadership, David Ben Gurion, who was already highly critical of Weizmann's lack of success in securing a Jewish army. Ben Gurion wanted Zionists to campaign immediately for the establishment of a Jewish commonwealth; Weizmann accepted the British position that the future of Palestine be deferred until after the war. Ben Gurion envisaged a totally independent Jewish state; Weizmann imagined a Jewish entity within the British mandatory power or within the Commonwealth. The one looked to Britain to *grant* Jewish statehood; the other looked to Jewish arms, if necessary, to *seize* it; one believed that discreet diplomacy within the British establishment would best achieve Zionist goals; the other insisted that worldwide Jewish pressure led by American Jewry must force the British to cede Palestine.[31] These long, simmering disagreements would eventually explode into an open clash. Berlin sided with Weizmann but he also managed to gain Ben Gurion's confidence.

In December 1941, Isaiah went to a late-night meeting with Roosevelt's confidant, Ben Cohen, at a Manhattan hotel. Cohen spent

Saturday in New York and then returned to Washington on the early-morning train from Grand Central Station. At midnight Isaiah knocked on what he thought was Cohen's door, only to have it opened, not by Cohen, but by a small, muscular man with a pronounced nose and a shock of white hair. Ben Gurion beckoned him into his room, and they talked politely about Plato before Isaiah completed his apologies and made his way to Cohen's room. This first meeting set the pattern: Ben Gurion seeking to seduce Isaiah away from the Weizmann camp with displays of philosophical erudition that never quite convinced. Isaiah enjoyed being pursued by both men. His relations with Weizmann were patriarchal and intense; while with Ben Gurion they were wary and more distant; but he managed to avoid being compromised in either camp.

For a time, Berlin must have thought that he could be as indiscreet as he wished in private about British policy, provided he toed the Foreign Office line in public. In September 1941, in a private letter, he let slip the remark that, while he was required to parrot the official line, the real reason against a Jewish fighting force was that it would antagonise the Arabs. This letter was intercepted by the British postal censors and passed to his superiors at the Ministry of Information. 'I believe,' one of them wrote in a confidential minute, 'that part of Mr Berlin's duties were to explain our policy to the Jews of the USA. If this report is correct, it does not seem that Mr Berlin is doing his job very well.' Another Ministry official added the damning comment, 'Yes, it looks as if his co-religionists have got him in a corner.'[32] In fact, Berlin had merely said out loud what every Jew knew to be the case – that the Foreign Office was the captive of Arab opinion. But calling a spade a spade is not a diplomatic virtue, and Isaiah was given to understand that he must never again let his Jewish loyalties get the better of British discretion.

At the time, he received no more than a gentle rap on the knuckles: certainly, the incident did not damage his career. He had displayed such a talent for making influential contacts that the British Embassy in Washington began to angle for his services.

On 7 December 1941 he lunched with David Ben Gurion. The talk mixed Zionist political gossip and Greek philosophy. Ben Gurion spoke in 'short, sharp bursts, punctuated by even more intense, absorbed brooding silences ... as if the apocalyptic vision by which he was possessed outran his powers of expression'.[33] This was political romanticism at its most self-dramatising and self-absorbed: Isaiah found it riveting as spectacle but untrustworthy as politics. At the time, he was convinced that Ben Gurion was wrong to seek to mobilise American Jewish opinion against British policy in Palestine; wrong because the Jewish lobby had little real influence; wrong because agitation would sow dissension between America and Britain. Only later did he realise that Ben Gurion's 'sense of reality' was just as shrewd as Weizmann's or his own.

After their lunch, Ben Gurion went on to Washington to see Ben Cohen, in the hope of arranging a meeting with Roosevelt. As soon as Isaiah hopped into a cab to head back to the Rockefeller Center, the cabby turned to him and broke the news that the Japanese had attacked Pearl Harbor. When he arrived at the office, British officials were in a state of celebration: the goal for which they had been working for more than a year, America's entry into the war, was now assured. Only Daphne Straight – half-American by marriage – was in tears.[34]

9

Isaiah's War: Washington, 1942–5

Berlin's press surveys for the Ministry of Information had proved so successful that he was now asked to do the same for the Foreign Office, working out of the British Embassy in Washington.[1] The Anglo-American alliance was at its apogee, American democracy was mobilised on the Allied side at last and two great leaders were working in concert. Berlin was exhilarated by Churchill and Roosevelt's 'appetite for the future', their sense that they were 'prepared to let the wave come in the full confidence that they will ride it triumphantly'.[2] Washington was filled to bursting with Quonset huts and temporary buildings, plywood office complexes, painted war-time grey or green to house a new army of war workers.[3] The whole city surged along on the wave of war. There were something like 3,000 British officials in Washington – half of the Oxbridge common rooms were serving in some capacity – and the old formalities of the British and American bureaucracies had been broken down by the influx of outsiders like Isaiah, and so he quickly felt at home. The weekly summary of American opinion gave him a licence to meet everyone who mattered, and he moved out into the overlapping worlds of war-time Washington with a social acumen that his colleagues at the embassy found astonishing. He was soon lunching with the major editorialists and columnists, Marquis Childs, Drew Pearson, Arthur Krock and Walter Lippmann. With Lippmann, he engaged in grand, formal and elaborate *tours d'horizon*, which, while global in scope, always seemed to bypass Palestine. Lippmann was sensitive about any subject that might engage his troubled Jewishness.[4] Isaiah quickly mastered the logic of newspaper leaks in Washington: if Krock was carrying a story about the Department of Labor, Berlin knew the material had been leaked by a rival department; he knew which secret sources worked for which columnist, which were reliable, which not. Washington, as his friend Chaim Weizmann wrote, was a 'regular whispering gallery, combining all the disadvantages of a great capital and a small village ... rumour and gossip are carried on invisible wings, with speedy and lightning rapidity and in most cases distorted'.[5] Berlin became Britain's ears in the whispering gallery.

Government departments, he soon discovered, were as aloof from each other as Oxford colleges. Professional relationships, on the other hand, were highly personal. In Washington you worked for Mr Ickes, or Mr Morgenthau or Mr Hull, which tended to make people indiscreet, since personal loyalties cut across institutional ties. Oxford connections also helped to open doors. Felix Frankfurter provided introductions to key figures in the White House. Berlin made friends with a circle of the brightest young New Dealers in Washington. This circle included Katharine and Philip Graham, then just taking over the *Washington Post* from her father, Eugene Mayer; Charles E. Bohlen, an aristocratic and highly intelligent State Department official, who was to be Roosevelt's interpreter and note-taker in his meetings with Stalin; George Kennan, another key State Department official, specialising in relations with the Russians; John Ferguson, a young Washington lawyer, then working for the Department of Justice; Donald Hiss, a State Department official; John Oakes, an official in intelligence; and Edward Prichard, a jovial and preternaturally quick young lawyer from Kentucky, former clerk of Felix Frankfurter's and now a member of the White House staff. Some of these men roomed together in a house called Hockley, and Isaiah was soon a fixture of dinner parties there. 'Prich', as Prichard was known, was a corpulent figure who joked when he was conscripted that they had reached the bottom of the barrel and were now coming for the barrel.[6] Later in the war, when Prichard returned from the army, he and Isaiah lived together in a rented house in Georgetown. Through these friendships Isaiah gained unrivalled access to some of the most influential and certainly the liveliest policy-makers in war-time Washington.

The All Souls connection opened all the doors in the embassy. John Foster was legal counsellor and the ambassador himself was a former fellow. Lord Halifax was vice-regal and remote, a 'being not of this century', who regarded most of his staff as Foreign Office pen-pushers, but he was unexpectedly warm with the very junior official from his old college.[7] In addition to Halifax, there was another All Souls fellow, Robert Brand, a senior partner in Lazard Freres, in charge of the British Food Mission.

In the winter of 1942, Berlin was invited to join a Washington lunch given by Jennifer Brand Polk, Bob Brand's daughter. He was warned that he would meet an absurd Central European adventuress who was bound to be a dreadful bore. Instead he found himself sitting beside the twenty-four-year-old Countess Patricia de Bendern, who turned out to be the daughter of Lord Queensberry and a relative, therefore, of Oscar Wilde's *jeune homme fatal*, Lord Alfred Douglas. Patricia's husband was then a prisoner of war in North Africa and she had come to America with her daughter and had enrolled at Radcliffe in Cambridge, Massachusetts. Isaiah found her 'wildly attractive': deep blue eyes, a gamine face, framed by soft brown hair in a pageboy cut; physically slight and delicate, seductively feminine. Like most society women of her time, she had no education to speak of, but she was highly intelligent and had a taste for clever men. It was obvious that she was not in love with her genial and inconsequential husband, and when Isaiah asked her why they had married, she said, 'Oh, because everyone else was so awful.'[8] She was from London's smart set, but she seemed bored by its smartness. At Radcliffe, she was busy re-inventing herself as a serious person, listening to F.O. Matthiessen's lectures on Henry James, taking cello lessons, entertaining Harvard professors in her apartment. She spoke well, Isaiah remembered, about Bach's unaccompanied cello suites, which she said were her favourite pieces of music. She was incorrigibly flirtatious and Isaiah found it intoxicating to be the object of her attentions. By the end of lunch, he felt himself succumbing. She invited him to spend the weekend in her flat in Cambridge. 'Nothing happened physically,' he recalled. 'She found me as unattractive as everyone else. But she clung to me for some reason. She wished to keep me.' He was soon included in the circle of clever Harvard academics who danced attendance upon her. He found her conversation entrancing, her gaiety and sense of humour irresistible.

Quite soon, he was in love for the first time in his life. Throughout the rest of 1942 he spent weekends with Patricia in Cambridge and saw her whenever she came to New York or Washington. Isaiah's friends found the relationship hard to fathom: this plump, jolly intellectual, with little *savoir-faire*, so obviously besotted with a notorious *femme fatale*; she so sexual, he so repressed; he so Jewish, and she, as one of Isaiah's friends put it, so 'super-goyissimo'.[9] She at least enjoyed the flattery of his attention. When he was away, either in Washington or back in London for consultations, she was sure to send him a tender note pulling him back to her. But he quickly realised that she was unreliable to a maddening degree, making appointments and then cancelling them, declaring herself his and then vanishing for months into some secret affair. If she was a deceiver, she was also irresistibly forgivable. The affair – if that is the word for such a frustratingly unconsummated business – continued throughout 1942.

By the summer of 1943 when Patricia fell in love with someone else, the affair passed beyond infatuation into something approaching real misery. The object of her attentions was a rich young Franco-Cuban graduate student at Harvard, Jacques Abreu, extremely handsome, Berlin remembered, and almost completely humourless. In December Patricia, Abreu and Isaiah went to see the musical *Oklahoma!* in New York and afterwards returned to the hotel, where Patricia and Abreu's rooms were next to Isaiah's. As he tried to sleep, he could hear the muffled sounds of love coming through the walls. Next morning when he checked out, he took the key with him. He held on to it for the rest of his life.[10]

In mid-1944 Patricia's husband escaped from a prisoner of war camp in Italy and fled to Switzerland, from where he sent a message, calling her home. Remorsefully she returned to Europe after D-Day, but continued to send Isaiah letters that adroitly maintained him in a state of suspended animation and hopeless expectation for another year.

Fortunately, his work consumed him. Instead of being tied down to a specific file or area of expertise in the embassy, Isaiah was free to range across all of official Washington, lunching, dining, gossiping, and once a week assembling the materials for a digest of American opinion to be sent to the Foreign Office, and through them to other Whitehall departments, including the Cabinet Office. To the Survey Section of the British Embassy came reports on public opinion from the British consulates around the country, as well as the weekly press summary from New York. Occasionally Isaiah would venture out of Washington and New York – he did visit Los Angeles, San Francisco, Chicago, Portland and Seattle – but the America he really knew stretched from mid-town Manhattan to the Potomac.[11]

Isaiah absorbed all of this material and then would dictate a digest in his own vivid and pungent language. He had begun dictating while doing the revisions of his Marx book, and for the rest of his life it remained his preferred method of composition. Dictation overcame his inhibition about the written word, but it taxed his long-suffering secretaries: they had to tune their hearing to the highly compressed, word-swallowing, intricate, clause-upon-clause flow of his thought. This rough version was then edited and some of Isaiah's more indiscreet pieces of gossip were excised by senior officials, before being signed and sent out under Halifax's name.[12]

Only on one occasion – at the very end of his time in Washington – did the ambassador personally alter Isaiah's despatches. It was a piece assessing the new President, Harry Truman, and it included the remark that Congress was likely to get on better with Truman than with his more 'imperious predecessor'. Halifax's hand shot out like a snake and his pen struck out the words 'more imperious'. The words referred to Roosevelt, but Winston, Halifax explained, would take that as a reference to himself.[13]

The range of Isaiah's sources, and the quality of the information he was able to extract from the inmost recesses of the American Government, impressed his superiors. Occasionally, however, he would be taken to task for some startling assertion. Is this true, thay would ask him? 'True,' Isaiah would gnomically reply, 'but at a deeper level.'[14]

An official version of his summary was cabled in cipher to the Foreign Office in London, while a letter incorporating all the gossip 'found too dazzling by the twilight denizens of Whitehall' found its way to Isaiah's friends – chiefly Herbert Nicholas – at 'Heartbreak House', the Ministry of Information.[15] These letters became known as the 'bootleg' version of the despatches, and themselves began to attract attention. This was a dangerous game, and Berlin had to caution Nicholas about distributing them too widely, since American friends were beginning to complain that inside information they had told him was reverberating back to Washington.

The circulation list of Isaiah's official summaries was small but select. The summaries were certainly read by Winston Churchill, Anthony Eden, the Cabinet Office, the Ministry of Information, senior levels of the Foreign Office, senior ambassadors and Cabinet ministers. They also reached the King. The voracious appetite for Washington political intelligence was one indication of the increasing subservience of the British towards American opinion. It now became a crucial factor to be weighed, investigated and reported on, before decisions could be made, and Isaiah had become its chief British purveyor. No wonder his stock rose out of all proportion to his relatively junior rank as a First Secretary. He himself was scathing about the new British tendency to wait until it was known which way the American cat would jump. In one of his 'bootleg' letters to H.G. Nicholas, he insisted that the British should make policy, whether or not the Americans could be counted on to support it.[16]

Palestine was the subject on which the British Government waited with particular attention to see which way the American cat would jump. After the fall of Tobruk in June 1942, when Palestine itself lay open to Rommel's North African army, American Zionist leaders began demanding that the British allow the creation of a Jewish fighting force. Isaiah's reports on this issue make clear that he had not been reduced to silence by earlier reprimands. He reported that 'the simplicity and humanity' of the demand that Jews fight as Jews had won many allies in the States. The British Government's arguments against a Jewish fighting force 'had been rebutted too often in the Zionist press to retain any plausibility'.[17] Only Weizmann's influence, Berlin argued, had prevented American Jewish circles turning irrevocably against the British position. Isaiah used every despatch to bolster Weizmann's position in British eyes. On 9 June 1942, for example, Isaiah counselled Halifax that the British Government 'would be well advised to make any eventual concession (re. the Jewish army) in the form of a concession to Dr Weizmann personally'.[18] Halifax forwarded just such advice to Churchill on 27 June, and these initiatives led to the formation of a Palestine Regiment in August, which, however, cruelly disappointed Zionist hopes because it was nothing more than a glorified Home Guard.[19]

Throughout this period Weizmann's influence on the American Jewish community was waning. In April 1942, at a meeting of Zionist organisations at the Biltmore Hotel in Washington, a declaration had been passed, largely at Ben Gurion's insistence, which formally protested the British ban on Jewish immigration to Palestine and committed the American community to campaign actively for a Jewish state in Palestine at the war's end. Weizmann's policy of seeking concessions from the British had got nowhere, while Ben Gurion's policy of direct challenge to the British was in the ascendant.

Berlin was never a fair-weather friend and he stuck with Weizmann. When he left Washington to return home to England in August 1942, he was carrying messages from the Chief for the Jewish Agency in London. When he returned to America in September, he brought Weizmann the latest news from headquarters. At this point, illness brought them still closer. Isaiah was struck down with pneumonia on his return and had to be hospitalised in New York. He was so weak that his legs felt like 'very inferior synthetic rubber'.[20] Isaiah's chief concern was to keep his mother in the dark about his condition, so he sent a stream of cheery telegrams: 'flourishing', 'monotonously well', 'physical condition superb', and passed off his pneumonia as a minor bout of sinusitis. He was in fact immobilised throughout the autumn of 1942, although he still managed to dictate political summaries from his New York hospital bed.[21] The Weizmanns joined in the 'mendacity front', sending Mendel and Marie reassuring messages of their own. Weizmann himself, worn out by the battles with Ben Gurion and discouraged by rebuffs from both the British and American Governments, had been hospitalised for exhaustion and spent the autumn recuperating at Grossinger's Resort in the Catskill Mountains in upstate New York. Isaiah joined them there and the old man, now sixty-seven, and Isaiah, thirty-four, took strolls in the woods and rested on the porch of the Weizmanns' cabin. Meyer Weisgal, one of Weizmann's intimates, joked to his Chief that he was bound to get plenty of rest, since Isaiah could be counted on to do all the talking.[22]

In January 1943, after a long convalescence, Isaiah returned to work, having confessed to his mother that he had been rather more ill than he had led her to believe. His curious double-act resumed: advising Halifax on how to cope with the Jewish lobby, while simultaneously advising Weizmann on how to handle Halifax. Weizmann, for his part, used Isaiah to keep the British Embassy informed of his dealings with the State Department. Weizmann proposed to Sumner Welles of the State Department that the Allies pay the ruler of Saudi Arabia a substantial sum, in return for his help in forcing the Arabs to concede a Jewish state. When Berlin reported this *démarche* to the Foreign Office, they reacted with fury. 'Weizmann is a child in these matters,' Harold Caccia of the Foreign Office seethed. It was absurd to suppose that Ibn Saud could be bribed into granting a Jewish state. Eden, the Foreign Secretary, energetically concurred. Creating a Jewish state in Palestine would lead to Arab uprisings, which would make those of the 1920s and 1930s seem like '*bagatelles*'. In April 1943 Eden secured Churchill's approval to inform Weizmann through the embassy in Washington that he was not entitled to stir up American Jewish opinion by repeating pro-Zionist remarks which Churchill had made to him privately. If Weizmann received this warning, he chose to ignore it.[23]

In May 1943 Isaiah informed the Foreign Office that Weizmann had told him it was impossible for a 'progressive minority' like the Jews to be ruled by a 'backward majority' in Palestine, and that the sooner the Great Powers forced the Arabs to concede this, the more easily the problems of the Middle East could be resolved. In his report, Isaiah let his own opinions momentarily appear in a glancing reference to the 'narrow policy' of the MacDonald White Paper of 1939, which had clamped down on Jewish immigration. Foreign Office officials annotated this report in exasperation:

> Dr Weizmann always repeats that the Arabs will acquiesce if they are told that they must accept Jewish immigration but that simply is not true. We have been warned that an explosion in Palestine is inevitable. When it occurs it will be due not to the 'narrow policy' of Malcolm MacDonald but to the intransigence of Ben Gurion and his like.[24]

Isaiah never saw these confidential minutes, but he was continually aware of the anti-Zionist bias of the officials who were reading his reports.

By the summer of 1943 the direct threat to Palestine from Rommel's troops had receded and Zionist underground organisations resumed their clandestine operations. The British administration in Palestine became

Riga, 1910

Petrograd, 1917, aged 8

Upper Addison Gardens,
London, 1923,
aged 14

London in the 1920s. *From left to right*: Isaiah, Aunt Ida Samunov,
Uncle Yitzhak Samunov, Marie and Mendel Berlin

Corpus Christi College,
1928-9

Isaiah (*far right*)
and friends at a Commem Ball,
New College Garden, 1931-2

British Information Services identification card

Shirley Morgan, Isaiah and Hershey Bar, Oxford 1946

Anna Akhmatova, taken on the day after Isaiah left Leningrad, 1946

In the 1940s

Marie and Mendel Berlin,
late 1940s

Isaiah and Mendel Berlin,
Venice, 1947

increasingly alarmed at the prospect of colonial insurrection there. Isaiah was sent confidential intelligence assessments of Jewish underground activity in Palestine and was asked for comments. He found these assessments both 'anti-Semitic and nonsensical'.[25] On the one hand, they maintained that the Jews must not be allowed to form a Jewish brigade to fight on the Allied side, because Jews were hopeless fighters; on the other, they must not be armed, lest they turn their guns against the British.

His loyalties were tested to breaking point in the summer of 1943. By then the British Government was becoming increasingly alarmed by the twin impact of Jewish agitation in Palestine and the Jewish lobby in America. The embassy in Cairo reported Arab concerns about Jewish pressure on British policy and, when British military moves to interdict illegal arms shipments to Jewish underground groups in Palestine were shelved, because of fears of an outcry in the States, Eden became worried that British policy was being immobilised by the American Jewish lobby. American oil interests in Saudi Arabia also had reason to be worried about the growing influence of Zionist organisations in Washington, and put substantial pressure on the already strongly pro-Arab State Department. In May 1943 Eden laid a memo before the British Cabinet outlining his concern that the Arab countries might not continue to support the war effort, if the result of victory was a Jewish state in Palestine. In June 1943 the American Ambassador in London expressed the same concerns to the British Government and proposed that Roosevelt and Churchill issue a joint statement condemning Zionist agitation and insisting that the Palestinian problem be deferred until after an Allied victory.

Isaiah heard rumours of the proposed joint declaration in early July from Nahum Goldmann, Weizmann's adjutant at the World Jewish Congress offices in Washington.[26] Berlin was genuinely shocked. Indians were agitating for independence for the sub-continent; Poles were clamouring for a free Poland at the war's end. Why should Zionist agitation alone be placed under a ban?

Isaiah decided to act. He secretly informed George Backer, a Zionist newspaper publisher, of the proposed declaration, and Backer immediately informed Henry Morgenthau, the Secretary of the Treasury. Having tipped off the Jewish lobby, Isaiah then told Halifax, much to the ambassador's consternation, that news of the declaration had leaked out.

Meanwhile, Morgenthau went to the President to demand cancellation of the declaration.[27] Roosevelt played for time and asked a senior adviser, Sam Rosenman, to consult with the British and with Jewish groups. Rosenman came to Isaiah and asked whether he could appease Jewish anger about the proposed declaration, to which Isaiah piously replied that he was 'of no possible use, if only in virtue of my official position'. As Isaiah expected, Jewish groups raised a howl of protest, and by 8 August the State Department had informed the British Government that it had withdrawn the declaration. Halifax, having informed the Foreign Office that the Jewish lobby was to blame, then asked Isaiah to establish how they had found out about the declaration, and how they had been able to mobilise opposition within the administration so effectively.

Isaiah now had to tell the Foreign Office a version of events that would conceal his own part in scuppering their initiative. His summary artfully told the story as French farce, and as an amusing case-study of how rumour ricocheted around 'the whispering gallery' of Washington politics. The deliberately light tone of his report had the desired effect: it helped to conceal his own part in the play.[28] He may have told the story as comedy, but he actually spent sleepless nights worrying that he would be found out. He had managed his conflict of loyalties with agility, humour and a certain amount of cunning, but when he had to choose, he had chosen his Jewish loyalties over his British ones. The episode troubled him. Long afterwards, when he might have wanted to reveal the part he had played, at least to Jewish audiences, he remained silent. Until he confided his role to me in a conversation at the end of his life, he always strenuously denied that the Jewish problem of double allegiance had ever haunted him.[29] But it had, and if he had once entertained thoughts that a Jew might work happily in the Foreign Office, the experience of 1943 cured him of that illusion for good.

For the rest of the war, Isaiah became the soul of discretion on Zionist matters. As proposals for eventual partition of Palestine began to be put about in late 1943, he reported on Weizmann's and Goldmann's reactions.[30] Shortly thereafter, Weizmann had a meeting in London with Churchill and the War Cabinet. Thanks to Berlin's summaries, Churchill could read the version of their meeting which Weizmann chose to circulate around Washington.[31] According to Weizmann, Churchill said that he remained a staunch pro-Zionist, that he would not forget how little the Arabs had contributed to the British cause in this war and that he would presently plunge 'into the pie and extract a real plum'. He then turned to Attlee and said, 'The Labour Party, at any rate, is committed to Zionism, isn't it?' whereat Attlee is reported to have nodded and added that his people would be even more enthusiastically against the White Paper if the Jews did not press them quite so much in Britain and America.

Attlee's remark might have been seen as an ominous warning of what was in store for Zionism when the Labour Party got into power in 1945. But for the moment this storm signal was not seen for what it was. As the war progressed, Isaiah's despatches became ever more assured, personal and even peremptory. On D-Day, for example, he met Rabbi Silver, the chief spokesman for Jewish matters in the Republican Party. Silver wanted the American Government to confront the British and force them to grant a Jewish state. In his reported version of their conversation, Isaiah cleverly used Weizmann's name and prestige to put over the Foreign Office position:

> I reported to him that no decision on Palestine would be published or implemented before the end of the war, and that Weizmann was himself somewhat opposed to partition, but in any case felt that the American government would never take a lead in settling this problem but would probably back the British govt in whatever it undertook to do in Palestine and that, therefore, Zionist pressure in the US seemed to him largely useless, and when it reached the pitch of 1943–4, damaging and harmful, since it provoked and irritated the British officials in London with whom he dealt without deflecting them from their policy.[32]

Playing one Zionist leader off against another, in the service of His Majesty's Government, earned Isaiah high marks from his superiors. On the margins of this report, a Foreign Office official wrote, 'Dr Berlin – Thirty–Love!'

Berlin in fact became convinced that the Foreign Office was exaggerating the strength of the American Jewish lobby. In a 1944 despatch he argued that 'Zionists have made little headway in enlisting widespread support for their views either in the press or in public opinion.' He knew privately that Roosevelt was much less pro-Jewish than the Jewish community assumed, and that there was no pro-Zionist momentum whatsoever within the administration. On Palestine questions, he argued, 'HMG could proceed resolutely to implement whatever course of action seemed to it desirable without excessive fear of repercussions on the part of the American public.'[33] If the White Paper policy – due to expire in 1944 – was changed, then the right public-relations policy for the British Government was to 'split the front', to isolate radical Zionists by despatching eminent British Jews like Lord Rothschild to talk to the leading moderates. With these figures safely in the British camp, the British Government had nothing to fear from either the American administration or the Jewish lobby.

Berlin's argument, though music to Foreign Office ears, alienated Zionists themselves. Blanche Dugdale, an important supporter of Weizmann's, heard Isaiah give a talk on American Jewish opinion at a meeting in London in early 1944. He maintained that Zionist forces in America made a great deal of noise but lacked the influence with the US administration to force the British hand. Dugdale let him know through Lewis Namier that she found his talk 'supercilious, cynical and not spoken like a Zionist'. In his mortally direct manner, Namier concurred. Years in embassy circles, he told Berlin, 'tend to desiccate one's style and petrify one's feelings'. Isaiah's double-life had become unconvincing.[34]

From August 1942 onwards, reports about the concentration camps began to reach Jewish organisations in Washington and New York.[35] The World Jewish Congress was informed that actual extermination was under way using crematoria. The Polish Government in exile in London communicated similar reports to officials in Washington and London. By early 1943 senior officials were aware that the Germans were planning wholesale·extermination. In February 1943 the Allies were approached by the Romanian Government with the proposal to trade 70,000 Romanian Jews in return for war *matériel* and cash. In April 1943 the Allied governments met in Bermuda to consider what to do about Jewish refugees from Nazi Europe in the post-war settlement.

In a meeting with Halifax, Weizmann implored the British Government to lift the 1939 White Paper ban on Jewish immigration. In a memorandum to the Bermuda Conference, he estimated the number of Jews likely to survive the Nazis at between four and five million. By late May 1943, in a melancholy conversation with Isaiah which he reported to the Foreign Office, Weizmann had drastically revised his estimates downwards: if the Jews absorbed behind the Iron Curtain were subtracted from the total, together with those likely to be exterminated by the Germans, he said, only a million Jews would survive and be available for emigration to Palestine. As Berlin reported, Weizmann went on:

> While he regarded this as tragic in itself, it seemed to him to make the Jewish problem more soluble along Zionist lines, since the old argument that Palestine alone, however widely its gates were opened, could not hope to absorb four or five million uprooted Jews, would no longer apply. A million was a manageable number.[36]

This was the first time that an oblique mention of the Holocaust figured in Berlin's discussions with Weizmann. Isaiah's only recorded reaction to these startling and disturbing figures was to ask Weizmann how the Arabs were likely to react to the million new arrivals:

> I put the usual question about the Arabs. He replied with the usual answer – that if the Arabs were clearly given to understand that they could not expect Palestine as an Arab National state or as part of one, they would acquiesce . . . I expressed doubts. They were left unresolved.

From late 1942 and early 1943 phrases about the 'overwhelming tragedy' and 'the horror' befalling European Jews began occurring in Weizmann's correspondence, as well as in that of major Jewish leaders like Stephen Wise. Yet it is clear that the full extent of what was happening – the mechanisation of death, the use of Zyklon B gas and crematoria, the mobilisation of the entire resources of a state for the purposes of racial extermination – escaped them entirely. In later life, Berlin insisted that the frame of possible expectation was limited by the folk memory of pogrom and by pre-war evidence of concentration camps. Most minds simply could not, or would not, travel the full distance to the conclusion that the emerging facts of 1943 seemed to warrant. Genocide itself, and by these awful means, remained inconceivable.[37]

The word 'extermination' figured in Berlin's own memos from May 1943 onwards, but he always claimed afterwards – with a sense of shame – that he was unaware of the Holocaust until the camps were liberated and pictures of Buchenwald, Dachau and Belsen were released in the late winter and spring of 1945. The only direct reference to these places in his official reports occurs as late as 28 April 1945. While he may have averted his gaze from a truth which others saw clearly enough, he was not alone in disbelieving what words like 'extermination' actually implied.

As to what the Allies should do to save the Jews, the official line – to which Isaiah subscribed – was that the only possible strategy was a rapid Allied victory. He always discounted the various schemes for bombing the railroad supply lines and the camps themselves, insisting that bombardment might have killed thousands of innocent inmates by mistake. The Allies could have done more, he believed, in warning Axis allies – Italy, Vichy France, Romania, Hungary, Bulgaria, Croatia – that they could not expect anything but a punitive peace, if they collaborated with the Nazis in genocide.[38] Within the Reich itself, however, nothing could be done. The regime was bent on extermination and nothing but its military conquest and unconditional surrender could have stopped it.

In February 1944 articles by Edgar Answel Mowrer in the *New York Post* and a book, *The Forgotten Ally*, by Pierre Van Passen insisted that the Allies were 'passively permitting the extermination of the European Jews when they could be saving a large number of them'. Isaiah was one of those consulted in a draft reply to these charges. The result was an entirely standard piece of Foreign Office press relations:

> The British and American governments are doing everything in their power, by warnings to Hitler and by negotiations with the neutrals, to put a stop to this massacre and to assist in the escape of its victims. For obvious reasons the full extent of their activity cannot be made public.[39]

Words like 'massacre' suggest that the magnitude of what was happening escaped Berlin's milieu entirely. It was as if his usual sense of reality, the capacity to infer the larger picture from a host of details, deserted him.

One wonders, for example, to what extent he thought of his relatives left in Riga. The last message that the family had received in London had been from Isaiah's maternal grandfather, Solomon Volschonok. He had written the family a postcard, in January 1940, in the dying days of the independent republic, before the Red Army marched in and severed all communication with the outside world. In fluent English, he wrote, 'Let God help you with all the Good!', going on to enquire about Shaja (*sic*) and informing them that in Riga there was nothing new to report.[40] On the bottom left-hand corner of the postcard – like a sinister premonition – was affixed the Swastika stamp of the German postal service, which had transmitted the postcard through Reich territory. It was the last communication they were to have with their Riga family. In July 1941 the German Army drove out the retreating Russians and behind them came the SS. In November and December 1941 the Jews of Riga were rounded up by Latvian fascists and German police and taken to sandy pits on the outskirts of the city, where they were shot and their bodies thrown into a mass grave. The Volschonoks and Schneersons of Riga – including Isaiah's maternal and paternal grandfathers – perished in this manner. He was not to learn their fate until the end of the war.

Their extermination was a fact he was prepared to mention but never to discuss. Nor did he write directly about the Holocaust in his later work. It was Stalin's crimes, not Hitler's, that roused his most intense imaginative response. This curious fact about him is more easily stated than explained. When asked, he would only say that he never had anything to say about the Holocaust that others had not said.[41] He actively despised the Holocaust industry and kept his distance from all rhetorical invocations of his people's horrible fate. Silence seemed more truthful.

But the experience of war-time Washington did bring home to him the drastic limits of his and Weizmann's liberal gradualism. He was shocked when the Jewish underground resumed its campaign of active resistance against British rule. In late 1944 the Stern gang assassinated the head of the British mandatory authority, Lord Moyne. One of Berlin's colleagues at the embassy, David Daiches, a Scottish literary academic who happened also to be Jewish, remembered that Berlin took him aside after Moyne's death and whispered, 'We shall have to think like Swedes', presumably meaning that, with their own people locked in a death-struggle with the British, as British Jews they would have to remain neutral.[42] Everything in Berlin led him to detest Zionist terrorism. The way forward was Weizmann's way, discreet lobbying behind the scenes. Yet, in the end, it was not Weizmann's manoeuvrings, but 'the physical sight of the dead and the dying in the camps, the photographs and films of the skeletons and the emaciated corpses, the children with swollen bellies and the pitiful heaps of broken human possessions', which made the Zionist case suddenly irresistible. 'A vast wave of horror and compassion and outraged human feeling spread over the earth.'[43] Added to this, the 1945 Labour Government's resistance to Zionism, the resulting spiral of Jewish terrorism and President Truman's unexpectedly determined support for a Jewish state: all these factors, entirely unforeseen at the time, produced a result that a lifetime of Weizmannite quiet diplomacy on its own might never have achieved. Isaiah never repented of his support for Weizmann, but he ruefully concluded that both he and Weizmann – 'the men of the centre' – had 'written on water', had 'built on shifting sands'.[44] Washington taught him that even great political figures rarely understood the history they were trying to shape to their own design, and that politics always had a potential for tragedy, because the forces it sought to master were never fully within human grasp.

One could get the impression that he did little else in Washington other than report on Jewish matters. Palestine actually occupied only a small part of his time, and an even smaller portion of his weekly summaries. As Isaiah took positive pleasure in pointing out to Zionist friends, for someone like Halifax, the future of Palestine was a marginal distraction.[45] The bulk of Isaiah's work was in fact taken up reporting every nuance of the President's relations with Congress, every manifestation of anti-British feeling among the unions, the newspaper columnists and the Irish, Indian, Czech and Polish minority groups in the American melting pot. These summaries attracted a growing following within Whitehall. In January 1944, after a particularly informative cable, Churchill sent Eden a note asking who actually wrote the summaries that went out under Halifax's name. Churchill, who loathed Halifax, was certain that such vivid despatches could not have issued from such a pallid pen.

The Foreign Office response that came across Churchill's desk a few days later described the author as a 'Mr Berlin, of Baltic Jewish extraction, by profession a philosopher'. On 27 January 1944 Churchill wrote to Eden: 'The summaries are certainly well written. I have a feeling that they make the most of everything and present a somewhat perfervid picture of American affairs.' Eden commented in his own hand: 'I agree. There is perhaps a too generous Oriental flavour.'[46]

By 'perfervid', Churchill meant ardent, close to feverish. By 'Oriental', Eden meant over-subtle, over-coloured, un-English. The 'Baltic Jewish' philosopher was undoubtedly clever, but he was not one of us. Nevertheless, the effect on Isaiah's prestige was immediate. It was not every day that a Prime Minister and a Foreign Secretary vied with each other to find the right adjective to categorise a junior official's reports.

Isaiah himself met Churchill only once, six months earlier in late August 1943. He was asked to take a confidential cable to the White House, where the Prime Minister was staying after the summit meeting in Quebec. Isaiah was shown up to Churchill's bedroom and was waiting, telegram in hand, when the Prime Minister, fresh from the bath, appeared dressed in his navy blue siren suit. He shook Isaiah's hand, took the telegram and said, with great vigour and emphasis, 'Splendid. Good work. Carry on', and then dismissed him with a benevolent wave. Isaiah went out into the night buoyed up by the old man's capacity to cheer on the forces of life, but also aware that Churchill had no idea who he was.[47]

In early February 1944 Clementine Churchill informed her husband that Irving Berlin was in London, and asked if he could he find time to thank him for his war work. Mrs Churchill envisaged a brief handshake. On the contrary, the Prime Minister said, he must come to lunch. Rather mystified, Mrs Churchill saw to it that Mr Berlin was invited to a luncheon party on 9 February in the Garden Room at 10 Downing Street, a little dining room directly beneath the Cabinet Room. The guests included Sir Alan Brooke, Commander of the Imperial General Staff, and the Duchess of Buccleuch, Molly Lascelles. Churchill's secretary, Jock Colville, recorded what happened. Berlin said little during the meal while Colville's mother, who thought he might be some kind of civil servant, kept trying to engage him on the subject of British social problems. At the head of the table, Churchill kept up a steady stream of talk about the war situation. At the end of lunch, Churchill turned and said, 'Now, Mr Berlin, tell us what in your opinion is the likelihood of my dear friend, the President, being re-elected for a fourth term.' Berlin, who spoke in a heavy Brooklyn accent, said he felt sure that Roosevelt's great name would ensure him victory. He added for good measure, 'But if he won't stand again, I don't think I'll vote at all.'

'You mean,' asked Churchill, 'that you think you'll have a vote?'

'I sincerely hope so.'

Churchill muttered that it was a good sign of Anglo-American co-operation if the Professor had a vote in America. Churchill's subsequent questions about the state and volume of war production in the States elicited only vague and noncommittal replies. Churchill, growing exasperated, asked Berlin when he thought the war would end. 'Mr Prime Minister, I shall tell my children and grandchildren that Winston Churchill asked *me* that question.' By now thoroughly confused, Churchill asked what was the most important thing that Mr Berlin had written. He replied, 'White Christmas'.

Sensing social disaster, Clementine Churchill said gently that they should all be grateful to Mr Berlin because he had been so generous. 'Generous?' her husband growled, looking about him in consternation. By this time Jock Colville was gently kicking the Prime Minister under the table. 'What are you kicking me for?' Churchill growled, and then turned his back on Berlin. Shortly thereafter the lunch broke up. Berlin returned to the hotel where he was staying with the producer Alexander Korda. He reported that it had been a puzzling lunch. He did not exactly seem to hit it off with the Prime Minister.[48]

Jock Colville then broke the case of mistaken identity to the Prime Minister, and a much-amused Churchill told the Cabinet. Soon the story was circulating in Whitehall and from there it leaked into the press, appearing in *Time* magazine in April 1944. Isaiah was in London at the time and, having heard the story from Jock Colville, realised that he had become a minor celebrity by mistake. 'The Irving-Winston-Isaiah affair' was going the rounds.[49] In London, Lord Beaverbrook rang up to ask Isaiah to dinner, and to offer him a column on his newspapers.[50] Formerly stand-offish All Souls grandees now sought his opinion. Whitehall colleagues wrote to him to say that his Washington despatches equalled the achievements of the great memoirists and diarists of the past: Creevey, Saint-Simon, Clarendon and Greville. His own chief, Lord Halifax, was heard delightedly shopping the story of the two Berlins around Washington.[51]

In November 1944 Isaiah was on such good terms with his boss that Halifax invited him to listen to the results of the presidential election contest between Roosevelt and Dewey on the radio in his private apartment at the embassy. He joined a select party that included Lord Keynes, his Russian wife Lydia Lopokova, and the Queen's brother, David Bowes-Lyon. Berlin's only previous meeting with Maynard Keynes – at a King's dinner in 1935 – had not been a success. He had come to read a philosophical paper on pleasure and when Keynes, who was seated beside him at high table, learned what the subject was, he said cuttingly that he might as well be giving a paper about the soup they were being served.[52] When they next met in Washington, the atmosphere was different. Berlin was introduced to Keynes as Professor Berlin, and when he firmly said he was not a professor, Keynes replied that he wasn't either, adding, 'I reject the indignity without the emolument.'

Over dinner at the Halifaxes' Isaiah chattered away to Lady Keynes in Russian, to Lord Keynes' mild but evident displeasure. After dinner, they all repaired to Halifax's study upstairs. As the expert on American politics, Isaiah was deputed to bring with him the *Washington Post* map of the electoral districts and to mark off the results as the radio announcers read them out. The radio droned on, 'Mississippi, 490 districts for Roosevelt, 10 for Dewey.' Lydia Keynes grew bored and began chattering away to Isaiah in heavily accented English: 'Do you like Roosevelt? People like him very much. Rosie. I like Rosie very much.' Maynard interjected, 'Not now, Lydia, not now.' Another half-hour passed. Lydia then asked Isaiah, 'Do you like Lord Halifax?' Halifax was sitting on an adjacent couch. She said, 'You know he is quite popular now, but it was not always so. Do you remember appeasement? It was terrible. Munich, appeasement, it was terrible.' Isaiah managed to muffle a snort of laughter and even Maynard did not interrupt her this time, clearly enjoying the mischief. The pallid host, Lord Halifax, looked down at his feet and patted his dog. 'Now now, Frankie,' he said to the dog. 'Enough of this politics.' He led the dog away and phoned Roosevelt's right-hand man,

Harry Hopkins. Halifax came back and said, 'I've talked to Harry and he says it's in the bag.' After that the party broke up.[53]

Whenever Keynes was in Washington, he and Berlin would meet, sometimes at Robert Brand's or at the embassy itself. Isaiah richly enjoyed the great man's company, though occasionally Keynes' provocative insouciance shocked him. Once, during a hot summer's dinner in 1944, Keynes asked, 'Have you ever noticed that Congress passes idiotic legislation in July and August? It's far too hot. Much too hot for white men. All right for niggers. No good for the likes of me.' Berlin also remained dubious about Keynes' grasp of American politics. He seemed to think that the despatch of some appropriate London *Times* editorial to the office of a recalcitrant southern senator would bring him round to appropriately enlightened views. 'Would this make a difference?' he would ask Isaiah. 'None whatever,' Isaiah replied. But he strongly approved of Keynes, the liberal internationalist. His Keynesian colours show through in a commentary on Friedrich Hayek's *The Road to Serfdom*, a work published in 1944 and immediately taken up by Wall Street Republicans in their battle against Keynes' Bretton Woods scheme, which, to the consternation of ideological free-marketeers, sought to bring stability to international currencies through central bank regulation. 'Wall Street looks on Hayek as the richest goldmine yet discovered and are peddling his views everywhere,' Isaiah sardonically concluded, in their battle against 'such sinister social incendiaries as Lord Keynes and the British Treasury'.[54]

Another episode from 1944 that casts light on Isaiah's politics was a memorable duel with Donald Maclean, then a colleague at the British Embassy and, unbeknownst to Isaiah, a Soviet agent. One day Maclean put his head round the door of Isaiah's office and said, 'I work with Pentagon and State Department people. They're all so pompous. I hear you know some New Dealers. Could you invite some?' Isaiah, who had Oxford friends in common with Maclean, agreed and got Kay Graham to arrange a dinner of young officials, including Ed Prichard.[55] Over dinner, Isaiah remarked in passing that he knew Alice Roosevelt Longworth, a cousin of the President, a *grande dame*, famous in Washington for her anti-New Deal opinions. Maclean, who had been drinking heavily, suddenly pounced: 'She's a horrible woman, with horrible views.' When Isaiah replied that he didn't see why he shouldn't spend time with people who had horrible views, Maclean angrily replied, 'I don't say you shouldn't see her. What I mean is that you should not have the kind of taste that would make you want to see her.' Seeing Mrs Longworth hardly proved that he had reactionary tastes, Isaiah responded. 'I won't say that at the twelfth hour you won't be on our side,' Maclean continued. 'But until then, you hunt with the hare and with the hounds.'

At this point, to Isaiah's astonishment – since he had first met Mrs Longworth at her father's house – Kay Graham weighed in on Maclean's side. The room was dividing rapidly into two camps, and Isaiah felt that he was in a Douglas Fairbanks film, where the hero has to jump onto the table to parry, with a single rapier, the thrusts of a hundred blades. It was a comic way of seeing things, but the argument was quite serious. Everyone was accusing him of siding with the arch-enemies of progressive folk everywhere. 'We're supposed to be fighting for civilisation against barbarism,' Isaiah remembers saying, with a sententiousness unusual for him. 'Civilisation means you're free to choose your friends.' Maclean would have none of this, and insisted that 'life was a war. In war, you had to know which side you were on.' The rest of the room, Kay Graham included, noisily concurred. Isaiah remained adamant. 'I can see that you should be judged by your friends, that I concede.' He was even prepared to envisage extreme situations in which one might have to sacrifice friends who had betrayed some essential trust, or some righteous cause. 'But until then you must be allowed to know them, even if people condemn you for it.'

Maclean would not let the matter rest. 'Life is a battle,' he repeated. 'We should know what side we're on and not have dealings with the other side.'

The evening broke up in acrimony, with Maclean tottering out into the garden to relieve himself. There were reparatory phone-calls from Kay Graham and a letter from Maclean contritely suggesting a lunch to make up. Isaiah duly appeared and Maclean asked him what he thought about Henry Wallace, Roosevelt's left-wing Vice-President. Isaiah said that he thought there might be a screw loose somewhere. Maclean again exploded and defended Wallace as the champion of all that was decent and progressive, at which point Isaiah concluded that friendship with him was impossible. As with Burgess, he had not the slightest inkling that Maclean was a spy. But the encounter remained in his mind as something more than an after-dinner disagreement. All his life he was to be reproached for the freedom of his friendships, for his capacity to be relatively indifferent to someone's views, provided that they had other redeeming virtues: in Alice Roosevelt Longworth's case, cheerful aristocratic hauteur, a sharp mind, a voluminous memory for Washington lore and gossip and, above all, a vitality which seemed, to Isaiah, to redeem her awful political views.[56] Ironically, he took the same view of Maclean's associate, Burgess: that sheer appetite for life redeemed his sordid love-life and peculiar political opinions. The Douglas Fairbanks duel with Donald Maclean was one of the small events in which a liberal temperament received its baptism of fire.

With the Allied invasion of Europe progressing towards inevitable victory and peace at last in sight, Arnold Toynbee offered Berlin a post in the Research Department of the Foreign Office, but he recoiled from the 'death in life atmosphere' of a 'cave of frustrated professors'.[57] He momentarily considered the idea of going to Paris as Ambassador Duff Cooper's press attaché.[58] He had met Cooper's wife, Diana, in an air-raid shelter in London, during a visit home in 1942, and had fallen for her icy beauty and lethal wit. But he could see that Paris was a step down from Washington; indeed, Whitehall was too. He regarded a Foreign Office career as a vegetarian diet after the satisfactions of a carnivore's feast at the centres of power.[59]

He tired of the weekly grind of the political summaries, telling a friend that he felt like an opera singer who had sung one too many mad scenes. But there was more than just fatigue in his growing restiveness at the embassy. Working for a vigorously anti-Zionist, pro-Arab Foreign Office was both exhausting and depressing. He felt worn down by the inner battle with his own exuberant indiscreetness. Finally he realised that he had a habit of 'seeing a pattern in the carpet' – the larger shape of events – and that this was an intellectual's, rather than a bureaucrat's, cast of mind.[60] The weekly opinion summaries were confining: he wanted to write with a bigger sweep. For all these reasons, therefore, he began to daydream of returning to New College and joked that he had in mind a vast work on European history in at least twenty-five volumes, which would keep him occupied in blameless drudgery for the rest of his life.

A chance encounter had set him thinking hard about the future direction of his intellectual life. Some time early in 1944 he lunched at the Harvard Faculty Club with the mathematical logician Harry Sheffer.[61] Sheffer was scathing about the damage done to philosophy by the pseudo-scientific pretensions of logical positivism. Scientific progress, he insisted, was simply not possible in philosophical fields like epistemology or ethics. 'To speak of a man learned in epistemology, or a scholar in ethics,' Isaiah remembered Sheffer saying, 'does not make sense; it is not that kind of study.' Only in strictly deductive fields like logic, or in empirical fields like experimental psychology, was progress of a scientific sort possible. Isaiah actually found Sheffer's condemnation of logical positivism too sweeping, but he came away from the encounter with renewed doubts about returning to philosophy. In the spring of 1944 he found himself on an interminable transatlantic flight to London. In those days the cabins were not pressurised and travellers had to spend the long hours in the dark, breathing through an oxygen tube. Unable to sleep – for fear that the tube would slip out of his mouth – Isaiah remained awake throughout the night in a dark, cold, droning aircraft, with nothing else to do but think. He always hated thinking alone, and this journey was singularly disagreeable. He went over what Sheffer had said and began to see pure philosophy as a field like criticism or poetry, in which it was not possible to add to the store of positive human knowledge. 'I gradually came to the conclusion,' he later wrote, 'that I should prefer a field in which one could hope to know more at the end of one's life than when one had begun.' When he landed the next morning, rumpled and bleary, he had decided to leave philosophy for the history of ideas.

He suggested to New College, where he had been teaching since 1938, that he would move into the history of philosophy, and proposed leaving ethics, logic and epistemology to his friend Herbert Hart. Hart was an old Oxford friend, from a Yorkshire Jewish family, by then married to another old friend, Jenifer Fischer Williams. He was the perfect choice to replace Isaiah at New College and duly did so in 1945. The other great Oxford philosophical figure of the 1930s, John Austin, had turned his formidable powers to managing the logistics for the D-Day landings. He was now due to return to Oxford, as was Stuart Hampshire, who had had an equally distinguished career in military intelligence, deciphering encoded German signals traffic. He was now trying to secure a fellowship at Balliol in order to resume his philosophical career. Isaiah urged Herbert Hart to contact Austin and Hampshire and put together the circle of the 1930s once again. As for Jenifer, who was giving up an important job at the Home Office, he warned Herbert that 'bringing a wife to Oxford is like bringing her to the Gold Coast – conditions are colonial'.[62]

It was now April 1945 and Berlin wanted to leave, but the Headmaster, as he now called Lord Halifax behind his back, was unwilling to let him go back to academic life.[63] On 12 April Franklin Roosevelt died, and Isaiah was given the task of assessing for an anxious British Government the momentous change that had occurred. The resulting despatch was one of the most acute of Isaiah's career. Roosevelt was being eulogised in death, he observed, but in life he had been one of the most bitterly hated figures in America. His achievement, Berlin went on, had been to alter 'perhaps in perpetuity, the concept of the duties and functions of the United States Government in general and of the Presidency in particular'. Turning to the future, he predicted that the main federal reforms of the New Deal would remain in place. Even if the extent of government interference was reduced with the coming of peace, the 'tradition of positive action towards social welfare' – which Roosevelt had initiated – would continue under Truman.[64] The bootleg version released to Nicholas and the Ministry of Information was considerably more candid:

> The truth about the White House is that while Truman is clearly sincere, decent ('I know he is decent, said Mr Ickes on the night of Mr Roosevelt's death, 'but can anyone mention any other attributes?') and liberal in a provincial mid-Western way, the best kind of American legionnaire, unexpectedly business-like, brisk, crisp and capable of getting on with people like Eden and Lyttelton, the whole thing is on such a minute scale, such a Dutch interior, that all these virtues cannot provide for the first really big crisis which general principles do not solve. Truman's predilection is quite simply for respectable, unfrightening hacks. 'Maybe I ought to have been a piano player in a whore house and not President of the United States,' he amiably observed to a friend of mine.[65]

Isaiah had wanted to go to San Francisco to join the British delegation at the conference establishing the United Nations that summer, but Halifax kept him in Washington drafting the weekly political summaries. In late May, however, he was flown out to assist the delegation with the Russian translation of the UN charter. This work brought him into close contact with an old friend, Charles (Chip) Bohlen, now US liaison on the Russian draft of the charter. Isaiah admired Bohlen's finely tuned sensitivity to language. Bohlen had been Roosevelt's personal translator and note-taker since the Moscow conference of 1943 and had sat in on meetings between the Big Three. It was Churchill who actually gave Bohlen most trouble as a translator. He was wont to throw out phrases like 'the depth of sublime unwisdom', which resisted any version in Russian.[66]

Bohlen now enlisted Isaiah's help with translation of the charter. The two spent two weeks together in the Veterans' Building in San Francisco, tossing Russian words back and forth, weighing their hidden connotations, to be certain that the Soviets were not slipping some useful ambiguity into their choice of treaty language. In the section dealing with the right of a member state to march its army through a second state in order to defend a third, Isaiah paused over the Russian word for 'passing through'. He convinced Bohlen that the Russian version implied a right not only to march through, but to stay, if need be. When this was pointed out to the Soviets, they protested that Soviet schoolchildren were already learning the proposed text by heart. It was too late to make any changes. Isaiah and Bohlen dug in their heels and eventually the Soviets conceded the point. On another occasion, the Russian translation implied that all British mandated territories should be abolished forthwith. Isaiah insisted on a change of wording, and Bohlen joked that Isaiah had saved the British Empire with a stroke of a pencil.[67]

Bohlen was sufficiently impressed to suggest to Halifax, as they flew back to Washington, that Isaiah be used again in further summit meetings with Stalin. Halifax agreed and recommended Berlin's appointment as a translator for Anthony Eden at the forthcoming Potsdam conference of the Allied leaders. In early July Isaiah flew to London, to prepare. Privately, he was not much enamoured of Eden and had been heard to refer to him, behind his back, as 'the sleeping beauty'.[68] For his part, Eden was not especially well disposed towards academics and intellectuals, especially witty and facetious ones. Days before his departure, the Foreign Office told Berlin that he was not going to

Potsdam after all. It is possible, though Isaiah never found out for certain, that his remark about the 'sleeping beauty' had caught up with him.[69]

His disappointment about Potsdam was severe but short-lived, for a beguiling alternative had come his way. Eighteen months earlier, on a visit to Washington in January 1944, Archibald Clark Kerr, the British Ambassador in Moscow, had talked to Isaiah about policy towards the Soviets. Casually, he suggested that Isaiah might like to come to Moscow and have a look around. Isaiah leaped at the prospect. Clark Kerr asked him when he would like to come. 'At once, tonight.' Clark Kerr laughed and said that he must have some conditions. 'None,' Isaiah replied. 'Unconditional surrender.'[70]

Clark Kerr returned to Moscow and the plan hung in the air for nearly eighteen months. As Isaiah wrote to a friend, he felt like one of the forlorn provincial women in Chekhov's *Three Sisters* who keep sighing, 'To Moscow, to Moscow.'[71] In May 1945 Clark Kerr reappeared in Washington on his way to the San Francisco conference. He renewed his offer and convinced Isaiah that it was genuine 'by the simple but irresistible device of waving a visa in front of me'.[72] This time, Isaiah did not repeat the mistakes of the Burgess affair. He made sure that the Foreign Office approved of Clark Kerr's plan. By early June it had been decided that he was to go to Moscow to prepare a long despatch about American-Soviet-British relations in the post-war world. The despatch was to be 'a grand affair', he ironically observed, a reference point 'for all time'.[73] He was to be in Moscow until early 1946, then return to Washington to draft his report. It would be his swan-song, his farewell aria as a British official. In late July 1945, by then back in England, Isaiah spent the weekend with Patricia Douglas at a country cottage she was renting after the collapse of her marriage. On 26 July they listened to the returns of the British General Election on the radio and danced a jig on the lawn at the news of the Labour landslide. With a charming ingenuousness, which this time Isaiah found it possible to resist, she proposed marriage.[74] Extricating himself from this new phase of his entanglement with her, he boarded a plane for Berlin and, after a night in company with Noel Annan, Goronwy Rees and other friends then serving with British Intelligence in the ruins of the German capital, flew on to Moscow.[75] He was in a state of high excitement. In a letter to his parents, he exclaimed in Russian, '*Chudno budet!* It will be wonderful!'[76]

10

Moscow, 1945

He was apprehensive about the journey, joking to a friend that he did not know what to bring with him – 'insecticide, shoe leather, sealskin hats or goodness knows what'.[1] In the event, Isaiah flew into Moscow on 8 September 1945 carrying winter clothing, small Swiss cigars with plastic holders and boots for Boris Pasternak, a gift from his sisters in Oxford.

He had longed to return – the idea of such a trip had been in his mind since his early twenties – but now that it was happening he was full of apprehension.[2] The Soviets might insist that he was a Soviet citizen, because he had been born in Latvia, and never let him out. He had a recurring nightmare of being arrested and he told himself – with uncharacteristic grimness – that if this were to happen, he would simply shoot himself.[3]

He didn't have time to dwell on his anxieties, because, with his usual good luck, he arrived in Moscow just in time for an embassy party, at which he made contacts that were to open doors to the Russian artistic community throughout his stay. The embassy – situated in an ornate merchant's palace on the river embankment directly opposite the Kremlin walls – was giving a dinner to celebrate the anniversary of its Russian-language news sheet, *Britansky soiuznik* (The British Ally). The guest of honour was a tired and irritable J.B. Priestley. During a misguided moment at the height of the British-Soviet war-time alliance, Priestley had written that Soviet literature was the conscience of the world.

Stalin's reward had been an official visit, complete with numbing tours of factories and collective farms.[4]

Priestley was exhausted and quickly retired to his hotel bed, leaving Isaiah with Lina Prokofiev, the composer's Catalan ex-wife; the theatre director Alexander Tairov; the critic and children's writer Korney Chukovsky; and the film director Sergei Eisenstein. To their astonishment, they were now talking to a British official who not only spoke fluent Russian, but whose very form of thinking, Tairov enthused, was 'entirely Russian'.

Each of the men at the table, Isaiah soon realised, was gripped by fear. Stalin had recently viewed the second part of Eisenstein's *Ivan the Terrible* and had taken Eisenstein's portrayal of the Tsar as an allegorical denunciation of his own increasingly paranoid and savage rule. Stalin had apparently reprimanded the director in person.[5] Not surprisingly, Eisenstein looked drawn and distracted. To draw him out, Isaiah asked him when he had been happiest. In the early 1920s, Eisenstein wistfully replied, when experimentation was still allowed. There had been a night in a Moscow theatre, he said, when they had let grease-smeared pigs loose in the audience. Those had been the days. The director Tairov, who had been dismissed from the Kamerny Theatre by Stalin in 1939, agreed that the 1920s had been a good time, but the pre-revolutionary days of the Moscow Art Theatre had been even better. Tairov fondly recalled the work of Vsevolod Meyerhold. For Isaiah, Meyerhold – whose experimental work had made Moscow the most important theatrical centre in Europe in the 1920s – was just a name. For these men, Meyerhold was also a fate and a warning. They knew only that he had disappeared: there were rumours that he had been seen in Tashkent during the war. In fact, he had been tortured and shot in 1940.[6] Of this Isaiah of course knew nothing. He asked them why all the artistic experimentation of the 1920s had come to an end. 'Things change,' Tairov said gloomily. Then, after a time, he added, 'Things also do not change. This is even worse', and stared down at the tablecloth in silence, looking old and broken.

From his first nights in Moscow, therefore, Isaiah was exposed to the atmosphere of gloom, shame and terror among 'the scared ones' who had managed to survive the Yezhovshchina, the whole-scale extermination of the Russian intelligentsia in 1937. In addition to the millions of ordinary people sent to labour camps or simply shot, the regime had exterminated the cultural élite, including the poet Osip Mandelstam, the brilliant short story writer Isaac Babel, the theatre director Meyerhold, the critic D.S. Mirsky and numberless others. By the time the killing and deportation were done, there was a vacant stillness in Russian culture, like a forest after an all-consuming fire.[7]

The pace of destruction slowed with the beginning of war. By 1941 some artists were allowed to join in the national struggle against the Germans: Boris Pasternak and Anna Akhmatova had given readings, and the party discovered that the moral authority of these dissident figures was an asset to be exploited. At a time when the language of patriotic appeal had been debased into crude slogans, these poets knew how to conjure up the most genuine source of national affection: love of the Russian language. Common soldiers knew their work by heart or carried their poems around with them on scraps of paper.[8] Now, in 1945, artists were gingerly testing the water – daring, for example, to accept invitations to the British Embassy. But no one at that dinner knew whether the slight relaxation of the war years was a harbinger of better times to come or whether the terror would return. As Isaiah was later to write, those who had survived were like Giotto's frescos of Jonah in the jaws of Leviathan, half-swallowed by the whale.[9]

The most assured of the three Russians was Korney Chukovsky, a critic and literary scholar of the pre-revolutionary era who had survived the purges of the 1930s by turning himself into a blameless and, as it happened, inspired children's writer. His widespread popularity managed, at least for the time being, to protect him and his family. With Isaiah he felt sufficiently secure to venture into nostalgic reminiscences of his penurious times in England before the revolution. At the embassy dinner table he took out of his vest-pocket the penny edition of Thomas Carlyle's *Sartor Resartus*, which he had used to teach himself English in London before the First World War. To Isaiah, he confessed a yearning for the novels of Trollope, especially the parsons and vicars of Barchester. His friend Ivy Litvinov, British-born wife of the disgraced ex-Foreign Minister, shared his love of Trollope but judged it too risky to send to England for more. Isaiah promised to oblige (and on his return to England duly sent Chukovsky a package full of Trollope).[10]

Isaiah now asked whether he might ask a favour in return. Could Chukovsky arrange a meeting with Boris Pasternak? Isaiah had read *My*

Sister Life and Maurice Bowra, who had published some of Pasternak's verses in a war-time anthology, had suggested that a visit might be possible. Chukovsky, who had a *dacha* near Pasternak's in the artist's colony at Peredelkino, a short train journey from Moscow, said that his relations with the poet were difficult, but he promised to help. Lina Prokofiev also volunteered to assist. With his knack for seizing the moment, Isaiah came away from his first nights in Moscow with an entrée to Russian writers that Western diplomats regularly stationed there could only envy. The Western community in Moscow lived – he later wrote – 'in a kind of zoo, with intercommunicating cages, but cut off by a high fence from the outside world'.[11] He had found a way out of the cage.

He ventured into that September Moscow, full of returning soldiers and stolid people from the countryside, a Moscow still gripped by the euphoria of that famous ceremony in August 1945 when the flags and banners of the defeated German legions had been flung onto the cobblestones of Red Square. Isaiah hadn't heard his native tongue being spoken in a city street since the age of eleven. He eavesdropped on conversations; he explored the streets of the Arbat quarter, descended into Stalin's Metro, listened to the women in the queues outside bread shops, absorbing the Russian life from which he had been separated for twenty-five years. He browsed in the catalogues of the Lenin Library and then edged into the reading rooms, where he watched, with some astonishment, as young graduate students thumbed their way through theses, dutifully copying out the quotations that were officially approved for citation in their own work. But it was the experience of being bathed in the language again which moved him most. In a letter home, he exclaimed: 'I had forgotten that such emotions and expressions existed.'[12]

It soon became obvious that he was being followed. The sensation that there were trench-coated figures sliding in and out of the crowd behind him was uncomfortable, but not especially alarming. If he was frightened, he gave little sign of it, except when he assured his parents that he was being 'most careful, well-behaved, discreet, etc.', and emphatically did not go out for walks alone at 3 a.m.[13] He lived in an embassy flat in the Arbat and told his family that he was at the ballet, theatre or opera every night – Chekhov's *Cherry Orchard*, Prokofiev's *Cinderella* and Tchaikovsky's *Onegin* were among the performances he saw. Most uncharacteristically, he even noticed the food he was eating: mushroom soups, *piroshkis*, *borscht*. He reported on the comic conversations he had with the maid in the embassy flat. 'They say Stalin is very ill,' she would venture.

'No, the American Ambassador saw him at Sochi and he was in excellent form,' Isaiah would reply.

'Do you read Trotsky much?'

'No.'

'He was a very good man, wasn't he?'

She was 'a nice old thing' and her bungling attempts to entrap him on behalf of her employers were endearing rather than menacing. He also overheard her whispering to another maid that he was a very strange customer – slept in until eleven: '*Sovsem ne Anglichanin*. Not at all like an Englishman.'[14]

Really, he told his parents, these were 'the fullest weeks of my life'. He was, he told them, 'bursting with impressions' and, when the first snows of autumn began to fall in October, his description of the scene, while ironic, was alive with feeling:

> Need I describe to you the crunching snow, the cupolas of the churches, the crisp air, the peasants, the fur caps, the Russian timbre of speech in the streets, the distant sound of Red Army men singing as they march? It is all like an almost vulgarly sentimental Repin illustration . . .[15]

In Moscow there were close family ties to renew. His father's brother, Leo, had settled in Moscow after the revolution and was now a professor of dietetics at the university. On two occasions Isaiah slipped out of a ballet performance at half-time, eluding his pursuers, in order to visit Leo and his wife and family in their Moscow flat – a cosy, cramped, book-lined refuge, full of Jewish cheer and Riga memories. On the second occasion the entire Berlin clan assembled – his uncles, Samuel and Solomon, and his aunt Evgenia, once married to Isaac Landoberg and now separated from him. The last contact between the English and Russian Berlins had been in 1935, when Mendel Berlin had visited Moscow with a timber delegation. So there was much catching up to do, enquiries about health and business, though not any reckoning together of the loss of the entire family who had remained in Riga. This doleful subject was not mentioned, even though by then Isaiah suspected that no one had survived.[16] Nor did the mild and charming Leo venture into political discussion. Even with his own nephew, in his own house, politics was simply too dangerous a subject. He did let slip one remark that brought the realities of Soviet life home into stark relief. When Isaiah suggested that life as a university professor might not be so bad after all, Leo asked him pointedly, 'Have you been to Florence? Have you been to Venice?' Isaiah nodded, and Leo replied with firm but quiet poignancy, 'We would like to go there too.'

Isaiah's antennae did pick up the impression that anti-Semitism, in abeyance during the war, was now making a return. One of his uncles, then still in Soviet army uniform, hinted as much, though he did not elaborate. But Isaiah had no inkling of what lay in store and Leo, for his part, was an innocent too. When asked whether he was worried that the NKVD would soon pay them a visit, Leo cheerfully replied that he was more likely to visit *them*. Like the intellectuals at the embassy, he must have hoped that the war signalled the end of their hardships. In reality, they were just beginning.

Back at the embassy, Isaiah was given a desk in the Chancery, but he had little to do apart from preparing a weekly digest of the press. Needless to say, the Russian newspapers were less diverting than the American. The propaganda was monochrome and the content was virtually the same in each. Indeed, the papers reminded him of the flat, cheerful and dissembling world of the English public-school magazine.[17] Very occasionally the grimmer realities of Soviet life slipped through: the fact, for example, that three trainloads of demobilised soldiers had been forgotten on a siding north of Odessa and had actually frozen to death.

Apart from such vignettes, the press gave Berlin no idea of what might be going on outside the 'intercommunicating cages' of the foreign community. Meetings with the political élite were few and far between, and when they occurred – even a brief encounter at an official cocktail party – every utterance had to be decoded for hidden meaning. At one such gathering on 7 November he fell into conversation with a senior official, whose name Isaiah did not catch but whom he judged to be of high rank, from the aura of apprehensive respect accorded him by the officials who stood around him and by the relative confidence with which he engaged in conversation.[18] He let Isaiah know that the party was worried by the unwillingness of the peasants to return to the collective farms after the war. The size of the crisis, the official said, was 'reminiscent of the twenties and early thirties', a reference to peasant resistance to collectivisation and Stalin's crushing response. Now, the official hinted, similar resistance was developing again. With undiplomatic directness, Isaiah next asked the official whether it was true that the old type of communist intellectuals, mostly Jewish – particularly Maxim Litvinov, former Foreign Minister, and Ivan Maisky, former ambassador in London – were being edged out of power. The commissar suavely reassured him that the evils of 'racialism' were denounced in the current issue of *Bolshevik*. The conversation, which until this point 'had been a dialogue against a slightly tense silence of the ten or eleven other persons present', now loosened up, and the Russians gathered round Isaiah to take him to task for British policy towards Russia during the war. The Russians believed that when Rudolf Hess had flown to Britain in 1940, he and Churchill had concluded a secret deal, giving the German dictator a free hand if he attacked the Russians. They professed to be puzzled by Britain's support for Russia in 1941 and chose to interpret it as a stab in Germany's back. Isaiah tried to disabuse them of such conspiracy theories, but 'the atmosphere was exactly that of a group of Mid-Western American businessmen who are told by a British official that Australia is not a colony'. There was no budging them: and the encounter left him with a deep sense that Soviet man was not, as optimists believed, pragmatic and susceptible to rational argument. Party doctrine had penetrated every crevice of consciousness.

At a literary salon, held in the house of a Madame Afinogenova, a short time later, Berlin had a taste of the toadying atmosphere that prevailed in intellectual life. He was invited to meet Ilya Selvinsky, an official poet who had been officially reprimanded a short time before for innocently proposing that socialist realism should be supplemented with a socialist romanticism. Selvinsky, naturally enough, was in a state of some agitation about his future, as he and Isaiah discussed contemporary literature in the stilted fashion typical of exchanges in that era. Who were the greatest contemporary British writers, Isaiah was asked? When he failed to cite Arthur Greenwood's *Love on the Dole* and other official classics of workers' literature, and suggested instead that the notorious bourgeois reactionary Virginia Woolf might actually prove the more enduring writer, he sensed a chill come over the room. Then Selvinsky said, with great vehemence and volume, that although he knew Russian writers were accused of conformism in the West, they welcomed the accusation. 'We conform because we find that whenever we deviate from the Party's directives, it always turns out that the Party was right and we were wrong.' An awkward and embarrassed silence descended on the company. Berlin realised that Selvinsky's words were intended for the microphones.[19]

An altogether freer and nobler atmosphere reigned in Peredelkino, the artists' colony where Chukovsky, Pasternak and other writers had their summer *dachas*. Isaiah, carrying the package of boots packed by Lydia and Josephine Pasternak and accompanied by Lina Prokofiev, journeyed out there by train on a sunlit autumn afternoon at the end of September. He found the poet, his wife and son seated around a rough wooden table in the back garden. Pasternak, then fifty-five years old, had a 'dark, melancholy, expressive face'.[20] The Oriental curvature of his lips and eyes gave him, as Marina Tsvetaeva had memorably said, the appearance of an Arab and his horse. When Berlin handed Pasternak the boots, the poet appeared to be embarrassed by his sisters' charity. Pasternak's wife, seeking to break the ice, asked how England was recovering from the effects of war. Before Isaiah could reply, Pasternak broke in and began recounting – in a low tenor monotone that did not allow interruptions – the story of the last time he had seen his sisters. It had been in June 1935, during his visit to Paris as official Soviet delegate to the International Writers' Congress in Defence of Culture, organised by André Malraux, Ilya Ehrenburg and other left-leaning anti-fascist intellectuals.[21] He had been despatched to Paris on Stalin's express command and Ilya Ehrenburg had given him a speech to read. But, instead of reading the prepared text, Pasternak told the writers packed into the vast hall at the Mutualité that they should keep out of politics. Do not organise resistance to fascism, he said. Writers should never organise. 'I implore you, do not organise.' Then he had fallen silent, while the whole hall waited in vain for him to continue. This silence, amplified by the microphone, had – in the memory of Soviet delegates at least – a 'devastating effect'. Pasternak's muteness recalls Isaac Babel's apocryphal remark to Soviet interrogators around this time that he was developing a 'new genre of silence'.[22]

When Pasternak took the train home to Moscow in 1935 after the conference, the feeling that he was being severed from the culture of Western Europe had borne in upon him with unhinging force. He kept the Secretary of the Writers' Union up all night in the sleeper with tearful and compulsive talk. Re-telling the story for Isaiah's benefit, he even suggested that his demented behaviour had gained him a reputation for madness, which served to protect him later. In the dark night that followed, Pasternak saw most of his friends executed or banished to labour camps. He himself was too eminent to be touched, but he was forced to abase himself in ways that were to torment him for the rest of his life. In 1936, when senior party figures Zinoviev and Kamenev were put on trial, accused of Trotskyism, the Soviet Writers' Union joined in, baying for their heads. In an article in *Pravda* entitled 'Wipe Them From the Face of the Earth', the union denounced Kamenev and Zinoviev as terrorists and demanded their execution. Pasternak was one of the sixteen writers who signed this appeal.[23]

Isaiah would have known nothing of this. He came to Peredelkino in an unquestioning spirit of idealisation. For him, Pasternak incarnated Russia's Silver Age, the artistic flowering of the last years of Tsarist rule. He had already noticed that these artists never spoke of the Soviet Union, only of Russia, and it was as an embodiment of his lost but native Russian culture that Isaiah sought him out. It was only on subsequent meetings that he began to grasp the shame that haunted all survivors of the era just passed.

Berlin was probably the first Westerner to hear the story of the ominous telephone conversation of 1934 between Pasternak and Stalin about the poet Osip Mandelstam, then under suspicion for having recited a savage poem attacking 'the Kremlin Mountaineer' at a small private gathering in Moscow. Pasternak at first thought the call was a practical joke and hung up. Stalin then called again, and Pasternak, realising that he was talking directly to the Leader, said, in his most ecstatic mode, that he had always known this would happen and hoped they would meet immediately and talk about ultimate matters of life and death, and the future of Russia. Stalin brushed all this aside and asked roughly whether Pasternak had been present when Mandelstam had read the poem. Pasternak equivocated; Stalin pressed him. Was Mandelstam a great poet, a master? Pasternak replied that this was not the issue – meaning that poets should be treated decently whatever the quality of their work. At which point Stalin famously interjected, 'If I were Mandelstam's friend I should have known better how to defend him', and put down the receiver. Mandelstam was then sent into the exile that ended with his death in the labour camp of Magadan in December 1938.[24]

In the autumn of 1945, however, Pasternak believed that all these episodes of horror and self-abasement were behind him. He was in an exalted, even euphoric mood. The war, for all its privations, had enabled Pasternak to identify himself and his work with the patriotic struggle. He gave more public readings of his poetry than at any previous time and discovered that when he stumbled for a line, voices from the hall would volunteer the missing words. For the first time in the Soviet period, he felt that he was not just a marooned remnant of a lost pre-revolutionary culture, but an active participant in his nation's fight for survival. This desire to join the struggle led him to write some hackneyed patriotic verse, On Early Trains, yet it was characteristic of his essential artistic honesty that its publication embarrassed him, and he was relieved when Isaiah told him that he had not read it.

In the shaded garden Pasternak 'spoke in magnificent slow-moving periods, with occasional intense rushes of words; his talk often overflowed the banks of grammatical structure'. When he was in full flight, he was like the dancer Nijinsky: he seemed to remain in the air longer than ordinary human beings.[25] Isaiah both admired Pasternak's unstoppable eloquence and kept a sceptical distance of his own. He remained dubious about Pasternak's view that the terror and the war had been a necessary purgatory for the Russian soul. When Pasternak was in prophetic mode, Isaiah found him obscure and sometimes incoherent. But there was no doubting his eloquence, his genius or his sense that, with the end of the war, his artistic life had approached a turning point. That afternoon in Peredelkino, Berlin became the first foreigner to learn that Pasternak had a new project – a novel about his own generation and their fate in the revolution and war. A few early chapters had been completed, and Isaiah was entrusted to take them back to Pasternak's sisters in Oxford. The work was then called 'Boys and Girls, The Story of a Russian Faust: from the unpublished papers of the Zhivago family'. Isaiah put the chapters under his arm and, on his return to England, delivered them unread.[26]

As they sat together in the garden in the slowly ebbing light, Pasternak began questioning Isaiah about Western writers and thinkers: Joyce,

Hemingway, the English philosopher of art Herbert Read. During the war Pasternak had been moved to discover that he had not been altogether forgotten in the West: some critical studies of his poetry had appeared, and Maurice Bowra had included one of his poems in his *Book of Russian Verse*, published in 1943; Pasternak's *Liuver's Childhood* had also been published in translation, and Isaiah gave him pleasure by telling him that he had read it. For Pasternak, every scrap of attention from the West was precious: it proved that he had not been buried alive. Indeed, his idealisation of the West was embarrassing. He seemed convinced that there had been 'a magnificent flowering of art and literature' that was beyond the reach of Russians. Berlin 'tried to indicate that our cultural development was less irresistibly triumphant than they generously supposed'. Idealisation, he suspected, was Pasternak's resistance to the exaggerated denigration of the West by the party. He did not challenge Pasternak; he simply listened as the poet, denied such an interlocutor for a decade, now resumed his dialogue with the culture from which he had been severed.

The clock had stopped in Russia, he told Isaiah, in 1928 or so, when relations with the outside world had been broken. Pasternak had little knowledge of any contemporary western writers. As for the Russian writers in emigration – Bunin, Nabokov, Khodasevich, Berberova – they could not even be mentioned. Russian literature, which had been one in 1914, had been cut in two.

But walls also divided the artists of Peredelkino from their own public. One of Pasternak's neighbours, Lydia Seifullina, joined them in the garden and, when Pasternak told Berlin that *The Soviet Encyclopedia* made no mention of his work after 1928, she chimed in, 'My fate is exactly the same. The last lines of the *Encyclopedia* article about me say, "Seifullina is at present in a state of psychological and artistic crisis." For twenty years,' she said sardonically, 'I have remained in the same state of crisis.' Then she added, 'We are like people in Pompei, you and I, Boris Leonidovich, buried by ashes in mid-sentence.'[27]

Seifullina asked about the fate of the poet Vladislav Khodasevich, not knowing that he had died in Paris in 1939. At this point Pasternak seems to have felt that Seifullina had been too candid. He grew visibly embarrassed and Isaiah decided to leave, promising to visit Pasternak again in Moscow. He walked over to Chukovsky's *dacha* – Chukovsky and Pasternak were not on speaking terms – where he met the writers Samuil Marshak and Lev Kassil. But he did not pay much attention to what they were saying – he had been overwhelmed by his encounter with Pasternak.

With the darkness coming on, he asked to be accompanied to the station. While waiting for the train, it began to rain and he took shelter with two young students beneath a railway shelter. Emboldened by the darkness, the two students began talking to the stranger from England. The girl – a history student – confessed that she couldn't understand why, if the Tsarist empire had been the prison-house that her textbooks said it was, the radicals and revolutionaries had been left in relative freedom to plot its downfall. Isaiah did not reply, but he could feel that she was rattling the bars. It was also obvious that they were much more attached to pre-revolutionary than post-revolutionary writers. When he asked them whether they liked contemporary Soviet writing, the girl replied pointedly, 'Do *you* like them?' Like the great poet he had just left, the students believed that across the walls that divided them from Europe lay a golden cultural realm from which they were for ever excluded. Just before the train arrived, he asked them why people still felt unable to speak their minds on social issues. 'If anyone tries,' the young man replied, in the darkness of the railway shelter, 'he is swept away as with a broom.'[28] When the train came, the three separated and journeyed to Moscow in silence, as if the conversation had never occurred.

Once back in Moscow, Isaiah visited Pasternak several times at the poet's apartment. They were always alone, with Pasternak seated behind a polished desk 'on which not a book or a scrap of paper was to be seen'. Pasternak spoke about his father, the artist Leonid Pasternak, whom Isaiah had met shortly before his death in Oxford. Leonid Pasternak had painted Tolstoy and had taken Boris to Tolstoy's deathbed at Astapovo in 1910.[29] Pasternak saw himself as the last authentic voice of that nineteenth-century Russian tradition. Berlin was the rarest of visitors from the lost world of Europe: a native Russian speaker who felt, just as he did, that the culture of the nineteenth century was his spiritual home. Both home and refuge: for, as Isaiah noticed, Pasternak seemed more or less untouched by modernism. He had read and admired *Ulysses*, but he had been insulated from Eliot, Stravinsky, Picasso, all the avatars of the twentieth-century rebellion against the Tolstoyan virtues in art. To the degree that modernism had aligned itself with revolution, and revolution had turned into tyranny, Pasternak had set himself – as did Berlin – against both.

As they talked together in Pasternak's Moscow flat, the poet revealed some of his torment at having collaborated with the regime, and his anguish at being Jewish. The two were deeply connected. He longed to be considered an authentic Russian patriot and to have his work accepted as the true voice of the Russian people: yet, as a Jew, he was never allowed to feel authentically Russian. Lacking this sense of authenticity, he had accommodated himself and deformed his talent in order to survive. This twin shame was a source of genuine self-torture. Isaiah had noticed how insistent Pasternak had been to point out that Peredelkino had once been part of the estate of the Russian patriot and Slavophile, Yuri Samarin. Pasternak wanted to identify, not with the liberal (and sometimes Jewish) intelligentsia, but with the more authentically Russian Slavophiles. 'This passionate, almost obsessive desire to be thought a Russian writer' led him to be sharply negative about his Jewish origins. He gave the impression, Isaiah tartly observed, of wishing that he had been born a flaxen-haired, blue-eyed peasant's son. Pasternak insisted that Jews should assimilate and said that he considered himself a believing, if idiosyncratic, Christian. The whole subject, Isaiah noticed, caused him 'visible distress'.[30] Ten years later, when Isaiah returned to Peredelkino, Pasternak handed him a manuscript and said he would publish in the West whatever the consequences. Berlin went away, read the chapters and immediately knew that Pasternak's crisis of identity had been resolved. He had put all his equivocations behind him in a single act of defiance and genius: the writing of *Zhivago*.

11

Leningrad, 1945

He heard that Leningrad's bookstores might have a richer store of pre-revolutionary material than that on sale to foreigners in Moscow. So it was books, not nostalgia, that lured Berlin to the city of his childhood. On 12 November he set off on the Red Arrow overnight sleeper in company with Brenda Tripp, an organic chemist, who represented the British Council. As she confided in her diary, he was shy, avoided contact with her and covered up his nervousness with a great deal of talk. After supper in the dining car they returned to their sleeper, he on the top bunk reading in his pyjamas, she on the bottom. When he turned out the light, she found it amusing that he dropped all the newspapers onto the floor, like a child tossing its toys out of a pram.[1]

After checking into the Astoria Hotel, scarcely heated but still in its pre-revolutionary glory, they both sought out his old apartment on Angliisky Prospekt. He lingered outside in the snow, taking in the dank atmosphere of the inner courtyard, as sordid and abandoned as when he had last seen it in Lenin's time. He ran his hands over the familiar broken railings of the little shop in the basement, the one with the misspelled sign 'Shamovar', where the old tinker had repaired samovars and other domestic goods. He felt himself suspended half in the too-real past, half in the unreal present.

In a melancholy daze, he wandered along the Neva embankment and then down Nevsky Prospekt. The tramcars were full to overflowing and crawled along 'like gigantic disabled wasps, covered with human barnacles'.[2] People in the streets looked shabbier and more emaciated than the Muscovites. The thousand-day blockade still marked every face. His eyes sought out survivors of the city he had once known: 'the worn and torn members of the old intelligentsia, their threadbare clothes flapping in the piercing wind and snow'. If the survivors were in tatters, the city itself was a haunting combination of devastation and grandeur. In the year that had passed since the siege had been lifted, the worst effects of the bombardment had been repaired. But the royal palaces and resorts on the outskirts of the city – Tsarskoye Selo, Peterhof, Oranienbaum – remained in ruins, and many of the city's façades were still pitted with shell bursts and shrapnel. Behind these façades – as Joseph Brodsky was to put it – 'among old pianos, worn-out rugs, dusty paintings in heavy bronze frames, leftovers of furniture (chairs least of all) consumed by the iron stoves during the siege – a faint life was beginning to glimmer'.[3]

At the top of the Nevsky, a day after his arrival, Berlin and Brenda Tripp came upon the Writers' Bookshop. Behind the counter of the outer room were shelves lined with pre-revolutionary books at prices considerably cheaper than in Moscow. There was also an inner room behind a curtain, which writers and critics used as a kind of club, going in there to get out of the cold, to browse and gossip. The manager of the shop was a 'small, thin, gay, baldish, red-haired Jew' named Gennady Moiseyevich Rachlin, who invited them into the inner sanctum.[4] Rachlin proudly informed Berlin that his bookshop was on the very site of Smirdin's famous establishment, once frequented by Belinsky and the Russian writers of the 1830s and 1840s. Figures in tattered coats were leafing through the old volumes and gossiping quietly among themselves. Russian literary life, Isaiah could see, was still indomitably alive. Rachlin was a kind of 'Leningrad Figaro': dictator of the city's book prices, chief purveyor of literature to the city's writers, indefatigable go-between, gossip, scold and club manager. He also arranged theatre tickets, lectures and contact with foreigners. He boasted of his roster of important clients: Molotov, the Foreign Minister; Beria, the head of the secret police; not to mention the Patriarch Alexis and the Leningrad rabbi. Rachlin had plans to open a shop in Moscow and seemed to believe that these various authorities would support him.

Isaiah struck up a conversation with one of the figures browsing in the back room. He turned out to be the critic and historian Vladimir Orlov. The siege, he told Isaiah, had been unimaginable: virtually all of the children born during those three years had died; Rachlin described how bodies lay in the streets, since it was impossible to bury them in the frozen ground. Into this very shop, he said, figures half-dead with cold and hunger had come clutching chapters ripped from old books, hoping to exchange them for food. Rachlin and Orlov had both been kept alive by special rations issued to intellectuals. Rachlin joked that for rationing purposes he had been classed as a 'second-rate writer': he could still taste the carpenter's glue that he had diluted with water and drunk as soup. More than a year after the lifting of the siege, some Leningraders were still giddy from undernourishment. Had it not been for Comrade Zhdanov's convoys across frozen Lake Ladoga in 1943, they would have perished. Yes, Rachlin insisted, it had been Comrade Zhdanov who had saved the city.[5]

Berlin asked about the fate of the city's writers. He mentioned two names: Mikhail Zoshchenko, whose mordant and melancholy satire *Scenes from the Bathhouse* had made him one of the most popular Soviet writers of the 1920s; and Anna Akhmatova, a poet of the pre-revolutionary era, who had not been allowed to publish anything since 1925. The regime had silenced them both but still considered them national treasures. When the Germans surrounded Leningrad in the autumn of 1941, Zhdanov had ordered them to be flown over the German lines to Moscow and from there to Tashkent, where they spent the war. Zoshchenko, it so happened, was now in the bookshop, slumped in a chair – yellow of complexion, withdrawn, incoherent, 'pale, weak and emaciated'. Isaiah shook his hand but did not have the heart to engage him in conversation.[6]

Isaiah had read Zoshchenko's *Scenes from the Bathhouse*, but as for Akhmatova's poetry, he had read nothing at all. She was just a fabled name from the vanished Czarist past, known to him because Maurice Bowra had translated some of her early poems and had included them in his war-time collection of Russian verse. Bowra did not even know whether she was still alive.[7] So Isaiah asked, in all innocence, whether she was, and the critic Orlov replied, to his astonishment, 'Why, yes of course, she lives not far from here on the Fontanka in Fontanny Dom.

Would you like to meet her?' It was, Isaiah remembered, as if he had been
invited to meet Christina Rossetti or some semi-mythological figure from
the history of literature.[8] In his excitement, he could only stammer that
he would indeed like to meet her. There and then Orlov made a phone-
call and returned to say that the poet would receive them that very
afternoon at three o'clock. Isaiah returned Brenda Tripp to the Astoria
and walked back to the bookshop.

In company with Orlov, he set off across the Anichkov Bridge, with its
statues of rearing bronze horses, along the Fontanka Canal on a snowy,
grey afternoon in failing light. Fontanny Dom was the eighteenth-
century palace of the Sheremetiev family. Its baroque yellow and white
plasterwork was pitted with shell fragments and in places worn away by
neglect. They passed beneath the Sheremetiev crest over the baroque
entrance, through rococo iron gates and into the interior courtyard.
Berlin and Orlov went up a dark, steep staircase to a third-floor
apartment – No. 44 – past five or six rooms ranged along a corridor. Most
of the apartment was occupied by Akhmatova's ex-husband, Nikolai
Punin, his wife and child. Akhmatova herself had a room looking over
the courtyard at the end of the hall. It was bare and denuded: no carpets
on the floor or curtains at the windows, just a small table, three chairs, a
wooden chest, a sofa, and near the bed a drawing of Akhmatova – head
bent, reclining on a couch – rapidly sketched by her friend Amedeo
Modigliani during her visit to Paris in 1911. It was the only icon of a
Europe she had last seen thirty-four years before. Now stately, grey-
haired, with a white shawl around her shoulders, she rose to greet her first
visitor from that lost continent. Isaiah bowed – it seemed appropriate –
for she looked like a tragic queen.

She was twenty years older than he, once a famous beauty, now
shabbily dressed, heavy, with shadows beneath her dark eyes, but of
proud carriage and coolly dignified expression. As they sat down on
rickety chairs at opposite ends of the room and began talking, Isaiah
knew her only as the brilliant and beautiful member of the pre-
revolutionary poetic circle known as the Acmeists; as the brightest star of
St Petersburg's war-time avant-garde and its meeting place, the Stray Dog
Café.[9] But of what had befallen her after the revolution, he knew
nothing.

There was nothing falsely melodramatic about her tragic air. Her first husband, Nikolai Gumilyov, had been executed in 1921 on trumped-up charges of plotting against Lenin. The years of terror had begun for her then, and not in 1937. Although she wrote continuously, she was not allowed to publish a line of her poetry between 1925 and 1940. During that time she had survived by working in the library of an agricultural institute, by translating and writing critical studies of Pushkin and Western writers like Benjamin Constant.[10] As all contact with the outside world was severed, Akhmatova and her fellow-poet Osip Mandelstam kept alive a fierce conviction that the tyranny that had divided them from Paris, London and Berlin would not endure for ever. As Mandelstam wrote in 1933 in his poem 'Ariosto':

> It's cold in Europe, Italy is dark,
> And power is barbarous like the hands of Peter the Great.
> Oh to throw wide open, as soon as possible
> A vast window on the Adriatic.
>
> ... Dear Ariosto, maybe a century shall pass –
> And we shall pour your azure and our black together
> Into one fraternal, vast, blue-black sea.
> We were there too. We too drank mead.[11]

Akhmatova had been there on the night in 1934 when Mandelstam was taken away for his first interrogation; and from then until his death in Magadan she stood by his wife, Nadezhda.[12] But in March 1938 the weight of the terror fell upon her directly. Her son Lev Gumilyov was arrested. For seventeen months she had no idea whether he was alive or dead. As terror sealed the lips of those around her, she made herself the poet of despair and abandonment:

> For seventeen months I've been crying out,
> Calling you home.
> I've flung myself at the hangman's feet,
> You are my son and my horror.
> Everything is confused forever,
> And it's not clear to me
> Who is a beast now, who is a man,

How long before the execution.[13]

For seventeen months she stood in the queues of women outside Kresty Prison in Leningrad, vainly seeking news. It was in these queues that she received what she always regarded as an imperative summons to an act of poetic witness:

> Then a woman with bluish lips, standing behind me, who, of course, had never heard me called by name, woke up from the stupor to which everyone had succumbed and whispered in my ear (everyone spoke in whispers there):
> 'Can you describe this?'
> And I answered: 'Yes, I can.'
> Then something that looked like a smile passed over what once had been her face.[14]

Akhmatova's poetic cycle – *Requiem* – kept her promise to that anonymous woman: it preserved in poetic memory the torments of a generation. In those days it was too dangerous to keep these poems in written form. Akhmatova's friend, the novelist Lydia Chukovskaya, remembered the bitter ceremony that used to conclude Akhmatova's whispered reading of these poems, how, when finished, she would hold the pages over the ashtray and silently burn them to ash.[15]

During her war-time evacuation to Tashkent between 1941 and 1944, Akhmatova lived in a airless top-floor room in the Hostel for Moscow Writers. Lydia Chukovskaya and Nadezhda Mandelstam lived there too, and for a time their conditions were eased. Akhmatova was allowed to publish a severely censored volume of *Selected Poems* and gave readings in hospitals for wounded soldiers. In May 1944 she was at last allowed to leave Tashkent. On her way home, she stopped in Moscow and gave a reading at the Polytechnic Museum, which ended with the audience rising and applauding her as a national figure, the incarnation of the victorious Russian language. She herself was terrified by this mark of respect and feared the attention it brought. She was right to do so, for, as Pasternak reported to her, Stalin himself supposedly asked Zhdanov, 'Who organised this standing ovation?'[16]

Akhmatova's return to Leningrad, in June 1944, proved to be desolate:

the city was a 'horrible spectre'; so many of her friends were dead; her rooms in the Fontanny Dom had been looted and smashed. She had hopes of being reunited with Victor Garshin, a Leningrad coroner with whom she had become close after leaving Punin. He met her at the station and told her that he had decided to marry someone else.[17] So, as she was meeting Isaiah, she was just coming to terms, at the age of fifty-six, with the prospect of living the rest of her life alone.

In the late summer of 1945 her son Lev, released earlier from Siberia to serve in the Soviet Army in Germany, at last returned home. She allowed herself to hope that her life might finally be about to improve. Certainly, without the fact of Lev's recent release – and thus the liberation of the hostage whose fate might have inclined her to caution – it is doubtful that she would have taken the risk of seeing a temporary First Secretary from the British Embassy in Moscow.

Vladimir Orlov and an 'academic lady' friend of Akhmatova's were with them as they talked and the conversation at first was formal and constrained. Berlin said he was glad to see her in good health, since 'nothing had been heard of her for many years'. She corrected him regally: an article about her had appeared in The Dublin Review and a thesis was being written about her work, so she had been told, in Bologna.[18] She might have been wondering at this point how much of her work Isaiah had actually read, and he was certainly apprehensive that she would realise he had read nothing.

Then she asked him how London had survived the war. He replied, as best he could, unaware that she had written 'To the Londoners' in 1940. In that poem she had expressed her horror at the thought of London being destroyed, but also her unshakeable belief in the unity of European culture, of which the nervous young British official sitting before her now was the unwitting symbol:

> Time, with an impassive hand, is writing
> The twenty-fourth drama of Shakespeare.
> We, the celebrants at this terrible feast,
> Would rather read Hamlet, Caesar or Lear
> There by the leaden river;
> We would rather, today, with torches and singing,
> Be bearing the dove Juliet to her grave,

Would rather peer in at Macbeth's windows,
Trembling with the hired assassin –
Only not this, not this, not this,
This we don't have the strength to read![19]

As they talked, Isaiah began hearing his name being shouted nearby. He thought it was an illusion, until the word 'Isaiah' echoing up from the courtyard below became too loud to ignore. He went to the window, looked down and to his horror saw Randolph Churchill, standing in the middle of the yard, bawling up at the window like a tipsy undergraduate in the quad at Christ Church. Berlin muttered an apology and fled, followed by Orlov. In the courtyard, Isaiah introduced the Soviet critic to the son of Mr Winston Churchill. No sooner had he shaken hands than Orlov fled. Now any chance of the meeting with Akhmatova passing unnoticed had been thrown away. Indeed, absurd rumours immediately began to circulate that Churchill was in Leningrad to reconnoitre a British rescue operation that would whisk Akhmatova to England. In fact, Churchill simply wanted Isaiah – whom he had known as an undergraduate – to return to the Astoria and explain to the hotel staff that the caviare he had just purchased should be placed on ice. Isaiah gritted his teeth, returned to the Astoria, safely united Churchill's caviare with the requisite ice and then telephoned Akhmatova to apologise and arrange another meeting. 'I shall wait for you at nine this evening,' came her reply.[20] There was a sovereign innocence in her decision: only a queen could have been so oblivious to the risk she was taking.

We know that she keenly awaited his return. Afterwards she dedicated some lines of a poem to those feelings of keen anticipation:

> But how
> gladly I heard his step
> on the stair, his touch on the bell
> as shy as a boy's fingertip
> touching his first girl.[21]

But when she opened the door to him, she was not alone. Another learned lady – an expert in Assyrian antiquities – was there and asked Berlin questions about English universities, while Akhmatova sat silent, keeping to herself. It was midnight before they were at last alone. The room was poorly lit; she sat in one corner, he in the other, smoking Swiss miniature cigars with their plastic handles. Her face was wreathed in shadow, his in smoke. She immediately began asking him about her Russian friends in emigration. He was able to tell her that he had met the composer Arthur Lourie in New York during the war. She had had a brief affair with Lourie, in the far-gone era when she had frequented the Stray Dog Café and he had composed futurist music for performance there. She asked after Boris Anrep, and Isaiah told her that he was at work as an artist in London. It must have seemed uncanny that this complete stranger should have known these old friends and proved able to restore the connection broken by revolution. It is easy to imagine her delight when Isaiah told her that he also knew Salomeya Andronikova Halpern, a Petersburg beauty of the Stray Dog era with whom Mandelstam had been briefly in love, and whom the whole Acmeist circle had admired both for her beauty and for her capacity to listen and inspire.[22] Isaiah told her that she had married a Russian lawyer, Alexander Halpern, and that they were living in New York. As Akhmatova later recorded, this young stranger had miraculously 'brought me Salome back from the dim pharaonic vault of the Stray Dog cabaret'.[23]

In her eyes, Isaiah was serving as messenger between the two Russian cultures – one in external exile, the other in internal exile – which had been split apart by the revolution. In the poems she wrote after his departure, she said that Europe was putting out its leaves: that a green shoot from the culture that had once been hers had at last coiled its way into the Fontanny Dom.[24]

But she was categorical about the question of emigration. Salome Andronikova, Boris Anrep and others might choose the road of exile, but she would never leave Russia. Her place was with her people and with her native language. And so the night acquired another significance for her: it was a moment in which to re-affirm her sense of destiny as the all-enduring Muse of her native tongue. Isaiah was quite sure he had never met anyone with such a genius for self-dramatisation – but, at the same time, he recognised that her claim to a tragic destiny was as genuine as that of anyone he had ever met.

He had always sought validation by genius: it mattered intensely to him that Virginia Woolf, Freud, Wittgenstein and Keynes had all seen his worth. But this encounter mattered more than any other. Here was the greatest living poet of his native language talking to him as if he had always belonged to her circle, as if he knew everyone she knew, had read everything that she had read, understood what she said and what she meant. In reality, of course, this was an illusion: he knew far less about her than she supposed. None the less, a moment of the purest communication, such as occurs only once or twice in any lifetime, was in the process of taking place.

In a rising tide of enthusiasm and nostalgia, she told him of her childhood on the Black Sea coast – 'a pagan, unbaptised land' – and of her lifelong affinity with 'an ancient, half-Greek, half-barbarian, deeply un-Russian culture' on Russia's southern shore. She recalled the Odessa she had known as a young woman, the brawling sea-port of Isaac Babel's stories, the meeting place of Jew and Bessarabian, Turk and Ukrainian. He told her stories of his childhood in Riga, of his early years in Petrograd, and how – when she was already a poet so famous that her admirers could recite the whole of her latest collection verbatim – he was still a child, alone in his father's study, reading Mayne Reid's cowboy stories.[25]

She told him of her marriage to Gumilyov and how, despite their separation and divorce, she had always remembered the laconic and unquestioning way he had accepted her talent. When she described the circumstances of his execution in 1921, tears came to her eyes. Then she began to recite from Byron's *Don Juan*. Her pronunciation was unintelligible, but she delivered the lines with such intense emotion that Isaiah had to rise and look out of the window to conceal his feelings.

Soon she was reciting her own poems, from *Anno Domini*, *The White Flock*, *From Six Books* and from *Cleopatra*, written in 1940, at one of the lowest ebbs when she wondered whether there was anything left but to die like the Egyptian queen by her own hand. She told him that poems like these had been the cause of the death of a better poet than she – but whether she meant Mandelstam or Gumilyov, Berlin could not tell, for she broke down again. Recovering, she began to recite the still unfinished *Poem without a Hero*, begun in Leningrad in 1940. It was, Isaiah later wrote, 'a kind of final memorial to her life as a poet, to the past of the city', in the 'form of a Twelfth-night carnival procession of masked figures'. Listening to her, he could not have known that in this work –

which she was to refine until 1962 – he would eventually figure as the mysterious 'Guest from the Future', 'the guest from beyond the looking glass'.

She then read from a manuscript copy of *Requiem*, much of it composed in the room where they sat together. This cycle of poems was her act of commemoration on behalf of all the tortured and disappeared of her generation:

> I'd like to name them all by name,
> But the list has been confiscated and is nowhere to be found.
>
> I have woven a wide mantle for them
> From their meagre, overheard words.
>
> I will remember them always and everywhere,
> I will never forget them no matter what comes.[26]

She broke off to describe the arrest of her son and husband, speaking – as Isaiah remembered – in a matter-of-fact voice of her vigil at the prison gates, of their humiliation at the hands of their jailers, of the desertion and betrayal of so many of their former friends. She kept interrupting herself. 'It is no good,' he remembered her saying, 'you come from a society of human beings, whereas here we are divided into human beings and . . .'[27] There had been years before the war when the circle of betrayal and denunciation bore down so harshly upon her that she had not been able to trust another living soul, except Nadezhda Mandelstam and Lydia Chukovskaya. Of Osip Mandelstam and his fate, she could not speak. She changed the subject and forced herself to recall better times in Tashkent during the war.

It was three in the morning when her son, Lev Gumilyov, arrived. He was two years younger than Isaiah – thirty-four to Isaiah's thirty-six – and phenomenally well read and educated, despite having been arrested at the age of twenty-four. He had read Proust and Joyce in the original, despite never having left the confines of the Soviet Union, and obviously thought of himself, like his mother, as preserving European standards of culture against the Soviet tide.[28] He had been arrested for the crime of having Nikolai Gumilyov and Anna Akhmatova as his parents. Now he seemed convinced that his misfortunes were over and that he would resume a scholar's life in his native city. He went into the kitchen alcove and found some boiled potatoes in a dish. His mother was embarrassed by the meagreness of their hospitality, but Isaiah remembered with pleasure how they divided the clutch of potatoes in the dish and ate them together in the near-dark room, by the glowing stove.

When her son had left, Isaiah asked Akhmatova to let him write down *Poem without a Hero* and *Requiem*. It is a sign of how hopeful she then was that she refused, promising that she would send him a volume of her collected verse, due to appear the following year. They then talked about their favourite authors and for the first time began to disagree. He shared her reverence for Pushkin, her distaste for Chekhov's 'mud-coloured world', but he could not share her love of Dostoyevsky, and she had no time for his affection for Turgenev.[29] These were not mere differences of taste: they marked the boundaries between their emotional worlds – Isaiah drawn to the lightness, delicacy and irony of Turgenev, but repelled by the violence, darkness and emotional intensity of Dostoyevsky; Akhmatova identifying with Dostoyevsky's intense depiction of inner states, and unable to bear the delicate subtleties of Turgenev. These differences in moral taste were of course also differences of circumstance. Turgenev's delicacy struck an easy chord in Isaiah's Oxford, but it is hard to imagine how it could find an audience in Stalin's Leningrad. Isaiah was drawn most to Russian writers – Herzen and Turgenev – who had fashioned their art in exile, while Akhmatova was drawn to the artists whose work was forged on Russian soil. He always contrasted 'the open, passionate, spontaneous, broad Russian nature' with the 'dry, calculating, inhibited, sophisticated' West, but the reality was that it was the mixture of the two – available only to exiles – which moved him most.[30] Nor was this their only disagreement. Isaiah idealised Tolstoy for the breadth of his historical vision, while Akhmatova was repelled by what she regarded as his sexual hypocrisy. In allowing Anna Karenina to be hounded to her death, she said, Tolstoy had capitulated to the philistine social conventions he said he condemned.

Isaiah was pleased to discover her scornful, sarcastic and slightly malicious side; then the queenly demeanour was replaced by something more humorous and human. He began to see that she was a consummate actress who had mastered a queenly role, but was shrewd and self-knowing enough to detach herself from it and see herself and others with an occasional glint of mockery. She spoke amusingly about Pasternak's recurrent crushes on her; how, in the 1920s, he would come over and sigh that he could not live without her, only to tire and beg his wife to come and take him back home.

She confessed how lonely she was, how desolate her Leningrad had become. She spoke of her past loves, for Gumilyov, Shileiko and Punin, and, moved by her confessional mode – but also perhaps to forestall her erotic interest in him – Isaiah confessed that he was in love with someone himself. He was veiled, but it was clear that he was referring to Patricia Douglas. Akhmatova seems to have passed on a wildly garbled version of these remarks about his love-life to Korney Chukovsky, whose memoirs, published years later, referred to Berlin as a Don Juan disembarking in Leningrad to add Akhmatova to the list of his conquests.[31] Akhmatova herself seems to have been responsible for this *malentendu*. It has hung over their encounter ever since. No Russian who reads *Cinque*, the poems she devoted to their evening together, has ever been able to believe that they did not sleep together.

In fact, they hardly touched. He remained on one side of the room, she on the other.[32] Far from being a Don Juan, he was a sexual neophyte alone in the apartment of a fabled seductress, who had enjoyed deep romantic attachments with half a dozen supremely talented men. She was already investing their meeting with mystical historical and erotic significance, while he fought shy of these undercurrents and kept a safe intellectual distance. Besides, he was also aware of more quotidian needs. He had already been there six hours and he wanted to go to the lavatory. But it would have broken the mood to do so, and in any case, the communal toilet was down the dark hallway. So he remained and listened, smoking another of his Swiss cigars. As she poured out the story of her love-life, he compared her to Donna Anna in *Don Giovanni* and, moving his cigar hand to and fro – a gesture she was to capture in a line of verse – traced Mozart's melody in the air between them.[33]

They had now been talking continuously for hours, ranging back and forth from the Stray Dog Café to the blockade, from Leningrad to Oxford, across the whole course of their century, weaving together a chain of associations and connections that was to bind them to each other for the rest of their lives. They had talked of the most intimate things and now they talked of the most abstract and otherworldly. He asked her whether the Renaissance was a real world to her, or an imaginary one, and she affirmed that it was the latter. All poetry and art, she said, were a 'form of nostalgia, a longing for a universal culture, as Goethe and Schlegel had conceived it, of what had been transmuted into art and thought – nature, love, death, despair and martyrdom, of a reality which had no history, nothing outside itself'.[34] That evening in the Fontanny Dom, in the bare and denuded room, with the potatoes in the dish, the Modigliani drawing, the cigar smoke slowly settling, Isaiah's life came as close as it ever did to the still perfection of art.

By then it was light outside and they could both hear the sound of freezing rain falling in the Fontanka. He rose and kissed her hand and walked back to the Astoria, dazed, 'turned over', exalted. He looked at his watch and discovered it was eleven in the morning. Brenda Tripp clearly remembered him saying, when he threw himself down on the bed of his room, 'I am in love, I am in love.'[35]

In his memory, there was nothing else of his visit to the city, only Akhmatova. In fact, he stayed for a week in total – making the obligatory pilgrimage to a performance of Glinka's *A Life for the Tsar* at the Mariinsky Theatre, visiting Rachlin at home in his apartment in company with Randolph Churchill, and paying a call on the city's more or less thuggish political leaders. But all this – recorded in his official reports – quickly passed from memory.

It is a sign of how fundamentally Akhmatova had moved him that, instead of the memorandum on Soviet foreign policy, which he had been sent to Moscow to compose, Berlin spent December writing 'A Note on Literature and the Arts in the RSFSR in the Closing Months of 1945'.[36] Its modest title belied its ambitions: it was nothing less than a history of Russian culture in the first half of the twentieth century, a chronicle of Akhmatova's fateful generation. It was probably the first Western account of Stalin's war against Russian culture. On every page there are traces of what she – Chukovsky and Pasternak as well – told him about their experiences in the years of persecution. He insisted that the authentic voice of Russian culture remained the 'ageing but articulate . . . deeply civilised, sensitive, fastidious and not to be deceived . . . pre-revolutionary Russian intelligentsia'. If anything, he idealised their courage and ignored their equivocations. For the rest of his life they remained the gold standard, the touchstone of moral integrity.

He had seen the audiences of office-workers and soldiers at the Maly and Marinsky Theatres and how they watched a play by Shakespeare or Griboyedov as if it were a scene from contemporary life; how they murmured approval or disapproval with an intense hunger absent in the sated West. If he idealised this hunger, he had some reason to. Akhmatova and Pasternak had told him how front-line soldiers had known some of Pasternak's lines by heart. Prisoners in the *gulag* sewed Akhmatova's poetry into hand-made, birch-bark-bound books, which they carried about in their rags.[37] This enduring sense that Russian culture would one day overthrow its Soviet shackles came from his night with Akhmatova. With his despatch completed in December 1945, Berlin's secondment to the British Embassy was over and he had to return to Washington. But he decided that he must see her one last time.

On 3 January 1946 he took the Red Arrow overnight and booked into the Astoria once again. He was due to leave for Helsinki from the Finland Station the next day. That afternoon he called again at No. 44, Fontanny Dom. She was alone, waiting for him, as regal as ever. She told him that the iron gates of the palace – always closed – had been open the morning he walked away. She had an instinct for portents and this, she believed, was one.[38] He gave her a copy of Kafka's *The Castle* in English and a collection of the Sitwells' verse. She presented him with volumes of her poetry, each inscribed in her own hand. One of these dedications referred to her longing to 'place the black viper on her dusky breast with an indifferent hand'. But she wrote that she had freed herself of Cleopatra's longing. She would endure. On a second volume she wrote out a quotation from *Poem without a Hero*, as if the lines, written long beforehand, had foretold their meeting:

No one knocks at my door, Only the mirror dreams of a mirror,
And quietness stands guard over quietness – A. 4 January 1946

On another, she inscribed lines composed after his first visit. As he was to discover, they formed part of *Cinque*, a cycle of love poems charting the course of her own enchantment, her battle against hope, her exhilaration and her sorrow at his departure.

1

As if on the rim of a cloud
I remember your words,

And because of my words to you,
Night became brighter than day.

Thus torn from the earth,
We rose up, like stars.

There was neither despair nor shame,
Not now, not afterward, not at the time.

But in real life, right now,
You hear how I am calling you.

And that door that you half opened,
I don't have the strength to slam.

2

Sounds die away in the ether,
And darkness overtakes the dusk.
In a world become mute for all time,
There are only two voices, yours and mine.
And to the almost bell-like sound
Of the wind from invisible Lake Ladoga,
The late-night dialogue turned into
The delicate shimmer of interlaced rainbows.

3

For so long I hated
To be pitied,
But one drop of your pity
And I go round as if the sun were in my body.
That's why there is dawn all around me.
I go around creating miracles,
That's why![39]

They parted without embracing or touching. At the train station on the border with Finland, a venerable Soviet lady customs official looked over the books, inscribed by the proscribed poet, bowed gravely and let him pass through the looking glass into the other world. Absently he journeyed through Helsinki, Stockholm and a Paris as 'clean, beautiful, silent and empty' as a tomb.[40] After a brief stop-over in England, he returned to Washington. But his thoughts stayed with Akhmatova, for in a letter written in late February he was still talking about his visit as 'the most thrilling thing that has ever, I think, happened to me'.[41]

He returned to the outside world; *she* to the solitude of Fontanny Dom. Her desolation – even her anger – found expression, a week after his departure, in the last two poems of *Cinque*:

4
You know yourself that I'm not going to celebrate
The most bitter day of our meeting.
What to leave you in remembrance?
My shade? What good is a ghost to you?
The dedication to a burnt drama
Of which not an ash remains,
Or the terrible New Year's portrait
Suddenly hurled from its frame?
Or the barely audible
Sound of birch embers,
Or that they didn't have time to tell me of
Another's love?

5
We hadn't breathed the poppies' somnolence,
And we ourselves don't know our sin.
What was in our stars
That destined us for sorrow?
And what kind of hellish brew
Did the January darkness bring us?
And what kind of invisible glow
Drove us out of our minds before dawn?[42]

Their encounter was one of those events which never ended, which spilled out consequences to the end of their lives. Within days of his departure, the secret police arrived while Akhmatova was out and clumsily installed microphones in her ceiling. They did not even bother to clean up the little piles of plaster they left behind on the floor.

In the St Petersburg headquarters of the security organs there are three volumes of files totalling 900 pages of denunciations, reports of phone taps, quotations from writings, confessions of those close to her. The files, which began in 1939, were titled 'Hidden Trotskyism and Anti-Soviet Attitudes'.[43] The only person to have seen them, KGB operative Oleg Kalugin, gave a lecture on the Akhmatova file to a conference in Moscow in 1993, organised by the Heinrich Böll Foundation. Kalugin disclosed that the KGB forced an unnamed Polish woman, who was translating Akhmatova's work, to inform on her. She told the KGB that the English spy Berlin had visited the poet on two occasions and had declared his love for her. Even through the coarse alembic of an informer's gaze, Akhmatova comes across as a regal and imperious figure, melancholy, proud and unafraid.

In April 1946 Akhmatova travelled to Moscow and, with Pasternak, gave a poetry reading in the Hall of Columns. A severely censored collection of her work had appeared and she read from it, wearing her severe black dress and a white shawl. Once again, as in 1944, she was frightened by the intensity of the adulation. As she later recorded, 'I knew I was doomed the moment a girl ran up to me and dropped down on her knees in the Hall of Columns after I finished reciting my poetry.'[44] That night, she was reunited with Pasternak and in his apartment they ate, drank and recited poetry together. They also discussed Isaiah. In a letter that Berlin received in July 1946, through the British Embassy, Pasternak told him:

When Akhmatova was here her every third [word] was – you. And so dramatically and mysteriously! At night, for example, in a taxi on the way back from some evening or reception, inspired and weary, and slightly in the clouds (*or* intoxicated) in French: *Notre ami* (that's you) *a dit, ou a promis*, etc. etc. In the end, those of her friends who were jealous of her [attachment] to you began to pester me with requests: Boris Leonidovich, please describe Berlin for us, who is he and what is he like? Then followed my praises and only then did their real torments begin. Everyone loves you and recalls you with great warmth.[45]

That summer Isaiah continued to keep them both in the forefront of his mind. He was back in England by then and, while standing on Oxford station platform, he approached the university Vice-Chancellor and suggested that Pasternak be proposed for an honorary degree. The Vice-Chancellor said that he had never heard of the name. In any event, he said, he disapproved of using degree ceremonies to make political gestures.[46]

Akhmatova was quite correct to fear the outpouring of emotion at her Moscow readings. Over the summer of 1946 the noose was slowly tightened. Nadezhda Mandelstam, who visited her at the Fontanny Dom, remembers that shadowy figures 'with ugly mugs'[47] shadowed them whenever they went out walking. Once, on returning home, they found the gates locked and were unaccountably held up by the door-keeper. When they were finally let into the courtyard, a flash-gun went off in an upstairs window: the operatives were taking their picture.

Then in August Akhmatova was in the Writers' Union, 'that idiotic old people's home', as she called it, and noticed that people were avoiding her glance and visibly edging away from her. On her way home she bought some fish and had it wrapped in a newspaper. She met Mikhail Zoshchenko by chance and he asked her in great distress what they were to do. She replied calmly that they must bear with it, not understanding why he seemed so agitated. When she got home and unwrapped the fish, she read in the newspaper that a party resolution had just censored the magazines *Zvezda* and *Leningrad* for publishing their works. A week later Andrei Zhdanov issued a party report in which Akhmatova's work was described as 'the portrait of a frantic little fine lady flitting between the boudoir and the chapel'. Her poetry was a reactionary concoction of 'sadness, longing, death, mysticism and doom'. She was a 'left-over from the old aristocratic culture', 'half-nun, half-harlot', or rather a 'harlot-nun, whose sin is mixed with prayer'. On 4 September 1946 she was expelled from the Writers' Union, and her book of poems – the one she had promised to send Isaiah – was pulped.[48]

Once again she had been consigned to darkness and purgatory, although – as the KGB recorded – there were anonymous neighbours and friends brave enough to leave bouquets of flowers and parcels of food at the door of 44 Fontanny Dom. Eventually these stopped and, with the re-arrest of Lev in 1949, once again for the crime of being her son, Akhmatova's desolation was complete.

She had no doubt that these catastrophes were all the result of Isaiah's visit. She did not blame him for this. It was her destiny that it be so. She always saw her situation in the grandest perspective. For her, Berlin's visit and Zhdanov's subsequent condemnation of her work marked nothing less than the beginning of the Cold War, the end of war-time co-operation with the Western allies and the resumption of ideological, moral and political war between two radically different world orders. Of Berlin's visit she wrote:

> He will not be a beloved husband to me
> But what we accomplish, he and I,
> Will disturb the Twentieth Century.[49]

This was grandiose, but not entirely wrong. She had been told, probably by Pasternak, that Stalin had reportedly read the KGB surveillance reports and had said to Zhdanov, 'So now our nun is consorting with British spies, is she?' When, therefore, she wrote in *Poem without a Hero* that her night with a visitor from the future would change history, she meant it seriously.

Isaiah had never calculated the consequences of his visits, either to her or to his family in Moscow, but as the years passed he began to realise how terrible these consequences had been. Throughout 1947 and 1948 the embassy in Moscow attempted to allay his anxieties about Akhmatova's fate. He heard that she was 'well and living quietly in her flat on a state pension of 600 r. a month'.[50] He wasn't to blame himself for the difficulties she had endured. Another letter painted an altogether bleaker picture. While Pasternak was left alone to write his novel, Akhmatova had lost her Writers' Union card and was in miserably reduced circumstances.[51] In mid-1947 the embassy forwarded a copy of Andrei Zhdanov's latest strictures on Soviet philosophy, and Isaiah could see that the ideological pressure of the party was as unrelenting as ever.[52] In April 1948 his friends in the Moscow embassy advised him that anti-foreign xenophobia was running so high that any attempt to make contact would only endanger her further.[53] For the next six years he had no further news.

These were among Akhmatova's darkest years. In desperation at her son's re-arrest she bowed to the regime, composing a few perfunctory and unconvincing odes to Comrade Stalin in an attempt to secure his release. This gesture was all the more humiliating because it was unsuccessful. For Stalin was not fooled. The ageing Kremlin Mountaineer could have read the astringent things she had said about him, in the file in the Leningrad KGB archives. There, so Oleg Kalugin reports, she greeted her fate with a certain grim relish, telling the Polish informant that she was proud of Stalin's unflagging interest in her, just as proud as she was of the anonymous bouquets left at her front door. People forget the fat cats, she said, but they do not forget those who suffer.[54]

Stalin died in 1953, but her ordeal continued. In May 1954 a party of English university students visited the Leningrad House of Writers. Akhmatova and Zoshchenko, tense, pale and at bay, were paraded in front of them. The only student who spoke Russian was Harry Shukman, then an undergraduate at Nottingham University. In all innocence, Shukman asked whether there was any place for satire in Soviet literature. The questions put both writers in an impossible position; a single word out of place would be pounced on by the party hacks in the room. Zoshchenko replied that there was room for satire – a foolhardy, if courageous remark, which was to cost him dear – and then fell silent. When asked for her opinion, Akhmatova snapped that she was in agreement – whether with Zoshchenko or with the decrees was deliberately left unclear – and then she too fell silent. She went home believing that the students had been sent by Isaiah. In fact, none of them was from Oxford and he had no knowledge of their visit.[55]

He never doubted that his visit to Akhmatova was the most important event in his life. He came away from Russia with a loathing for Soviet tyranny, which was to inform nearly everything he wrote in defence of Western liberalism and political liberty thereafter. His fierce polemic against historical determinism was animated by what he had learned from her, namely that history could be made to bow before the sheer stubbornness of a human conscience.[56]

But his visit to Russia also left him with a burden of guilt. Everyone but him paid a price for his visit. Between 1948 and 1953 the wave of anti-Semitism rose to a crest. Soviet Jewish institutions and publications were closed down as part of a general crack-down on supposedly nationalist and 'cosmopolitan' manifestations in Soviet life. This culminated in 1952 with the arrest, trial and execution of fifteen prominent Jewish doctors for plotting the murder of Stalin. Isaiah's uncle Leo was rounded up and accused of belonging to a British spy ring that included his brother Mendel and his nephew Isaiah. The accusers linked Mendel's visit to the timber mission in 1935 with Isaiah's visit in 1945 and alleged that British Intelligence had placed Leo in the university dietetics clinic in order to gather information on the health of Stalin and other Soviet leaders. The purpose of Isaiah's visit, so the interrogators insisted, was to take Leo's information back to British authorities in London. Leo Berlin was beaten until he attempted suicide. Then, simply to bring his tortures to an end, he confessed that he was indeed a British spy. He was held in prison for over a year and released in February 1954, after Stalin's death.[57] He was walking in the streets in Moscow, still weak and undernourished, when he saw one of his torturers cross the road in front of him. He suffered a heart attack and died alone in the snowy streets.[58]

12

The Tribe, 1946–8

Akhmatova and the war had changed him. The thirty-seven-year-old who returned to Oxford in April 1946 was a more seasoned and accomplished figure than the naïve accomplice of Guy Burgess' transatlantic expedition in June 1940. He had proved himself, and the world's view of him shifted accordingly. The prestige of the Washington despatches gave him a reputation in Whitehall that percolated through to the upper reaches of London society. Berlin became someone it was creditable or amusing to know. Society hostesses invited him to dinner; the BBC asked him to broadcast.[1] In 1945 Lord Beaverbrook invited him to write a column for *Express* newspapers.[2] As Isaiah later recalled, 'I behaved like a Swiss governess, an attempt on whose virtue was being made.' It was easy to refuse, but the old devil's courtship was flattering. Oxford figures who had condescended to Isaiah before the war now deferred to his opinions. By 1951 he was being seriously considered as a candidate for the Wardenship of All Souls; in 1953, for the Wardenship of Nuffield College.[3] His reputation began to ripple out around him. In 1951 Freddie Ayer told Berlin that when he had been introduced at a party in London as 'the cleverest man in England', someone exclaimed, 'Oh, so you must be Isaiah Berlin.'[4]

He was one of only eight people whom Churchill consulted on the general structure and historical detail of his memoir of the 1930s, *The Gathering Storm*. William Deakin, a fellow of Wadham, who had got to know Isaiah in New York during the war, was Churchill's chief assistant on the memoirs and persuaded Churchill to use Berlin as a sounding board.[5] In December 1947 Churchill despatched the first six chapters and asked for a general reaction. In February 1948 Berlin replied bluntly that the book took too long to get into its stride. The early chapters were 'too episodic and insubstantial to act as an adequate scaffolding' for the later ones.[6] Moreover, Churchill's account of why Stalin had executed Soviet Marshal Tukhachevsky in 1937 was based on an unreliable rumour. He also drew Churchill's attention to one of his passing remarks. In 1933 he had said that Hitler's hostility to the Jews was unjustified, though 'if the Jews were acting against their country, they must be put in their place'. Such an aside, Berlin observed, was liable to be misconstrued. Churchill took the criticisms seriously, revised the manuscript accordingly and sent Isaiah an honorarium of 200 guineas.

Other signs of recognition began to come his way. *Foreign Affairs*, the journal of the American foreign policy establishment, asked him to contribute, and the two articles he wrote for them – one on political ideas in the twentieth century and another on Stalin's art of government – made his reputation in America as an expert on Russian affairs.[7] Chatham House and then the Labour, Conservative and Liberal Party summer schools asked him to lecture.[8] The Foreign Office sent him reports and memos from Moscow, asking for comments.[9] In the summer of 1947 Oliver Franks asked for Berlin's services at the Paris Conference on the establishment of the Marshall Plan for Europe. At the conference, the Europeans, Isaiah sardonically observed, behaved like 'lofty and demanding beggars' approaching an 'apprehensive millionaire'. Drafting the tortuous language of international compromise did not appeal to him, and after only two weeks he returned to Oxford.[10]

If he had changed, so had Oxford. The colleges were flooded with demobilised servicemen taking up their education where they had left off in 1939. At New College he was soon teaching an unheard-of eighteen hours a week – the history of political thought, a course on the philosophy of Bishop Berkeley, tutorials on epistemology.[11] He was an eccentric teacher, often taking tutorials in pyjamas and dressing-gown, or actually in bed. His rooms at New College were dominated by a huge gramophone with an outsized horn, and his mantelpiece contained a diverting range of bric-à-brac: the 'Austin' sign from an Oxford garage; a number of Woolworth sixpenny toys; a clockwork mouse and a car; in addition to a piece of seaside rock in the shape and colours of a public-school tie. A student, Ronald Hope, was reading an essay when he looked up to see Isaiah winding the mechanical mouse and letting it run around the carpet.[12] Another undergraduate, Isabel Roberts, remembers him announcing the essay topic 'There are no such things as natural rights', and then waving in the direction of his bookshelves. 'A lot of sawdust written on this topic – a lot of sawdust. Don't read any of it. Go away and think.'[13]

He didn't bore his students, but they often bored him. At one rather uncharacteristic low ebb in 1946, he wrote that they were 'dull and polite and spiritless with too much army life [in them], scores and scores of them cluttering up every available chink of time and space, morning and afternoon and evening'.[14] As for his colleagues – apart from Herbert Hart, Stuart Hampshire and David Cecil – they were all, he said sourly, 'devoted grey nonentities and hacks'. By 1950 he had extricated himself from tutorial teaching at New College and returned to All Souls, in the hope that 'monastic' retreat would allow him, at last, to write.

Akhmatova had rekindled his intellectual passion for Russia, but in Oxford there were few to share it. Intellectual history fell between stools, neglected by philosophy, history and politics alike. Stuart Hampshire noticed that Berlin had become a spectator rather than a participant in the circle of academic philosophers and that he was looking elsewhere for intellectual company.[15] From 1949 onwards he began regular academic pilgrimages to America – to Harvard, Bryn Mawr and Princeton – where intellectual history, especially of the Russian nineteenth century, had academic standing.

Another avenue of escape from Oxford lay in London where the sacred monsters, the society hostesses, took him up. There were Lady Colefax's lunches at Lord North Street, as well as invitations from Lady Cunard and later from Marietta Tree at Ditchley Park in Oxfordshire. His entry into high society raised eyebrows among his friends. Clarissa Churchill – who went on to marry Anthony Eden – regarded Isaiah's socialising with perplexed disappointment. He might have become a sage. Instead, she thought, he had allowed himself to become a salon conversationalist, an intellectual acrobat in the society circus.[16]

This reproach has shadowed his reputation, but it relies on a caricature of the austerity with which intellectual life is supposed to be lived. Parties, in fact, were one place where good ideas occurred to him. One of his best thoughts, for example, began its life as a party game. Just before the war, Lord Oxford – a hereditary Catholic peer then studying classics at Balliol – told Isaiah that he had come across a line from the Greek poet Archilochus.[17] It had all the elegance and mystery of a Japanese haiku: 'The fox knows many things, but the hedgehog knows one big thing.' Isaiah immediately began dividing the great minds of the past into hedgehogs and foxes: Goethe and Pushkin were foxes; Dostoyevsky and Tolstoy were hedgehogs. The distinction dramatised the ultimate incompatibility between types of artistic personality and the moralities of creative life. In 1951 the distinction recurred to him when he was working on a study of Leo Tolstoy's sense of history: it seemed to capture the fissure between Tolstoy's fox-like gift as a novelist for conveying the fine detail of human life and his hedgehog-like search for an over-arching theory of human existence.

This was also a fissure within himself. Most of his friends saw him as an arch-fox – nimble, cunning, quick-witted, darting from subject to subject, eluding pursuit. Yet he was also the type of fox who longs to be a hedgehog – to know one thing, to feel one thing more truly than anything else. It would take more than a decade for him to discover what this was.

Because his own frivolity and worldliness so often came under attack, a search for a personal intellectual morality became a central feature of his writing. He was looking for a path between heavy-going engagement and mandarin detachment. He wanted to be serious without being solemn, to defend beliefs without being dogmatic and to be entertaining without being facile. He shared the English suspicion of the continental intellectual. French intellectuals, for example, enjoyed enormous prestige in the post-war period. But what exactly did a French intellectual *know*?

Raymond Aron became the only French figure whom Isaiah respected. Isaiah called upon him in Paris in 1950 and they kept in contact thereafter. Aron was liberal, anti-communist, Jewish, sceptical – all these things about him appealed to Isaiah – but he was too intellectually vain to become a close friend. He seemed piqued that the young Oxford don did not appear to regard himself as an Aronian, while Berlin thought Aron was a superb political journalist but a weak historian of ideas.[18]

At least in France a certain Cartesian lucidity was respected. As for Germany, Berlin was impatient with the lofty obscurity of the German philosophical tradition, and when it was accompanied by the low service of fascism, his impatience turned to scorn. He was repelled by the special pleading with which Heidegger had sought to explain his complicity with the Nazi regime. Of Heidegger's world view, Isaiah wrote scathingly in 1949 that it was 'vaguely tragic but too remote to bring home the sense of the crimes and horrors of the immediate past, relieving the burden of particular guilt by a misty disquisition on its nature in general'.[19]

Rejecting continental models of the life of the mind did not bring Berlin any closer to the models on offer in Oxford. Having written his Marx, he knew that he was not cut out to be a scholar in the British mould. His talent was for synthesis, not for scholarship; the essay, not the monograph. The audience he cared about was the educated middle classes, not the specialists, though he knew he must earn their respect. Besides, he loved company too much to spend the best years of his life in the library.

Before the war he had taken his intellectual purposes from sources outside himself. Now he had to find sustaining motives within. He had reached a fork in the road: either he would develop a serious intellectual engagement of his own or decline into what he feared most, a 'chatterbox'. Around him, the best thinkers of his generation were defining themselves. Karl Popper, for example, had spent the war in New Zealand writing The Open Society and its Enemies.[20] Isaiah was influenced by Popper's impassioned defence of liberal values, but he and Popper were very different: Popper a sceptical rationalist, Isaiah a more intuitive thinker, interested – as Popper never was – in inner anguish, personal dilemmas, and the conflict between human values.

However different they were, they both took their stand against the Marxist intellectuals – E.H. Carr, then embarked on a long history of the Bolshevik Revolution; Isaac Deutscher, the biographer of Trotsky; and Christopher Hill, the historian of the Puritan Revolution, then at Balliol. In the 1930s Isaiah had been friendly with Christopher Hill, exchanging notes and books about Russian and European precursors of Marx. But in 1947 Hill's Lenin and the Russian Revolution asserted that the Bolsheviks had been right to dissolve the Constituent Assembly of 1917 because ordinary peasants had no confidence in it. In any event, Hill argued, the socialist revolutionary party, who were well represented in the Constituent Assembly, did not truly speak for the interests of the ordinary peasants who had voted for them. This passage made Isaiah doubly indignant: he felt that it falsified the historical record and it denied that ordinary human agents – in this case the much-abused Russian peasantry – could be trusted to know what was best for them. Hill got word of Isaiah's reaction, but a meeting failed to restore their relationship. The easy friendships of the 1930s were over; from now on, liberals and Marxists were on opposing sides.[21]

In this context of increasing polarisation Berlin went his own way, searching for his own agenda and his own version of intellectual commitment. The first large-scale piece of research and writing that he undertook after the war was a study of the nineteenth-century critic Vissarion Belinsky, who was responsible for creating the image of the Russian intellectual as moral witness, and for the idea of the poet as defender of the Russian language. In this sense, Belinsky made Akhmatova's moral career possible. But the study of Belinsky was also a way of developing Berlin's own vocation. He was coming to see ideas exactly as Belinsky did, as what human beings lived for and by: 'something wider and more intrinsic to the human beings who hold them than opinions or even principles ... [they] are indeed the central complex of relations of a man towards himself and to the external world'.[22] Out of Belinsky and the Russians came the outlines of a distinctive intellectual project: in place of logical or semantic analysis, Isaiah would study how ideas permeated and gave shape to the intellectual vocation itself; how intellectual seriousness was itself elaborated and defended from epoch to epoch. But in making himself the historian of the Russian intellectual vocation, he ended up demonstrating to himself why a much lighter, more ironical and politically detached style suited his own nature. Belinsky had invented Russian intellectual moral seriousness, but he had also legitimised a certain style of moral fanaticism. Who was to claim Belinsky as his spiritual ancestor but Lenin himself? Compared to this, independent intellectual scepticism of a Berlinian sort had something to be said for it.

The problem was that Isaiah hated writing. As he confessed to a friend, 'spoken words vanish and no responsibility lingers; and one is freed from these embarrassing witnesses of one's momentary states'.[23] Writing meant taking responsibility, and he avoided responsibility of any kind. He had no children, no dependants, few official duties. He had consciously prolonged his adolescence. He was approaching middle age, unmarried, unsettled, condemned to a future as a minor Oxford personality.

In a letter to a friend, he lamented:

> ... I go careering from pillar to post like an American student perpetually harassed by examinations, perpetually judging and being judged, unable to achieve even a moment of the large calm, the minimum of tranquillity which all tolerable lives require ... I know nothing, I have written nothing, I have not said what I wish to say. I no longer remember what it was I would wish to say. Presently someone will notice how empty my activity is, the bluff will be called, the game over.[24]

When the frenetic pace of work and social life brought on one of his periodic collapses and he had to go into a nursing home for a rest, his friend Stuart Hampshire begged him to impose an 'economy of spirit' upon himself: to rein himself in, channel his energies, stop dissipating it in a thousand directions.[25] Berlin was aware that being an intellectual entertainer for the rich was a trap into which Jews were especially liable to fall. He would have to secure his reputation by more unequivocal means than mere talk.

As the exigencies of his situation were borne in upon him, he had a rare but galling experience of English anti-Semitism. Thanks to his connection with Churchill, he had been befriended by the Conservative politician Oliver Lyttelton, who, charmed by Berlin's vivid talk, put him up for membership at the St James's Club in the summer of 1950, only to discover that several members were 'determined to have no one of Jewish extraction in the Club'.[26] Berlin immediately withdrew his name and was then proposed and accepted for Brooks' club, an even more distinguished establishment just down the street. But his rejection at the St James's reminded him that there were still invisible doors barring entry into the Gentile world.

At end of the war, there were new pressures forcing him to choose between his Jewish and British identities. Jews were flooding out of refugee camps to Palestine; underground groups were waging open war on the British mandate authorities there. When the Attlee government attempted to continue the pre-war restrictions on Jewish immigration, when it turned away ships containing desperate European refugees, British Jews felt their twin loyalties begin to come apart. By 1946 Weizmann's long-standing Anglophilia stood exposed as bankrupt. Political momentum was in the hands of those who had taken up the gun. On 22 July 1946 Jewish underground units, commanded by Menachem Begin, blew up the King David Hotel in Jerusalem, which housed the British administration, killing ninety-one people. Weizmann struggled in vain to halt the tide of Jewish terrorism. He consulted Isaiah over the speech he was to give at the Zionist Congress at Basel in December 1946 and Isaiah contributed a strong paragraph condemning Jewish terror: 'Terrorism insults our history; it mocks the ideals for which a Jewish society must stand; it contaminates our banner; it compromises our appeal to the world's liberal conscience.'[27] Weizmann commented to his associate Meyer Weisgal, 'Isaiah's paragraph about terrorism has some punch, hasn't it?'[28] But the speech did nothing to retrieve Weizmann's political authority. By the conclusion of the congress he had been stripped of his leadership of the Jewish Agency and cast into the wilderness. Enraged and rejected, the ageing, near-blind Weizmann dreamed of leading a rump of moderate followers, Isaiah included, out of the movement.[29] This came to nothing and Ben Gurion's associates in the Jewish Agency began seeking to draw Isaiah into their camp. In January 1947 he received a call from Moshe Shertok, a senior official in the Jewish Agency, offering him the direction of the Agency's work in Eastern and Central Europe. Shertok was seeking to draw able Weizmannites away from 'the Chief', but Isaiah refused to be seduced.[30]

By the summer of 1947 4000 Jewish underground fighters had pinned down 80,000 British troops, dug into fortified command posts known as 'Bevingrads', after the Foreign Minister, Ernest Bevin. Weizmann commanded Berlin to visit him.[31] In late July 1947 Berlin unwillingly set sail for Palestine in company with his father. On the voyage, he was irritated by Mendel's constant need for company, but for the first time he saw his father, then sixty-four, with the detachment that comes from at last achieving adulthood himself. As he wrote to his mother, she had thrown a tent over both of their lives, so that Mendel had remained protected from life, amiable, kindly, decent and innocent, a man 'with no natural bristles'. Mendel, for his part, wrote home commenting sadly on the gulf between them. Marie wrote back from Baden, where she was taking the waters, to say rather wisely that such a gap was natural. All the same, she said, he was still 'our Shaiele'.[32]

As the boat meandered from Marseilles to Athens, from Alexandria to Haifa, Isaiah talked to the Jewish emigrants in steerage. British warships were turning back other vessels loaded with refugees, but these emigrants were among the small minority who had legal papers for Palestine. They were crammed below decks, with only the most basic possessions, and had been pushed from one refugee camp to another, before securing passage to Palestine. But they were now, he reported to his mother, 'within solution of all their moral problems – and material as well. They are afraid neither of life nor death – what more can be said?'[33]

When the boat finally docked in Haifa, the Jews on board would have been surprised to observe one of their own being met at the quay by the British assistant district commissioner, Lord Oxford – Isaiah's friend from Oxford days – and an armed British escort.[34] Haifa itself was in a state of tension. Only weeks before, British marines had boarded the *Exodus*, a ship bound for Haifa with 4,500 Jewish refugees on board. They had wrested control of the ship from its defenders, towed it into the port of Haifa and compelled the refugees to disembark for forcible transfer back to the refugee camps in Germany. At the same time, two British sergeants were found hanging in a eucalyptus grove in Natanya, executed by a Jewish underground fighting force in retaliation for British executions of their own fighters. The British and the Jews were at war and here was Berlin journeying south from Haifa in a British official car, to stay with Weizmann. The atmosphere was so tense that when he arrived in Weizmann's home town and asked directions to the Chief's house, one Rehovot resident he questioned looked him in the eye and said coolly, 'No idea.' Even Jews in his home town loathed Weizmann for his willingness to talk to the British. Indeed, these talks continued while Isaiah was staying in Rehovot. The British military governor of the local district dined with Weizmann, and the local Haganah detachment de-mined the road for the governor's arrival and then re-mined it when he departed.[35]

Weizmann – nearly blind by now – blundered about his walled garden, raging against the stupidity of the British and the folly of his fellow-Jews.

He had just given another speech imploring his people to put their trust in the British, only to be hissed at for his pains. Isaiah asked him why he had gone so far and Weizmann shot back, 'Everyone in this country goes too far. I don't see why I shouldn't.'[36]

He begged Isaiah to leave Oxford, to cease teaching Gentiles and take up his rightful place as his chief of staff. But Isaiah was shrewd enough to see how things really were: there was no staff to be chief *of*. When Berlin turned him down, Weizmann was furious. He couldn't understand how a Jew could prefer to remain in the Diaspora when the fate of the homeland hung in the balance. Isaiah remembers him muttering, 'Your friend, Felix Frankfurter, sits there among those Gentiles, seven days a week. How can he? What is he doing?' In letters to Frankfurter, Berlin confided that Weizmann had become a 'huge, bitter tragic ruin', a man 'all his life wedded to power' now 'stripped of it most remorselessly'.[37] Berlin felt sure that he should not give up Oxford for a career in Palestine. Jewish politics was too sharply polarised. He feared he would be torn to pieces.[38] He also realised that he had no place there. The emerging Israeli society was Middle Eastern, Hebrew-speaking and instinctively anti-British. The Zionist project was creating a kind of Jew with whom he had nothing in common. In the *kibbutzim* in Galilee, he met brown-skinned Mediterranean people who looked like the Cypriots or Maltese, untroubled, unpolished and unafraid. The chasm between these *sabras* and European Jews was bound to grow.[39] There is an irony in all of this: a life-long Zionist discovering that he had no place in Zion.

With some relief, Isaiah excused himself from the Weizmanns and went to Jerusalem to visit Aunt Ida Samunov and other members of the Berlin clan. One of them was in the thick of the struggle for independence. His uncle by marriage, Isaac Landoberg, had fled Russia for Palestine in the early 1920s, changed his name to Yitzhak Sadeh and was now a Jewish underground fighter living in Tel Aviv on the run from the British authorities.[40] Having fought the French Vichyite forces in Lebanon and Syria on the British side in 1943, he had become one of the architects of the *Palmach*, the élite strike-force of the underground Jewish army. While not personally involved in terrorism, Sadeh was an enthusiastic advocate of direct military action against the British. Berlin ought to have disapproved, but he was captivated by 'Big Isaac', as the British had called him, so obviously one of life's irregulars. The slender, elegant and rather vain man whom Isaiah remembered from Petrograd was now plump, bearded and unkempt, but as cheerful as ever and enthralled by the dangers of an underground existence. They met in a back-street café in Tel Aviv. Isaiah worried that someone in the café might tip off the British authorities, but Yitzhak laughed off the risks. He had no feeling against the British, he said. He even admired British institutions; but most colonial administrators were frightful philistines. It was impossible to talk to them about books, ideas, music or history. Submission to Arab rule – which was clearly what the Colonial Office had in mind – was unthinkable. Isaiah came away from Sadeh and from Palestine convinced that partition and independence had become inevitable and that he belonged back in England.[41]

The British announced that they were handing the Palestine problem over to the UN, and the UN decided in November 1947 on partition. The Jews accepted partition while the Arabs rejected it, and both sides inside Palestine prepared for war as the British departed. Palestinian Arabs began fleeing, driven out by massacres and reprisals. On 14 May 1948 David Ben Gurion proclaimed the independence of the state of Israel, and Syrian, Lebanese and Egyptian forces attacked while the British-trained and armed Arab Legion crossed the Jordan and laid siege to Jerusalem. Jews around the world believed that the British, having abandoned Palestine, had sided with the Arabs.[42] On 6 June 1948, as the fate of Jerusalem hung in the balance, Isaiah wrote to congratulate Weizmann on his election as Israel's first President and furiously criticised British complicity in the attack on the new state. He told Weizmann that the Foreign Office had persuaded themselves that a Jewish state must be crushed before it 'falls within the Soviet orbit ideologically and politically'.[43] He ended by offering to approach Winston Churchill, then Leader of the Opposition, to urge him to mount an attack on the Labour government's policy. Weizmann wrote back, with sovereign calm, to say that Churchill should not be disturbed. By then, of course, even Weizmann could see that the old Zionist strategy of whispering in the ears of sympathetic British politicians was useless: now the fate of Israel depended on the force of its arms and on figures like Yitzhak Sadeh who were at this moment leading units of the *Palmach* against Egyptian command posts in the Negev and Sinai deserts.

As the young state struggled for survival, Isaiah continued to feel occasional qualms of conscience about his detachment. The siege of Jerusalem continued through the summer of 1948, and he contacted Leo Amery, an All Souls colleague and former Colonial Secretary, to see whether pressure could be put on the Arab governments to relax their grip on the city.[44]

In September 1948, with Israel gaining the upper hand in its fight to survive, Isaiah wrote to Weizmann making it clear that, while he would always remain a Zionist, he would not align his life with the new state. He said he would never turn his back on Israel and insisted that his association with Weizmann gave him more pride than anything else. He acknowledged that to choose Oxford 'in an hour of crisis for our own people may seem unpardonable egoism and even a kind of levity', but if he did not settle down and do some serious work, 'I should become worthless in my own eyes.'[45]

This letter was both his most passionate declaration of allegiance and simultaneously a declaration of independence – from Weizmann, from Israel and from Zionism. Over the next three years, as the state of Israel took shape, Ben Gurion himself, and senior officials like Abba Ebban, Teddy Kollek and Walter Eytan (Isaiah's contemporary at St Paul's, now a senior official in the Israeli foreign office) were to plead with him to come and live in Israel.[46]

Weizmann was both gracious and shrewd enough to relinquish his hold, but his wife Vera refused to let go so easily. As late as 1951 she was still imploring Isaiah to settle in Israel.[47] But he had begun to detach himself from Weizmann's orbit after 1948. While he continued to visit the Chief whenever he came to rest and recuperate in Switzerland, he found his visits to 'the old monster' ever more difficult. Weizmann lived for power and hated the marginalised, purely ceremonial character of his office. Abba Ebban told Isaiah that when he visited Weizmann and asked him what he was doing, Weizmann growled, 'Doing? I am said to be the symbol of the state of Israel. I sit here and symbolise.'[48] When Berlin visited him again in 1950, he was still the King of the Jews, still the scathing observer of the follies of lesser men. Yet there was a pathos about him now and a bitterness that made their encounters painful. He was now, Isaiah said, like a 'sick old lion'.[49] When Vera Weizmann proposed that Isaiah become her husband's biographer, Isaiah delicately excused himself.

After staying with Weizmann at Rehovot, it was a relief to look up Yitzhak Sadeh again. He was living in a small house in Jaffa, decorated with trophies of his battles with the Egyptians in the war of independence – helmets, flags, daggers – and, in a prominent position in the room, a large bottle of vodka, a gift from the Soviet Ambassador. He was living with a 'sniperette', a partisan fighter of the 1948 war. There were photographs of him with his arms around his young protégés, Moshe Dayan and Yigal Allon, and snapshots taken in captured Egyptian dugouts in the Negev. He was absolutely delighted when Isaiah called him a Jewish Garibaldi.[50]

Isaiah loved 'Reb Yitzhak's' enthusiasm for the new Israel but did not share it himself. As he wrote to Felix Frankfurter, 'the trouble about the Israelis is not only their partly unconscious conviction born of experience that virtue always loses and only toughness pays, but a great provincialism and blindness to outside opinion'. It is doubtful that Israelis ever knew how disparaging he was in private about a state that he defended in public. Would Ben Gurion, for example, have continued to seek Isaiah's company whenever he was in England, as he did in December 1950, had he known how sceptical Isaiah actually was? The Prime Minister arrived incognito, with his bodyguards, prowled about the bookshops and then spent the evening at The Mitre, drinking tumblers of port and excitedly discussing everything from Plato's philosophy to the role and significance of elephants in Indian fables. Ben Gurion struck Isaiah as a vivid 'peasant leader': rough, ruthless and cunning. He denounced Berlin's way of life and offered him the directorship of the Israeli Foreign Office, but Isaiah refused.[51] Despite this, the Prime Minister considered using Isaiah as a secret go-between with Churchill in 1951, when the Israeli Prime Minister thought of approaching the British with the idea of a joint seizure of Sinai from the Egyptians.[52] The plan was preposterous and happily did not go much further than Ben Gurion's own mind, but the fact that he thought of Isaiah for the mission suggests how much in the confidence of the Israeli leadership he then was.

In a lecture on Israel to the Anglo-Israel Association in 1953, Berlin praised the country because it allowed Jews to escape their stereotypes and escape their history. They no longer had to be 'sophisticated, chess-playing, café intellectuals'. After a history of martyrdom, they had earned the right to 'normality', 'wholesomeness', even 'dullness'. If the Israelis did not 'wish to spend their lives in mourning for the six million Jewish dead', that too was their right. They would never forget the Holocaust, but neither were they required to live their lives as 'gloomy heirs of a black tragedy'.[53]

When Weizmann died in November 1952, Vera sent Isaiah a heartbroken account of her husband's final hours and soon afterwards redoubled her demands that he become his biographer. Isaiah duly contributed an obituary to The Times, but privately he confessed that the Chief had been 'too ruthless and large-scale, and too public-minded with too little private life, to be good'.[54] Publicly, he praised Weizmann as 'the first totally free Jew of the modern world'.

If Weizmann's death finally resolved the issue of whether to embrace a Zionist career, it did not resolve the question of how to live as a Jew within British society. The creation of the state of Israel changed the nature of the question. In May 1950 the anti-communist writer Arthur Koestler, famous for Darkness at Noon, gave an interview to The Jewish Chronicle in which he argued that Jews in the Diaspora had only two possible choices: either to assimilate fully and discard their Jewishness or to emigrate and lead a fully Jewish life in Israel. Anything in between was false.[55] This was a direct challenge to Isaiah's own position and he decided to confront Koestler's arguments head-on. His essay 'Jewish Slavery and Emancipation' was published in The Jewish Chronicle, in the autumn of 1951. Until Israel existed, Berlin argued, no Jew was free to live a purely Jewish life, undeformed by the scrutiny, pressure and repression of non-Jews. The creation of the state of Israel was a victory for freedom precisely because it 'restored to Jews not merely their personal dignity and status as human beings, but what is vastly more important, their right to choose as individuals how they shall live'.[56] But this did not mean that the only free life for a Jew had to be lived in Israel.

Koestler's either/or choice of assimilation or emigration was an exercise in intellectual bullying: 'there are too many individuals in the world who do not choose to see life in the form of radical choices between one course and another and whom we do not condemn for this reason. "Out of the crooked timber of humanity," said a great philosopher, "no straight thing was ever made."' Jews should have the same right to fashion their own lives as any other people – to choose assimilation, emigration, separation, any option that met the test of a self-chosen life. Berlin's

Zionism was a defence of Israel as the necessary condition not for Jewish belonging but for Jewish freedom.

Berlin denied that there had to be only one way to live a Jewish life. Religious Jews believed that the preservation of Judaism as a faith was an 'absolute obligation', to which everything else must be sacrificed. Equally, most secular Jews believed that the preservation of Jewish values might be worth any sacrifice. Still others might well ask themselves whether the survival of Judaism over the millennia justified the 'unbelievable cost in blood and tears'. Had the Jews assimilated successfully, had they disappeared completely as a distinct people and religion, they might have been spared their martyrdom.

Isaiah never believed that total assimilation was possible, but the point was: how could Jews be sure that such an alternative might not have been better for them? For him, as Avishai Margalit remarked, Jewish suffering could never be a blessing; it was always a curse. There was an eerie chill in the way he imagined that it might have been better to assimilate and disappear, than survive and suffer. But he was one of those Jews who, as he remarked of Proust, 'turns his very rootlessness into the kind of Archimedean point outside all the worlds, the better to assess them from'.[57] Because he was able to question his own commitments, he could see that the core values of others might be contestable. What one person valued another would reject; key values – freedom and belonging – were in conflict. These central conclusions were hammered out in his relation to his own Jewishness. One Jew would find his identity in Israel, another in Britain; one would find it in religious faith, another in keeping to Jewish customs, and still another in abandoning Judaism altogether. It was a form of intellectual tyranny to suppose that one of these choices must be right for everyone. Were the claims of religion and tradition to prevail over an individual's right to shape his life as he wished, Jews would only substitute the self-imposed slavery of their own community for the Gentile-imposed slavery they had endured for millennia.

'Jewish Slavery and Emancipation' was also an unsparing portrait of his inner experience as a Jew in Gentile society. A Jew, he said, was like an anthropologist studying a tribe. He could only prosper if he made himself more of an expert on the customs of the tribes than the natives. Hence the poignant passion of the Jew for institutions that admit him but do not allow him truly to belong. Hence the 'fantastic over-development of their faculties for detecting trends, and discriminating shades and hues of changing individual and social situations, often before they are noticed anywhere else'.[58] His own social success was due to exactly such finely tuned radar. Now, he could see that these sensitivities were something of a deformation. For they made him too eager for Gentile approval and this in itself built up a dialectic of rejection: the more sensitive he became, the more his self-consciousness stuck out, the more he lay himself open to exclusion and rejection.

Another metaphor in the essay captured the inner essence of his experience of Jewishness in even starker terms. He liked telling a joke about a hunchbacked American inventor named Steinmetz, who was walking past Temple Emanuel Synagogue on Fifth Avenue in New York with Otto Kahn, a financier who, though Jewish by origin, had thoroughly assimilated. Kahn looked up at the synagogue and said, 'I used to attend services there', to which Steinmetz tartly replied, 'And I used to be a hunchback.'[59] This story must have been the basis for a long passage in 'Jewish Slavery' in which Berlin argued that being a Jew was like having a hunchback. Each Jew reacted differently to his hump: some pretended they had no hump at all; others gloried in their humps and showed them to all the world; while a third group, 'timid and respectful cripples', wore voluminous cloaks to conceal their deformed contours. The hunchback metaphor makes uneasy reading. It says something for the complexity of his inner life that Berlin should have made such subliminal connections between Jewishness and deformity and yet openly declared his Jewishness to the end of his days.

A Jewish colleague at All Souls, Keith Joseph, later a minister in Mrs Thatcher's administration, reproached him for publishing the hunchback passage. Jews might think such thoughts, but uttering them was a betrayal of the tribe.[60] Berlin now felt embarrassed about his candour. He never allowed republication of 'Jewish Slavery and Emancipation' and it remains hidden in a forgotten *Festschrift*.

The essay had one important sequel. In it Isaiah had made a glancing reference to T.S. Eliot, including him as one of those 'fearful thinkers', 'those souls filled with terror' who sought to place Jews 'beyond the borders of the city' because their critical and discontented spirit jeopardised the unity of European Christian civilisation.[61] This critical reference to Eliot was somewhat surprising, since Isaiah had known the poet since the early 1930s, admired him deeply as a poet and had written for Eliot's quarterly magazine *Criterion*.[62] After the war, Eliot had occasionally consulted him on philosophical manuscripts sent in to Faber. In December 1948 Eliot had been awarded the Nobel Prize for Literature.

Berlin's view of Eliot changed as controversy about the poet's opinions began to emerge. In 1950 Emmanuel Litvinoff, a Jewish poet and man of letters, read to a London audience, which included Eliot and Stephen Spender, a poem entitled 'To T.S. Eliot', which took the poet to task for his references to the Jewish people. After Litvinoff had finished reading his work, Stephen Spender rose to defend his friend against accusations of anti-Semitism. Eliot himself, his head bowed, was heard to mutter, 'It's a good poem, a very good poem.'[63] Thus a controversy about the exact nature of Eliot's opinions was already under way when the editor of *The Jewish Chronicle* sent Eliot a copy of 'Jewish Slavery and Emancipation' after it appeared in its pages in October 1951.

In a letter to Berlin in November 1951, Eliot began by insisting that he had never advocated mass migration of the Jews out of the Diaspora and that for him 'the Jewish problem is not a racial problem at all, but a religious problem'.[64] Isaiah would not let the matter drop. Was it not the case, he replied, that in the lectures delivered at the University of Virginia in 1934 and later published as *After Strange Gods*, Eliot had said that a modern society could not achieve cultural and spiritual unity so long as there were Jews in its midst? He quoted Eliot's words back to him: 'reasons of race and religion make any large number of free-thinking Jews undesirable'.[65] So much for Eliot's insistence that 'race' had nothing to do with the 'Jewish problem'. After pointedly referring to the fact that these lectures were delivered a year after Hitler came to power, Isaiah accepted that Eliot had never advocated 'methods of barbarism', but he went on:

Am I profoundly mistaken if I think that, at any rate in 1934, you thought it a pity that large groups of 'free thinking Jews' should complicate the lives of otherwise fairly homogeneous Anglo-Saxon Christian communities? and that it were better otherwise? and that if this could be done by humane means, and persuasion and without coercion, it would be better for such communities if their Jewish neighbours, or a sufficiently large proportion of them, were put 'beyond the borders of the city'?

Eliot's reply apologised for the dubious sentence in the 1934 Virginia lectures, 'the sentence of which you complain (with justice) would of course never have appeared at all at that time, if I had been aware of what was going to happen, indeed had already begun, in Germany ... I still do not understand why the word "race" occurs in the sentence, because my emphasis was on the adjective "free-thinking".[66] Eliot was unwilling to abandon the word 'race' altogether – there might be something in the idea of 'racial inferiority' and 'superiority' after all, he said, if understood merely as a way of saying that some cultures and societies had proven more successful than others. But whether or not Jews were a race, they certainly were a culture and, in his view, cultures could not survive without a religious backbone. The key question, therefore, was whether Jewish religion could or should survive:

> From a Christian point of view, the Jewish Faith is finished, because it finds its continuation in the Catholic Faith. Theoretically, the only proper consummation is that all Jews should become Catholic Christians. The trouble is, that this ought to have happened long ago: partly because of the stiff neckedness of your people; and largely – perhaps chiefly, the apportionment is not immediately relevant – because of the misbehaviour of those who called themselves Christians, this did not happen.

Secularisation, Eliot went on, was unlikely to bring peace between Christians and Jews. If both discarded their faith, Jews would still be on the outside looking in. For the Gentile majority would always remain within an essentially Christian culture, while the Jewish minority that abandons its religion would find no home within Christian culture. 'This is what my adjective "free-thinking" implies,' he continued. In a secular modern culture, the Jews were condemned to an eternity of alienation, discontent and self-dislike. He concluded:

> The only possibilities are: that Jews should maintain their own culture by maintaining their own religion (and I do not see why

there should not be Jewish communities in a Western civilisation) or else that they should be assimilated completely – affirming that the only real assimilation would be by acceptance of Christianity.

Berlin did not reply to this – but he had already indicated in 'Jewish Slavery' that total assimilation (that is, abandonment of the Jewish faith) was impossible. So there was nothing more to say. Feeling that he did not want to associate Eliot with Koestler's views and not wishing to offend the poet, Berlin removed all reference to Eliot in the version of the essay when it appeared in an Israeli *Festschrift*. Much later in life, he felt that his politeness had shaded into obsequiousness.[67]

Beyond these concessions to good manners, Berlin did not give ground on the substance of the difference between them. The divide was not merely between a secular Jew and a believing Anglo-Catholic, but between a liberal individualist and a conservative with an abiding conviction that individualism was corroding European civilisation. Isaiah's Jewishness made it as evident to him, as it was to Eliot, that individuals must have secure cultural belonging if they are to be genuinely free. A Jew whose culture has vanished around him is no longer free to be a Jew. To this degree he could share something with Eliot. He could see, as Eliot did, that individuals in modern societies were incorrigibly divided about the nature of the good and that the faiths men professed were in irremediable contention. In place of cultural unity there was now an irreducible conflict between competing human goods.[68] For Eliot, this was a matter of regret; for Isaiah, an unchangeable fact about the modern world, indeed about human life as such, and one that he was to make the central focus of his later work.

13

Cold War, 1949–53

In January 1949 Berlin took up the first of a quarter-century of part-time appointments at American universities. Just as he had to make his peace with Israel, so he had to make his peace with America. He was attached to the Russian Research Center at Harvard and, besides pursuing his own research on the Russian intelligentsia, was supposed to teach an undergraduate course on Russian thought. Maurice Bowra, who had been at Harvard a short time earlier giving the Norton Lectures, wrote Isaiah a teasing letter about his instructional duties:

> In that admirable publication 'Courses of Instruction' p. 161 under 'International and Regional Studies' I see that Mr Berlin of Oxford University will lecture on 'The Development of Revolutionary Ideas in Russia' on Mon, Wed and Fri at 9. Now 9 in this country means 9 a.m. and Monday is Monday all the world over. No doubt you have given thought to this, but I feel it my duty to point it out.[1]

For a middle-aged Oxford don used to the semi-ecclesiastical splendour of College dinners, it must have been a lowering experience to stand in line with a tray in the Lowell House cafeteria in a queue of teenage Americans. At first, Isaiah was miserable. He struggled through his lecture course in an agony of self-consciousness: avoiding the serried stares of his listeners and fixing his eyes on the ceiling over their heads.

He burrowed into Widener Library, dug deep into Russian sources, but missed London society and, after the excitement of his Washington years, felt that Cambridge, Massachusetts, was flat and monochromatic. His students didn't seem to know how to read or write, at least 'not as these activities are understood at our best universities'. Their thoughts came out higgledy-piggledy, from the 'buzzing, booming confusion of their minds'.[2] The worst seemed deaf to irony, while the best seemed beset with guilt. He thought their guilt about the uselessness of art and scholarship was just another form of philistinism.

The contrast between the tormented moral language of the Russian intellectuals he was reading about in Widener and the blandly psychological discourse of the eager young American undergraduates he met at dinner in Lowell House gave him food for thought. They seemed baffled by the idea that life's essential problems might not always be soluble. The more Berlin thought about it, the more this seemed to be a central symptom of the age. 'All misery or evil [is] considered,' he wrote, 'as a bad state, a species of psychological malaise, needing in the first place a remedy.'[3] But this was to misunderstand what made life worth living. When this culture of therapy was linked to energetic social welfarism – in Attlee's Britain and Truman's America – the result was soulless social conformity.

Something was germinating in his mind, but for the moment he registered only the dreariness of post-war American academe. His colleagues at the Russian Research Center spent their time 'deducing unexciting conclusions from devious and suspect material'. In letters to E.H. Carr and Alan Bullock, Isaiah wrote scathingly about the positivist pedantry of American social science.[4] He probably had not read much of it, but this did not prevent him from remarking that American academics wrote with all the grace of a deep-sea diver sitting down to a dinner party.[5]

As the months passed, he made friends and his spirits lifted. As in London, his social acumen never deserted him. The grandest Boston hostesses – Mrs Warren and Mrs Chandler – invited him to their afternoon teas. Unlike London, where talk at a society dinner table was often racy and amusing, Boston high-society talk was a parody of Henry James.[6]

He had more to say to Merle Fainsod, the Harvard political scientist who specialised in the governance of the Soviet Union; the great Italian scholar and anti-fascist hero, Gaetano Salvemeni, then working in the next office in Widener Library; Irving Singer, a young philosophy graduate student; Elliot Perkins, master of Lowell House; Perry Miller, the brilliant author of *The New England Mind*; and Arthur Schlesinger Jr., a young American historian just achieving fame for his *Age of Jackson*.[7] Schlesinger, whom Berlin had first met in Washington during the war, became a close friend: they were both gregarious liberals, avid for gossip and intrigue, impatient with academe, fascinated with power and influence.

On every available weekend, he took the train down to Washington to revisit his old haunts. In just three years, the atmosphere in the city had changed. The Churchill-Roosevelt Grand Alliance was just a memory: Truman and Attlee had quarrelled openly about Palestine, and Britain's fall from grace in American eyes was only too evident. In place of the naïve self-confidence that Isaiah had so admired, there was a new mood of morose self-doubt about the communist threat. In January 1949 communist troops seized Peking and by midsummer most of China was in communist hands. In Washington 'Who lost China?' was the question of the hour, and the hunt for scapegoats – fellow-travellers, Marxist intellectuals, spies in government agencies – was already under way. Berlin's old friends were gloomy and, in Joe Alsop's case, convinced that the republic's days were numbered.[8]

Disaster had overtaken Edward Prichard. He had been convicted for ballot-stuffing in a Democratic election in Kentucky in 1948, and despite the intercession of his powerful Washington friends, had lost his appeal and was serving time in a federal penitentiary. He wrote poignant letters to Isaiah admitting his guilt and lamenting the hubris of youth.[9]

In May 1949 Isaiah travelled out to Wellfleet on Cape Cod to renew his acquaintance with the critic Edmund Wilson. Berlin had admired *Axel's Castle* and the two men had first met over lunch at the Princeton Club in New York in the spring of 1946. Isaiah was fascinated by Wilson's appearance, 'thickset, red-faced, pot-bellied . . . not unlike President Hoover', and by his extraordinary vehemence. He spoke 'in a curiously strangled voice, with gaps between his sentences, as if ideas jostled and thrashed about inside him'.[10] Berlin thought Wilson's political ideas were sometimes mad – for example, his intransigent isolationism during the war – but he admired his intellectual seriousness, and the fearless way he plunged into new languages (Hebrew and Russian, for example), when setting off on a new project. Wilson was intrigued by Berlin's 'double Russian – and British – personality', and by the end of a breathless weekend of non-stop argument, interspersed with some heavy drinking by Wilson, they had become enduring friends.[11]

Before he returned to England that summer, Isaiah gave a lecture at Mount Holyoke College in eastern Massachusetts on 'Democracy, Communism and the Individual'. He had warmed to American undergraduates and was now writing to English friends about how agreeable it was to sit like a bishop at confirmation surrounded by 'hundreds of very serious young women in blue jeans, moccasins [and] white socks'. They reminded him of the Russian intellectual women of 1880, who, when asked what they did, replied, 'I walk and think.'[12]

The root of communism, he told these serious young women, lay in the eighteenth-century belief – expressed in its most extreme form by Rousseau – that there was one right way for human beings to live. This belief, he went on, 'denies that different ideals of life' might not be 'altogether reconcilable with each other'; liberty, equality and fraternity, for example, were 'beautiful but incompatible'.[13] Communism had inherited this faith and Stalin's 'engineers of human souls' had sought to mould human beings into identical shapes. This same utopian temptation also threatened Western democracies, wherever planners believed that there must be one answer for all questions, and wherever experts conceived of society as 'one vast hospital' and interpreted all human discontent as maladjustment. Democracy, he told the undergraduates, did not mean rule by planners and experts, but by citizens.

Having delivered this worthy but hardly incendiary sermon, Berlin was appalled to read in the *New York Times* the next day that he had been urging American universities to take up Marxist studies. The story was buried on the inside pages and later editions dropped it altogether, but Isaiah wrote a nervous letter to the editor insisting that he had been misunderstood. Marxism should certainly be taught in American universities, but only by teachers 'sufficiently critical to take account of the errors and distortions in which Marxism abounds'.[14] Then he wrote to the Provost of Harvard assuring him that he was not a communist fellow-traveller and asked George Kennan at the State Department to write a reassuring note to the FBI liaison officer at State.[15] Kennan duly informed the FBI that his friend 'was probably the greatest and wisest student of Soviet affairs in the whole Anglo-Saxon world'. After a week, Isaiah wrote shamefacedly to Alice James:

> I am indeed anti-communist, but perhaps when heretics are being burnt right and left it is not the bravest thing in the world to declare one's loyalty to the burners, particularly when one disapproves of the Inquisition.[16]

The inquisition was indeed under way – a US Congressional Committee was investigating supposed communists in academe and the defence industries; Senator McCarthy was just about to begin his sinister career. Alger Hiss had been dismissed from the State Department as a security risk and was being dragged through the courts. All of Isaiah's closest friends – the Frankfurters, the Alsops, the Schlesingers – were appalled at the poisonous atmosphere of intimidation and denunciation. It seems obvious that Isaiah was panicked by this atmosphere: he had been prudent, but he had hardly been brave.

Although he sided with American liberals, he knew their battles were not really his. While the Frankfurters contributed to the Hiss defence, Isaiah maintained a degree of detachment towards the case which taxed their patience. On a weekend in Washington he reportedly said to Mrs Alice Roosevelt Longworth that he thought Hiss was 'a little guilty and a little innocent', and Mrs Longworth promptly repeated this remark in Marion Frankfurter's hearing. When Mrs Frankfurter took him to task, Isaiah, now back in Oxford, replied that the battles of the Cold War seemed far away. He was happy to be safe within the monastery walls, 'sublimely unaware of the outside world'.[17]

He did not refuse all gestures of solidarity. When Robert Oppenheimer, director of the Institute for Advanced Study at Princeton, was denied a security clearance because of his alleged communist sympathies, Isaiah joined others in writing letters of protest. But he remained aloof. In June 1951 Guy Burgess bolted to the Soviet Union; while other friends professed shock and moral dismay, Isaiah remained unperturbed, though he was more irritated than pleased when in 1953 Burgess sent a cheeky note from Moscow, via Roy Harrod, conveying his regards.[18]

Berlin gave every assistance to Peter Wright, the 'spy catcher' from British Intelligence, who called in search of any other accomplices Burgess might have had inside academe or the Establishment. Burgess' defection did sow panic among his English friends, especially Goronwy Rees, who had been a particularly close friend in the late 1930s.[19] After Burgess' defection, Rees lived in terror that he would be denounced as a spy – which he was not. In 1956, in a confused attempt both to clear himself and mount a pre-emptive strike at what he feared might be a campaign of denunciation and defamation by Burgess himself, Rees collaborated with a popular tabloid, *The People*, in writing a wild denunciation of the Foreign Office as a nest of fellow-travellers and spies. In this piece, he suggested that Berlin might have been working unwittingly for Burgess.[20] Berlin wrote him an icy note making it clear that he never 'became a member of any organisation Guy was working for. Nor have I ever been sent on any secret mission anywhere by anyone; nor was I Guy's assistant.' Even here, angry as he was with Rees, he eventually re-established their friendship and, as for Burgess' treachery, while Berlin certainly did not look Burgess up when he visited Moscow in 1956, he never disavowed his friendship.

This aloofness from the intense intellectual and emotional conflicts of the Cold War struck Albert Einstein when he met Berlin at Princeton in March 1952. Frankfurter had provided a fulsome letter of introduction and the two talked amiably enough in Einstein's study about Soviet foreign policy. Afterwards, Einstein wrote to Frankfurter that Isaiah seemed to him like a highly intelligent 'spectator in God's big but mostly not very attractive theater'.[21] Isaiah's reaction to Einstein was equivocal. He was a genius, but in political matters he seemed an innocent. Einstein seemed to suppose that no decent man could have enemies on the left. Psychologically, he was inaccessible, with – as Isaiah reported to Vera Weizmann – 'the inhumanity of a child'.[22] Berlin wondered whether a genius for pure abstraction could only be cultivated at the expense of any 'close personal relationship'. But there were two aspects of Einstein's thought which made an indelible impression, or at least accorded deeply with Berlin's central commitments. One was his 'sense of reality'. There was only one world, Berlin wrote of Einstein, and this was 'the world of human experience; it alone was real'. This sense of reality – that the world was as it seems, and that it could be known by patient and careful research – was the only sure guarantee against ideological intoxication. The second aspect of Einstein's thought which appealed deeply was that he managed to reconcile a consistent internationalism and a hatred of nationalism with a steady commitment to Zionism. By his very being, Einstein seemed to demonstrate that you could be both a Zionist and a cosmopolitan, and as Berlin sought to reconcile these opposing tendencies within himself, Einstein's example was a reassurance and an inspiration.

In the autumn of 1949 Berlin gave a talk on BBC radio on the 'Anglo-American predicament', which showed how deeply he had been affected by his sojourn in the United States and how thoroughly Anglo-American his essential loyalties had become. He insisted that Britain must recognise that its ultimate interests lay neither with the empire nor with Europe, but with the United States. The article has a ring of prescience in its acceptance of British decline and American hegemony. But it angered both right and left. Lord Beaverbrook, who must have been offended that Berlin had turned down his offer to work for him, now took his revenge in the form of an unsigned piece in the *Evening Standard*, which tore into him for his defeatism about the empire and his subservience towards the Americans.[23] Isaiah's views were hardly more popular on the left. Both Harold Laski and Isaiah's Oxford colleague G.D.H. Cole disliked the unwelcome thought that a commitment to the American capitalist camp precluded too much socialist collectivism at home.

The middle ground became more tenuous still with the publication of Berlin's panegyric to Churchill in 1949.[24] 'Winston Churchill in 1940' is deservedly famous as one of the essays that created the Churchillian myth. It was a brilliant examination, both ironic and admiring, of the structure of Churchillian rhetoric: how an archaic and baroque prose style was self-consciously forged in order to align the Churchillian persona with the grand sweep of English history, and how his speeches created the flattering mirror of myth in which the English people could see their best features heroically enhanced. Since Isaiah's own emerging prose style was self-consciously archaic – a superbly personal pastiche of the rolling periods of Macaulay and Carlyle – his remarks on the rhetoric of archaic ponderousness as a form of psychological defence mechanism can be read autobiographically. 'Since we think largely in words,' he remarks at one point, 'they necessarily take on the property of serving as an armour.'[25] Since his own writing triggered understandable anxieties about commitment, self-disclosure and inauthenticity, he was fascinated by Churchill's armour, by his artistic ability to create adamantine moral conviction in the face of chaos without and darkness within. It was the intensity of Isaiah's own identification with the Churchillian project of creating a believable rhetoric that raised the article above political hagiography.

But hagiography is what his left-wing friends took it to be. Half of the country had voted Churchill out of office in 1945 and regarded him as a reactionary relic. In 1949 an election beckoned. Churchill was about to lead the Conservative attack on the Attlee record, and here was a supposed liberal singing his praises as the 'largest human being of our time'. Harold Laski, the leading intellectual within the Labour Party, wrote two angry letters attacking Isaiah for failing to mention Churchill's 'lack of magnanimity, his power to be meanly aggressive, his long-term capacity for revenge' and his 'coarse and often malignant brutality'.[26] Isaiah did not pay much heed to this: he regarded Laski as a myth-making mediocrity. But it was less easy to be rebuked by his old friend Rachmilievitch. It did not matter that 'Rach' was now entering a twilight of depression and mental illness from which he never recovered. On this occasion, he was stingingly accurate:

> It is not the business of a member of the Labour party to write an 'objective' account about the role of Churchill, it is after all not an obituary, it is a heroisation of the still alive and acting Churchill, appearing 2 months before the election.[27]

Rachmilievitch's mistake was to assume that his old friend was a Labour supporter. While Berlin had voted for Labour in the landslide of 1945, he had good reason to loathe Labour for their stubborn refusal to grant a Jewish state in Palestine and was never comfortable with the mixture of 'minor public school morality', Methodist unction and technocratic busy-bodying which served as the well-springs of Labour activism.[28] Compared to this, Churchill seemed both grand and life-enhancing. Isaiah particularly enjoyed a Churchillian remark reported to him by his friend John Sparrow. When Sparrow had mired conversation in some abstruse academic complexity, the great man had cut him short 'Do not darken counsel, young man.'[29]

Churchill's own reaction to Berlin's fulsome praise took some time in coming. William Deakin laid it on his desk and waited for Churchill to make a comment. Finally, getting none, he prompted Churchill and the old man winked and growled, 'Too good to be true.'[30]

Berlin and Churchill met in December 1949 at Oliver Lyttelton's house. By then the Irving Berlin story had entered political lore and Churchill bowed his head and said that Mr Berlin must be aware of the 'solecism' he had been so unfortunate to commit in his regard.[31] Churchill was then absorbed in his own painting and he strode from room to room, peering at every picture, commenting loudly on the technique and the brush-strokes, while an eddy of dinner guests followed nervously behind. At the dinner table, he made a remark that Isaiah reported to Vera Weizmann with obvious approval: 'Never mind whether the choices are good or bad; what we must have is a great multiplicity of them and not a miserable grey on grey.'[32]

Since, only too evidently, Labour was the 'miserable grey on grey', Isaiah's vote in the elections of 1950 ought to have been a foregone conclusion. In fact he admired Churchill but never actually liked him. At the same dinner, the old lion roared that he was looking forward to returning to power and pitching into the fight with Stalin. With real ferocity, he said he thought both Italy and France might fall to the communists, and he contemplated the possibility of renewed war in Europe with obvious delight. Berlin was both enthralled and repelled. 'He was too coarse, too brutal, and I didn't want him back in.' So he voted for the Liberals instead.[33]

In convictions he was a liberal social democrat, but he was more comfortable socially among Conservatives. He tried to have it both ways and, inevitably, this opened him to charges of being two-faced. But here too he was a fox who longed to be a hedgehog. What he admired about Churchill, after all, was his adamantine firmness of purpose and hedgehog-like consistency. But how could a liberal outsider hope to be a hedgehog?

Out of this inner tension, this drive to find a core of belief, even if it stood betwixt and between, came Berlin's longest and most significant essay to date: 'Political Ideas in the Twentieth Century', published in

Foreign Affairs in the spring of 1950. The essay can be read as a Cold War text, as a Western liberal's defence of freedom against the Soviet threat. But it made more uncomfortable reading than that. Both Soviet Marxism and post-war Western social democracy were prey to the same twentieth-century rationalist illusion: that, with sufficient social engineering, human evils could be abolished and individuals happily assimilated into a seamless social consensus. To be sure, Soviet Marxism was more ruthless in its contempt for democracy and human rights. But Western liberals could not remain complacent. The human desire to be relieved of the burden of choice might lead the West to hand the dilemmas of public and private life over to experts, politicians, psychotherapists and other 'engineers of human souls'. In an anticipation of what Daniel Bell was to call 'the end of ideology', Isaiah observed that fundamental disagreement about political and moral ends had been displaced by a technical disagreement about means. This technocratic style of politics displaced moral disagreement: it did not resolve it. In fact, beneath a bland managerial consensus, ardently opposed principles continued to contend. Having condemned modernity for bland managerial consensus, Berlin now – rather contradictorily – criticised its shrill polarisation. 'Liberals with a taste for private life' and a distaste for organised political movements were 'despised by all the embattled parties in the great ideological wars of our time'.[34]

In these wars, he belonged on the liberal left, but he warned his own side that their goals were in conflict. For every supposed gain in social justice there might be a corresponding loss of freedom. This conflict between ends was bound to defy smooth managerial solutions. The best that could be hoped for was some 'logically untidy, flexible and even ambiguous compromise'. What the age calls for, Isaiah concluded, 'is not (as we are often told) more faith, or stronger leadership, or more scientific organisation. Rather it is the opposite – less Messianic ardour, more enlightened scepticism, more toleration of idiosyncrasies.' Fighting injustice was essential, but men 'do not live only by fighting evils'. They live by choosing their own goals – a vast variety of them, seldom predictable, at times incompatible'. It was individual freedom, to choose well or ill, which had to be defended, not some ultimate vision of the human good. Since no disposition was faultless, no disposition was final. His motto in politics, he concluded, was: *surtout pas trop de zèle*.

The left's reaction was predictable. E.H. Carr, writing later in *The Times*, remarked that a thinker who warned against the dangers of strong belief was unlikely to believe anything very much at all.[35] The reaction on the centre right was more enthusiastic. The powerful publisher of *Time* magazine, Henry R. Luce, and the editor of the *Washington Post*, Herbert Elliston, wrote to congratulate Berlin on his *Foreign Affairs* article, but both wished there had been a more ringing expression of faith in Western democracy.[36] When Elliston wrote to ask him to pen a credo for Cold War liberals, Isaiah replied ironically:

> Certainly I do not think that the answer to communism is a counter faith, equally fervent, militant etc.; because one must fight the devil with the devil's weapons. To begin with, nothing is less likely to create a 'faith' than perpetual reiteration of the fact that we are looking for one, must find one, are lost without one etc. etc.[37]

Other friends, like the Russian *émigré* composer Nicolas Nabokov, believed in a militant cultural crusade against the communist threat, and when the American Central Intelligence Agency began funding the Congress of Cultural Freedom, Nabokov became its secretary in Paris. The Congress' activities included covert funding of *Encounter* magazine, founded in 1953 by Stephen Spender and Irving Kristol; *Tempo Presente* in Italy, edited by Nicolo Chiaromonte; *Preuves* in Paris; and *Der Monat* in Germany.[38] Berlin certainly knew all the major figures in these Cold War publications, as well as people like Michael Josselson, who were active agents of the CIA in Europe. He also had no difficulty, then or later, in thinking of himself as a Cold War intellectual. But he certainly had no official or unofficial relationship with either British Intelligence or the CIA, and he had no foreknowledge that the CIA was covertly funding the magazines to which he contributed, though he may have heard rumours and may have had his suspicions. As he later explained, 'I did not in the slightest object to American sources supplying the money – I was (and am) pro-American and anti-Soviet, and if the source had been declared I would not have minded in the least ... What I and others like me minded very much was that a periodical which claimed to be independent, over and over again, turned out to be in the pay of

American secret Intelligence.'[39] But this did not become public knowledge until 1967. Until then, Berlin contributed to *Encounter*, but it would be far-fetched to regard the studies of the Russian intelligentsia, which he published there between 1954 and 1956, as blows in the ideological struggle.[40]

Nor were his *Foreign Affairs* articles simply pieces of Cold War propaganda. They were serious attempts to understand the totalitarian temptation in the twentieth century as a whole and, while they gained a wide and influential readership, some of his more *engagé* friends like Charles Bohlen felt they failed to denounce the evils of communism with sufficient energy.[41] George Kennan, the architect and philosopher of America's post-war policy of containment towards the Soviet Union, praised 'Political Ideas in the Twentieth Century' as 'one of the really important statements about our own times', but felt the concluding condemnation of the Soviet Union was too perfunctory.[42] He observed correctly that what Berlin loathed about fascism and communism was their moral cynicism, their shared contempt for ordinary human beings. Both had sought to indoctrinate men into abandoning their faith in their own judgement. Kennan's letter drew from Berlin one of his most thoughtful expressions of his convictions. He agreed with Kennan that the core of his moral outlook lay in a fierce dislike of attempts to deny human beings their right to moral sovereignty. Communism and fascism alike were guilty of this in the very way they sought to indoctrinate their adherents and liquidate their enemies. He dwelt at length on the most sombre example: how Nazi executioners had deceived Jews into peacefully going to their deaths by reassuring them that the cattle cars were taking them towards 're-settlement' in the East:

Why does this deception, which may in fact have diminished the anguish of the victims, arouse a really unutterable kind of horror in us? . . . Surely because we cannot bear the thought of human beings denied their last rights – of knowing the truth, of acting with at least the freedom of the condemned, of being able to face their destruction with fear or courage, according to their temperaments, but at least as human beings, armed with the power of choice.[43]

There was, he came to see, a continuum of denials of the human right to know one's fate and they could lead, he now saw, to the gas chamber. The Holocaust was not solely responsible for fixing this theme at the centre of his thought thereafter. A confluence of pressures put it there: rising moral distaste for the Marxist theory of false consciousness and the Soviet 'engineers of human souls'. But anti-communist conviction alone was insufficient to account for the vehemence, consistency and determination with which he defended the embattled sovereignty of private judgement and the right of human beings to know their fate and meet it with their eyes open. Here Auschwitz did play a subliminal part. It was the thought of his own people, indecently deceived, going blindly to their deaths, which turned a theme into a conviction, an idea into a commitment.

The fox had discovered that he was a hedgehog after all. He had found 'the one big thing' that was to order his intellectual life thereafter: the theme of freedom and its betrayal. In 1950 and 1951 he read furiously the works of the *philosophes*: Diderot, Helvetius, Holbach, La Mettrie, Voltaire; he also began, for the first time, reading German Romanticism: Schelling, Herder, Fichte. In February and March 1952 he gave the Mary Flexner Lectures 'On Political Ideas in the Romantic Age' at Bryn Mawr College in Pennsylvania. Here, for the first time, he began to assemble his historical vision of the transition between Enlightenment and Romantic ideals of freedom.

The Enlightenment *philosophes*, he told the Bryn Mawr undergraduates, assumed that human values could be derived from facts about human nature. They believed that all men wanted the same things and that these things were not in conflict. The entire Western agenda of ameliorative reform derived from this optimistic rationalism. Berlin's dilemma was how to rescue what was positive in the Enlightenment project from what was tyrannous. What was positive was clear enough: the attack on religious authority and dogma; the campaign for human rights and personal freedom against state tyranny; the faith in human reason itself. In these respects, Isaiah himself was Voltairian to the core. He could see, however, that Enlightenment rationalism was deeply flawed. Human values could not be securely derived from human nature. This was what the Romantic thinkers had understood. Values were created by men in their struggle to master themselves, their society and the natural world. Values, therefore, were historical, relative to the cultures that engendered them and contradictory, since human nature itself was contradictory.

Enlightenment rationalism supposed that conflicts between values were a heritage of mis-education or injustice and could be swept away by rational reforms, by indoctrinating individuals into believing that their individual interests could be fully realised by working exclusively for the common good. Both Rousseau and Robespierre envisaged just such a state, in which freedom was experienced as submission to rational necessity.

In the four Bryn Mawr lectures, he set out the distinction he was later to make famous between negative and positive liberty. Only at this stage, he called them 'liberal' and 'romantic'.[44] Until Rousseau, liberty had always been understood negatively, as the absence of obstacles to courses of thought and action. With Rousseau, and then with the Romantics, came the idea of liberty being achieved only when men are able to realise their innermost natures. Liberty became synonymous with self-creation and self-expression. A person who enjoyed negative liberty – freedom of action or thought – might none the less lack positive liberty, the capacity to develop his or her innermost nature to the full.

Berlin evidently approved of the ideals of self-realisation. The danger lay in the idea, latent in Enlightenment rationalism and Romanticism alike, that men might be so blinded to their true natures – by ignorance, custom or injustice – that they could only be 'freed' by those revolutionaries or social engineers who understood their objective needs better than they did themselves:

> This is one of the most powerful and dangerous arguments in the entire history of human thought. Let us trace its steps again. Objective good can be discovered only by the use of reason; to impose it on others is only to activate the dormant reason within them; to liberate people is to do just that for them which, were they rational, they would do for themselves, no matter what they in fact say they want; therefore some forms of the most violent coercion are tantamount to the most absolute freedom.[45]

To free a man, Isaiah insisted, was to free him from obstacles – prejudice, tyranny, discrimination – to the exercise of his own free choice. It did not mean telling him how to use his freedom.

There is little here that Berlin claimed was original. The tyrannous fallacies of Enlightenment rationalism had been denounced since Kant; and among his modern contemporaries, Karl Popper and Jacob Talmon had also traced the totalitarianism of the twentieth century to Rousseau.[46] What was distinctive was Berlin's emphasis on human dividedness: the self was torn by competing impulses; the ends and goals that human beings pursued were in conflict. Berlin made human dividedness, both inner and outer, the very rationale for a liberal polity. A free society was a good society because it accepted the conflict among human goods and maintained, through its democratic institutions, the forum in which this conflict could be managed peacefully.

Both public and private choice had to take place in the absence of certainties. The compromises that made liberal society viable were rarely painless and sometimes they involved real damage and harm. Is it true, he pointedly asked, 'that all tragedy is merely due to error, fallibility, that all questions are answerable, that all ills are in principle always curable, that everything must come out well in the end . . .?'[47] Tragedy was intrinsic to choice because all choice entailed significant loss.

He had few brushes with tragedy himself, but he did have a deep sense of inner dividedness. His deepest loyalties were not conveniently layered one on top of the other. They were in conflict, and their resolution was painful and protracted. What made him magnetic company for his friends – his labile, multi-faceted self – was in fact sharply divided: a fox who longed to be a hedgehog; a solitary thinker who longed for society; a liberal, often torn by the displeasure his middle course earned him from friends on the left and right. This helps to explain the unique acuteness with which he zeroed in on the Enlightenment fallacy that each of us harboured a single, unproblematic inner nature from which our values and our interests could be deduced.

This was history of ideas in the service of philosophical world view. His method was high abstraction and grand synthesis. He focused on what the Oxford philosopher R.G. Collingwood called 'the absolute pre-suppositions' of both Enlightenment and Romantic modes of thought. He believed in striding right into the citadel of a thinker's assumptions, seizing the ruling concept and ignoring the earthworks of qualification and elaboration. The project was highly ambitious, but also drastically abstract. The whole complex and contradictory phenomenon of the Enlightenment was reduced to a single set of propositions about freedom; the Romantic movement was similarly simplified. While his work on the Russian intelligentsia displayed an unerring sense of context, nuance and difference between one thinker and the next, his pursuit of the distinction between Enlightenment and Romantic modes of thought drastically over-simplified the antithesis.

His lecturing style of grand generalisation did not always satisfy scholars, and it did not always satisfy him, but it proved enormously successful as broadcasting. Since 1946 he had developed a friendship with Anna ('Niouta') Kallin, a brilliant and sardonic radio-talks producer of Russian-Jewish extraction, who had grown up in the Russian emigration in Berlin and had been a mistress of the fiery expressionist painter Oskar Kokoschka. After a war spent monitoring Russian broadcasts at the BBC monitoring station in Caversham, she had been recruited for Radio 3, the BBC's adventure in serious intellectual broadcasting, in 1946. She was an inspired producer of radio talks, a fearless exile who seemed to unite a British conception of public service with the Russian conception of the intellectual as a moral authority.[48] She was responsible for bringing an extraordinarily high-brow and difficult kind of talk to the post-war British air-waves: discussions between Graham Greene, Elizabeth Bowen and V.S. Pritchett on the role of the artist in society; Bertrand Russell and Father Copleston on the existence of God; Noel Annan on Lytton Strachey and his critics; and Berlin on Belinsky.

In the autumn of 1952, at Kallin's urging, he re-worked the four Flexner Lectures, which had been organised by topic, into six lectures on individual thinkers – from Helvétius to de Maistre – for BBC Third Programme for Radio 3. In order to maintain what he called 'the noble lie of spontaneity', he delivered each of the six hour-long talks extemporaneously from notes alone in the BBC studios at Broadcasting House. It was a terrifying experience, 'a kind of agonised bawling into a machine', but the reaction to this prodigious feat of studied verbal improvisation was admiring and even awed. Over six weeks in October and November 1952 hundreds of thousands of people tuned in, mostly from the educated middle classes, to listen to fiendishly difficult hour-long talks, delivered in a clipped, rapid-fire Oxford accent. These were the lectures that led Eliot, in his barbed way, to congratulate Isaiah for his 'torrential eloquence'; and the conservative philosopher Michael Oakeshott to praise him, in equally barbed fashion, as the 'Paganini of the platform'. Lydia Keynes – Maynard Keynes' widow – wrote to say that Isaiah's 'stammerings and stutterings' were 'cosy and appropriate' and the more conventional signs of public attention poured in: anonymous ladies knitted him red socks; cranks sent him manuscripts.[49] After it was over, he had his characteristic second thoughts, confessing to Marion Frankfurter that he was ashamed of 'broadcasting too much, too popularly'.[50] But he was also gratified and surprised by the response. The head of Radio 3 hailed the talks as a landmark in British broadcasting, and they were certainly a landmark in Berlin's life. The search to find his own intellectual vocation had been a central preoccupation since his return from the war. With the broadcast of 'Freedom and its Betrayal', that struggle resolved itself. The BBC provided him with a platform and a new audience. He had become a public intellectual – in the Russian mould, but in an English idiom.

Despite his radio success, university audiences were the ones that still mattered most. In the Auguste Comte Lecture at the London School of Economics in May 1953 – with Karl Popper and Michael Oakeshott in the audience – he mounted a sustained attack on doctrines of 'historical inevitability' in a paper entitled 'History as an Alibi'. The fame he had acquired from 'Freedom and its Betrayal' guaranteed a full turnout; his nervousness was increased by Oakeshott's barbed encomium to his skills as a lecturer; and he had ludicrously overprepared. The text was much too long for delivery and he began abridging it as he went, wildly putting pages aside, struggling to keep the argumentative thread together, talking in an ever faster, high-pitched gabble.[51] When he staggered to a conclusion, the reactions were perfunctory and he came away, not for the last time, with the uneasy feeling that his peers were asking themselves whether his reputation was deserved.

He re-worked the LSE lecture into a radio talk and then rounded it off in its final form as 'Historical Inevitability'. It is an impressive statement of his most fundamental beliefs.[52] He conceded that the realm in which human beings could be said to exercise freedom had been shown by modern science to be circumscribed. Biology, behavioural psychology and genetics had all underscored the extent to which human beings were subject to the laws of nature. But he insisted that the moral vocabulary that human beings everywhere employ was no less a fact about human nature. This vocabulary assumed that human beings were unique, among other species, in their capacity for moral choice. Such an assumption informed every feature of human language: it was not reasonable to suppose that such a pervasive and constitutive feature of discourse proceeded from an illusion that science was bound, one day, to disperse.

Human beings were not marionettes; they were not the playthings of vast impersonal forces; their behaviour and their mental universe might be shaped by their class position, their race, their gender or their cultural traditions, but as individuals they retained the capacity for moral choice, and to that extent they remained free of these determining factors. Hence, it was appropriate to praise or blame them for their historical conduct. Those who insisted that the historian's function was to understand rather than judge the past were wrong; as were those who maintained that the more we understood the past, the less we were able to apply our moral standards to the alien circumstances of the past. The relativist charter *Tout comprendre, c'est tout pardonner* was false. The function of historical understanding was to identify the precise range within which historical actors enjoyed room for manoeuvre, to understand how and why they used their freedom, and to evaluate their actions by the standard of what real alternatives were possible to them at the time.

'Historical Inevitability' was a defence of the intellectual as moralist, and therefore an apologia *pro sua vita*. But it was more. The political implications of the argument were that a society of free individuals and free institutions depended on the possibility of individual responsibility and free choice. People's willingness to defend liberal society could be undermined if they came to be cynical or sceptical about their own powers of moral agency, if they accepted a view of themselves as moral marionettes, as dupes and playthings of political manipulators. The various styles of determinism – historical, scientific, psychological – were doing just that, and they were seductive because they were comforting. The lure of deterministic theory, he told the LSE audience, lay in our 'desire to resign our responsibility, to cease from judging provided we be not judged ourselves and, above all, are not compelled to judge ourselves – from a desire to flee for refuge to some vast, amoral, impersonal, monolithic whole, nature, or history, or class, or race, or the "harsh realities of our time".[53]

There was nothing abstract about this insistence on facing up to personal responsibilities. For in his own life – as his intellectual views were assuming their mature shape – his dilemmas were becoming especially acute. In both his writing and his life, he had reached the moment of truth.

14

Late Awakening

In June 1949 he passed a gloomy fortieth birthday at Harvard. It was a 'dreadful hump to cross', he confessed. He found it difficult to admit that he had actually become an adult:

> I cannot quite think of myself as on the side of authority, judgement etc. and I hear myself chatter and the only excuse for it is that one is full of unsifted ideas and too chock-a-bloc to have time to think and too warm-blooded to reckon the consequences and so on, and this is absurd when one is viewed as an old bachelor.[1]

Despite a frantically busy social life, darting down on the train to society dinners in London, he was unsettled and late at night, when he returned to his rooms at New College, he was often lonely. He told close friends that he wanted to get married, but they found the idea hard to imagine. He seemed to take no interest in their children; lacked the most elementary domestic skills; and still remained tied to his parents. He celebrated the Jewish high holy days with them, visited them in Hollycroft Avenue, Hampstead, whenever he was in London and even took holidays in French hotels and German spas in their company.

Oxford colleges have always served as homes for permanently arrested adolescents. Safe in their embrace, he might well have remained a sexless don. But he knew this was no solution. His relationship with Patricia

Douglas had ignited strong, if unconsummated longings and he knew that flight into monastic seclusion was out of the question. She continued her infuriating and inflaming dance with him for well over four years after the war. When he was in Moscow she wrote longing letters, coquettishly scolding him for wrapping himself in the mystery of Russia; when he returned, he found she was deep in some new affair. They would make plans to go to the music festival in Aix-en-Provence and then she would fail to show up. As she careered in and out of affairs and marriages, now in Paris, now in Ireland, he would receive plaintive letters that made her seem irresistible. But when they were together, she would soon flee to a man who was more confidently sexual. The situation became intolerable and he found that he could only keep his balance by refusing to see her.

His emotional state in this period is laid bare by his translation of Ivan Turgenev's *First Love*.² It is the story of a boy's awakening to love, told in retrospect by a sadder and older man. In order to test his renderings into English, Isaiah enlisted the help of a beautiful friend, Shirley Morgan, then working at the Foreign Office. There are photographs of the two of them, lounging on an Oxford river bank or in a punt – Shirley in a light cotton print dress, Isaiah, heavy-set and formal in a three-piece suit, with a Hershey chocolate bar raised to cover his face from the photographer. With Shirley, Isaiah played the *curé* as usual: listening to the stories of her suitors, who included Freddie Ayer, whom he had warned her against, and the Marquis of Anglesey, whom she eventually married.³

Since *First Love* was a tender study of infatuation, its translation provided Isaiah with an indirect means of exploring his own feelings for Patricia. Was it right, he asked Shirley, to say that your heart 'turned over' when your loving glance was first returned? Or should he say the heart 'slipped its moorings'? While at Harvard, Isaiah actually consulted Vladimir Nabokov – then a research fellow in lepidoptera at the Harvard zoology department – on how to translate this particular passage. Nabokov's suggestion – 'my heart went pit a pat' – left Isaiah unimpressed. Finally, he settled on 'my heart leaped within me'.⁴

First Love tells the story of an adolescent swept into love and into adulthood by the force of his unrequited passion for a young woman who is older and more experienced than himself. As the story progresses, the young man discovers why the woman, Zinaida, refuses the deeper commitment he longs for. She is in fact in love with an older man. In the climactic scenes, he discovers who this older man is. One night, hidden in the shadows, he watches Zinaida and the man alone at an open window. They are talking when suddenly the boy realises that the man is his father. He then watches in horror as his father raises his horse-whip and strikes her bare arm. The watching boy's shock is intense: 'It was all I could do to prevent myself from crying out. Zinaida quivered – looked silently at my father – and raising her arm slowly to her lips, kissed the scar which glowed crimson upon it.'[5]

This is an unforgettable image of love in its maddest intensity. Isaiah's identification was with the watching boy: with his choked sense of being still trapped in adolescence, able to watch, but not to take part or even fully understand the passion of adults. It is not too much to say that *First Love* expresses all the anguish that he had felt years earlier in the New York hotel, listening to Patricia and her lover on the other side of the partition wall. The first edition of the translation, when it appeared in 1950, was dedicated to her. But it was a bitter kind of parting gift, for by then he knew that the affair was hopeless. In subsequent editions, he removed the inscription 'To P de B' (Patricia de Bendern) from the dedication page.

His experience with Patricia might have confirmed him – or imprisoned him – in the role of the sexless bachelor. But instead of marking the end of his erotic life, it was the beginning. For he fell out of love with Patricia in the most efficient of all available ways, by falling in love with someone else. His choice was surprising: a married woman with children, whom he had known since the 1930s. She was a vivacious, attractive, highly intelligent woman of strong political opinions, who had briefly been a communist before the war. Her marriage was enduring but unhappy. She was married to a brilliant, abstracted and otherworldly don. She was adventurous in her sexual life, and one might have expected that it was she who took the initiative. But this was not the case. He took to his bed with a cold in midsummer 1950, and when she came to take care of him, he pulled her down on to the bed. She was astonished and then moved that he could display such feelings. For him, the experience undammed a reservoir. The change was complete. At the relatively ripe old age of forty-one, he had begun adult sexual life. They started an intense affair in his college rooms, in her house, in fields and churchyards around Oxford and on one occasion, during their absence, in his parents' house in Hampstead. They had some close scrapes: colleagues, children and friends all came within inches of discovering them, but Isaiah seemed to relish the danger. He was a naïve rather than a sentimental lover, eager rather than accomplished, but capable, so she discovered, of intense physical tenderness. Behind the protective screen of brilliant talk, there was a capacity for intimacy that perhaps not even he had suspected.[6]

Isaiah never asked her to leave her husband, knowing that she would probably have refused. Very soon, however, *he* decided that he must tell him of his feelings. It must have been an excruciating moment: they were close friends and the man in question was decency personified. 'I'm in love with your wife,' Isaiah blurted out, to which the husband replied, 'That's not possible'. So the affair continued but Isaiah felt compelled to repeat his confession, and this time the husband came home – so she remembers – shaking his head and saying, 'Isaiah keeps going mad. He says *again* he's in love with you.'

Before the war Berlin had been censorious about the betrayals and subterfuges of his friends. By his own admission, he had been priggish in matters of personal relations. Now he was engaged in duplicities he had been quick to reprove in others. The experience knocked some of the priggishness out of him; made him less quick to judge and blame; more respectful of the tidal power of feeling, and more aware of the frailty of the locks and dams built to keep the tides in check.

The affair continued for several years, but Berlin's affections slowly began to transfer towards another woman, also married to an Oxford colleague, also with children. Aline Halban was a slim, sportive and aristocratic Frenchwoman in her late thirties, born into a distinguished section of the Jewish community of Paris. Her father was Baron Pierre de Gunzbourg, the Russian-born son of Baron Horace Gunzburg, an illustrious banker and philanthropist of pre-revolutionary St Petersburg. Her father had settled in Paris and had married the daughter of a Jewish family from Alsace, who had made their fortune in heating oil.[7] Aline grew up in a large family mansion in the Avenue d'Iéna in the 16th *arrondissement*. It was a significantly less observant Jewish household than Isaiah's. Aline grew up as an assimilated Parisian, conscious of her Russian and Jewish origins, but fundamentally French in language, culture and outlook.

Her sheltered life was rudely shattered just before the war by the death in quick succession of her sister, a brother, and her young husband. At the age of twenty-four, she was a widow with an infant son. Then the war came and the entire basis of French Jewish assimilation collapsed with the defeat of France. In 1940 she fled south to escape the Germans, lodging first in Biarritz and then in Nice. When the Vichy regime published its anti-Jewish edicts, she determined to escape and in early 1941 managed to reach New York, via a boat from Lisbon, with her son, soon followed by her parents.[8] On that boat had been Isaiah, on his way to his posting in New York. He had noticed the tall, elegant, shy woman and had wondered who she was.

They met again during the war in New York, through the auspices of the Rothschilds at a house in the Hamptons on Long Island. She was there to play golf with Cecile Rothschild. He thought, with a certain *frisson*, that she cut a fine figure. She was considerably less impressed: couldn't follow what Isaiah said, couldn't make out his age and thought he looked dumpy and unprepossessing in a crumpled white suit. They met again at the Hotel Pierre in New York some time later, and the same pattern repeated itself: she barely noticed him.

In 1943 she met Hans Halban, a physicist of Austrian extraction who had worked on the French nuclear programme and had escaped to America in 1940, carrying with him important information about the production of heavy water, a component in the manufacture of atomic weapons. He was then working on secret research for the Manhattan Project.[9] They were married and went to Montreal, where he directed a research laboratory for the duration of the war. In 1946, as Isaiah was about to leave America to return to Oxford, he met Aline again. Her marriage seemed to have crushed her. The accomplished and stylish woman he had met in 1942 was now meek, submissive and obviously unhappy, though she said nothing about it.

Hans Halban was invited to take up a post in Oxford and when they moved there in 1946, Isaiah became part of their life, taking Aline to concerts, dining at their house and gradually becoming a family friend. She felt at ease with him; he made her laugh and provided her with a safe and blameless escape from a marriage that was becoming more difficult by the year.

In 1949, when he went to Harvard, she was on the same boat heading to visit her mother, and they spent ten happy days together on a crossing which included Marietta and Ronald Tree and other friends. The trip became an adventure: the ship ran aground off Cherbourg and they didn't reach New York until twelve days later. It was on board ship that they became inseparable friends, yet even at this period, while she was increasingly unhappy in her marriage, the thought did not cross her mind that Isaiah might be a possible partner. The thought obviously never occurred to Hans Halban, who let her drive him across France to the Aix festival in the summer of 1952.

By mid-1953 Aline was coming to Isaiah's rooms at All Souls almost every day to work with him on a French translation of 'The Hedgehog and the Fox', then just in the process of appearing in the Weidenfeld and Nicolson edition. Weidenfeld had been shrewd enough to see the commercial potential locked up in an obscure essay, 'Lev Tolstoy's Historical Scepticism', which Isaiah had published in *Oxford Slavonic Papers* in 1951. By retitling it 'The Hedgehog and the Fox' and putting it out for a general readership with additions by Isaiah, Weidenfeld did more for Isaiah's public reputation than any other publisher. The essay concluded with the most memorable image of human anguish in Berlin's writings, his picture of Tolstoy at Astapovo:

> At once insanely proud and filled with hatred, omniscient and doubting everything, cold and violently passionate, contemptuous and self-abasing, tormented and detached, surrounded by an adoring family, by devoted followers, by the admiration of the entire civilised world, and yet almost wholly isolated, he is the most tragic of the great writers, a desperate old man, beyond human aid, wandering self-blinded at Colonus.[10]

As Aline and Isaiah worked together on the translation of this, the most compelling of all his essays, they came still closer together. He was spontaneous and phenomenally agile of mind, but also affectionate and full of life. She felt that early deaths – of her sister, her husband and a brother who died as a young conscript before the war – had left her frozen. Isaiah seemed capable of thawing her out.

But still she could see how different they were: despite a common Jewishness, she was Parisian French and aristocratic; he a Russian Jew from the commercial classes. As she once said: 'I was Western Europe; he was Eastern Europe.'[11]

He could sense that she was withdrawn, that she had developed a protective shell. He called her the 'odalisque': an ambiguous compliment, which praised her beauty while expressing perplexity at her melancholy passivity. As he wrote to a friend, 'I like her very much. She is beautifully bred and altogether charming: and lives in a curiously detached . . . way in Oxford, to which she does not belong in any sense and which she reacts to in a half sleep-walking fashion.'[12]

In the summer of 1953 Isaiah's father was diagnosed with leukaemia. The nature of his illness was kept from him by his doctors, but Isaiah was told the truth. In September he left for a semester at Harvard, knowing that his father was unlikely to recover. Isaiah had always believed that truth entailed certain obligations and that a dying man was entitled to know the reality of his situation. But now face to face with his own father, he found it impossible to live up to his own maxims. He arrived home in December to find his father in hospital, alert and without pain, but clearly dying. They spent two days together, his father still not exactly aware of his condition, asking his son whether there was an after-life and his son not having the heart to tell him that he believed there was no such thing. Mendel met his death with the same gentle, retiring and slightly baffled air with which he had dealt with life. He slipped into a coma and died in his sleep on 15 December 1953, aged seventy.

For a week or so the Jewish rituals of burial and mourning kept both Isaiah and his mother occupied, and Isaiah remarked to a friend about the hidden wisdom of a religion in which he himself did not believe. But thereafter, in January and February, the full force of loss began to hit him. He may not have believed in the rituals, but he followed them punctiliously, ordering services to be held on every anniversary of his father's death. Throughout the winter of 1954 he found it hard to look at his father's hand-writing without being overcome by sorrow and a certain remorse. As he remarked sadly to his friend, Anna Kallin, he had always thought of his father as a kind of younger brother, whom he had to teach about life.[13] Now he understood that his father had sheltered him, taken the responsibilities on his shoulders, allowed Isaiah to remain the untroubled adolescent. For the first time, he realised, he was 'in the front line', responsible for his mother, for himself, for his own life at last. The 'abnormality and bleakness' of this depressed him deeply.[14] Altogether, his father's death 'had a far deeper and more devastating effect' on him than he had expected.[15] It was the most serious emotional crisis of his life. He was deeply depressed throughout the winter of 1954. But he did not turn in upon himself. He poured out his feelings in letters to friends and reached out to Aline.

Before Easter 1954, in a depressed and anguished state of mind, he asked Aline to give him a lift into London so that he could attend a meeting about the disposal of his father's bristles business. On the journey, he 'declared himself' and touched her hand. She kept entirely silent throughout but remembered thinking: 'Damn.' His touch moved her, but it was deeply unwelcome. She was a married woman with three children, struggling to maintain the façade of a difficult marriage. But her unhappiness was such that she began to see him clandestinely. At Easter they had an hour-long conversation on the phone. Isaiah went on to stay with his mother at the Hotel Ruhl in Nice. There he received a letter from Aline breaking off their relations. Hans Halban had overheard their conversation and threatened to divorce her and take the children. For two days Isaiah was prostrated, unable to get out of bed.[16]

On his return to Oxford, she telephoned him – 'in a strangled voice' – and invited him to drinks at Headington House, the splendid three-storey Georgian house she had purchased for her family. It was her husband's idea to keep on good terms. Halban seems to have thought it impolitic to force the issue to a break. Both Berlin and Halban were Oxford figures. The matter had to be handled with delicacy. But by then, Isaiah cordially disliked him.[17]

But Hans Halban was also suffering greatly: he had intercepted their phone-calls; he employed private detectives to track their movements; and once, on Deauville beach, Aline found him frantically piecing together a letter of Isaiah's that she had read and torn up.[18] His anguish was unmistakable. At the drinks party Aline appeared, drained and miserable, while Isaiah kept his distance from her and maintained a stilted conversation with Halban.

Soon afterwards Aline phoned and said that she must see him. 'I am a prisoner,' she said. 'Will you take me in?' They began meeting again in the summer of 1954, driving out into the country together. But one day, having arranged to meet her in the High Street opposite All Souls, Berlin crossed the road only to see that Halban had got word of the rendezvous and had come to confront them both. Isaiah continued across the street, bowed to both of them, went into the chemist's directly opposite, blindly purchased items he did not need, and returned to his rooms in All Souls, feeling – so he remembered – 'more dead than alive'. Soon afterwards Halban called and asked Isaiah to come to Headington House for a meeting.

As Isaiah remembered it, Halban said, 'This is a difficult situation, let's talk about it.' But it was Isaiah who did the talking. He remembered saying, 'Look, you're entirely right. Justice is entirely on your side. You're married to her. You love her. There's nothing I can say. I fully understand your position. You needn't expound it to me. There's only one thing I'd like to say. Let me give you a piece of advice. It's not entirely unbiased, as you will see. If you keep someone in prison, the prisoner is more anxious to get out than the jailer is to keep her in. This will not end well. If you stop her from seeing me, this will not go on indefinitely. Sooner or later, it's bound to be broken, even if I do nothing at all.'

This urbane disquisition on the psychology of freedom appears to have taken Halban by surprise. He said he would think about it and sent Isaiah into the garden to see Aline. She was wandering to and fro amidst the roses, twisting a handkerchief in her hand. She was just telling Isaiah that she felt sorry for her husband when Halban rushed into the garden with a note. It read: 'I accept your proposal. You may see her once a week.'

It was a desperate measure. The marriage was like a cracked vase. But Isaiah too was giving way under the strain. By this time, he wanted Aline desperately but she continued to feel tormented by residual loyalty to her husband and anxiety about the impact upon the children. In late autumn Isaiah was hospitalised with pericarditis – an irregularity of the heartbeat, which left him dizzy and breathless. It was an obvious symptom of emotional exhaustion.

At the end of 1954 Hans Halban was approached by the French Government and asked to return to Paris to head up a new nuclear physics laboratory. When he proposed to Aline that they accept, she said she could not accompany him. This was the end of the marriage. Isaiah was standing in the porter's lodge at All Souls talking to a friend when Aline rang through with the news. It was over. Halban had left for Paris. He had agreed to a separation. Two weeks later, in the Oxford botanical garden, he proposed marriage. To his dismay, she wondered why it was necessary. He persisted. He wanted something 'solid and definite'. She relented and they announced their engagement.

Isaiah presented Aline to his mother, who, having been alarmed, at the height of his infatuation with Patricia Douglas, that he might marry a Gentile, was now overjoyed that he was returning to the fold. Whatever ambivalence a powerfully protective mother would have had towards a prospective daughter-in-law, this was balanced by pride that her family should be marrying into the de Gunzburg family, whom all Russian Jews had respected for their philanthropy. She told a friend that she had 'trained herself' to be parted from Isaiah, and while marriage was a 'deeper and much more definite parting', she hoped, by practising 'a self-imposed discipline' and not interfering in his life, to 'gain Aline's devotion'.[19]

Aline's mother – a *grande dame* of great vigour and charm – had met Isaiah and liked him, but when her daughter broke the news of their impending marriage, she exclaimed, '*Mais il est inépousable.*'[20] Almost all of Isaiah's friends, male and female, registered the same surprise. He was the least marriageable man they knew.

The news that they were to be married, once the divorce was finalised in Paris, filtered down to Isaiah's friends through the winter and spring of 1955. But there was still one person who knew nothing. The woman he had been in love with two years before chanced to hear the news, from a mutual friend, at an All Souls lunch, following the conferring of honorary degrees in June 1955. Her shock and disappointment were intense. She came to Isaiah's rooms and he could only comfort her as best he could: 'Cry, child, cry.'

It is a testament to her lack of rancour, the depth of his attachment (and Aline's forbearance) that they remained close friends, mocking each other's politics and exchanging confessions throughout the rest of Isaiah's life.

In the summer of 1955 Aline and Isaiah journeyed through the south of France together, travelling as man and wife. By then, both felt that they had never been so much in love in their lives. It seemed a revelation to Aline that this middle-aged bachelor, so notoriously *inépousable*, should have been able to 'thaw her out' and restore her animation, confidence and appetite for life. They had already developed a running joke about the French, with Aline defending the country of her birth, its culture and civilisation, and Isaiah grumbling that they measured out their emotions by the thimbleful.[21]

While staying in Avignon, they went to see the art collector Douglas Cooper, at his château in the Vaucluse. They lunched in company with Cooper, and the philosopher Richard Wollheim and his wife Anne. Isaiah told a long story about the death of the Spanish poet Lope de Vega. Assured that he was now finally at death's door, de Vega was able to confess one final (for a poet) sacrilegious thought: 'Alors, Dante m'embête' – 'Well then, Dante bores me.'[22] This caused much laughter at lunch. Afterwards, Cooper and Wollheim went off to a bullfight at Nîmes, where Cooper was to meet Pablo Picasso.

Aline and Isaiah returned in the evening to find Cooper's château ablaze with light and servants scurrying to and fro. In the forecourt was an enormous Mercedes. Inside, they found Pablo Picasso, his mistress Jacqueline, his son Paolo, Jean Cocteau, the artist Tériade and his mistress. Picasso and Wollheim went upstairs into the attic to look at an early still life which Cooper had just bought. Picasso had not seen it since he had painted it. He bent over the picture, stood back and then muttered, 'C'est bien ça, c'est quelque chose.'

After dinner, Picasso talked amusingly about how it was that, whenever he was invited to Moscow and proposed an exhibition of his own work, the invitation was mysteriously withdrawn.[23] Isaiah was always drawn to genius, and such was the force of Picasso's personality that he was uncharacteristically silent throughout dinner. Picasso was about to leave when Isaiah approached and began telling him the story of Lope de Vega's dying words. The result was disastrous. As Isaiah ploughed on, Picasso's face darkened with displeasure. Death was a strictly forbidden subject in Picasso's presence; a story about the death of a famous Spaniard was worse; and worst of all was a story in which a Spanish artist's dying words were held up to apparent ridicule. Picasso stormed out and the huge Mercedes roared off into the night. Isaiah remained at a loss to understand what he had done wrong. For once in his life, his uncanny social antennae had failed him.

His uncharacteristic obliviousness has to be seen as the exaltation of a man deeply in love. As Aline and Isaiah continued through France to Rome, where Isaiah was to attend a historians' conference, he wrote an ecstatic letter to his mother saying, 'I am about thirty years younger than I have ever been: *rien à dire*.'[24] This state of happiness continued as they drove south into Italy. When they sent telegrams to friends or signed joint letters, they amalgamated their names: *Isaialine*.

In Rome, Isaiah met the first Soviet historians allowed out of Russia since Stalin's death. The Khrushchev thaw was just getting under way and many Western observers thought a genuinely new era had dawned. Isaiah remained sceptical. When Isaac Deutscher announced in *The Times* that the *ancien régime* was mellowing, Berlin thought the argument was 'clever rubbish'.[25] As he reported to his mother, the Soviet historians were full of hearty *bonhomie*, but it all seemed like a performance, carefully orchestrated by their party bosses. His own analysis of Soviet politics, 'Generalissimo Stalin and the Art of Government', had outlined the 'zig-zag' pattern of Soviet behaviour, now loosening, now tightening the reins of repression, in order to keep their enemies off-balance. The new thaw was a 'zig' in the pattern; a 'zag' was sure to follow shortly.[26]

He spent the autumn of 1955 lecturing at the University of Chicago. He met the conservative political philosopher Leo Strauss, and they talked about Hobbes and Machiavelli. Strauss was one of those who remained sceptical both about Berlin's scholarship and about his liberal project in general.[27] Through Arthur Schlesinger Jr., Berlin made the acquaintance of Adlai Stevenson, former Governor of Illinois and Democratic candidate for President. Unlike most intellectuals, who admired Stevenson this side of idolatry, Berlin was unimpressed. He thought Stevenson was neither a genuine intellectual nor a genuine man of action, and he was always most admiring of politicians, like Truman or Weizmann, who were men of action.[28]

Like a star tenor, Isaiah was now drawing large crowds, and American universities made flattering offers, but his attention was elsewhere. The absence from Aline was painful – she was in Oxford and Paris finalising the divorce – but it gave them both time and space to reflect on each other. To his mother Isaiah confided that 1955 had been 'the most triumphant' year of his life: 'I am happily in love. It is an astonishing sensation ... To live on a perpetually rising wave of very strong, very calm, very real emotion is a luxury not known to me before.'[29]

In a letter to Aline, he struck a note of alarm – partly genuine, partly ironic – about his approaching loss of independence. He also commented, in a jocular way, about the submerged connection between the dramas in his personal life and the development of his political ideas:

> It is a far stranger transformation of my life than of yours; till 45 I lived without knowing this sensation of irrecoverable loss of independence. I am trying to write notes for politics lectures on why people think a feeling of necessity is freedom. I am certainly tied hand and foot. Am I unfree? Is this what political 'love' for leaders produces? Is fanatical devotion, violent love = self realisation, or is there some calm deep feeling which is not tied to 'images' and goes on in some even, mystical fashion?[30]

He could now look back on the decade that had elapsed since his return from Washington as the most transforming period of his life. He had left analytical philosophy and found his own voice as a historian and moralist. He had faced up to the conflicting claims that threatened to divide him as a Zionist and as a Jew, and he had resolved his position in the Diaspora. He had been tempted by America and had overcome it. His liberalism was always to have a different inflection from theirs. Finally, he had overcome his emotional hesitations and was about to embark on married life. He joked to a friend that if he had to write an autobiography, he would call it 'Late Awakening'.[31] But awaken he had. All of these struggles – for an identity as a Jew, an intellectual, a liberal and a man – had converged simultaneously and out of this moment he emerged with the work that was to make him famous and with the woman who was to share the rest of his life. On 7 February 1956, at Hampstead Synagogue, he and Aline were married. Three days later he moved into Headington House, where he lived for the rest of his life.

15

Fame, 1957–63

In August 1956 Aline and her three boys, together with Isaiah, booked into the Pensione Argentina in Paraggi, a small village of shops, guest houses and *trattorie* around a sandy cove a mile from Portofino on Italy's Ligurian coast. Home movies taken by Aline from that summer concentrate on her children, sleek as seals, diving from the jetty, climbing in and out of boats, more or less ignoring a cluster of adults on the crowded beach: Stuart Hampshire and his son Julian, David Cecil (with his trousers rolled up), Lady Diana Cooper in a broad-brimmed hat, just arrived off a shipping magnate's yacht, and an improbably bronzed Isaiah in swimming trunks, standing in the water, gesticulating and brimming over with talk. He did not swim – his weakened left arm prevented that – but he would remain waist-high in the water, occasionally ducking to keep cool, keeping up a steady stream of jokes and speculation with the friends who swam nearby. He liked to compare the national characteristics of the swimmers. The English looked 'as if they are about to be medically examined', he decided, while the French 'wear too little and behave as if in a nightclub'. The only foreigners who were perfectly at ease, he concluded with a certain regret, were the Germans.[1]

He was experimenting with step-fatherhood that summer. He had an ambiguous position in the household, as a sort of resident Russian uncle. He had never wanted children of his own and was uneasy about displacing their father, now installed in Paris. Isaiah's diplomatic skills did not desert him, however, and he forged a useful alliance with the children's nanny, Miss Lee, who did much to smooth his way with her charges. As the children grew older, he helped them into schools and colleges, wrote them affectionate letters and provided them with dispassionate advice. They gradually discovered they *could* get a word in edgeways into his monologues.[2]

The Pensione Argentina was to be the family's summer home for most of the next decade. They occupied a whole floor and took all their meals there. Isaiah worked most mornings in his room or in a deckchair on the roof. Even though marriage to Aline gave him the means to retire from active academic life, he never considered doing so. Instead, the decade after his marriage proved to be one of the most creative periods in his life. It was then that he began his studies of Vico and Herder, and it was in Paraggi that he began composing the most famous of his lectures. On one memorable Dictabelt from the summer of 1957 or 1958 one can hear him intone over the crackle and hiss, 'Two Concepts of Freedom – no . . . of Liberty.'

He was now forty-eight years old, newly married, intensely happy, at the height of his productive powers and on the brink of fame. But his attitude towards success was complex. When he was approached by Harold Macmillan with the offer of a knighthood in the spring of 1957, his first instinct was to turn it down. He felt, as he wrote to T.S. Eliot, that he was being asked to wear a funny paper hat.[3] When he told his mother of his decision to refuse it, her eyes filled with tears and he decided that he must accept it after all.[4] When the knighthood became public, his old love, Patricia Douglas, wrote him a feline letter congratulating him for his services to conversation.[5] This barb stuck in his flesh. Throughout 1957 he was troubled with ailments – a flickering eyelid, an arrhythmic heartbeat – which indicate psychic distress.[6] He loved quoting the stern admonition he had read on a grave in an English churchyard: 'Avoid shame.' Now *Sir* Isaiah, he wondered whether he *had* avoided it.

He remained neurotic about his press coverage. He had already broken off relations with Robert Kee after an article of his in *Picture Post* made much of Berlin's size and volubility.[7] During the 1960s icy letters were sent to the *New Yorker*, *The Sunday Times*, and the *Daily Telegraph*, complaining about articles which, even though they were laudatory, made him feel ashamed that he had permitted them.[8]

Recognition engendered a particular kind of self-consciousness, which he began to explore in an essay on 'The Naïveté of Verdi', based on Schiller's distinction between the 'naïve' and 'sentimental' artist. A 'naïve' artist like Verdi was unselfconscious: he was at one with the Italian Risorgimento and all his work spoke for and to that world. 'Sentimental' artists like Wagner made their art out of their own alienation, their own inability to identify fully with their times or with their milieu. Berlin himself loved 'naïve' art, especially Verdi, but he excelled in the highly 'sentimental' – that is, self-conscious cultural forms, like analysis, criticism and theory.[9]

He thought of this self-consciousness as especially Jewish. If so, how was it to be lifted? In an essay on Disraeli and Marx, Berlin argued that Disraeli tried to escape Jewishness by identifying romantically with the British aristocracy and the Victorian monarchy. Marx, his apparent antithesis, overcame Jewish alienation by identifying with the proletariat. Both classes – the aristocracy and the proletariat – were free of middle-class snobbery and self-consciousness. There is something of Disraeli in Berlin's lifelong affection for aristocrats like David Cecil. The quality he admired in the well-born was the indifference to convention that went with a sense of being at ease. But how was a Jew ever to be fully at ease? Zionism, Berlin always argued, offered Jews one avenue of escape from self-consciousness. It promised them a land where they could be themselves, safe among their own, no longer required to 'fit in', to 'pass', to accommodate and please anyone but their own. He made the case for Zionism, but he knew that he could never be fully at home in Israel. So where did that leave him?

Marriage certainly helped: he was no longer a sexual or social outsider. Aline had given him ultimate belonging, and with it came that sense of being at home with himself, which his friends remarked upon after his marriage. But his intellectual life itself played a part. He overcame self-consciousness through empathy, by identifying himself with the imaginative dilemmas of the historical figures he wrote about. He knew he could never be a 'naïve' artist himself, but close friends like Robert Silvers, then just beginning the *New York Review of Books*, were right to think of his temperament as essentially artistic.[10] All of Berlin's best essays displayed a genius for transposing himself into antithetical minds and imagining the world as it must appear through their eyes. This allowed him to explore his own dilemma – about commitment, about self-consciousness itself – in disguise. He sometimes worried that he became such a good ventriloquist that no one could tell where Berlin started and Herzen, Turgenev, Tolstoy or Disraeli stopped. But this gift allowed both escape and protection: he could see how he must look through alien eyes, and the sight in general reassured him. He could rightly say, by his mid-fifties at least, that he had left behind most of the burdens of Jewish self-consciousness. He knew who he was and, thanks to empathy, he knew how he seemed to others. His friends came to think of him as one of the freest men they had ever known.[11] There was a spontaneity, an effervescence, a bubbling over, which his friends loved in him and which he liked in himself. He was genuinely at home with his body, with nakedness, physical afflictions, his weakened arm. The women who loved him all attested to his capacity to give of himself and to be absorbed in their life. Despite all this, his acutely sensitive relations to press attention suggest that he never entirely dropped his guard towards a Gentile world that he feared celebrated his brilliance to his face, while casting doubt upon him when his back was turned.

Despite anxieties about being thought too forward, he applied early in 1957 to succeed G.D.H. Cole as Chichele Professor of Social and Political Theory. Isaiah had been encouraged to apply, but he had some worries about the outcome. He knew that his only major work was the study of Marx, published nearly twenty years before. While he enjoyed a private reputation among professional philosophers, his public reputation depended on the fame of his radio lectures. The three Oxford grandees who wrote in support of his application qualified their praise for his quickness of mind with carefully phrased doubts about his limitations. The philosopher Gilbert Ryle said that Berlin had admitted he was no 'ice-breaker' in philosophy. A chair in political thought, on the other hand, would suit his talents. Richard Pares, Berlin's historian colleague at All Souls, confessed that he found too much 'rhetorical cumulation' in Isaiah's 'Historical Inevitability' and that the BBC lectures were almost 'too exciting' by the standards of sober scholarship. Charles Webster observed that Berlin had not yet produced 'the larger work of synthesis which is confidently awaited'.[12]

Their caveats mirrored his own. Yet both he and they were to be proven mistaken, since his professorship was an unquestionable success. The lectures he gave to packed halls of undergraduates between the autumn of 1957 and 1965 established him as one of the most exciting teachers in the Oxford of his day. Those who heard him lecture never forgot the experience – how he once said, with memorable bite: 'whenever you hear a man speak of "realism", you may always be sure that this is the prelude to some bloody deed'. Listening was like an 'airborne adventure', in which Berlin took the audience on a swooping flight over the intellectual landscapes of the past, leaving them at the end of the hour to file out onto the High Street 'slightly dazed', their feet not quite touching the ground.[13]

Those who listened to Berlin at the height of his powers simply did not believe that his fluency on the lecture platform cost him dread before and gloom afterwards. Lectures always involved compulsive over-preparation, endless refining from sixty pages to thirty, then to ten, and finally to single-headings on a single piece of paper, which were ignored when he entered the seance-like state of performance. Even then, his nerves did not desert him, and he would stare up at the steam-pipes, windows or chandeliers over the audience's heads, lest he be rendered speechless by a questioning gaze. The price of his uncanny oral fluency was an anxiety that he was 'a mere rattle', someone who, he said, cast 'bogus pearls before real swine'.[14] Yet for all his doubts, his professorship helped start an extraordinary revival of Oxford political theory. With J.L. Austin's death in 1960, Oxford analytical philosophy lost its driving force, while political philosophy and the history of political theory embarked upon a renaissance. Berlin presided over an ecumenical revival of serious political thinking – Marxist, Hegelian, liberal – which continues to this day.

'Two Concepts of Liberty' was delivered as his inaugural lecture as Chichele Professor to a packed hall in the Schools Building in Oxford on 31 October 1958. He was characteristically gloomy beforehand.[15] He had spent two summers in Paraggi dictating and re-dictating the lecture, cutting it back from four hours to a deliverable length. He had shown it to close friends like Herbert Hart and came away convinced that he was about to give vent to a series of sonorous platitudes.[16] In reality, it was to be the most influential lecture he ever delivered.

Key elements of his creed were already in place: the inaugural lecture offered him the chance to bring them together into a single coherent statement. He recast the earlier contrast between 'liberal' and 'romantic' conceptions of freedom into a sharper distinction between negative and positive liberty. This distinguished the liberal credo from its Jacobin, socialist and communist cousins. As he put it, with blunt succinctness, liberals 'want to curb authority as such', while the rest 'want it placed in their own hands'.[17] Negative liberty was the core of a properly liberal political creed: leaving individuals alone to do what they want, provided that their actions did not interfere with the liberty of others. Positive liberty was the core of all emancipatory theories of politics, from socialist to communist: for all such doctrines wish to use political power to free human beings to realise some hidden, blocked or repressed potential.

The European Enlightenment, he argued, was divided by a central contradiction: between maintaining that men should be free to choose and insisting that they should only be free to choose what it would be rational to desire. Marx had been an authentic child of Kant: the socialist utopia was intended to emancipate the individual and make possible the self-direction that Kant had defended as the essence of a rational life. But the result had been a communist tyranny built conceptually on the doctrine of false consciousness – the idea that men might be so alienated by bourgeois conditions from their true needs and true selves that they would have to be re-educated by the state and forced to be free. This was the 'strange reversal' to which the doctrine of 'positive liberty' – 'freedom to' – was fatally prone: to begin with an ideal of freedom as self-mastery and to end with the dictatorship of the proletariat and Stalin's engineers of human souls.

The sense of Berlin's position was that a liberal does not believe in a hierarchy of inner selves (higher, lower, true, false) or believe that there can ever be a political solution to the experience of inner human division. Human beings are what they are, and a liberal politics deals only with what human beings say they want. Their preferences can be argued with and persuasion is possible, but coercion – in the name of what they might prefer, if they could only see it more clearly – is always illegitimate. The revealed preferences of ordinary men and women must be the limit and also the arbiter of all practical politics.

The lecture was a strong defence of the liberty of the individual, rather than a defence of democratic government as such. Democratic self-government 'on the whole provide[s] a better guarantee' of negative freedom than other regimes, but only 'on the whole'.[18] A liberal might have to defend liberty (of, say, a minority) against a democratic tyranny. Such a conflict of values was intrinsic in modern political life.

A second conflict of values – between privacy and participation – ensued. Against the weight of the whole republican tradition, which had always made political participation and citizenship the redeeming arena of human life, Berlin tacitly defended political quietism, or at least the liberty of those who wanted to keep out of politics. He was highly sceptical, therefore, about the idea held since Aristotle that men were 'political animals'. The desire to participate was simply the desire to be recognised by one's own group, and the desire to belong. There was no reason to suppose that participation, the exercise of citizenship, improved human character. Politics was an inescapable element of human affairs, he argued, simply because human goals were in conflict. Politics was not an emancipatory activity, merely a necessary one.

'Two Concepts' was consciously crafted for an era of de-colonisation, and its message towards colonial peoples demanding their liberty was highly sceptical. He warned that national liberation movements that claimed to be fighting for liberty against a colonial oppressor were not necessarily fighting for liberty, but for recognition of their distinctiveness as a national people and for the status of national independence. Berlin was not unsympathetic to these instincts – indeed, as a Zionist, his liberalism was unusually receptive to this craving for recognition and status. But to call national liberation a fight for liberty was to mistake the motives behind such colonial revolts, and hence to guarantee disillusion when they fail to deliver the emancipation they promised.

A distinctive psychology had now come into place within Isaiah's liberal philosophy. It viewed human beings as divided creatures, often required to choose between private and public claims, between reason and emotion and, crucially, between conflicting political values. 'Two Concepts' was an attack on the faith common to classical republicanism, to Marxism and to utopian socialism, that politics could liberate men from these inner and outer conflicts.

Many of his listeners on the left took the lecture to be a defence of *laissez-faire* individualism. But the robust after-life of 'Two Concepts' would be inexplicable if it had been only a defence of the status quo; instead, it was its psychology – its view of human beings choosing between often incompatible and incommensurable goals, which gave it such influence.

In practical politics, Berlin was neither a conservative nor a *laissez-faire* individualist, but a New Deal liberal, convinced that individuals could not be free if they were poor, miserable and under-educated. Liberty was only liberty if enjoyed in some degree of social equality. But he challenged the whole post-war social democratic tradition by pointing out that the values at the heart of it – equality, liberty and justice – contradicted each other. For example, it might be necessary to increase taxation on the incomes of the few in order to bring greater justice to the many, but it was a perversion of language to pretend that no one's liberty would suffer as a result. In a passage that comes closest to being the core of his political ideas, he wrote:

> Everything is what it is: liberty is liberty, not equality or fairness or justice or culture, or human happiness or a quiet conscience. If the liberty of myself or my class or nation depends on the misery of a number of other human beings, the system which promotes this is unjust and immoral. But if I curtail or lose my freedom, in order to lessen the shame of such inequality, and do not thereby materially increase the individual liberty of others, an absolute loss of liberty occurs. This may be compensated for by a gain in justice or in happiness or peace, but the loss remains, and it is a confusion of values to say that although my 'liberal' individual freedom may go by the board, some other kind of freedom – social or economic – is increased.[19]

All serious political choice involved loss, not merely trade-offs or compromises but genuine sacrifice of desirable ends: so much liberty sacrificed for so much equality or justice sacrificed for the sake of mercy, and so on. 'If, as I believe, the ends of men are many, and not all of them are in principle compatible with each other, then the possibility of conflict – and of tragedy – can never wholly be eliminated from human life, either personal or social.'[20] Loss was inevitable, because values were in conflict and because human reason was incorrigibly imperfect. Reason

Isaiah Berlin by Cecil Beaton, 1955

In the 1950s

Isaiah and Aline
Berlin on board the
Queen Mary, at the time
of their marriage, 1955-6

Stuart Hampshire, Isaiah and Nicolas Nabokov on the lawn,
Headington House, 1960s

Isaiah Berlin by Clive Barda, late 1960s

At Headington House,
1950s, with Peter and
Phillipe Halban

Peraggi 3.9.58:
I look as if I were in terrible agony
but I have just emerged from Diving
& the water is still blinding me — I
am in a more ecstatic state of
pleasure — how photographs can mislead!

On holiday in Italy, 1980s

Bathing at Paraggi,
September 1958

With contributors to the first *Festschrift* in his honour,
edited by Alan Ryan, at Wolfson College, 1979.

From left to right, back row: Pat Utechin, (Isaiah's secretary), H.L.A [Herbert] Hart,
G.A [Jerry] Cohen, Henry Hardy, Charles Taylor, Bernard Williams, Richard
Wollheim, Stuart Hampshire; *Front row*: Robert Wokler, Alan Ryan, Isaiah Berlin,
Robin Milner-Gulland, Patrick Gardiner, Larry Siedentop

Isaiah and Aline (*right*), with Elena Bonner and Andrei Sakharov at Headington House, June 1989, when Sakharov received his honorary degree

With Stephen Spender, early 1990s

Isaiah Berlin by Deborah Elliott.
In the Codrington Library, All Souls, January 1988

could clarify the facts, but choice itself was an act of will, instinct and emotion and as such a gamble made in the dark.

'Two Concepts of Liberty' made it clear what liberalism stood against. But it was less clear about what liberalism was for – that is, how much social justice was compatible with negative liberty, indeed how much justice was *required*. The polemic against positive freedom carried Berlin away from these questions and left his commitments to social justice unspecified. He might have taken this question further had his life gone in another direction. Morton White invited Berlin in 1958 to conduct a seminar on liberalism at Harvard with John Rawls and, had he accepted, Berlin might have found himself pressed to take his arguments further. He did not accept White's invitation, and the consequences of a sustained encounter between Rawls and Berlin remain in the domain of the might-have-been.[21] When the American revival of liberal theory came in the 1970s, with the publication of Rawls' A *Theory of Justice*, it took a Rawlsian rather than a Berlinian form. The feature that distinguished Berlin from Rawls was his emphasis on the ultimate incompatibility of values, and hence the tragic quality of liberal choice.

The other source of difficulty in the lecture was that Isaiah did not explain why negative liberty should have priority over other political values. He disagreed with John Stuart Mill's view that liberty was the 'necessary condition for the growth of human genius'. As his own visit to Akhmatova had taught him, individual genius could flower under the most adverse and illiberal conditions. Freedom and human flourishing were in a contingent rather than necessary relation, just as human flourishing was only contingently dependent on knowledge. The truth had never made men free, and freedom did not always make men better.[22] Berlin's central objective was to separate a defence of liberty from any claim that it had an emancipating or improving effect on human nature.

Indeed, the only defence he offered of liberty's priority in politics was in terms of pluralism. If values were in conflict, then liberty's priority was procedural. A regime of negative freedom was the best guarantee of the public discussion of choices that a free social life required. But this left the justification of liberty trapped in a circle: freedom was required to make freedom possible. He never professed to be bothered by his own failure to ground the defence of liberty on ultimate principles. He tartly suggested that secular rationalists who sought unassailable guarantees for political principles were succumbing, without realising it, to nostalgia for the kinds of consolations once offered by religious faith. Berlin dismissed the very idea of seeking ultimate guarantees at all. 'Principles are not less sacred because their duration cannot be guaranteed.'[23]

'Two Concepts' immediately came under fire, even from close friends.[24] It put into question the élitist paternalism of his own milieu. George Kennan wrote to Berlin to ask whether the American electorate of 'this sprawling, careless, lethargic country before me – this 175 million people stumbling thoughtlessly into self-indulgence, bad habits, decadence and political apathy' could really be trusted with negative liberty. Wasn't there a case for an élite to tell them, or at least suggest, how they might best use their freedom? No reply from Berlin can be found, but it was a fixed principle of his that so-called élites – intellectual or otherwise – had no business presuming that they knew better than the man or woman in the street.[25] From the other end of the spectrum, philosophical conservatives like Leo Strauss and Alan Bloom at Chicago welcomed Berlin's critique of the totalitarian temptation, but were uncomfortable with his equally adamant attack on their idea that the good – in politics and morals – was non-contradictory and could be proclaimed, *ex cathedra*, from the pulpits of the University of Chicago.[26]

Critics on the left singled out Berlin's sceptical attitude towards democracy and political participation. The idea of 'participatory democracy' was just beginning to make its transit through the ideological firmament of the 1960s and Steven Lukes, a young tutor in Oxford, argued that 'Two Concepts' might be seen as an apologia for voter apathy. Berlin replied – he said the same to Bernard Crick – that he believed in citizenship as much as any liberal: what he refused to believe was that citizenship made men better.[27] Karl Popper wrote to Berlin to congratulate him on his lecture, but also to criticise him for attacking the Kantian idea of men emancipating themselves and achieving self-mastery.[28] Again, Berlin held firm to his central theme, which was to dissociate the defence of liberty from liberation, personal or social.[29] A rather different defence of the ideal of self-realisation came from the Canadian philosopher Charles Taylor. He argued that Berlin's account of positive freedom was a caricature: Kantian self-realisation did not necessarily lead to totalitarian tyranny. Individuals could use their freedom to transform themselves through knowledge and self-understanding. Liberty had an emancipatory potential; if this wasn't realised, Berlin's defence of liberty collapsed into a mere apologia for *laissez-faire*. It gave no adequate account of why freedom mattered so much to individuals.[30]

Isaiah was no controversialist: but he gave no ground on the matter. It seemed to him that the conflicts that might rage within the self were incorrigible. Emancipatory justifications for freedom finessed rather than confronted this difficulty, for individuals disagreed about what emancipation might mean and what forms it should take. The impression that he was a thinker who buckled under pressure is false: it is the unyielding quality of his scepticism that has guaranteed intellectual longevity to his work. Berlin had no programme of moderate political reform to propagate; he was not interested in enjoying or cultivating active political influence. He had no interest in policy. The original aspect of his political philosophy lay in his psychology of the divided human self and his insight into the human susceptibility to utopias promising release from the burden of moral choice. From these central intuitions, he never wavered.

In the light of this, it is interesting to look at how he positioned himself in the political controversies of the times. He never had any difficulty thinking of himself as a Cold Warrior, as a liberal defender of the capitalist world and its freedoms. But he was often uncomfortable with the company he was forced to keep and uneasy at joining public campaigns. In 1956 Anthony Blunt, director of the Courtauld Institute, appealed to Berlin to sign a declaration condemning the Soviet invasion of Hungary.[31] This appeal, Blunt said, was necessary 'in order to stir up opinion' in the US. The incident highlighted all the dangers of joining the 'stage army of the good'. By then, Isaiah knew that Blunt's friend and lover, Guy Burgess, had fled to the Soviet Union, but he had no inkling that Blunt himself had been a Soviet agent and that Blunt's petition was breathtaking in its bad faith. Yet Berlin's loathing of the regime behind the Iron Curtain never wavered and, over the next decade, he continuously signed appeals on behalf of imprisoned Hungarian dissidents such as Istvan Bibo and Tibor Dery.[32]

Berlin was also unusual among liberals of the 1950s in not being taken in by the Khrushchev thaw. A visit to Moscow in the summer of 1956 – as a honeymoon journey with Aline – left him convinced that the Soviet regime was still expansionist and repressive at heart. The Politburo, whom he had met at an embassy reception, made him think of a thuggish group of Oxford college porters, 'at once smooth and brutal, class conscious and corrupt, hideously jovial and with an easy gangsterish flow of sentimental reminiscence'.[33]

During that visit to Moscow, Berlin took Aline to visit Pasternak at Peredelkino.[34] There the writer told him that he had already sent the manuscript of *Dr Zhivago* to his Italian publishers and was determined to see it published. Berlin begged Pasternak to consider the consequences for himself and his family.[35] Martyrdom was a moral temptation like any other and should be resisted. Pasternak flared up and Isaiah knew it was hopeless to press his case. Back in his room in the British Embassy in Moscow, Berlin read the manuscript – one of the first Westerners to do so – and concluded immediately that it was a masterpiece. On his return, Isaiah was instrumental in securing British publication of *Dr Zhivago*.[36] But he remained haunted by the memory of having put Akhmatova in danger. When *Dr Zhivago* appeared in the autumn of 1958, Berlin was appalled that his Oxford colleague and friend George Katkov read portions of the manuscript on the Russian service of the BBC.[37] This made official retribution against Pasternak inevitable. Berlin broke angrily with Katkov over the issue. When the Soviet regime forced Pasternak to refuse the Nobel Prize and began the harassment that contributed to his early death in 1960, Isaiah felt his own caution had been vindicated.

In 1958 Dimitry Shostakovich came to Oxford to receive an honorary degree, along with the French composer Francis Poulenc. Shostakovich arrived at Headington House in an official embassy car flanked by Soviet officials. The composer was small, shy and looked like a 'chemist from western Canada'. Whenever his minders were around, he referred to them as his dear friends, and a nervous spasm would cross his face. But at a musical evening with Poulenc at Alexandra and Hugh Trevor-Roper's, the Russian composer was transformed. As soon as a pair of musicians began playing his cello sonata, Shostakovich, who had been huddling in the corner like a frightened animal, shot to his feet, ran over to the score and insisted that the players had made an error. It was discovered that they were working from a Western score, altered by the cellist Gregor Piatigorsky. These alterations Shostakovich angrily crossed out with a pencil, substituting the correct version. Isaiah then suggested that Shostakovich go to the piano and play. He performed a prelude and fugue with such passion and flair that everything they had heard by Poulenc sounded pale and polite by comparison. The haunted, persecuted expression left Shostakovich's face only during those minutes when he was at the piano.[38]

The last of Isaiah's encounters with the great figures of the Russian intelligentsia occurred in 1965, when he and Maurice Bowra managed to persuade their university to grant Anna Akhmatova an honorary degree. He had telephoned her in Moscow in 1956, and she had received the news of his marriage in icy silence. They had both decided it was not safe to meet. When she duly appeared in Oxford in June 1965, Isaiah was shocked to see how she had aged. She had gained weight and he thought, a little unkindly, that she resembled Catherine the Great. But she carried herself like an empress and delivered herself of her opinions with imperial force. When she arrived outside Headington House and surveyed the splendid garden, the three-storey Georgian house and Isaiah's new wife, she observed caustically: 'So the bird is now in its golden cage.'[39] The spark that had leaped between them twenty years before was now extinguished. He could only secure her the recognition in the West that was her due; she could only acknowledge it with regal hauteur. He accompanied her as she stood in the Sheldonian and heard herself acclaimed in Latin as 'an embodiment of the past, who can console the present and provide hope for the future'. Afterwards he was in attendance at the Randolph Hotel when she received Russian visitors who had come from all over the world to pay court to her. He was there too when she read from her verse, intoning the deep and sonorous rhythms into a tape recorder.[40] She departed for Paris and home, and Isaiah never saw her again. She died the following year. His anti-communism had always been a declaration of allegiance to the intelligentsia of whom she was the last surviving heroine. After her death, he exclaimed to a friend that he would always think of her as an 'uncontaminated', 'unbroken' and 'morally impeccable' reproach to all the Marxist fellow-travellers who believed that individuals could never stand up to the march of history.[41]

Berlin's unbending suspicion of the Soviet system led him to part company with the large number of his Oxford friends who joined the Campaign for Nuclear Disarmament. In 1958 when Philip Toynbee asked for a statement in support of unilateral nuclear disarmament, Berlin replied – with rather uncharacteristic bravado – that liberal principles were of little meaning unless one was prepared to risk one's very survival in their defence:

> Unless there is some point at which you are prepared to fight against whatever odds, and whatever the threat may be, not merely to yourself, but to anybody, all principles become flexible, all codes melt, and all ends in themselves for which we live disappear.[42]

In November 1960 Ignazio Silone and Nicolo Chiaromonte, illustrious Italian liberals, asked him to sign a manifesto supporting the FLN uprising against French rule in Algeria.[43] Berlin accepted the Algerian right to self-determination and condemned the brutality of the French war of counter-insurgency, but he could not endorse the FLN's use of terrorism against civilian targets.[44] This loathing of the use of violence was applied consistently, even to Zionists. When he met Menachem Begin in the lift of the King David Hotel, the very hotel that Begin's men had blown up in 1946 with the loss of ninety lives, Berlin refused to shake his hand.[45]

In May 1961, when the Kennedy administration sponsored the abortive invasion of Cuba by Cuban exiles, Kenneth Tynan, the drama critic, wrote to Berlin asking him to sign an appeal condemning the operation. Isaiah declined on the grounds that Castro 'may not be a Communist but I think he cares as little for civil liberties as Lenin or Trotsky'. Tynan's reply – that Castro was less repressive than many other Latin American dictators – may have been true, but Berlin would have none of it. Castro might be 'progressive', but his human rights record forfeited any right to support.[46]

These commitments – on Hungary, Cuba, Algeria and CND – were consistent with liberal principles, but they earned Berlin growing suspicion on the left. Perry Anderson of the *New Left Review* attacked him in a memorable article for being one of the European immigrants to Britain who had done most to serve up to the English a self-congratulatory picture of their own supposedly liberal virtues.[47] Berlin indeed saw no reason to disagree: he loved England and told her so.

Left-wing resentment came to a boil over the Isaac Deutscher affair.

There had never been much love lost between the two men. Deutscher had drawn blood with a scathing review in the *Observer* of Berlin's lecture on historical inevitability, and Berlin was antagonised by Deutscher's political dogmatism and his hostility to Zionism. In 1963 Deutscher, who was then completing his monumental biography of Trotsky, was being considered for a professorship in political studies at Sussex University. Berlin, who served on the university's academic advisory board, was asked by the Vice-Chancellor for his opinion of Deutscher's academic credentials. Berlin's reply – that Deutscher was 'the only man whose presence in the same academic community as myself I should find morally intolerable' – put paid to Deutscher's chances.[48] Berlin hastened to say that he would have supported the claims of a C. Wright Mills or an Eric Hobsbawm, for they did not subordinate scholarship to ideology.

The Deutscher affair burst into flame in 1969 when the radical magazine *Black Dwarf* published the confidential correspondence and denounced Isaiah as an anti-communist witch-hunter. His own part in the affair troubled Berlin: he maintained that if Deutscher had been offered a chair in Marxist thought, he would have had no objection. The difficulty lay in supposing that Deutscher could be counted on to teach non-Marxist concepts with the fairness requisite in a university teacher. This was a fair enough application of the standards of liberal tolerance in a university, but Isaiah muddied the waters considerably by claiming that he himself remained a man of the left. In reality, as the Deutscher affair shows, he was not of that political family at all.

He was in fact committed to exploring and widening the divide that separated liberalism from socialism. Just how wide he believed this divide to be came through when the Labour politician Richard Crossman wrote to him in 1963, praising his essay 'Does Political Theory Still Exist?', but taking Berlin to task for giving such short shrift to the British democratic socialist tradition represented by Laski, Tawney, Lindsay and T.H. Green. Laski, Berlin tartly replied, was a 'shallow rhetorician', while Lindsay's ideas were like London buses: they loomed up and disappeared again into the rhetorical fog. Only Tawney retained his respect, for the moral seriousness of his politics and the quality of his historical learning.[49]

Berlin's polemics with the left continued throughout the 1960s. In

1961 E.H. Carr devoted a portion of the Trevelyan Lectures at Cambridge to an attack on Berlin's 'Historical Inevitability'. Carr questioned whether Berlin believed in the possibility of historical explanation at all, given his indifference to social and economic factors, and given his apparent belief that historians should be chiefly concerned not with explanation but with moral evaluation. Surely, Carr argued, no one seriously supposed that a historian's task was to bother with the question of whether Hitler or Cromwell were bad fellows. Their task was rather to understand the factors that had enabled them to come to power and the forces which their rule unleashed.

Carr's lectures were highly public events, re-broadcast on the BBC, published weekly in *The Listener* and eventually assembled in the hugely influential text *What is History?* Replying to Carr was a challenge that Berlin could not duck. In a series of letters to *The Listener*, as well as in private exchanges with Carr himself, Berlin insisted that Marxist theory put an almost exclusive emphasis on abstract socio-economic causation and neglected the importance of the ideas, beliefs and intentions of individuals.[50] This falsified causation itself and robbed 'historical language of the evaluative force which it has in common speech, in the interests of an amoral objectivity'.[51] Moreover, the supposed moral objectivity of Marxist historiography was bogus. Carr's history was the story of the rise and eventual triumph of the 'progressive' forces – the proletariat and the Bolshevik party. They were judged to be 'progressive', Berlin insisted, simply because they had succeeded. For Carr, 'the failures and the minorities belong, in Trotsky's famous words, to the rubbish heap of history'. For Carr, the task of the historian was to pick the winners. In a letter of reply to Berlin, Carr professed to be 'puzzled by this winner and loser business'. If he were writing a history of cricket, he said, he would give space to the batsman who scored hundreds of runs, not to the 'nice young man who muffed the catch'. Berlin remained on genial personal terms with Carr throughout the controversy, but the gulf between them was unbridgeable. Berlin insisted that the 'losers' questions were as pertinent as the 'winners' answers.

The duel with Marxists was not the only area in which Isaiah was forced to apply liberal political principles in practice. He sometimes found himself wavering uncomfortably. In the first days of Anthony Eden's ill-fated Suez operation to seize the canal from Nasser in 1956,

Berlin wrote to Clarissa Eden, lending her husband his support.[52] As the operation continued, however, it dawned on him that even if the invasion succeeded, Britain and France would have to occupy Egypt, or at least the canal zone, in the teeth of aroused Arab nationalist opposition, and that such colonial policing operations were doomed to failure.[53] From then on, he turned against Eden's Suez policy, but this volte-face – relatively rare – troubled him. He realised that he had allowed his pro-Israeli convictions to pull him in one direction and his anti-colonialist inclinations to pull in the other.

He often found it deeply uncomfortable to be asked to give concrete political advice. In 1958 David Ben Gurion asked fifty sages, including Berlin, whether the time had come to challenge the Orthodox rabbi's monopoly over how the Jewishness of new immigrants and converts to Judaism should be ascertained. The question sharply divided Israeli society and had caused governments to fall. At issue was the very definition of who was a Jew: did children of certain mixed marriages belong? Berlin was resolutely secular, but he replied that for Ben Gurion to force the issue now would sow needless contention between secular and religious Jews. 'The status of the Jews is unique and anomalous, composed of national, cultural, religious strands, inextricably intertwined. To attempt either to affirm their indissolubility, or to attempt the separation of these strands, must inevitably lead to deep and bitter disagreement.'[54] He recommended that Ben Gurion avoid a *Kulturkampf* with the religious parties, but he ducked out of further involvement in the controversy by saying that Jews in the Diaspora, like himself, should not meddle in Israeli affairs.[55]

He was more comfortable outside the political realm altogether, collaborating with artists. In 1958, through Nicolas Nabokov, he met the composer Igor Stravinsky and his friend and amanuensis, Robert Craft.[56] Stravinsky, he reported to a friend, was 'far tinier than anyone supposes' and his face had a 'ceaseless mobility', which made him fascinating to watch.[57] Berlin was drawn to Stravinsky's vitality and even enjoyed his malice. For example, when asked his opinion of Benjamin Britten, Stravinsky replied suavely, 'Such a marvellous accompanist.' And Berlin could not help but warm to someone who, when asked for his opinion of Wagner, replied, 'If you listen to *Parsifal*,' articulating that word slowly and distinctly, 'you hear many very disagreeable sounds.'[58]

In October 1961, at a lunch in Headington House, the composer said that he had been asked by the state of Israel to compose a piece in honour of the Jerusalem Festival. Did Berlin have any ideas for a suitable libretto? Isaiah hurried upstairs to his library and came down with a copy of the Hebrew Bible. Thumbing through it, he first suggested the biblical account of Creation in the book of Genesis, but Stravinsky thought the result would be too long: 'like a British weekend'. Then Berlin suggested Abraham's binding of Isaac, the moment when, in obedience to God's command, a father prepares to sacrifice his own son. Berlin read out a few of the Hebrew sounds – *elim, elohim* – and Stravinsky seemed to listen intently to their musical rhythm. A collaboration began.[59] Berlin sent Stravinsky a complete transliteration of the Hebrew text with an English translation beneath.[60] When the work was ready, Berlin was invited to Jerusalem to watch the dress rehearsals and first performance. He found the music of the Abraham and Isaac Cantata baffling, but he found the spectacle of Stravinsky on the podium riveting. The composer came to the podium, looking as frail as a porcelain doll, but when he said *Shalom* in a faint voice, the Israeli audience applauded wildly. As the music was performed, the audience, 'a forest of white and blue shirts and mops of rough white hair', seemed bewildered, having 'no idea what the sounds were meant to convey or whether they were meant to be anything at all', but applauding none the less at the end, because they understood the compliment that Stravinsky had intended to the Jewish tradition. As for Stravinsky, he enjoyed Israel thoroughly, sat in the King David Hotel restaurant, drank quantities of Irish whiskey and behaved benignly to everyone. He was even amused by the spectacle of Berlin persuading the band leader of the hotel restaurant to cease playing lush waltz tunes in the composer's hearing.[61]

Throughout the 1960s, Berlin continued to spend semesters in the United States, first at Harvard, then at the City University of New York, which gave him a part-time chair. Oxford had never provided much of a home for his idiosyncratic blend of philosophy, ethics and intellectual history. It was to the States that he went for congenial academic company: the Russian scholars Martin Malia, Adam Ulam, Richard Pipes, Marc Raeff and James Billington; the critics Edmund Wilson and Lionel Trilling; the historian and Democratic political activist Arthur Schlesinger Jr.; the philosopher and historian of ideas Morton White.

Berlin now was in such demand that his tours in America took on the quality of a royal progress, much to the irritation of Edmund Wilson, who confided to his diary that his old friend was 'behaving more and more like royalty'.[62] Other friends also noticed that Isaiah had become a grand figure. In his diary, Stephen Spender recorded this exchange with a lift attendant in New York:

'Did you read Sir Eesiah Berlin's article in *The New York Times* about the Historic Past?'

'I'm afraid not.'

'Well, Sir Eesiah's right. You can't know nothing about the past until you're dead.'[63]

In the autumn of 1962 Berlin established himself alone in Lowell House, Harvard, to prepare the Storrs Lectures at Yale on three turning points in political thought: the Greeks, Machiavelli and Romanticism. But most weekends he spent in New York or Washington in glittering company. It was Camelot's hour of glory, and many of the friends he had first met in war-time Washington had been drawn into the Kennedy court: Arthur Schlesinger was a special counsel to the President; Walt Rostow and McGeorge Bundy were White House advisers; Phil Graham and his wife, Kay, were publishers of the *Washington Post*; while Joe Alsop was the most influential columnist of the day. Other figures, like George Kennan and Charles Bohlen, were Presidential counsellors on foreign affairs.

In mid-October 1962 Joe Alsop invited Isaiah to a small private dinner in honour of Chip Bohlen, who was leaving to take up his post as American Ambassador in Paris. Kay and Philip Graham, Arthur Schlesinger, the Bohlens and the French Ambassador and his wife were there. Berlin watched the President arrive with Mrs Kennedy, and circle the room shaking hands like Napoleon greeting his marshals.[64] There was the same intensity, complicity and adoration, the same cult of toughness and ruthlessness. Before dinner, the President took Chip Bohlen out into the Alsops' garden and the two could be seen strolling up and down, deep in conversation.

Over dinner the President joked in the breezy style of a Palm Beach playboy, eyeing Berlin suspiciously, so Isaiah thought, 'like a man of action faced with a notorious, possibly unintelligible or even ironical intellectual'.[65] After dinner he took Berlin aside and his manner became intense and business-like. Why were the Russians not making more trouble in Berlin, Kennedy wanted to know? What did Russians typically do when backed into a political corner? Berlin replied as best he could, while Kennedy listened with terrifying attention. As Isaiah later recalled to Schlesinger, 'I've never known a man who listened to every single word that one uttered more attentively. His eyes protruded slightly, he leant forward towards one, and one was made to feel nervous and responsible by the fact that every word registered.'

Kennedy invited Berlin to compare Khrushchev's intentions with Stalin's and then said that someone should write a book on Stalin's philosophy. 'In what sense do you mean philosophy?' Berlin asked, and the President replied that every great political leader had a particular set of principles that he followed. Berlin didn't think Stalin had a philosophy worth the name, but he did not press the point. Kennedy seemed obsessed with greatness: whenever he mentioned Stalin, Lenin or Churchill, 'his eyes shone with a particular glitter'. But there was none of the ease of a great man about him. Berlin sensed that, for the President, life was a series of hurdles to be crossed by means of enormous inner concentration and effort. He also had the sinking sensation that all his Washington friends were waiting, on the edge of the conversation, to see how he was faring, and his own impression was that he was not faring well at all. After a half-hour grilling the President rose, rejoined the company and said, cordially but firmly, 'You must go sit next to Jackie. She wants to bring you out.' She turned out to have a sharper and shrewder intelligence than her exterior had led Berlin to believe. She was cutting about Adlai Stevenson, whom she seemed to despise as much as her husband did. Isaiah found himself feeling sorry for her, because there seemed to be an edge of melancholy and exclusion to everything she said. Their conversation turned to her fears for what her husband would do after his Presidency. As he wrote to Aline afterwards, she said 'she had a horror of her future after J. ceased to be President. Boston would be terrible (it is). And he, J. would lapse into his family's habits, which were worthless. Oddly frank.'[66]

The next morning, the President announced that American over-flights of Cuba had discovered Soviet missiles on Cuban soil. The President had first seen these photographs on the morning of Alsop's dinner party. His conversation in the garden with Chip Bohlen had been about how to confront the Russians with the information. With his uncanny ability to be at the right place at the right time, Isaiah had been centre-stage on the first night of the Cuban Missile Crisis. As he thought back over the evening, he was astonished at the President's sang-froid and good humour.

As the crisis unfolded, Berlin watched the President's speeches on television in the company of undergraduates at Lowell House and went to overflow meetings at Harvard's Sanders Theatre, where large crowds were addressed by not very competent orators. As usual, Isaiah stood apart from the general atmosphere of worry, and told his cleaning lady, when she anxiously asked him whether there would be a war, that there could not be one.[67]

Once the crisis was over, the White House called again to invite him to a small dinner organised by Mrs Kennedy to celebrate. The President was in 'a glow of absolute happiness', though he confided that Cuba No. 2 would never quite expunge the stain of Cuba No. 1 (the Bay of Pigs fiasco). This time talking with the President was easier, though Berlin confessed in a letter to Noel Annan that he was 'really no good at a round table discussion of ICBM's, of middle-range weapons, the strategic importance of Assam or even the secrets of the British Minister of Defence'.[68] As for Kennedy, Berlin had the sense of someone consciously striving to attain a place in history, striving to be equal to the great duel with the Soviet Union. He remarked that he did not expect to have a quiet term of office and obviously believed that in Khrushchev he had found his Moriarty. It was also clear that he was haunted by his father's reputation as an appeaser and that the Munich analogy led the President to believe that 'resistance must be offered *at once*' to any incursion on the Russians' part. Kennedy's self-dramatising quality, this perception of himself as a character with a fate and a destiny, Berlin found both fascinating and unappealing. When he relaxed sufficiently to tell the President 'a rather frivolous story' about Lenin's private life, the President cut him off abruptly, apparently displeased that historical figures should be discussed with such levity.

Despite this *froideur*, a further invitation rapidly arrived, this time to lecture at the informal seminar held at Bobby and Ethel Kennedy's home, Hickory Hill. Berlin knew that his rival A.J. Ayer had lectured there and had not been a conspicuous success; the militantly anti-religious Ayer had poured such ridicule on Ethel Kennedy's attempts as a good Catholic to introduce Thomas Aquinas into the discussion that Bobby had hissed, 'Drop it, Ethel.' Berlin at first refused the invitation but, after appeals by the British Ambassador, agreed. The President asked for the meeting to be held in the White House. The seminar was conducted after dinner on 12 December, attended by McGeorge Bundy, Robert McNamara, Arthur Schlesinger, Robert Kennedy, Walt Rostow and other key figures of the administration, together with their wives. Aline Berlin attended and found the President captivatingly good company. After dinner, with the President sitting in his rocking chair, listening intently, Berlin rose to speak. Had he been more ambitious, more policy-minded, more of a Cold Warrior, he might have chosen a subject calculated for the President's ear. Instead he chose to talk about artistic commitment among the nineteenth-century Russian intelligentsia. In his seminar, he tried to explain how communism, imported into Europe as a 'secular, theoretical, abstract doctrine', was transformed by its contact with the earnest Russian intelligentsia and their belief in the social functions of thought and returned to Europe, in Leninist form, as a 'fiery, sectarian, quasi-religious faith'. Even for such a relatively intellectual subject, Berlin felt the full force of the President's tense, omnivorous attention. At the end of the talk, the President asked him what had been the fate of the intelligentsia after the revolution – who had collaborated, who resisted, and what difference the reaction of the intelligentsia had made to the course of the revolution.[69] Again, Berlin had the sense of a President measuring everyone, weighing who would stand up to pressure, who would break and at what point, as if such questions were the ones he insistently posed to himself.

Later that month Berlin, together with Stuart Hampshire, was in the lobby of New York's Carlyle Hotel on his way up to see his mother-in-law. The lifts were blocked and no one was allowed to leave the lobby. Suddenly the hall filled with a moving wedge of secret-service agents and policemen, behind whom briskly walked the President. He spied Isaiah, walked over, shook his hand and asked him what he was doing there. Berlin said he was just a fan, waiting for his autograph. The President laughed, complimented him again on his lecture and said that they must meet again. Then he walked to the car and was gone.

Berlin was obviously flattered by the President's attention, but he remained less star-struck by Kennedy than were his friends. He was not drawn towards the flame of power. There was no reservoir of frustration within him about the passive, spectatorial limitations of intellectual life that a powerful man could exploit. He enjoyed the spectacle of Camelot, but it left him fundamentally unmoved. Camelot's interest in *him* represents the high point of his reputation on the American East Coast. After the visits to the Kennedy White House, he would never enjoy quite such favour again. He was also shrewd enough to see that the relative prestige of the English in Washington had suffered a drastic decline since the Roosevelt years. As he wrote to Robert Oppenheimer, director of the Institute of Advanced Study at Princeton, only Russia, China and the United States were fully 'real' to American policy-makers; in their eyes, Europe lacked any strongly discernible personality.[70] When he returned to Oxford in 1963, Berlin felt – for the first time – that he was returning to a diminished and second-rate country.

He was at Sussex University, just about to mount the platform to give a lecture in November 1963, when he was told of the President's assassination. For about ten minutes he found himself unable to speak. Then, without commenting on the news or referring to it in any way, he went out and read his scheduled lecture on Machiavelli.[71]

16

Liberal at Bay, 1963–71

By the early 1960s Berlin had a unique reputation, neither as a historian nor a philosopher, but as an idiosyncratic combination of the two. This approach put him in a class of his own, but it raised doubts in critics' minds as to what exactly he was up to. Since his most distinctive insights were presented as glosses on the thoughts of others – Herzen, Vico, Machiavelli – his own originality lay concealed. But this method suited his cast of mind. He lacked John Rawls' or Herbert Hart's capacity for sustained abstract exposition. Thinking, for him, was always a dialogue either with a friend or with a book. A blank sheet of paper aroused dread; a page of Vico stimulated spark after spark of reflection. The results might have been a series of clever but miscellaneous essays had the whole project not been held together by an overarching commitment to defend the validity of liberal principles in the face of their apparent historical relativity.

He became convinced, by the early 1960s, that this issue had only become salient in Western philosophy with the birth of the Romantic age. In 'Sources of Romantic Thought', the Mellon Lectures at the National Gallery of Art in Washington in March and April 1965 – another prodigious exercise in prepared extemporisation before a huge audience – he made the controversial claim that, until the Romantic era, the very idea that values might be in conflict had not arisen. Until the Romantics, serious philosophical opinion held that for any genuine question there must be one true answer; that these truths were accessible to all human beings; and that all the true answers to true questions must be compatible with each other.[1]

He knew that this triad of rationalist dogmas simplified the contradictory impulses of the Enlightenment. But he simplified deliberately in order to illuminate the philosophical problem that Romanticism had bequeathed to modernity when it cast these tenets into doubt. First, in conceiving Man as an expressive creature, who creates his own nature and his own identity through labour and art, the Romantics decisively historicised human nature. Since human nature was not always one and the same, the truth would not always appear the same to each human group. Each culture had its own centre of gravity – what Herder called its *Schwerpunkt*.[2] It was unintelligible, therefore, to believe that all human societies were stretched out in a caravan called progress, heading towards the same horizon line.

By the 1820s, thanks to the Romantics, none of the legs of the rationalist tripod were standing: the idea that there was one right answer to all human questions; that the truth was the same to all human beings; and that human values could never contradict each other. Out of this assault on the assumptions of Western rationalism there emerged a new set of values – sincerity, authenticity and toleration – which had never been admired before. It had never occurred to John Calvin or Ignatius Loyola to suppose that the truths of the other side in the religious wars might be worthy of respect.[3] They were damnable heresies. By 1820 sincerity itself had become a virtue, and authenticity – backing up sincerity by commitment – came to be valued irrespective of the content of belief. After Herder, European culture embraced toleration as the recognition of the plurality of truth and value. Added to this, the Romantics introduced the idea that cultural variety was in itself a good thing. Sincerity, authenticity, toleration and variety – these new values formed the presuppositions of modern liberal individualism. Moreover, the Romantic conception of tragedy transformed modern politics. Until the Romantics, it was believed that tragedy arose from error or human fallibility. But in the world revealed by the Romantics, tragedy was unavoidable: men were bound to disagree about the ultimate ends of life; these ends themselves were in conflict. Not all good things could be had at once. Conflict of values and tragic loss were unavoidable.

Why was Berlin himself so drawn to the tragic register in Romantic thought? Despite outward success and inward happiness, his own self-image in the 1960s was of a man beset: disliked by the left, held in suspicion by the right; too sceptical to be trusted by the committed; too committed to be at home among defenders of the status quo. He managed these conflicts with a gay, sardonic public surface; but underneath, he was often troubled with a sense, if not of tragedy, then certainly of the inevitability of losing someone or something dear whenever he made a commitment. The conflicts within were not merely about political alignment. They were centrally about his intellectual morality. The very form of his lectures – panoramic generalisation addressed to a general audience – caused him deep inner apprehension. Before the Mellon Lectures, his stepson Philippe Halban remembered that he was in a state of almost comical agitation, restless, doubtful, convinced that they would be a dreadful failure.[4] In fact, they were a resounding success and all six lectures were broadcast on BBC Radio in August and September 1966 to an almost universally favourable response.[5] Yet acclaim never stilled the voices within. Some hint of these suppressed inner doubts about the very legitimacy of his own thinking surface in a letter to Richard Crossman in January 1963:

> Myself, I am caught between all fires: you think me a cautious and subtle evader and craven pedant; almost everyone else blames me for intemperate polemics, over-wild generalisations, insufficient caution and dedication to minute analysis, and not enough intellectual neutralism. So I'm damned if I do, and I'm damned if I don't.[6]

To one of his closest friends throughout the 1960s and 1970s, the Nuffield sociologist Jean Floud, Berlin confessed that he was much more inwardly divided than he seemed: his sense of the conflict of moral ends arose from his own inner experience:

> The *only* truth which I have ever found out for myself is, I think, this one: of the unavoidability of conflicting ends: hence anti-eighteenth century, anti-Herbert [Hart], anti-positivism, romanticism and all. All central beliefs on human matters spring from a

personal predicament: so with Plato (I am sure), Kant, Hume, Spinoza, Freud, Marx etc . . . The contrast between my cheerful and feckless façade, and unquiet constant perturbations and apprehension within, is too odd.[7]

What gave his thought its resonance was this sense of his own inner divisions, and while Berlin never explicitly carried his own autobiography into his intellectual work, it was always at work within, pushing him to stress the potential for tragedy whenever people were forced to choose between sides of their natures.

This sense of the tragic deepened his thought and oriented his work towards questions he had not been able to face. Up to this point, references to the extermination of his own people were rare and his intellectual gaze focused on Soviet, rather than Nazi, totalitarianism. From the late 1950s, he began to think about fascism seriously, tracing the remote intellectual antecedents of Nazism back to the Romantics. In their emphasis on the distinctiveness of German *Kultur*, the Romantics shattered the unity of European culture for ever:

If I am a German I seek German virtues, I write German music, I rediscover ancient German laws, I cultivate everything within me which makes me as rich, as expressive, as many-sided, as full a German as it is possible for me to be . . . That is the romantic ideal at its fullest. The old pre-suppositions have vanished overnight. What is the common ideal of life? The very notion has lost relevance.[8]

The Romantics bequeathed the tyranny of identity politics: the obsessional elaboration of an identity distinguishably one's own, safe from contamination or impingement by other races, religions, genders or nationalities. It is significant that an expatriate who had to forge an identity for himself should have been so sceptical about Romantic self-creation as an ideal. Self-creation might be innocuous, occasionally noble, in conditions of freedom, but in the hands of a Napoleon or a Hitler, it could degenerate into a justification for moulding human clay into instruments of their own diabolical will. Romanticism gave the world not just the heroic figure of Beethoven in his garret but Hitler as artist of a nation:

> As the artist blends colours and the composer sounds, so the political demiurge imposes his will upon his raw material – average, ungifted human beings, largely unconscious of the possibilities dormant within them – and shapes them into a splendid work of art – a state or an army, or some great political, military, religious, juridical structure. This may entail suffering: but like discords in music it is indispensable to the harmony and effect of the whole. The victims of these great creative operations must take comfort, and indeed be exalted, by the consciousness that they are thereby lifted to a height which their own lower natures could never by themselves have achieved.[9]

Romanticism's contribution to political irrationalism in the twentieth century was the glorification of the leader as artistic demiurge. It also helped to fracture the idea of a single human species whose members were equally entitled to the same forms of moral consideration:

> The division of mankind into two groups – men proper, and some other, lower, order of beings, inferior races, inferior cultures, subhuman creatures, nations or classes condemned by history – is something new in human history. It is a denial of common humanity – a premise upon which all previous humanism, religious and secular, had stood.[10]

The curse of the twentieth century, Berlin argued, has been that both of its major utopias – Hitler's and Stalin's – rejected the very idea of the indivisibility of the human species. A communist true believer did not even attempt to persuade a bourgeois or aristocrat of the truth of communist principles: they were class enemies, to be re-educated or disposed of. Likewise, fascists did not deign to reason with Jews, gypsies or other racial enemies. They were to be extirpated as vermin. Romanticism's denial that all human beings were everywhere the same could lead ultimately to the denial that they deserved to exist.

In his long essay on another precursor of fascism, Joseph de Maistre,

Berlin focused on the romanticisation of violence. De Maistre's conception of Man was of a violent artist whose desire for self-immolation was 'as fundamental as [his] desire for self-preservation or happiness'.[11] When the Romantics exalted conflict, then storm and stress and finally violence, they provided the intellectual soil in which the seeds of Nazism could take root. Berlin was imprecise about how these influences worked through into Nazi ideology. In what historical sense was de Maistre a 'precursor' of fascism? Hitler had never heard his name. But again, a historical genealogy of fascism was not what Berlin really had in mind. His problem was philosophical: trying to understand how the Enlightenment faith in moral universals should have been transformed into the Romantic exaltation of all that was irrational in human nature.[12]

What made him unusual was that he deliberately moved out beyond the well-lit playing area of academic liberalism, where John Rawls, Herbert Hart and Ronald Dworkin were re-fashioning the heritage of Kant and Mill to fit the modern age, into the dark undergrowth of modern irrationalism. Berlin was the only liberal thinker of real consequence to take the trouble to enter the mental worlds of liberalism's sworn enemies.

Where did this leave him? What, in the end, could he salvage from the Romantic attack on his own premises? The key text here is 'European Unity and its Vicissitudes', a sombre lecture delivered in 1959 to the European Cultural Foundation in Amsterdam. Its essential purpose was to understand what values had survived Hitler and Stalin with their legitimacy intact. His list was bare and to the point: there is such a thing as human nature, for we all share the same 'physical, physiological and nervous structure', the same body, the same capacity to feel pain.[13] Moreover, we are moral beings: we would not qualify as human if moral considerations, however false or inadequate, were absent from our deliberations. And from this common ground – of a shared body and a shared language of moral discourse – we know the inhuman when we encounter it. He had no convincing argument as to why men and women, who had imbibed the culture of European universalism through Goethe and Schiller, should have treated their fellows as so much vermin. All he could say was that to regard human beings as vermin was to reason from demonstrably false premises. But why such reasoning should have become persuasive to the entire political class of a great nation, and to millions of their supporters in Europe, he could not say. But then who can?

What Isaiah could affirm was that the century's experience of infamy had brought the European conscience back to its senses. 'Because these rules were flouted, we have been forced to become conscious of them.' Since the Second World War there had been a return to 'the ancient notion of natural law' – sustained this time not by faith *in*, but fear *of*, mankind.[14] It was now clear, he argued, where ideas of racial superiority and theories of the dictatorship of the proletariat, these twin denials of human universality, were bound to lead. The human race had at last performed all the necessary experiments: it was no longer possible to deny that mankind must either respect the universality of the species or perish altogether. Apart from these fragmentary suggestions, he never explored further how faith in moral universals might be strengthened. He had an aversion to sermons. The most he would ever say was that 'the first public obligation' of any politics whatever was 'to avoid extremes of suffering'.[15]

Where did these ventures into darkness leave him? Larry Siedentop, a one-time pupil of Berlin, remarked that his teacher liked to venture out into the Romantic irrational by day, but always returned to the Enlightenment at nightfall.[16] This does catch something of the ambiguity of Berlin's intellectual odyssey in the 1950s and 1960s. But in the end, his adventures into the dark and exalted world of the European Romantics made it impossible for him ever to fully return to the calm and classical light of the Enlightenment. He believed in reason, but not overmuch; he believed in moral universals, but he knew they had scant purchase on fanatics. Human beings were never less than ingenious in justifying their own abominations. He hoped that Europe had learned from its journey into the abyss; he deeply believed that the concentration camps offered the most conclusive justification ever for the necessity of a universal moral law. But towards even his own moderately hopeful propositions, he remained what he had always been: a wise, watchful and incurably realist sceptic.

By the time he delivered the Mellon Lectures in 1965, Berlin was fifty-five. In a mysterious way the impulses that had powered the most formidably creative period of his intellectual life now began to wane. Since the visit to Harvard in January 1949 he had written the work on which his reputation was to depend. All of the competing identities within him, as Jew, Russian and Englishman, had to be forged together for this exceptionally single-minded achievement to be possible. Once that impulsion to speak had spent itself, he was done.

By the 1960s he was almost as famous a sight in Oxford as the Sheldonian Theatre or the Radcliffe Camera. But he knew that being an Oxford character was a fate to be avoided. He had only to look at Maurice Bowra to see why. His old friend now drank too much, shouted a great deal, told boring stories about the 1930s and 'went for arsers', his phrase for falling on his backside.[17]

Berlin's marriage to Aline had saved him from the fate of a Bowraesque bachelorhood and his own intellectual youthfulness kept him from becoming a fossil. He had never cultivated the friendship of younger generations – but they had gravitated naturally to him, since he was free of the hauteur usually associated with academic grandees. As a result, he was at the centre of the revival of political thought – especially among young Marxists – in the 1960s. Though he disagreed with his Marxist or *Marxisant* graduate students, their moral urgency reminded him of his beloved nineteenth-century Russian intelligentsia. But when a young colleague, Norman Birnbaum, claimed that alienation was a necessary 'metaphysical beginning point' for his search 'for a way out of the present discontents', Berlin dismissed the concept as a typical piece of Central European secular theology, more likely to confuse than clarify the discontents, whatever they were. The idea of alienation 'pre-supposed the possibility of some kind of terrestrial paradise – an ideal state of affairs which is the solution of all problems and the harmonisation of all values'.[18] This was precisely what he had set his liberalism against. Berlin also remained dubious about the proposition, central to the 1960s' Marxist revival, that there was a meaningful distinction between the young and old Marx, between the humanist of the 1840s and the positivistic revolutionary of the 1850s. As he wrote to the Harvard Russian scholar Richard Pipes, there was no liberal humanist Marx to be saved from the Stalinist consequences; there was only the young Marx, who believed in 'swift blows and putsches', and the older one who was resigned to a longer revolutionary build-up.[19]

Berlin's visits to American campuses in the 1960s took him right into the radical cauldron. At one point during the Columbia student strike of 1968, he gave a lecture so close to the police lines that his friends told him to wet a handkerchief to place over his mouth and eyes in case tear-gas canisters were fired in his vicinity. His Marxist graduate students Bert Ollmann and Marshall Berman attended the lecture, ready to defend him against hecklers, and if necessary against physical attack.[20] It was not an auspicious time to be a liberal philosopher.

Unlike many of his own generation – Stephen Spender and Yehudi Menuhin, for example, who prided themselves on communing with 'the young' – Berlin felt little attraction to the turbulence of the times. He saw the 1960s' revolution as an uprising against the boredom, security and lack of existential challenge in the post-war capitalist boom. The anger, he thought, was 'about psychological malaise, hypocrisy, lack of love, lack of understanding, lack of acceptance, "alienation", class consciousness and class education and not oppression of the majority by a wicked or deluded minority'.[21]

Typically, he explored the discontents of the 1960s by returning to the past, through a study of the early twentieth-century anarcho-syndicalist philosopher Georges Sorel. Berlin imagined that Sorel would have had no difficulty understanding Franz Fanon, the Black Panthers, Che Guevara and all those in revolt against imperialism, capitalism and the rule of technocratic experts. Berlin displayed a certain ironic sympathy both for Sorel and the revolutionaries of the 1960s in their loathing of 'a society of consumers without authentic moral values of their own, sunk in vulgarity and boredom in the midst of mounting affluence, blind to sublimity and moral grandeur'.[22] But it was ironic sympathy only. In what purported to be a paraphrase of Sorel's views, but which actually expressed one of his own deeply felt paradoxes, Berlin wrote that 'if faith in reason is delusive, it is only by the use of rational methods, by knowledge and self-knowledge . . . that this could be discovered and established'.[23] The revolutionary cult of violence, the exaltation of revolt for its own sake, the loathing of reason were all too dangerous to indulge.

His distaste for the philosophy of the 1960s grew as the decade progressed. In 1962 he had met Herbert Marcuse at Harvard and thought him an amiable German café intellectual. As Marcuse grew into his role as guru of the student revolution, Berlin became increasingly disenchanted. Then in 1969, while reading an issue of *Encounter*, he came upon Marcuse's remark that 'the world of the concentration camps was not an exceptionally monstrous society. What we saw there was the image, in a sense the quintessence, of the infernal society into which we are plunged every day.'[24] This caused a rare explosion of intellectual fury. In a letter to Jean Floud, Berlin exclaimed:

> Wd you trust such a man with *anything*? Would you think him capable of telling the truth or behaving honourably, in *any* circumstances? Old charmer indeed! To hell with them all . . .'[25]

In one of the few examples of a genuine rant in his correspondence, he went on to excoriate the milieu that had produced Marcuse:

> the terrible twisted *Mitteleuropa* in which nothing is straight, simple, truthful, all human relations and all political attitudes are twisted into ghastly shapes by these awful casualties who, because *they* are crippled, recognise nothing pure and firm in the world!

It was not just Marcuse, but Hannah Arendt whom Isaiah had in mind. He had first met her in 1942 when she was working with a Zionist relief organisation and then later in the early 1950s, when she was part of the *Partisan Review* circle with Dwight MacDonald and Mary McCarthy. When he met her the second time, she had recanted her Zionism and he distrusted someone who had changed position on so fundamental a question.[26] He also thought that certain of her ideas – for example, that the classical Greeks did not respect work – were wrong and thus weakened much-praised books like *The Human Condition*. His dislike reached a peak over her 1962 book, *Eichmann in Jerusalem: A Report on the Banality of Evil*. Isaiah himself had been in Jerusalem during the Eichmann trial and, like Arendt, had been struck by the banality of the bespectacled defendant in the glass cage. But he was genuinely infuriated by her argument that European Jewry might have resisted the Holocaust more effectively. He could only take this personally. The thought that his own people, the gentle, inoffensive, unheroic Volschonoks and Schneersons of Riga, should be criticised from the safety of New York for having failed to stand up to the SS struck him as a piece of monstrous moral conceit.[27] No moral judgement whatsoever was possible from conditions of safety on the behaviour of human beings in conditions of danger. Even active collaboration could not be condemned outright.[28]

This distaste for the fashionable intellectuals of the 1960s – Arendt and Marcuse – deepened into something approaching intellectual despair when he surveyed the student revolutionaries themselves. Berlin was in America when armed black students took over the campus at Cornell; he was told by Harvard colleagues that they feared students might set fire to the books in the Widener Library; he witnessed an earnest concern for university reform by moderate students being hijacked by a violent nihilism, which refused even to justify its own destructiveness. As he wrote to Bernard Williams from New York in early 1969:

Is there something we genuinely do not understand about people who refuse to give rational answers to questions about what they want, how they intend to do it, what their principles [are], how they estimate the moral cost?[29]

The whole experience of the 1960s made him uneasily aware that he had not understood the nihilist consequences of the Romantic esteem for sincerity and authenticity. In the Christ-like bearded figures roaming the campus and streets of New York, he could see Romanticism carried to its extreme.[30] In a letter to his old friend Niouta Kallin, with whom he had made his BBC radio broadcasts, Isaiah confessed the depth of his alienation from the Romantic nihilists of his day:

I feel depressed by the rapid growth of barbarism – I daresay every generation has – among our young men. The revolutionaries of my day had some respect for knowledge and intelligence and tried to learn from the enemy in order to use the weapons – whatever they may have been – philosophy or history or mathematics or technology for their own ends. This generation is complacently ignorant, uses mechanical formulae to dispose of anything that may be difficult or complicated, hates history on the whole, wishes to throw off the past (which I can understand if it is a return to a still older past) – the future cannot be returned to or used, it is only a hollow word! The old nihilists at least thought they respected science – these ones confuse crudity and sincerity and when culture is mentioned their hands really do automatically reach for a paving stone. But I must not go on with this lamentation, it sounds like some decayed liberal from Turgenev.[31]

On the great issue of the day – Vietnam – Berlin took a position that satisfied no one, not even himself. Some of the Americans he became closest to in the 1960s – such as Robert Silvers, the founder editor of the *New York Review of Books* – were passionate in their opposition to the war. Others, like Arthur Schlesinger and McGeorge Bundy, were burdened by their role in the American build-up in Vietnam during the Kennedy presidency; while still others, like Joe Alsop, were intransigently in favour of pursuing a military victory. Berlin congratulated himself on remaining on good terms with friends who could barely stand to be in the same room.[32] But his detachment irritated those who believed that the issues at stake were too serious for detachment.

In 1967 he was asked to contribute to *Authors Take Sides on Vietnam*, a collection of pro- and anti-war statements by prominent intellectual figures on both sides of the Atlantic. In a short and equivocal contribution, Berlin argued that Vietnam was a much more ambiguous issue than Spain in the 1930s. Then he had been certain that republican Spain deserved support. On Vietnam, he believed that the Americans should not have intervened but, having committed themselves, they could not withdraw precipitously, lest the South Vietnamese be massacred by communist forces. He accepted the key propositions of both sides: that the American intervention was wrong; and that the domino theory – the likely collapse of other pro-Western regimes in the region, following a communist victory in Vietnam – happened to be true. He simply did not see how American policy could keep the dominoes from falling. This position satisfied neither the student radicals nor conservative friends like Alsop.[33]

Berlin wanted to believe that the united scorn of both left and right vindicated the moderation and good sense of his position, but in reality he often felt friendless and equivocal in a moral atmosphere of passionate faction and aroused sincerity. He joked to the Canadian politician John Roberts, who had been a graduate student at Oxford, that he was now being treated 'as an old mastodon of liberalism', as a 'last feeble echo of J.S. Mill to be treated gently as a harmless, respectable old relic'.[34] He was joking, of course, but not much.

Earlier than most, he sensed that the entire Cold War period was drawing to a close. As he wrote to McGeorge Bundy, 'the cultural cold war – two large armies operating against each other – seems to me to have broken up into confused skirmishes all over the place, inside and between old armies'.[35] He no longer knew which army to fight for. One symptom of the new confusions was the spectacle in France and Italy of students, drawn from the bourgeoisie, marching into revolutionary battle, ultimately against the reactionaries in the communist-dominated trade unions. As Isaiah wrote to the Italian historian Franco Venturi, 'the rebellion of the repentant bourgeoisie against the complacent and oppressive proletariat is one of the queerer phenomena of our time'.[36]

As the 1960s turned into the 1970s, Berlin identified more and more with the figure of Turgenev, another person who had endured the suspicion and dislike of left and right. He confessed to his friend, the Polish historian of Panslavism, Andrzej Walicki:

> I go on thinking about Turgenev: caught in a situation not all unlike our own, unable, as he said himself, 'to simplify himself', constantly attacked by both sides, constantly anxious to please the young and yet, when the crisis comes, unable to commit himself totally, although perfectly able to demean himself before authority and incur the wrath of Herzen and those to the left of him.[37]

In October 1970 for the Romanes Lecture, delivered before a packed audience at the Sheldonian Theatre in Oxford, Berlin chose the theme of 'Fathers and Sons' in Turgenev's writing. The lecture was a defence of liberal moderation in a radical era.[38] He drew transparent parallels between Turgenev's perplexity towards the radicals of the 1870s and his own. Like Turgenev, Isaiah was fascinated by radical temperaments, but incapable of being a radical himself. Like Turgenev, he had a preternatural gift of empathy, 'an ability to enter into beliefs, feelings and attitudes alien and at times acutely antipathetic to his own'.[39] Like Turgenev, he could not enter into radicalism sufficiently to surrender his own detached and ironic scepticism.

The essay on Turgenev was also an oblique portrait of the liberal temperament, of the psychology required of good citizens in a liberal polity. Empathy was, for Berlin, the core liberal aptitude – the capacity to be open, receptive, unafraid in the face of opinions, temperaments, passions alien to one's own. Empathy committed you to leave the stockades of liberal reason itself in order to understand reason's limited purchase on a world propelled by passionate conviction and radical intensity. Empathy of this sort did not imply relativist indulgence: it meant coolly establishing what could be negotiated across the frontiers between convictions and what could not. The result was a moral psychology of liberal life which, while unsystematic, was as deep as anything within the liberal canon since Adam Smith's *Theory of Moral Sentiments*.[40]

Turgenev occasioned a still more intimate encounter with another liberal dilemma: the problem of courage. Turgenev was accused throughout his career of ingratiating himself with the authorities and the revolutionaries alike, and of securing the trust of neither side. Even Herzen, who respected his literary genius, thought Turgenev an equivocating old maid in politics. Such, in crude terms, was the charge whispered behind Berlin's back throughout his steady ascent through the upper reaches of English life: that he had run with the hares and hunted with the hounds: that he had wanted to be thought a man of the left, but actually felt most comfortable among the right. All of these failings amounted to the single indictment that he lacked the existential courage to stand and be counted.

The charge of cowardice bothered him all his life. But his work does not have the shape of a man eager to please at any cost. His liberal theory was intransigent in its emphasis on the necessity of tragic choice and in its commitment to negative rather than positive liberty. His theoretical claims remained provoking rather than mollifying: they were the work of a mind prepared to push its own scepticism very far indeed; and, in the key arguments of his life – with E.H. Carr, Isaac Deutscher, T.S. Eliot, Arthur Koestler, Adam von Trott – Berlin gave no ground at all. Nor had he been a smooth *suiviste*: he had made his career on his own terms. He left academic philosophy and followed a highly idiosyncratic path of his own in the borderlands between history and philosophy, without mentors to guide him or disciples to follow. This might not take courage but it certainly indicates a temperament prepared to take intellectual risks. He also knew how to take risks in his personal life. He sought out the love of a married woman with children and eventually made her his wife. Of all the risks he ever took, it was the one most worth taking.

Yet the issue of courage caused him real anguish.[41] This in itself is interesting: that he should have believed that intelligence and achievement could not redeem failures of will. This issue also tormented his hero, Turgenev. In the last year of his life, when he knew he was already dying of cancer, Turgenev dictated a story called 'A Fire at Sea', which recounted the experience of a young Russian on board a Baltic ferry after it catches fire on the crossing from St Petersburg to Lübeck. Turgenev re-created all the young man's terror as the adults around him lost their composure and their dignity. He himself had survived just such a fire as a young man, so it was maliciously rumoured, by promising a sailor half his estate if the man could save him from the flames. 'A Fire at Sea' was thus a dying man's attempt to confront the rumours of cowardice that had haunted him all his life. What seems to have drawn Berlin to Turgenev's story was his touching candour about the failings of his youth. Yes, Turgenev admitted, he had briefly lost his head – and had indeed offered money to a sailor if he would save him. But he had regained his composure within seconds and later helped others into lifeboats before himself. Berlin translated the story and read it on BBC Radio in 1957, subsequently republishing it himself with an introductory note. In this note, he argued that Turgenev 'represents his own conduct as that of an innocent, confused, romantically inclined young man, neither a hero nor a coward, slightly cynical, slightly absurd, but above all amiable, sympathetic and human'.[42] Beyond identifying deeply with an old man's defence of his younger self, Berlin obviously could see that a larger issue was at stake. The point was that romantic standards of heroism were a form of moral tyranny: men should be judged, not by whether they are willing to risk their lives, but by whether they kept their heads, morally and politically, when others lost theirs. By these modest yet not unexacting standards, both men passed the test they had set themselves.

17

Wolfson, 1966–75

In the autumn of 1965, while Isaiah was at Princeton, he was telephoned by the Oxford Vice-Chancellor with an unlikely proposition: would he consider becoming the first principal of Iffley College? It was a new institution barely in existence, one of two created to provide homes for dons who taught in the Oxford faculties but did not have fellowships in existing colleges, because they worked in subjects for which there was insufficient undergraduate teaching demand. Some two-thirds of these dons were in medicine and the natural sciences; the rest were in various humanities disciplines, university administration and the social sciences. Iffley was also supposed to provide a home for graduate students in these disciplines. A theoretical chemist had been approached for the principalship, but he declined when the university declared itself unable to help raise the funds for a new college building. The new fellows of the college then suggested Berlin.[1] But Iffley hardly existed: the statutes setting it up had only been ratified in May; it had no purpose-built buildings of its own, just a converted family house – No. 15 – on the Banbury Road. The university had allocated a substantial site for a future college building, but it was far outside Oxford and while four great Oxford colleges – Merton, All Souls, Christ Church and St John's – were stumping up funds to help with Iffley's running costs in its early years, there was insufficient capital for a new building.[2]

On first impressions, Berlin thought Iffley could never be more than a 'waste-paper basket'[3] where the University deposited faculty for whom no real college could find a place. Throughout the 1960s the natural science faculties were growing; more graduate students were arriving, but Oxford wasn't responding adequately to these pressures. If something was not done, there would soon be too many people who, while teaching at Oxford, lacked proper college facilities of their own.

It is not obvious why this issue should have mattered to Berlin. He had little interest in science and certainly no close friendships among scientists. As for the social sciences, he was a long-standing sceptic.[4] Twelve years before he had turned down one opportunity to become head of an Oxford house – Nuffield College.[5] Here was an offer to run a rag-bag college out of a single stucco-fronted house on the Banbury Road. The proposition, on the face of it, seemed absurd.

To the Vice-Chancellor's evident surprise, and perhaps to his own as well, Berlin said that he might consider it. He told Aline that he had the idea of turning it into a proper graduate college. On his return from the United States, he met a delegation of fellows, led by Frank Jessup, and discovered that they were his sort of people; unstuffy, intelligent, amusing and – on the issue of their exclusion from Oxford college life – properly indignant. When they complained of their treatment at other colleges, Isaiah found himself sympathetic for reasons intimately connected with his own memories of being an outsider. The excuses the scientists knew other colleges to be making – 'They work in labs, they don't come into college much ... there's no room in the common room' – sounded to him exactly like the excuses that rich nations offered in order to deny poor immigrants asylum.[6] This meeting seems to have tipped the balance. As an expatriate, he had a particular understanding of belonging: the chance to create a new community for those who had none suddenly had deep appeal. But remaining in 15 Banbury Road and running the college like a club for homeless scientists was not an option Berlin was prepared to consider. So he set one condition: if he couldn't raise the money within six months, the deal was off.[7]

When he heard that Berlin was considering Iffley, the distinguished historian Alan Bullock said that he was being 'quixotic'; the philosopher Herbert Hart thought the job sounded 'repellent'; Maurice Bowra said he could not understand leaving the splendours of All Souls for a miserable house up the Banbury Road; William Hayter, Warden of New College, thought Berlin mad; and the Balliol philosophy fellow, Marcus Dick, exploded: 'The idea of your wasting your extraordinary gifts and your time taking college meetings and sitting on committees horrifies me.'[8]

He had some explaining to do. He complained that he was tired of his professorship: lecturing to undergraduates had become a burden, and he felt that he was too much of a historian for a chair whose proper centre of gravity was political theory and philosophy.[9] A professor of politics ought to propagate doctrine, he said, and he had none to propagate. Besides, there was no interest in the history of ideas in Oxford. He felt isolated and only found an echo for his ideas in America. Accordingly, if he could raise the money, his plan was to take the Iffley job and continue with his professorship at the City University of New York for one term in every six.

He confessed to a pang at the thought of leaving All Souls and giving up his rooms with the beautiful view of the quad and the Radcliffe Camera. But apart from that, he was ready to go. He was disillusioned by what he felt was the stagnant mediocrity settling over the college. When All Souls turned down a brilliant, if difficult Austrian logician for a fellowship, Berlin felt that the college had sacrificed its intellectual standards.[10] By the mid-1960s the college was under increasing attack for failing to share its wealth with the university and for doing nothing for graduate teaching. Berlin believed that reform was long overdue. Three options were possible: first, it could begin to accept graduate students and commit itself to graduate education. This proposal, which Berlin supported, went nowhere. A second possibility, a marriage between St Antony's and All Souls, to create a Princeton-style Institute of Advanced Study at Oxford, was rebuffed by both colleges. The third option, which was to open up All Souls by offering visiting fellowships, found favour and went into operation in 1967. Sensing that All Souls would do nothing further for graduate education, Berlin seized on the Iffley offer: it gave him a chance to found a graduate college on his own.[11]

As usual he was lucky: the moment turned out to be extraordinarily propitious. It was already clear that Lord Franks' Report into the state of education at Oxford – due to be published in June 1966 – was going to recommend a substantial increase in Oxford's commitment to graduate education, especially in the sciences.[12] Berlin had discussed its possible recommendations with his friend Jean Floud, who served on the Franks

Commission. It now dawned on him that doing something for graduate students and for the 'non-dons', the faculty lecturers who didn't have college fellowships, might be a way to repay Oxford for what it had done for him. He wrote to Marcus Dick that if he could contribute something to Oxford of a concrete and lasting nature, 'I should feel better about my life in general. Better than if I had produced three good books.'[13] He said this in public, but in private he confessed, 'I have a secret desire to escape from something, I expect, although I rationalise it, naturally, as the purest high mindedness.'[14] What he was escaping from may have been the Romanticism project, whose looming outline now began to seem daunting. If anything, his self-doubt as an intellectual had grown with the years. As he had confessed to a correspondent in 1963, 'I have not the slightest faith in anything I write myself. It is exactly like money – if you make it yourself, it seems a forgery.'[15] Running a college offered a creditable escape. Yet it would be wrong to see the next decade as an exercise in flight or sublimation. Like many intellectuals, Berlin longed to prove his capacity for practical business. After a lifetime of consciously evading responsibility, he was seeking it now, and on risky terms, not taking over an established Oxford house but founding one from scratch.

The first problem to overcome was the Iffley site, which was too small and two miles from town. A site had to be found closer to Oxford if donors were to be attracted and if the college were to become a real part of the university. Once again, Berlin's luck held. In November, just as he was conditionally accepting the Iffley offer, the Haldane family agreed to sell the university their lease on a nine-acre site at the end of Linton Road in north Oxford. After some politicking, the site was made available to the new college.[16] The Haldane home, a large brick pile in which the scientist John Scott Haldane had conducted his First World War experiments on the impact of poison gases on human respiration, would have to be demolished and a new building erected on the sloping meadows and marshes that led down to the River Cherwell.[17] But where was the money to be found?

Berlin had never raised money in his life. It was time to use his connections. First, he made contact with McGeorge Bundy, then just about to take over as President of the Ford Foundation.[18] He had known Bundy since Harvard and they had kept in touch when Bundy was at the White House. Berlin had great respect for Bundy as an administrator and as an adviser of presidents, but his candid assessment to Maurice Bowra in 1963 had been that 'he clearly does not mind walking over corpses'. This was all right, Berlin added, provided the corpse was not his own.[19]

His appeal to the Ford Foundation played on American *noblesse oblige* towards the faltering British ally: a new college was necessary to prevent the brain-drain of Britain's best scientists and scholars; it was needed to renew Oxford itself.[20] These were persuasive arguments, but most persuasive of all was Berlin himself. His presence made the proposal intellectually respectable. As Ford later made clear, Isaiah's involvement was the *sine qua non* of their decision to get involved.[21] Once again, Berlin's timing and luck were uncanny: as an incoming president, Bundy enjoyed a honeymoon with his Trustees, which allowed him to get his way.[22] By February 1966 Bundy had committed Ford to the project, provided matching funds from a British donor could be found.

As the most respected Jewish figure in British intellectual life, Berlin knew that the doors of Jewish philanthropy were open to him. He marched straight through the most imposing door of all, to Sir Isaac Wolfson, founder president of Great Universal Stores. Wolfson was a shrewd and pious Glaswegian, full of jokes and vitality, who had made a large fortune by dint of enormous flair and acumen in the retail trade and mail-order. The Wolfson Foundation had existed since 1955 and had already made substantial grants to the Oxbridge colleges. Its founder had now reached the stage where he wanted to set the seal on his university benefactions. Isaac Wolfson reminded Isaiah of a great medieval merchant prince, while his son Leonard seemed a modern man of business, punctilious, if silent and inscrutable.[23] At his first lunch at the Ritz with Leonard Wolfson, Isaiah laid out the prospect of being associated in a joint venture with the greatest American foundation. Wolfson said that there was to be one condition: Iffley would have to be called Wolfson College.[24] Berlin immediately agreed, and he remembered saying, 'If you want your name immortalised, a college will do it better than a hospital. Wolfson College really will be immortal.'[25] By February 1966 Isaac and Leonard Wolfson had tentatively agreed, subject to the approval of their board.

Euphoria proved short-lived. Word reached Isaac Wolfson that Anthony Crosland, Secretary of State for Education in the Labour government, believed that money should be going to the red-brick universities instead.[26] Sir Solly Zuckerman, chief scientific adviser to the government, a professor at Birmingham and a member of the Wolfson Foundation board, also argued that money should be channelled away from Oxbridge.[27] The irony was that Zuckerman's resentment at Oxford may have owed something to the fact that as a young university demonstrator in anatomy he had been one of those 'non-dons' who had not been elected to a college fellowship.[28] This did not make him any less ferocious an opponent of the very project that proposed to remedy the injustice he felt he had suffered. His opposition proved formidable, especially because Oxford as a whole was on the defensive in the egalitarian ethos of the times. Isaiah was frankly exasperated, as he confessed to a friend:

> It is impossible to convey in America the full degree of prejudice against Oxford and Cambridge in the present Labour government – equality is a noble idea – and in its interests Oxford and Cambridge require reform – but when the desire for social justice takes resentful and emotional forms, it leads to repression and gratuitous damage rather than reform.[29]

To Lord Franks, then completing his report on the university, Isaiah wrote, 'the fashion is for egalitarianism – where it can well be fatal'.[30] The proposed college would be like Covent Garden, Berlin said, a national centre of excellence, but, like all such centres, it was bound to provoke the ire of a certain type of egalitarian social democrat. In fact, Berlin's plans were themselves egalitarian. There was to be no high table; spouses would have common-room rights; there would be a crèche for children and family living quarters. The fellowship was to be a genuine democracy.

But in the winter of 1966 this was all in the domain of pious intentions. The risk was that the Wolfson Foundation would pull out of the project altogether. To save the college, Berlin had to call on reserves of political acumen that his friends never suspected. He mobilised all the Oxford heads of houses, together with two Nobel Prize-winning scientists – Sir John Cockroft of Cambridge and Lord Florey, Provost of Queen's – behind the proposed college; then he sought out Crosland and succeeded in changing his mind.[31] Finally, knowing how much difference it would make to the Wolfsons if the Prime Minister himself, Harold Wilson, were known to approve, Berlin contacted Thomas Balogh, Wilson's chief economic adviser, and asked him to put in a good word.

Isaac Wolfson rang Berlin a few days later complaining that he had been telephoned by some Hungarian communist. This was Balogh. Then Balogh rang, equally irritable, to say that Isaac Wolfson had been rude to *him*. Clutching at straws, Berlin suggested absurdly that Wolfson must have mistaken Balogh for Max *Beloff* and pleaded that Balogh try again. Balogh was as good as his word. When Wolfson asked him whether he would put his *own* money into the college, Balogh said he certainly would. It would 'combine quality with democracy'.[32] Berlin could not have put it better himself. Soon Wolfson had received a call from the Prime Minister assuring him of his support – though Wilson grumbled to Berlin, when they met, that a lot of arm-twisting had gone on to get it this far. Indeed it had, but the college was back on track.

It was still necessary to steer the proposal through the full meeting of the Wolfson Foundation board, scheduled for June 1966. McGeorge Bundy flew over from New York, while Berlin flew in from Jerusalem, suffering from pneumonia. The Wolfsons, *père et fils*, kept silent, observing the fray. The chief remaining opponent was Zuckerman. It helped proceedings that Bundy had taken an immediate and sustained dislike to Zuckerman. Both had been in the Bahamas meetings between President Kennedy and Prime Minister Macmillan in 1962, and Bundy had come away believing that Zuckerman could not be trusted.[33] All of Zuckerman's suppressed resentment at Oxford now surfaced and he launched into a blistering attack on it as the graveyard of British science. Sir John Cockcroft heard him out and then murmured from the other end of the table, 'Solly, you go too far.'[34] Indeed he had. When it came to his turn, Bundy disregarded Zuckerman and firmly declared Ford's support. He then turned to Leonard Wolfson and asked whether he was in favour. When Wolfson said he was, Zuckerman gathered up his papers and stormed out, Berlin remembered gleefully, like the moustachioed villain of a melodrama. All this time Berlin – who was feeling more dead than alive from his pneumonia – had said not a word.

The deed was done. Ford had committed $4.5 million and Wolfson £1.5 million. It was Ford's largest single benefaction in Europe and the biggest donation to Oxford since the foundation of Nuffield College.

Letters of astonished, even envious congratulation poured in from friends.[35] Other colleges, especially St Antony's, which had been pursuing Ford money for years, were discomfited by Berlin's success, and to set matters right Berlin put in a word with Bundy. This was among the reasons why St Antony's eventually did receive $3 million of Ford funding.[36]

In July 1966 Iffley College was renamed Wolfson, Berlin accepted its presidency and in the autumn the fledgling institution settled into its temporary nest on the Banbury Road. Conditions were cramped: there were thirty-six fellows and they could not hope to find a berth in a house with only six modest rooms. But the basement was converted into a common room and straitened circumstances produced a special camaraderie.

Having found the money, Berlin now had to recruit a team. He enlisted a blue-ribbon committee of trustees – Leonard Wolfson, two Nobel Prize-winning scientists, Lord Florey and Peter Medawar, together with Dame Janet Vaughan of Somerville. To provide the committee with the ballast of worldly *savoir-faire*, he brought in two of his oldest friends, Sylvester Gates, a Vice-President of National Westminster Bank, and Sir John Foster, MP, his old colleague and mentor from All Souls.[37] Berlin had the good sense to realise that he was no administrator. For his right-hand man he chose the Corpus historian Michael Brock, as Vice-President and Bursar. Berlin proved an acute judge of character, for Brock was precise, methodical, hard-working, loyal and already versed in the intricacies of university politics.

Now that the team had been chosen, their most urgent task was to find an architect. Most university building in England in the 1960s had been afflicted by the parsimony imposed by government spending limits, and Berlin was determined to create an institution that would rise above the cheap and soon dilapidated modernism of so many of the new universities. He and the fellows took the business of finding an architect seriously. They were looking for someone who could translate the Oxford college into a modern idiom. Great names in architecture – I.M. Pei, Gordon Bunshaft and Philip Johnson – [38] were mentioned, but Berlin warned against choosing anyone who thought himself a Michaelangelo, while regarding the Wolfson fellows as a very inferior version of the Pope.[39] He and a team of fellows toured in buses, visiting many grim examples of modern brutalism, both in England and as far away as Finland and Holland.

The building that impressed them most was the Cripps Building, St John's College, Cambridge. It was elegant, discreetly sited and seemed to be born out of a real understanding of college life. When he toured it, Berlin's concern for detail was revealing: he asked about the sound-proofing, checked the students' rooms, toilet facilities and study space, and ran his hands over the travertine facing on the exterior.[40] Because it had been funded by a private donor and a rich Cambridge college, the Cripps Building had the well-built and unostentatiously splendid finish Berlin was looking for. In May 1967 the Wolfson fellows and the Trustees settled on the architects of the St John's building, Philip Powell and Hidalgo Moya. These two were enthusiastic: it is not every day that an architect is asked to design a whole academic village. A site plan was approved, laying out the quads, the wings of study-bedrooms, the library, and the most remarkable feature, the harbour-like marina for punts, which instead of bringing the building to the river, brought the river to the building. Demolition of the lugubrious Haldane pile was completed, and in May 1968 the Queen laid the foundation stone, while Berlin and the Wolfsons looked on.

Berlin's involvement with the details of the architectural plan was close and passionate. He was especially bothered by the 'crank-shape' of the B block. Throughout the summer of 1968, as the final design took shape in the architects' offices, Berlin sent Powell and Moya a stream of postcards from his and Aline's summer home in Paraggi. Each one displayed an aerial view of the harbour of nearby Portofino, and Berlin kept drawing their attention to the gentle curve of the buildings around the port. 'Don't you see,' he wrote to the doubtful architects, 'this is the way to do it.' Instead of forcing the building into 'rectilineal rigours', why not imitate the Renaissance curvature of the harbour, so much more suited to the 'sylvan scene' of the River Cherwell. The postcards are an interesting example of Berlin in persuasive mode, playful, joking but relentless. In the end, the architects gave way and, when the block arose on the banks of the Cherwell, it had a gently curving shape. In college lore, it was to become known as the Berlin Wall.[41] Aline brought her own quiet but determined aesthetic sense to bear as well, closely scrutinising the plans and gently pointing out to the architects that some of the proposed pillars were rather too thin. The pillars went up as per the drawing, but when Powell returned to the building twenty years later, he confessed that she had been right.[42]

In the summer of 1968 the college moved up the Banbury Road, from No. 15 to No. 60 and in the autumn accepted its first twenty-five graduate students. The college now had a dining hall, common room, committee rooms and an embryonic library – thanks to gifts from Berlin and Sir Ronald Syme – and even a croquet lawn.[43] But it lacked student accommodation and, to fill this need, it purchased houses down the Linton Road.

A college assembled out of a miscellaneous collection of north Oxford brick houses was quite a change from the regal elegance of All Souls, but both Isaiah and Aline seem to have loved what came to be called the 'years in the galleys' on the Banbury Road.[44] One early student pioneer remembered coming into the common room and spying a figure in black ferreting through the newspaper rack at lightning speed. The student introduced himself: 'My name is Stephen Grounds and I come from Birmingham.' The figure turned and said, 'And my name is Isaiah Berlin and I come from Riga,' whereupon the student found himself lifted up into the vertiginous climb of a Berlin conversation.[45]

This atmosphere, unusually intimate for an Oxford college, meant that the student revolution of the late 1960s largely bypassed Banbury Road. Graduate students were admitted to the General Meetings of the college along with fellows, and graduate representatives served on the governing body as well. The place, in Berlin's words, was to be 'new, untrammelled and unpyramided'. Just as he wished, the barriers between faculty and students present in the other Oxford colleges were dismantled: no high table; common rooms common to all; gowns to be worn only on special occasions. In addition, there was to be a crèche and family accommodation.[46]

Meanwhile, at the end of Linton Road, the new college building was slowly rising on the Cherwell site. Michael Brock struggled to keep the architect and the contractor within budget and on deadline, and while they did their best, British inflation, running high in those years, worked against them. By early 1971 it was clear that the project was going to overrun both in cost and time.[47] But despite escalating costs and delays, Berlin and Brock remained as keen as ever that the college should not be meanly appointed and that the finish – the furniture, the carpets, the skirting – should be decent. To their relief, once committed, both Ford and Wolfson never wavered. On Sir Isaac's initiative, the Wolfson Foundation contributed the white Carrara marble that provides a gleaming finish to the entrance to the dining hall, and on Leonard Wolfson's initiative, made an additional payment to ensure that hardwood trim was used throughout the buildings. By the time the project was completed, the Wolfson Foundation had contributed far more than their original financial commitment.[48]

There were days when Berlin felt that his life had been swallowed up by considerations about furniture, budgets, contractors' delays, the supply of marble and hardwood trim. His own letters from the period are full of rueful lament, but the tone is mocking rather than genuinely regretful:

> I become a bureaucrat and all is over. Intellect, imagination, love of art, pleasure, friends, all is absorbed in the managerial world of which we have become a part. This is perhaps a slight exaggeration.[49]

Despite this tide of detail – and the fact that he spent one term in six in New York – he still managed to shape the intellectual identity of the college, attracting a growing number of extremely distinguished fellows, among them Niko Tinbergen, who was to win the Nobel Prize for his studies in animal behaviour in 1973. Isaiah's own presence began to attract graduate students in political philosophy and the history of ideas. By 1970 there were over fifty fellows and seventy graduate students, and Banbury Road was in ceaseless activity: student societies, research colloquia, committee meetings and elections. When Solly Zuckerman paid the college a visit, he asked to see the list of fellows and, after long and careful scrutiny, pronounced that Berlin had helped select one of the most impressive rosters in Oxbridge.[50] Even *he* came round in the end.

While his friends worried that Berlin was frittering his intellectual life away in administration, the truth was that Wolfson College gave Isaiah a new lease of life. He had always had an intense feeling for institutions. Now, he had the chance to create his own community and he revelled in it. As President, he demonstrated an entrepreneurial flair, a capacity for leadership and a political cunning that perhaps not even he had suspected. Those who worked closely with him – Michael Brock, Cecilia Dick, the domestic bursar, and the secretarial staff – remember Banbury Road as a time of high spirits. Berlin proposed, in jest, for example, that Wolfson's motto should be that lugubrious misanthropic tag: *Homo homini lupus* – Man is Wolf to Man. Brock especially remembered him in his office dictating letters on his Grundig machine, clicking the record button on and off, interspersing dictation with remarks and jokes to people in the room. His Scottish secretary had to transcribe these tapes, occasionally with comic results. One letter, placed before him for signature, contained the sentence: 'I am therefore obliged with the greatest regret (Ho Ho) to decline your flattering invitation.'[51] He shuddered to think how such a reply would have been received.

Much to her friends' surprise, Aline also enormously enjoyed the Wolfson years: fellows and students were frequently invited to garden parties and receptions at Headington House and she felt accepted among the fellowship, as she had never been at All Souls.[52]

Berlin's intellectual productivity declined during the Wolfson years, but his writing by no means stopped – essays on Georges Sorel, the famous comparison between Disraeli and Marx, the Romanes Lecture on Turgenev all appeared during his time as President. And honours continued to descend: in 1971 the greatest of all, the Order of Merit. It was a decoration granted by the Queen herself and reserved for twenty-four men and women whose unusual distinction had added significantly to the lustre of the nation. Characteristically, the honour unleashed yet another wave of embarrassment: he and Aline fled the country.[53] With the OM, he felt, the systematic over-estimation of his talents had reached its dubious climax. But when the news reached 60 Banbury Road, a spontaneous party erupted, which Michael Brock remembered as the most anarchic and enjoyable celebration he ever attended.

Berlin had a strong sense of narrative drama: he likened the creation of Wolfson to a steeple-chase, some riders unhorsed, others clearing their fences – some easily, others by the narrowest of margins. At other times, he felt he was a commander in the middle of shot and shell, with news from the battlefields – the building site, the committee rooms, the Wolfson Foundation – being brought to him by breathless courier. These metaphors were semi-comic, but they also suggested how deeply invested he was in the process. By the winter of 1974 the buildings were more or less complete. The long march to Linton Road was over.[54]

The founding of Wolfson College was important for Oxford. By the mid-1960s there was a danger that Oxford might decline into the Salamanca of English intellectual life, bypassed like the old Spanish medieval university.[55] Wolfson was part of a larger process of renewal, symbolised by the Franks Report, which prevented Oxford from falling victim to the Salamanca syndrome. With the foundation of Wolfson, the natural and social sciences were given a new college community of their own and this helped the university to strengthen its reputation in these fields. Certainly, the quality of Wolfson helped to lure high-quality graduate students from around the world, and its fellowship became among the most cosmopolitan in the Oxford system.

The creation of Wolfson mattered greatly to Berlin, because it allowed him to thank Oxford; enabled him to silence that inner voice which doubted he had the capacity for practical business; and because the college itself, when the new buildings opened in 1974, bore the imprint of his convictions and character. To the claims that can be made on his behalf, as the most historically minded of twentieth-century liberal philosophers and the most philosophical of historians of ideas, there should be added a third claim: that he was the only philosopher to leave behind him an institution in the image of his own ideals.

All through this period, indeed since his father's death, he had made a point of visiting his mother once a month at their home in Hollycroft Avenue, Hampstead. A passport photograph of her, taken for a visit to Israel in the 1960s, shows a tiny woman with white hair, distinctively dark eyes and a half-smile, with all the mild gentleness of the very old, yet still full of humour and force of character. Every Passover Seder was celebrated in her presence: Isaiah read the scriptures in Hebrew, Aline attended and afterwards the Polish maid served the Passover meal. She met all his close friends, pronouncing some acceptable, entering reservations about others; listened eagerly to the gossip; took as much part in his busy life as Isaiah allowed and then pined and reproached when he had to leave and get back to Oxford. It was the oldest and most basic relationship in his life, and it only began to ebb away in the last several years, when her health failed in her early nineties, and she required constant nursing.[56] At the end, when she was bedridden and drifting in and out of consciousness, Aline and Isaiah, who were sitting at her bedside, suddenly heard her sing the *Marseillaise* – in Russian. Isaiah's heart leaped – some buried memory of revolutionary Petrograd, a snatch of a song borne on the air, had risen within her. But she never repeated it again.[57] One mid-February morning in 1974 her nurses phoned him to say that she had not awakened. She was ninety-four years old.

Old friends rallied to give him comfort. He confessed to Herbert Hart and to Jean Floud that he felt as if the roof of his life had blown off.[58] The word that kept recurring to him was *Zerrissenheit*. It meant being torn to pieces. For a week or so he was in deep mourning, weighing his loss and looking back over the terrain he had travelled in her company. He suddenly felt horribly alone. Life seemed to have lost its story-line and his own existence seemed accidental. The link to the most intimate of his loyalties had been snapped. She had been the real unacknowledged source of his Herderian beliefs – in Jewishness, in belonging, in the very necessity of having roots.[59] She had given him that existential certainty, that confidence in his own judgement, which had allowed him to *live* his life and not merely inhabit it, as his father had done. With her death, he told a friend, the pillars that held up his life had cracked; while the cracks would soon be covered over with makeshift plaster, the pillars would never be as solid again.[60] Martin Gilbert, the biographer of Churchill, managed to grasp the extent of Isaiah's loss when he wrote, 'she must have been vastly proud of all that you had achieved on that long road from Riga'.[61] Isaiah buried her next to his father in Willesden Green Jewish Cemetery on 14 February 1974. It had indeed been a long road from Riga, and now the last person to have accompanied every step was gone.

18

Retrospect, 1975–97

Within a month of his mother's funeral, Berlin had resumed the same hectic pace as before, lecturing in America, dashing off to Jerusalem to sit on a committee awarding the Rothschild scholarships, then spending the summer in Paraggi, where he and Aline had built a house. In the autumn of 1974 he finally moved from the Banbury Road into his new offices in Wolfson College. In late autumn the new buildings were opened by Harold Macmillan, Chancellor of the University, with Isaac and Leonard Wolfson on hand. In his speech of dedication, Macmillan paid tribute to the Wolfsons but also to the college's President. 'I just want you each to ask yourself this simple question about him as a man: if you happened to be in a mood of melancholy or frustration, who would you rather see come into your room than Isaiah Berlin?'[1]

Berlin stayed on through that autumn and winter to hear Mstislav Rostropovich dedicate the new dining hall with a noble performance of a Bach unaccompanied cello suite. He could have stayed on, but the work of creation was done, and it was the creation of an institution, rather than its administration, that had excited him. Besides – and this was a central feature of his character – he was always lightly invested in his roles. He threw himself into what he did, but always kept back some part of himself. His identity never seems to have depended on any of his achievements. So it was relatively easy to leave Wolfson in March 1975 and not look back. His presence remained there, intangibly in the ethos of the place, and tangibly in Derek Hill's portrait of him, in Wolfson library, which depicts him as he was in his late sixties, wearing a three-piece suit, seated in a chair, legs crossed, looking out at the world with a wary, fox-like expression, tensely alive and sceptical.[2]

Retirement from Wolfson was made easier by the fact that he had been elected, in 1974, to the Presidency of the British Academy, the chief institution for the promotion and recognition of humanities and social science research in Britain. Being President was not a full-time job, and he found time for long trips to Australia and Japan during his tenure, but it did put Berlin at the centre of British academic politics in the 1970s. Like many venerable British institutions of that period, the Academy inhabited magnificent quarters – Burlington House off Piccadilly, next door to the Berlins' flat at Albany – but it was perennially short of money, staff and office space. Presiding over the Academy confronted him with Britain's relative economic decline and its dire impact on Britain's university culture. After a visit to a sister academy in Bavaria, Berlin observed that there was more room in the *corridors* of the Bavarian academy than in all the offices in Burlington House.[3] Compared to the support that Germany had lavished on the Max Planck Institutes and France on the Centre National de Recherche Scientifique, the British Academy was the Cinderella of academic research in Europe. The 1970s were an especially inauspicious time for British academic life. Inflation was eroding the value of the pound and reducing the Academy's capacity to support research institutes overseas and its programmes for foreign scholars. At home, the Academy's government grant was insufficient to enable it to maintain scholarly journals, learned societies and grants for humanities research. For Berlin, the experience heightened his sense of living in a society in post-imperial decline. As usual, however, he made light of the difficulties and in his first Presidential Address in 1975, after admitting that cuts would have to be made in the Academy's research grants, he observed that 'poverty marvellously sharpens one's powers of discriminating between . . . projects . . . that have a spark of real life in them, and those which move, when they move at all, at a gentlemanly and unhurried pace with the end not necessarily in sight at all'.[4] He did his best to encourage the former and weed out the latter.

As at Wolfson, he surprised his peers by his political astuteness and appetite for business, securing a better-than-expected grant settlement from a hard-pressed Department of Education and Science; persuading the Prime Minister, James Callaghan, to attend the annual dinner; and convincing the Wolfson Foundation to endow a series of visiting fellowships, both for foreign scholars and British researchers seeking to travel abroad. Berlin guided the Academy serenely through four years and handed the Presidency over to Sir Kenneth Dover late in 1978. In his parting address, he observed that in their sister academy in Thailand senior fellows were known as 'the million-year-old turtles'. It was a class, he said, 'I myself propose to join.'[5]

He was now nearly seventy, a million-year-old turtle indeed, and he had relinquished all his public positions except his seat on the Covent Garden board and his place as a trustee of the National Gallery. He was as active as ever on the board of Covent Garden, proposing singers, repertoires, conductors, watching performances intently, but otherwise there were now few fixed points in his calendar other than concerts.[6]

One major challenge remained. He had been stung by criticism that he had never written a major and magisterial work and he now set out to rectify that omission. He told friends that he was going to spend his time reading books on the German Romantics and revising his Mellon Lectures on the roots of Romanticism. A fixed routine ensued: weekends at Headington House, weekdays at Albany, mornings in the British Library, lunch with friends at his clubs, the Athenaeum or Brooks', or at the front window table of his favourite restaurant, Casale Franco on Jermyn Street. For several years the work in the British Library consumed him. Graduate students, burrowing away at their theses, would be surprised to see a venerable European gentleman in an impeccable three-piece suit seated at a table in the North Library, surrounded by piles of books, which he solemnly consumed one by one. He told correspondents that he was covered in the dust of ancient German texts, reading happily and adding to his enormous store-house of notes.[7]

Then, for mysterious reasons, he faltered. What he called the 'huge rag bag of notes on romanticism' now appalled and intimidated him. They were 'unreadable, unsystematic, not stupid (for the most part) but dust and ashes compared to real thinkers'.[8] He told Richard Pipes that his hatred of working was growing and that he kept at it 'out of sheer shame and some ancient sense of duty derived from all those severe and persecuted ancestors'.[9] By the early 1980s, he was no longer visiting the

North Library, and the project came to a standstill. A fundamental internal obstacle arose to prevent completion. He couldn't bear to re-write the original lectures and, when he tried to pull together a new synthesis from his notes, he despaired of his own 'reckless truisms', feeling a hundred exceptions or qualifications tugging at his intellectual conscience, forcing modifications that muddied the original bright outline and caused him to lose confidence in the project altogether.[10]

Friends who had read the original Mellon Lectures entreated Berlin to allow them to be revised and published as they were, but he refused, perhaps feeling that their appearance would be a standing advertisement of his failure to complete the more ambitious project. Other friends tried to help him to clear space in his life to bring the project to completion. James Billington, a historian of Russian culture, a former student of Isaiah's and now Librarian of Congress, invited Berlin to Washington to spend an autumn in the library, taking his research further. He had a pleasant enough autumn, making the acquaintance of one of his heroes, Andrei Sakharov, then also a guest of Billington's, but the Romanticism project went no further.[11] The failure galled Berlin. This, after all, was what had always been whispered: that he was incapable of a work of grand synthesis. From time to time he would struggle to revive the project, but gradually the door on the room he had set aside in Headington for Romanticism closed and the notes for the project remained there, fading and gathering dust.

He regretted this but perhaps sensed that he had always been best as an essayist, either sharply focusing on a single figure whose mind and work he entered as if his own or offering a panoramic sweep over some grand topic. The architecture of a large multi-chapter work simply didn't suit his type of mind, and if he felt he had failed, he was not one to curse his own limits.

With Romanticism left behind, one might have expected him to feel depressed, as men often are at the end of their professional lives. It might have been a time of gloomy retrospect and failing powers, resentment at being ignored and bafflement at the course of events in the larger world. If this is the common lot of men in old age, it was not to be his. If anything, the last twenty years of his life were among the happiest.[12] He managed to avoid most, if not all, of the reefs of old age. The times conspired to provide a kind of vindication: he lived long enough to greet the fall of communism. He was not the type to be triumphant, and when commentators suggested that his kind of liberalism was the sole ideology to have survived the century with its legitimacy intact, he thought the idea absurdly overblown. But it gave him deep and quiet satisfaction to know that the party of Akhmatova and Pasternak, the party that had refused the radiant tomorrow, had won out in the end.

On the personal plane, his marriage had matured into a deep mutual dependency. He joked that he and Aline were a real 'Darby and Joan', exemplary figures of domestic bliss. For more than forty years, they did everything together, concerts, sojourns at beloved musical festivals like Salzburg and Pesaro, annual visits to Jerusalem and New York, holidays, lecture tours and also sharing the quiet of Headington House, listening to music, reading in the downstairs sitting room, the one with the cosy sofas facing out through French windows onto the flower garden, the one with Leonid Pasternak's wonderful late-nineteenth-century group portrait, all in black and dark browns, of Russian composers and writers – Isaiah's true soul-mates – deep in discussion. This was where they were most peaceful, alone in the quiet of the studies and sitting rooms of Headington House. They turned into inveterate television watchers, especially of opera, concerts and late-night discussion programmes, especially ones with intellectuals. While Isaiah found these mostly comic spectacles – to which he contributed a mocking counterpoint from his easy chair – he loved to keep in touch with the latest trends and fashions in ideas, however absurd. He no longer bothered to read structural, post-structural, deconstructionist texts, but those who did found themselves systematically quizzed for their gist.

He was not a selfish or self-absorbed man but he was often astonishingly oblivious of the invisible support, mostly provided by Aline, which furnished him with such a full social life. It was she who made it possible for them to entertain constantly, so that he was always surrounded at Headington House by a huge circle of old friends. Well into their eighties they lived an amazingly intricate, non-stop social life, an often dizzying succession of concerts, dinners and receptions in at least three cities. At times, she found his appetite for social life wearying and then they would stay at home at Headington to recuperate and recharge. Isaiah's appetite for parties was inexhaustible: he loved being where the talk was brisk and funny and the people were full of life. This was an essential feature of his character. His social instincts were shrewd but they were also uncalculating, a product more of his sheer effervescence than of social ambition. Aline was of a more retiring nature and the gentle brake she applied to his social appetites was good for him. It brought him home, forced him to reflect and settle. By the late 1970s, Aline's children were grown-up and having families of their own; contented summers were spent in the house they had built on the hill above the beach at Paraggi. Down at the beach on the hot August afternoons Isaiah would stand, up to his waist in the water, as he had always done, surrounded by his friends, talking and joking. In his late seventies he could be observed, dressed in an improbable pair of baggy khaki shorts, a T-shirt and walking shoes, sauntering down the goat tracks from their house on the hill to the little town of Santa Margherita, with some beloved Haydn string quartet playing through the earphones of his Sony Walkman. He always talked to the *contadini* he passed, and they hailed him as *il Professore*. It delighted him at the end of his life that he was granted honorary citizenship of Santa Margherita.

Another essential support was provided by the Portuguese couple Casimiro and Claudina Botelho, whom Aline hired in the late 1970s to look after Headington House. Claudina, a fine-featured woman with superb culinary taste, provided the meals which became such a part of the allure of Headington House for anyone who was a guest there, while Casimiro became a kind of batman to Isaiah, a devoted and affectionate friend who looked after his every need, chauffeuring him to his appointments, back and forth between London and Oxford. The bond between them became very close and 'Caz' later looked back on their relationship with astonishment: he could not recall that a peremptory word had ever passed between them.

These relationships spared Isaiah the keenest indignities of old age. Indeed, he was looked after in high style. Equanimity and good cheer were relatively easy in the circumstances. Moreover, his constitution held up until his final illness. In 1979 atrial fibrillation caused him anxiety; and in 1981 one of his vocal cords gave out, leaving him all but voiceless for four months.[13] A specialist in New York told him the vocal cord would recover, but when his voice returned it was lower and deeper than before, halfway between a growl and a whisper.[14] But he could still sing his favourite tunes in a piping warble and even the extinction of his voice came as a deliverance, since it gave him an excuse to give up lecturing. If one had suggested to him that he was philosophical about getting older, he would have wondered what there was to be philosophical about. In any case, he had never believed in the consolations of philosophy. He had always been a Humean and his scepticism towards metaphysics, towards reaching after ultimate questions, served him well in old age. Everything, as Bishop Butler had said, is what it is and not another thing. Why should we desire to be deceived? If history had no libretto, why should an ordinary life have one? He was impatient both with those who repined at old age and those who pontificated about the wisdom that was supposed to accompany advancing years. When correspondents wrote to him to ask questions about such things as 'the meaning of life', he could be exceedingly brisk:

> As for the meaning of life, I do not believe that it has any. I do not at all ask what it is, but I suspect it has none and this is a source of great comfort to me. We make of it what we can and that is all there is about it. Those who seek for some deep cosmic all-embracing ... libretto or God are, believe me, pathetically mistaken.[15]

In his thirties and forties, he had often seemed ill at ease with himself, overweight and uncomfortable. Now, as he moved into his seventies, he gave an impression of serenity, like a man coming into his own. He cut a distinguished, even handsome figure strolling along Oxford's High Street or sauntering down Jermyn Street in the middle of London, in a brown fedora and Loden coat of best-quality material, whistling softly to himself. Serenity, of course, was easy in his circumstances. He was loved, respected, secure and in good health. Indeed, thanks to a young editor, he now entered into a period of ever-growing acclaim.

Early in 1974 a post-graduate philosophy student at Wolfson, Henry Hardy, approached Berlin and proposed to collect, re-edit and reissue his essays. He had joined Wolfson in 1972, got to know Berlin and admired his work, but certainly did not know it intimately. He was aware that the published essays were distributed through dozens of *Festschriften*, symposia, scholarly journals, pamphlets and printed lectures. Hardy already had enough editorial experience to have 'acquired a strong taste for the kind of editorial work that makes possible the publication of a book which otherwise would not have appeared'.[16] Berlin himself had not kept track of his own bibliography and no longer remembered what he had written, let alone where it had appeared. He seemed to welcome the obscurity in which some of his work was languishing and worried how it would look if restored to the light of day. Although he had assembled *Four Essays on Liberty* and *Vico and Herder*, he seemed content to let the rest remain forgotten. At a deeper level, there was a certain implication of impending obituary about the idea of bringing his *oeuvre* together. He joked that Hardy had in mind the publication of his 'posthumous writings' and while it was a joke, it also indicated a very real resistance to the whole project. Perhaps too his heart sank at all the work that might be involved. But it irritated him that people whispered that he was a salon conversationalist who published little. Close friends like Maurice Bowra were to jibe that 'like Our Lord and Socrates, he does not publish much'. Berlin could see that this earnest young editor might be able to give the lie to this untruth.[17] So he agreed to Hardy's proposal in 1974 and there began a twenty-three-year editorial relationship that was to transform Berlin's reputation.

It is a credit to each of them that they were able to see past their differences. The editor was everything Berlin had never been able to force himself to become: methodical, even pedantic, as he cheerfully admitted himself; an indefatigable bloodhound on the trail of unsourced or inaccurate quotations. There were plenty of these littered about Berlin's essays. He had never been a rigorous scholar: many of Berlin's 'quotations' were paraphrases of the original, often in pithier form, and while he had a phenomenal memory for quotations, he had often forgotten where he had come across them.[18] In any event, he had dictated most of his work and in the full spate of composition he had hardly wanted to stop for footnotes. His essays were elaborate and intricate castles of thought, but when Hardy came upon them, they were standing up without much in the way of foundations. All of these scholarly supports Hardy now proposed to insert like steel girders under an old house.

Hardy came to love Berlin and treasure their association, but he also had the independence never to wish to become a disciple, and Berlin was uncomfortable with disciples in any event. The two never became especially close, and though they lived in the same city, Hardy was punctilious about not imposing on Berlin's time. He preferred to write letters in search of clarifications and suggestions, rather than talk on the phone or meet face-to-face. Nor did their judgements always coincide: Hardy generally believed that all unpublished work of a certain standard deserved publication sooner or later; Berlin worried that his reputation would suffer if too much appeared. Sometimes one of Hardy's manuscripts of a new Berlin collection would sit on Berlin's desk for a year or more, waiting until he could face reading it.

But the relationship, while occasionally trying to both sides, was immensely productive. Hardy ferreted Berlin's works out of scholarly journals and had soon produced a bibliography of over 130 items, covering the period from his earliest undergraduate publications in 1929 down to *Vico and Herder* in 1976. In 1978 there appeared the first of Hardy's collections, *Russian Thinkers* (co-edited with the Russian scholar Aileen Kelly), bringing together Berlin's essays on Herzen, Belinsky, Turgenev and Tolstoy. In quick succession followed *Concepts and Categories*, his philosophical essays; and *Against the Current*, his essays in the history of ideas, including classic texts like the famous comparison of Disraeli and Marx. For *Personal Impressions*, his *éloges* of famous contemporaries, Berlin added his essay on his meetings with Akhmatova and Pasternak. The effect of these volumes was to keep Berlin steadily before the public throughout his retirement. While some hostile critics continued to maintain that he was a mere salon virtuoso, Hardy's work began to tilt the balance of his reputation. It was apparent to most critics that he was a major philosophical thinker, whose combination of historical, moral and political enquiry made him *sui generis*. There was no one, certainly not in England, remotely like him.

When Hardy began in the mid-1970s he worked whenever his other commitments allowed. In 1977 he became an editor at Oxford University Press and saw to it that editions of Berlin's work were reissued by the press in paperback. At first he supposed that the Berlin project merely meant re-editing work that had already found its way into print. In late 1988, when Berlin asked him to become one of his literary executors, Hardy asked whether there were any unpublished manuscripts. Berlin said there might be and Hardy made a search of Headington House from top to bottom. He uncovered an astonishing jumble of letters and unfinished manuscripts, some stuffed in old suitcases from Hollycroft Avenue or thrown into boxes when Berlin had vacated his rooms at New College in the 1950s and All Souls in the 1960s. All of the lectures on 'Freedom and its Betrayal' were there; the Mellon Lectures on Romanticism; the Storrs Lectures at Yale; an unfinished manuscript on the eighteenth-century German anti-rationalist Johann Georg Hamann; the St Paul's school report cards and family photographs kept by Berlin's mother; and above all, more than sixty years of correspondence with some of the most famous men and women of his time. In all, Hardy calculated, there were more than a million words of unpublished lectures and essays, together with many million more of letters. It soon became apparent that putting this material into order and bringing it to a publishable state was to be Hardy's life's work. With the help of the Bodleian Library archivists, he began arranging the material in date order and putting manuscripts together. By 1990 Alan Bullock had secured support from the Wolfson Foundation and other sources, and Wolfson had awarded Hardy a non-stipendiary fellowship; he began constituting a Berlin archive and seeing it through publication.

The work of preparing this material for publication required prodigious tenacity and inventiveness – for example, using an ultra-violet filter to render visible a page of a typescript bleached into illegibility by the sun.[19] When piecing together the 40,000-word essay on Hamann, written in the early 1960s and then discarded unfinished, Hardy realised that a crucial section of one of its main chapters was missing. In the basement at Headington he found the Dictabelts on which the original dictation had been made, but no machine to play them on. With the help of the National Sound Archive and the National Science Museum, a surviving example of the machine was found, the Dictabelts were played and, over the crackle and hiss, Berlin could clearly be heard dictating the missing pages – some 4,000 words in all. Hardy transcribed the missing material and, after further editorial reconstruction, the completed manuscript was finally published in 1993 as *The Magus of the North*.[20]

Berlin himself regarded Hardy's work of resurrection with bemused detachment and occasional irritation, followed by growing gratitude and pride. He told everyone that Hardy had transformed his reputation. Most of the lectures and essays dated from the golden period between about 1952 and 1966: now Isaiah could see that he *had* been extraordinarily productive. The question arises as to why Berlin should have been so careless about what he had written; why he should have completed monographs on de Maistre and Hamann and then abandoned them as unfinished torsos; why he should have completed no fewer than seven lecture series and failed to publish any of them. Whether he intended to abandon them or actually had one eye on posterity, without Hardy's prodigious feats of resurrection they would never have seen the light of day.

Nor was Hardy the only one to set about revaluating and re-estimating Berlin's reputation. Pupils, friends and admirers produced two *Festschriften*: one for his seventieth birthday, initiated by Henry Hardy and edited by Alan Ryan, helping to establish his centrality as a philosopher of freedom; the second for his eightieth, edited by Avishai and Edna Margalit, exploring his work in the philosophy of moral pluralism.[21] Besides these marks of recognition from his closest friends, Isaiah received honorary doctorates from Harvard, Yale, Oxford and Cambridge, Athens, Bologna, Toronto and many other universities. By the late 1970s he was England's most celebrated public intellectual, even though he rarely took public positions and shied away from publicity. He and Aline became guests at Buckingham Palace and Downing Street, when an Israeli dignitary or a person of intellect was being honoured. At Downing Street, during Mrs Thatcher's Premiership, he was presented to Mikhail Gorbachev, who, on shaking his hand, said with a characteristic mixture of twinkle and menace, 'We know all about you.' Berlin was less entranced with Gorbachev than many of his liberal friends, believing that any attempt to revivify Leninist idealism and save the communist system was doomed to failure.[22] He lived to be proved right.

To the annoyance of his left-wing friends, Berlin accepted invitations to Downing Street and he rather enjoyed Mrs Thatcher's company. Whenever they met she would ask him what he was working on and when he replied not very much, she would shake her finger at him in mock reproach: 'You must work, Isaiah, you must work.' 'Yes, madam,' he would dutifully reply.[23]

In 1979 he was awarded Israel's most prestigious literary honour, the Jerusalem Prize; in 1983 he was one of the recipients of the Erasmus Prize; and in 1988 he was honoured with the Agnelli Prize for contributions to the ethical understanding of advanced societies. He professed to be mystified by this last honour, since he claimed he had never written anything on the subject. He appreciated the recognition, worried that he was being over-praised and richly enjoyed the comedy of laudatory occasions. The Agnelli Prize, for example, was awarded in Turin opera house in front of over a thousand people, including the former German Chancellor Helmut Schmidt, the American banker and financier Felix Rohatyn and his old friend, the publisher Lord Weidenfeld. Berlin was seated beside the Fiat automobile magnate, Giovanni Agnelli, who fidgeted throughout the musical interludes – Beethoven's Emperor Concerto and Tchaikovsky's Fifth Symphony. Seeing that his benefactor was tiring of all the high culture and fine speeches, Berlin advised Agnelli to while away the tedium by thinking of something agreeable. Agnelli brightened up and whispered that he would turn over in his mind – slowly and voluptuously – all the most beautiful women he had ever known. This he confided, *sotto voce*, would take at least three-quarters or even a whole hour. He assumed a beatific expression, ignored the music and speeches and fell into a 'delicious reverie'.[24]

Berlin enjoyed the fun and frivolity of these occasions, but they were also moments to take stock. This was not easy, for he had never had a very strong sense of his own intellectual agenda. Indeed, it was only when others began to take up his ideas in the late 1970s and the 1980s that he began to understand the extent of their hidden coherence. Now he could look back and see the path he had been following. For the Agnelli Prize, he attempted to express the one big thing that the hedgehog had known all along. The essay he composed – 'The Pursuit of the Ideal' – was too long, not merely for Signor Agnelli, but for the rest of the audience in the Turin opera house – so a sharply abbreviated form was read, not by Berlin himself (since both his voice and his Italian were too weak for the occasion), but by his Italian publisher. 'The Pursuit of the Ideal' made plain that all the disparate studies of Machiavelli, Vico, Herder, Herzen and Tolstoy were not separate exercises but a sustained philosophical enquiry into the history of human values.[25] These studies had taught him, he said, that value systems – Christian mercy as compared with Roman *virtù*, for example – were sufficient unto themselves and incommensurable with those of other epochs. Progress was possible in science and technology, but there was no such libretto in ethics. The virtues and values of late modernity were neither better nor worse than those of the medieval age: they were incommensurable with them.

This position led easily to relativism, to the proposition that human conduct could only be judged by internal, variable or contextual standards. Berlin's friend and colleague Arnoldo Momigliano had suggested as much in a review of *Vico and Herder* in 1976.[26] If so, Berlin's liberal tolerance rested on nothing more than a queasy live and let live.

Berlin insisted that Momigliano had confused relativism and pluralism. No matter how different value systems might be, to be called human they had to refer to recognisably human needs and purposes. 'Forms of life differ. Ends, moral principles, are many. But not infinitely many: they must be within the human horizon.'[27] In the light of this common horizon, certain ultimate and non-relativist standards of evaluation were recognised as common by all human cultures. But if all cultures recognised certain crimes, they did not all recognise the same virtues. It was a rationalist form of arrogance to suppose that these differences could be put down to superstition or ignorance. Variety, including moral variety, was built into the constitution of humankind. Such differences, if within the human horizon, were entitled to respect and should be guaranteed by a regime of liberty.

Moreover, systems of values were never internally consistent. The conflict of values – liberty versus equality; justice versus mercy; tolerance versus order; liberty versus social justice; resistance versus prudence – was intrinsic to human life. Liberty ought to have a certain priority – without some modicum of it, he said, 'there is no choice and therefore no possibility of remaining human as we understand the word' – but even liberty might have to be curtailed in the interests of social justice.[28] In 'The Pursuit of the Ideal', this least political of men mounted a defence of the necessity of politics; this least conflictual of men insisted on the inescapability of moral conflict; and this least tragic of men taught the necessity of tragic choice. 'Some of the Great Goods cannot live together. That is a conceptual truth. We are doomed to choose, and every choice may entail an irreparable loss.'[29] The crimes of the century – and he now viewed his own century as the worst in recorded history – were the result of a faith in final solutions, and hence the failure to be reconciled to the limits of human reason and to the inevitability of loss and error.[30]

These were indeed the core beliefs – in moral pluralism, liberal freedom and their mutual entailment. A huge literature has ensued on Berlin's pluralism, for reasons that left him bemused, but which in retrospect seem clear enough.[31] In a post-imperial world, cultural world views – religious, secular, Western, Eastern, Christian, Islamic – compete for allegiance in conditions of increasing equality. Working out how these ethical world views can inhabit the same political space has given especial salience to the problem of moral pluralism. Then there has been the fragmentation within Western values themselves. The re-emergence of moral disagreement within liberal polities as previously suppressed or non-enfranchised groups (women, children, homosexuals) secured a political voice, all helped to make Berlin's question – how to mediate between opposing moral worlds – the central issue of late modern politics. Berlin himself had never given much thought to these features of late Western society. Indeed, the burden of his argument was that moral conflict was a feature of the human situation *tout court*, not just of modern times. He had never sought to make his work 'relevant', but now it suddenly spoke to his times in ways he never intended.

He never claimed to have been the first to think about pluralism.[32] But Berlin had reason to believe that he was the first to argue that pluralism *entailed* liberalism – that is, if human beings disagreed about ultimate ends, the political system that best enabled them to adjudicate these conflicts was one which privileged their liberty, for only conditions of liberty could enable them to make the compromises between values necessary to maintain a free social life. Beyond the obvious circularity of this argument, the real difficulty, as John Gray has argued, is that a pluralist logically cannot put liberty first.[33] Liberty is simply one of the values that must be reconciled with others; it is not the trump card. If so, why should a free society be valued above all? Berlin's later work opened up these questions, even though it failed to supply adequate answers. At the same time, the very incompleteness of his writing increased its power of suggestion and he lived to see his work debated to the end of his days.[34] Correspondents wrote in to ask him to clarify his thought so often that his secretary, Pat Utechin, used to groan at the very mention of 'pluralism', since it was bound to mean a painful morning, taking down dictation of an immensely long, obscure and difficult attempt on Berlin's part to explain himself once again.[35]

He would have denied it, but he was now looking back, seeking to discern the hidden threads that held his life together. In a warmly nostalgic letter to Mary Fisher (Bennett) – who had been his devoted friend since her father had been Warden of New College – Berlin said he was distressed to discover that his life was 'divided into compartments':

> connected with couplings which one *can* walk on, but with effort; discontinuities: Russia; Prep school; St Paul's; Oxford before the war; Washington; Oxford + London (too much of the latter) after the war; marriage & Headington: all, not exactly sealed off, but divided by gaps & held together by links: not 'organic' & and not quite my own: I *hate* change, breaks walls, & seemed doomed to them . . .[36]

He exaggerated the discontinuities because he was embarrassed that he had seen so little of Mary since the war and wanted to stress that the neglect was symptomatic. But to an incredible degree he kept his oldest friendships going – Maurice Bowra, David Cecil, Shiela Sokolov Grant, Stephen Spender, Nicolas Nabokov, Noel Annan and above all, Stuart Hampshire. And he had kept up his defining affiliations: membership of All Souls and life in Headington, Albany and Paraggi. The continuities, not the discontinuities, are striking, and they must have contributed to that fixed sense of knowing who he was, of being well in his skin, which everyone noticed as he entered the autumn and winter of his life.

He was fortunate too that his oldest friends were alive to keep him company. The oldest and most intimate of these were Stephen Spender and Stuart Hampshire, distinguished, witty, handsome, white-haired Englishmen, with all the worldliness and conviction of the 1930s undiminished in both of them. At the end of his life, Spender sent his old friend a poem by a ninth-century Chinese writer, which was an elegy for their lifelong friendship:

> We are growing old together, you and I;
> Let us ask ourselves, what is age like?
> The idle head, still uncombed at noon.
> Propped on a staff, sometimes a walk abroad;
> Or all day sitting with closed doors.

One dares not look in the mirror's polished face;
One cannot read small-letter books.
Deeper and deeper, one's love of old friends;
Fewer and fewer, one's dealings with young men.
One thing only, the pleasure of idle talk,
Is great as ever, when you and I meet.[37]

Spender died in 1993, and Berlin wrote to Natasha Spender sadly recalling how much they had loved going to listen to Artur Schnabel together; how Stuart Hampshire had said in admiration, once while they were talking about Stephen, that 'there is nothing between him and the object'; and how it seemed impossible to realise that he would never see him again.[38] In his eighties, this fabric of continuity, provided by old male friends, slowly began to unravel. Bowra, Cecil, Spender were now gone. Others, like Shiela Sokolov Grant, Mary Fisher and Jean Floud, he saw less frequently. He went to funerals, composed memorials to his friends, wrote affectionate letters to their families – which always emphasised that words were sticks, insufficient to their purpose – and scanned the obituary pages for the demise of his contemporaries. These rituals of departure could only have made him aware of the imminence of his own. Once, while coming out of Lord Goodman's memorial service, at which Lord Annan had given the tribute, Berlin took Annan aside and whispered, with a wink, 'I want to book you for mine.'[39]

His sense of humour flowed from his vitality, and it helped to keep night thoughts at bay. He joked about his own longevity, recalling the words of a Sicilian brigand on his death-bed who was asked by a priest to pardon his enemies: 'Father, I have none, for I have killed them all.' But he missed some friends keenly and became aware, in fact, that ageing had rendered him more, not less, susceptible to the misfortunes of others. As he told Morton White:

The proposition that the longer one lives the more indifferent one becomes to the ills that beset one or one's dearest is totally false; I suffer much more from this than I used to, and I now realise that there must have been a long period of my life when I was, comparatively speaking, too little sensitive to the misfortunes of others, however close, certainly of my friends . . .[40]

Although he lost his oldest friends, he managed, even in his seventies and eighties, to make new and much younger ones. The most important of these friendships was with the Brendel family, with Alfred, the pianist, and his wife Reni and their three children. They were drawn together by a common passion for Schubert, Beethoven and Mozart, but they were soon discussing and arguing about every subject. Brendel had grown up in fascist Croatia during the war and he found Berlin's willingness to speak positively about nationalism a mystifying bias, which he could only attribute to Berlin's Zionism. As an expatriate pianist making his living on the concert stages of the world, he had no similar longing to belong.[41] But they agreed much more than they disagreed – for example, sharing exactly the same trio of fixed dislikes: 'noise, cigarette smoke and fanatics'. Both had a strong sense of the absurd and could be seen at the Brendel house in Hampstead, laughing together at some private joke, Brendel's eyes alight with demonic glee, Isaiah shaking his shoulders and laughing soundlessly.

Brendel was a deeply thoughtful and literate man whose work as a performer was free of grandiosity, showmanship or false sentiment. His playing displayed a sureness of emotional pitch and a philosophical understanding of the meaning of nobility and pathos in music. Berlin also admired his ferocious dedication. Next to the photographs of Liszt in his practice room, there was a sign in German which read: 'Art is Nice, but it is a Lot of Hard Work.' Brendel, for his part, drew on Berlin's extraordinary memory for performance and repertoire stretching back to the 1930s, and despite the fact that Isaiah did not read music, they developed an intimate kind of shorthand for their musical conversations, with Berlin sometimes humming melodies or tapping them out on his knee and Brendel identifying them and then running through the various ways these themes might be played. Reni Brendel became one of the major confidantes of Isaiah's old age, telephoning him almost daily, visiting him as often as a busy life made possible. She was to become the last in a line of vivacious and able women who were drawn to his vitality and whose *joie de vivre* revived his own.

While he would have denied it, Isaiah was also making a few well-chosen farewells. In late March, 1988, Isaiah went back to St Petersburg and Moscow, where Brendel gave two recitals. He walked for the last time through the rainy streets of St Petersburg, past the Fountain House and Akhmatova's apartment.[42] He made a dry-eyed and unsentimental farewell to the city of his childhood and to the rendezvous which, more than any other, had changed his life.

19

Epilogue

He had never kept a diary and he had ruled out autobiography. He thought self-absorption was a bore. *Après moi le déluge* was the motto. But this did not prevent him from making attempts to put his life in order. I entered his life as a biographer in 1987 to assist him in the work of remembering. He was wary at first, telling the old stories in routine fashion, and only after several years beginning to stray from the well-worn grooves into subjects and themes he had buried within himself. During one of these long sessions over the tape recorder in his rooms in Albany, I asked him the central question about the relation between his life and his work: how a person who had not lived a tragic life should have put such emphasis on tragic choice and shown such empathy for people racked with inner conflict. His reply was brisk: 'My life is the opposite of my views . . . I believe all choice is painful, not that choice is painful to me.'[1] If this were true, his work was a demonstration, not of what it owed to his life, but what it owed to his capacity to imagine lives other than his own.

When I asked him about his serene, mysterious well-being, he replied in his calm deflationary style that he was happy because he was superficial. 'I live much more on the surface than people suppose.' So his life, he wanted me to understand, was a testament to the virtues of the lightness of being.

For the Jerusalem Prize, awarded before his seventieth birthday, he wrote what turned out to be his only venture into extended intellectual autobiography, detailing the three strands in his life – Russian, English and Jewish – which he had braided into the single skein of his identity.[2] From the Russian thinkers, his beloved Herzen and Turgenev, he had taken his fascination with ideas and his sense that they had the power to enslave men, no less than nature or institutions. From the Russian tradition too came a sense of the essentially admonitory and moral function of the intellectual.[3] From the British side, he took his empiricism, the conviction that the world was as our senses held it to be. A Jerusalem audience with bitter memories of the British Mandate might not have been happy about it, but he also ascribed to the English the entire content of his political beliefs: toleration, free discussion, respect for the opinions of others. As for the third and final strand, he told his Jerusalem audience that he owed to Judaism the fact that his liberalism had given such room to the human need to belong. It had been a mistake for the philosophers of the Enlightenment to suppose that men and women could live their lives according to abstract principles, cosmopolitan values and what he called 'idealistic but hollow doctrinaire internationalism'. He went on:

> This rejection of natural ties seems to me noble but misguided. When men complain of loneliness, what they mean is that nobody understands what they are saying: to be understood is to share a common past, common feelings and language, common assumptions, possibility of intimate communications – in short, to share common forms of life.

To be a Jew, he said, was to have a special understanding of this loneliness. It was also to know how deeply men and women needed to be at home somewhere in the world. Belonging was more than possession of land and statehood; it was the condition of being understood itself.

He paid due tribute to what he owed his people, but he knew that he was not necessarily understood better or more truly in Israel than anywhere else; or even that he himself understood Israel especially well. The last twenty years of his life saw him ever more perplexed, angered and depressed by what had happened to his Zionist dreams. He had believed in partition since the Peel Commission of 1937, and to the end of his life he saw himself as a two-state Zionist, committed both to the state of Israel and to sharing the land with the Palestinians. Indeed, the situation embodied exactly those conflicts between competing goods that his own philosophical view regarded as inescapable in moral life. In a conflict between two rights of self-determination of equal validity, he could not envisage any other solution than for Israel to cede significant parts of the occupied territories to a Palestinian authority. This steady conviction set him against the Begin and Shamir governments. Quietly, in interviews and letters to Israeli friends, he aligned himself with Peace Now, but vehement public stands were not in his nature and, in any event, he always believed that advice from outside, even if proffered by a Jew, would always be rejected.[4] Still, the thought that he had not stood up to be counted nagged at his conscience.

As he re-thought his relations to Israel, so too he gave new thought to Judaism. Nothing was recanted, but much was made plain that had been implicit. In matters of faith, he remained what his friend Jerry Cohen called a 'verificationist atheist', faithful to the anti-metaphysical convictions of Oxford logical positivism of the 1930s.[5] But he was a sceptic rather than a heretic and he expressed this radical scepticism gently, assuring the former Chief Rabbi, Immanuel Jakobovits, that he would certainly like to believe in God and an after-life, but had simply no evidence that such things existed.[6] Yet religious scepticism lived happily with religious observance. Wherever he was in the world on Yom Kippur, he made a point of fasting and going to synagogue. As long as his mother was alive, he celebrated the Passover every year in her house. After her death, the ceremonies were held either at Headington House or at the home of Peter Oppenheimer and his family in Oxford. Oppenheimer, an economics don and leading figure in the Oxford Orthodox community, was linked by marriage to the Oxford Pasternaks, so he and Berlin were bound by things Jewish and Russian alike. The Passover Seder was sometimes a grand social occasion, with Lord Rothschild, Lord Goodman, the painter R.B. Kitaj and Murray Perahia, the pianist, in attendance.[7] At other times, it was more intimate, with only the Oppenheimers and Aline's children and grandchildren. The passages were read and sung in Hebrew, and Berlin took a full part, sometimes explaining the significance of certain features of the ritual to the younger children. The celebration of freedom within his tradition meant a great deal to him, and he never missed it. The same held for Rosh Hashanah. If he was in Jerusalem, he celebrated the New Year with his friends Avishai and Edna Margalit and their children.

Many of his Jewish friends were surprised that Berlin never took his Judaism in the direction of Reform.[8] The Reform movement was supposed to purify Judaism of archaisms and adapt its ethical message for a modern day. But Berlin was adamant that if there was to be observance, it had to be as authentic, as traditional, as close to the ancient faith as possible. He joked, 'The orthodox synagogue is the synagogue I am not attending.' But he did attend twice a year and these observances were essential scaffolding for his calendar, ritual returns to his origins, which were something more than ancestor worship. For all his scepticism, his respect for the religious content of the ritual was unfeigned. He was repelled by the callow anti-clericalism of the Voltairian Enlightenment and had traced most of the evils of the twentieth century to the idolatry of secular reason. 'Stone-dry atheists,' he once wrote, 'don't understand what men live by.'[9] He respected the Jewish tradition – and religious feeling in general – precisely because it taught men the limits of their reason. In a letter written in 1981, commenting on Peter Oppenheimer's 'sermon' at the Oxford synagogue on Rosh Hashanah, Berlin observed:

> the validity of a religion shd not, in my view, depend on its moral implications: it is transcendent, absolute, orders things which, in human terms, may be horrifying (as so often in the more blood-shedding exploits in the O.T. [Old Testament]) but *are* the essence of a truly religious attitude . . .[10]

In retrospect, it seems obvious why, when Igor Stravinsky had asked him to provide a libretto for a cantata on a religious theme, Berlin had thought immediately of the binding of Isaac. Here was religious law at its most peremptory and inhuman, yet this was precisely what commanded Berlin's respect. He could vividly imagine Abraham leading his son up the stony hill to the place of sacrifice. Here, at the heart of his own tradition, was the *terribilità*, the awesome and implacable necessity which he had admired in the noblest music, the grandeur on a scale that dwarfed the merely human. To be sure, he was repelled by Abraham's blind submission and by the cruelty of the command itself – but these emotions were easy. With his usual fascination for states of mind radically alien to his own, he was gripped by the human capacity to obey a command beyond its own understanding.[11]

It is possible that this deep understanding of necessity – of aspects of life that could only be experienced as a command or a fate – saved him from raging at the dying of the light. This was not a religious attitude exactly, but it did involve an acceptance, even a resignation, which might have been more difficult had he been of a more rationalist temperament.

He gave more and more thought to dying, discussing it with close friends in a bemused way, as if admiring a distant view or a perplexing painting.[12] He did admit to being afraid of dying, but he thought it was incoherent to fear death itself. It was at the age of eighty-six that he quoted Epicurus to a journalist: 'Why are you afraid of death? Where you are, death is not. Where death is, you are not. What is it that you fear?' Death, he insisted, often quoting a remark of Wittgenstein's, 'is not an event in life'.[13]

He thought it nonsensical to suppose that his own life had a plan or a destiny; that he had made manifest the direction or purpose which had been latent within. Such order as it appeared to have was only apparent after it was lived. Prospectively, life had no shape whatever. Its shape was made in the living. Characteristically, these thoughts were expressed only as an aside in a text written towards the end of his life, in response to a request from a Chinese academic for an account of his work to be included in a Chinese guide to Anglo-American philosophy. It delighted Berlin to think of his work reaching the last bastion of an at least nominal faith in communism. In this essay, he quoted his beloved Herzen, and came as close as he ever did to spelling out a personal credo:

'Where is the song before it is sung?' Where indeed? 'Nowhere' is the answer – one creates the song by singing it, by composing it. So, too, life is created by those who live it, step by step.

The song held his attention to the very end. One of his favourite rituals, conducted in the upstairs study at Headington House with his secretary, Pat Utechin, was the booking of concert tickets, as far in advance as possible. It was a gamble on life to be planning for Glyndebourne,

Salzburg or Pesaro two years hence, when he was eighty-six, but when he had given Pat Utechin his instructions and the diary was well and truly filled in, he would sit back and sigh with satisfaction. Once, as she went away and left him alone, she looked back and saw him in his armchair, quietly murmuring to himself, in a voice at once sad and full of pleasure, 'I do so *love* music.'[14]

In 1996 the National Portrait Gallery offered Lucian Freud an open commission to paint a portrait of his own choosing. He asked if he could paint Isaiah. The two men had first met in Maresfield Gardens in October 1938, when they took tea in the garden with Freud's grandfather. Over Viennese cakes Lucian had told Sigmund that he had been to see *Romeo and Juliet*. The old man laughed: 'I thought you were your own Romeo.' Now, in a studio in a house on Kensington Church Street, Lucian, aged seventy-four, and Isaiah, aged eighty-six, met again. There were more than a dozen sittings, and they took up the better part of the mornings. Isaiah sat in an old battered armchair while Freud sketched him first in pencil and then began to paint him in oils. The time passed in gossip and then in silence, broken by the sound of charcoal on paper and paint on canvas. As Freud worked, Isaiah passed in and out of sleep. In the charcoal drawing, roughly eight by ten inches, Isaiah's eyes are closed, his head back against the back of the armchair, his mouth shut, the curvature of his upper lip is perfectly caught, as is the shape of his bare forehead and his cheeks sunken and hollowed with age. In the oil painting, not much larger than a regular sheet of paper, Isaiah is shown leaning back with his head resting on the back of the battered armchair. Unlike the pencil sketch, his eyes are open. He is looking away to the left, full of melancholy, at something we cannot see. The portrait was never finished.[15]

On 17 July 1997 he came into Aline's room in the small hours of the morning. He had been vomiting and was fighting for breath. An ambulance was called and he was taken to hospital, where doctors struggled to restore his breathing and clear the vomit inhaled into his lungs. There had been episodes of vomiting before, but this time he came down with pneumonia. He was in hospital for a month, unable to see anybody except Aline and one or two of his closest friends. Acute constriction of his oesophagus made it painful to swallow and also dangerous, since he risked choking and ingesting more fluid into his lungs. As a result he began to lose weight and his heart was weakened by recurrent fits of choking. For the first time, his closest friends found him genuinely depressed and unhappy. When Pat Utechin said gently that he had no choice but to grin and bear it, he said he was bearing it all right, but grinning was becoming impossible. Yet a certain spark remained. Once Bernard Williams arrived to find Isaiah asleep in his room and Reni Brendel, fresh from the country in her riding gear, reading the paper and waiting for Isaiah to awake. The two talked about him for many minutes while Berlin slept. After a while, they gently woke him. Had he heard what they were saying? He smiled, 'Every word.'[16]

When he returned to Headington House in August, he was weak and too ill either to read or to receive any but his very oldest friends. With the assistance of Casimiro and Claudina Botelho, Aline and his friends now tried to revive him. They did their best, but he was dejected and told Gerry Cohen, his successor in the Chichele chair of political theory, that life had lost its savour. His stamina was diminishing by the day. Yet he struggled on, determined to keep to old, life-giving routines. Pat Utechin still came for the morning ritual of dictation and, up to the end of October, he was replying to his correspondence.

The abiding passions and themes passed through his life once more in the final weeks. He received a letter from Anatoly Nayman, the friend and biographer of Akhmatova, enclosing some reflections on Akhmatova's love of Dante. Berlin had a special affection for Nayman and for the Russian generation of the 1960s who had so courageously kept faith with the best of the Russian pre-revolutionary tradition, and so his farewell letter to Nayman – the last he ever wrote – was marked with a special tenderness.[17]

But there were other farewells still more painful to make. It plagued him that he had done so little to help the beleaguered Israeli liberals who still stood by the idea of giving land for peace. Like his hero Turgenev who, when dying of cancer, had dictated 'A Fire at Sea' to Pauline Viardot, to acquit himself of a charge of cowardice, Berlin dictated a public appeal for political compromise in Israel. On 16 October 1997, on no one's initiative but his own, he composed a statement imploring Israelis to accept a final partition of the land with the Palestinians. Jerusalem must remain the capital of the Jewish state, but he urged

Israelis to agree to an international UN guarantee for the right of Muslims to have access to the Holy Places of Jerusalem and for Palestinians to have a right of abode in Jerusalem under international guarantee. The alternative, he warned, was an interminable cycle of terrorist chauvinism on both sides and savage war. The appeal was sent to his closest Israeli friends, Avishai and Edna Margalit. He was putting order into his life, making peace with his conscience.[18]

On 23 October 1997 the Prime Minister, Tony Blair, wrote to Berlin about the future of the European left. In an interview, conducted by Steven Lukes in 1991, but only published in *Prospect* magazine and excerpted in the *Sunday Telegraph* in September 1997, Berlin had wondered aloud whether the left as such had any future at all. Where, he asked, were the new ideas?[19] Liberalism and socialism had always been *frères ennemis*. Berlin's doctrine of negative liberty had been a plea for human freedom against even the best-intentioned socialist paternalism. Blair wanted to argue with this. Wasn't it true, the Prime Minister wanted to know, that 'the limitations of negative liberty' in Western societies had motivated generations of people to find some model of society that went beyond 'laissez-faire'? Surely, he suggested, 'positive liberty' had its validity, 'whatever its depredations in the Soviet model'.[20] Berlin's ideas retained all their capacity to provoke, but he was now too ill even to reply to a Prime Minister.

In the last week of October, Isaiah asked to see me. He was seated in the easy chair by the door of the downstairs study in Headington House, books and journals scattered unread on the table by his elbow. He was gaunt and pale, and his immaculate tweed suit hung loosely about him. At one point I helped him shift his weight in the chair, and as I lifted him, I was shocked to feel the bones of his ribcage beneath his suit. He was weak but lucid, with a feverish intensity I could not remember in previous meetings. He reviewed the more or less grim options that lay before him. The doctors were saying that the constriction of his oesophagus and the loss of weight left them no option but to insert a feeding tube in his stomach. He thought this was a dreary possibility, but he was resigned to it: there were no good choices left, he said, with a little shrug. But this was not what he really wanted to say. I drew my chair up until our knees were almost touching and he leaned forward and talked in a hectic whisper, ranging back and forward across the whole expanse of his life, correcting possible misapprehensions about this or that detail, worrying that I might have misunderstood certain confessions and asides. It pained me to think that he had been worrying about biographical truth. He needed all his strength for more important things. But I couldn't get him to change the subject. He wanted to leave the record straight. This too was painful, because it was out of character. All along, he had said he didn't mind what sense I made of his life. This had freed both of us. His carefully cultivated indifference to my project had been a form of generosity, an attempt to lighten the weight of our friendship. But now we were both facing the moment of closure, when suddenly words took on an urgency they had never had before. Time, which had stretched out before us over so many afternoons in the past, when the clock on the mantelpiece sounded the hours and the talk ranged over the whole of his life, now seemed fearfully short. His strength was ebbing away before my eyes. He had just enough energy for one more thought. In a voice just above a whisper, he said how much he loved Aline and how much she had been the centre of his life. This was what he most wanted me to understand. I said I did understand. And then I took his hands and tried to reassure him that I would do my best. What I meant – though I did not manage to say it – was that I would do my best not to betray him. I would repay the trust he had placed in me so easily, with so little calculation, ten years before. I wonder to this day whether he knew what I was trying to say. When I left, I bent over his chair and kissed him once on each cheek and once for good measure as we had always done. After Aline saw me out and I walked down the driveway, I passed the window of the downstairs study and saw him there, for the last time, his head sunk forward, asleep.

He went into hospital on the afternoon of 4 November to have the feeding tube fitted into his stomach. He was recovering from the operation on the evening of the next day when he had another attack of choking and died immediately. On Friday 7 November – as every paper in Britain and most in North America and Europe carried his obituary, and as the papers in Israel carried the text of his final appeal for peace – he was buried in the Jewish section of Oxford's Wolvercote Cemetery. His family and friends spaded wet earth onto his grave, and afterwards the Chief Rabbi intoned, in both Hebrew and English:

Tehi nishmato tserurah betsror hachaim. May his soul be bound in the bonds of everlasting life. *Vehi zichro barukch.* And may his memory always be a blessing.

In the days following his death, newspapers and magazines on both sides of the Atlantic accorded him the space in their obituary pages usually reserved for statesmen. The tone of most pieces was reflective and respectful, but there was venom from the left and right and these pieces confirmed what he had always believed: that for all his success, the ground on which he stood had always been narrower than most people supposed and his liberalism had always been embattled.[21] But it was also clear that he had been loved, especially by the English who had given him his home. In an article in the *Daily Telegraph*, his All Souls colleague William Waldegrave said, 'if you had asked me to show you what I meant by the ideal of Englishness, I would have taken you to see a Latvian, Jewish, German, Italian mixture of all the cultures of Europe. I would have taken you to see Isaiah Berlin.'[22]

At memorial commemorations in the Hampstead Synagogue, Oxford's Sheldonian Theatre and the British Embassy in Washington, his closest friends tried to capture what he had meant to them, to remember what had been so distinctive. In Washington, Kay Graham recalled that when he was asked to speak more slowly if he wanted Americans to understand him, he had replied, 'Yes I know, I know, I know. But if I did, I should be quite a different person, quite a different person.'[23] In Oxford his friend from Jerusalem, Avishai Margalit, remembered Isaiah as 'the prince of the exiles'. Noel Annan said that Isaiah had taught him 'to think more clearly, to feel more deeply, to hope, and to put my trust in life'.[24] Stuart Hampshire, white-haired, leaning on a stick, his voice suddenly breaking, paid tribute to his 'life-creating friend'. Bernard Williams said that he would always think of Isaiah listening to music, 'slightly bent forward, head on one side, listening, beyond any talk, any arguments, any history'.[25]

At the commemorative farewells there was music from every quarter of his past, the laments of the cantor, a Bach *sarabande* played by Isaac Stern, the *andante* from Beethoven's quartet, opus 130, and the *andante sostenuto* of the Schubert B-flat Major sonata, played into the stillness of the Hampstead Synagogue by Alfred Brendel. The pianist's tribute to the man he wished had been his father carried all that was inexpressible in the mourning of those who had loved him. When the final notes had died away and the audience in the synagogue filed into the winter streets of north London, many were seized by a common presentiment that such events had never been complete without Isaiah's judgement of them. For the first time we were leaving a grand occasion without being able to enjoy the whispered coda that had always marked the essential conclusion to such occasions. The source of all the verdicts that had mattered was now gone.

When he was eighty-five, I asked Isaiah what had most surprised him about his life. 'The mere fact that I should have lived so peacefully and so happily through so many horrors.'[26] A survivor's guilt always shadowed his happiness. How could he forget the darkness? It had claimed his very own. It had been 'the worst century there has ever been', in wanton destruction of innocent human life and in murderous unreason masking itself as reason. It was this sense of ambient darkness that gave a sombre eloquence to the best of his writing and passion to his intellectual vocation. But he did not allow the times to dictate to his nature. Biography is the art of the singular and he was absolutely singular: the voice, the mind, the playfulness of both, the lightness of his being and the gravity of his best ideas were all one of a kind. In a dark century, he showed what a life of the mind should be: sceptical, ironical, dispassionate and free.

Acknowledgements

Aline Berlin spent hours talking to me about Isaiah, shared her letters from him and offered me hospitality at Headington House, Albany and Paraggi. It is not easy to see your life set down on the page, and the temptation must be great to put limits and barriers in a biographer's way. This makes it all the more extraordinary that she put none in mine. I thank her for her forbearance.

As Berlin's editor and literary trustee, Henry Hardy collected Berlin's letters from hundreds of sources; sorted his unpublished manuscripts and prepared them for publication; and collected an archive of papers, photographs, tape-recordings and videos. In addition, he gave me hours of his time, correcting my mistakes and pointing me towards sources I had neglected. He deserves no blame for any inaccuracies which remain and deserves a lion's share of the credit for such accuracy as has been achieved. His collaboration with me was a model of generosity, and his work on the Berlin archive has set an extraordinary standard of scholarly accuracy.

The Cerberus guarding the gate of Isaiah Berlin's life for over twenty-five years was his secretary, Mrs Pat Utechin. I am grateful to her for securing appointments for me at short notice, correcting countless strange errors in earlier drafts of this book, and for sharing her memories of 'the boss'.

While working in Oxford, I was able to stay in the President's Lodgings at Magdalen College, thanks to Anthony Smith. He has provided me with hospitality and affection for over twenty years and has listened to me worrying about my books more often than he must care to remember.

I interviewed many friends, colleagues and students of Sir Isaiah and wish to thank them all for their co-operation and assistance. Where their comments figure in the manuscript, their contribution is noted in the endnotes. In this connection, I want particularly to acknowledge: Peter and Philippe Halban, Herbert and Jenifer Hart, Stuart Hampshire, Stephen and Natasha Spender, Alfred and Irene Brendel, Noel and Gabrielle Annan, Jean Floud, George Weidenfeld, William Deakin, William Hayter, Avishai and Edna Margalit, Robert Silvers, Arthur Schlesinger Jr., Daphne Straight, Clarissa Avon, Brenda Tripp, John Gray, Richard Wollheim, Bernard Williams, Richard Wilberforce, Michael Brock, Ralph Dahrendorf, Harry Shukman, Katharine Graham, Eric Hobsbawm, Steven Lukes, Gerald Cohen, Berel Rodal, Ian Buruma, Tim Garton Ash, Ben Rogers, David Butler, Andrzej Walicki, Bernard Wasserstein, Peter Oppenheimer, Leonard Wolfson, David Daiches, Edward Mortimer, Shiela Sokolov Grant, Cressida Ridley, Mary Bennett, Dimitri Obolensky, Nicholas Henderson, Max Beloff, David Cesarani, Isabel Roberts, Ronald Hope, Michael Goldman, Norman Davies, Shirley Anglesey, Charles Taylor, Larry Siedentop and Jonathan Sacks.

Michael Brock, former Vice-President and Bursar of Wolfson College, provided invaluable assistance on Berlin's years as President of the College.

It is impossible to thank individually all of the hundreds of people and institutions who responded to the appeal by Henry Hardy and myself for copies of Berlin's correspondence. We received support and co-operation from research libraries and institutions around the world, with one exception, All Souls. It is regrettable that a community of scholars who depend for their work on accepted conventions of access to archival material should deny a biographer access to papers on a fellow who was a credit to their institution for over sixty years.

I hope that those of Isaiah's friends and colleagues who go in search of their names in my index will not be disappointed if they do not find themselves in my pages. The range of his acquaintance was so large that inclusiveness had to be sacrificed for narrative coherence. Similarly, everyone who knew him had their own Isaiah. I have included as many of these versions of the man as I can, and I hope that those who have not found their version will at least find themselves surprised by the variety of other Isaiahs on display in these pages.

Thanks too to Briony Glassco (Walton), actress, mother of three and wife, for the enthusiasm and *joie de vivre* which she brought to her research for this project.

The fellows of St Antony's College, Oxford, were kind enough to elect me to an Alistair Horne Fellowship while I was working on this biography. I especially want to thank my benefactor, Alastair Horne, for his generosity. Thanks too to the staff of the London Library and the Wiener Library for bibliographical help.

I was lucky that my editor at Chatto, Jenny Uglow, is an accomplished biographer in her own right and was able to bring to my book her sense of how to bring a life alive. She was ably assisted by the editorial team at Chatto, led by Alison Samuel. Her predecessor, Jonathan Burnham, made the book welcome and I remember his acumen and advice with affection and respect. In New York, Sara Bershtel at Metropolitan Books provided an incomparable line edit, and, in Toronto, Cynthia Good and her team provided their usual high standard of editorial assistance.

I wish to thank the following persons for reading the manuscript and making suggestions: Suzanna Zsohar, Bernard and Patricia Williams, Pat Utechin, Aline Berlin, Reni Brendel, Avishai Margalit and Henry Hardy. I also wish to thank Douglas Matthews, former Librarian of the London Library, for his help in preparing the index.

The mistakes which remain, alas, are mine.

Text and picture acknowledgements: I would like to thank the following for permission to include quotations from published works: Zephyr Press, Boston, for Anna Akhmatova, *The Complete Poems*, translated by Judith Hemschemeyer and edited by Roberta Reeder (1989); Angel Books, London, for Osip Mandelstam, *The Eyesight of Wasps*, translated by James Greene (1989); John Stalworthy and the *Oxford Magazine* for 'The Guest from the Future: a tryptych, 1940-88' (1989). Extracts from the unpublished letters of A.J. Ayer are reproduced by courtesy of the Estate of A.J. Ayer; the extract from Elizabeth Bowen's letter of 27 September 1935 is reproduced by permission of Curtis Brown Limited, London; the extract from T. S. Eliot's letter of 9 February 1952 is reproduced by permission of Mrs Valerie Eliot; from Boris Pasternak's unpublished letter of 26 July 1946 by permission of The Pasternak Trust; extracts from the correspondence of Stephen Spender appear by courtesy of the Estate of Stephen Spender, and from an unpublished letter of 23 October 1997 by courtesy of the Prime Minister.

I would also like to thank Aline Berlin, and Henry Hardy and the Berlin Archive, Wolfson College, Oxford, for providing many photographs, and granting their kind permission to reproduce them. I am grateful to the Estate of Cecil Beaton, and to Clive Barda, Deborah Elliot and Steve Pyke for permission to include their portraits of Isaiah Berlin; to Pat Utechin for her photograph of Sir Isaiah and Lady Berlin with Andrei Sakharov and Elena Bonner: to Patricia Williams for her photograph of Isaiah in his holiday hat; and to John Murray, publishers, and Europaïsche Verlaganstalt, for the portrait of Anna Akhmatova, included in *The Guest From the Future* by György Dalos (1998).

Notes

The chief source was my series of interviews, beginning in December 1988 and continuing until late October 1997, with Berlin himself. These occurred on such a frequent basis or in such informal settings – in concert intervals or over dinner or on walks – that it was sometimes impossible to take notes. Where tapes or transcripts were made, these have been lodged with Henry Hardy's Berlin Archive at Wolfson College. These interviews are cited as MI/IV IB, followed, where possible, with the date of the interview and the page of the transcript. The archive is closed to researchers until Henry Hardy has completed his edition of Berlin's letters.

The other major source was the collection of correspondence, to and from Berlin, in the Berlin Archive at Wolfson College. Here I cite as follows: IB to (name of correspondent), followed by the date – day, month, year.

Interviews with other sources are cited as MI/IV, followed by the name of the person interviewed, together with the date of the interview. Few of these interviews were either taped or transcribed, but where they have been, the tapes have been lodged with the Berlin Archive at Wolfson.

The definitive listing of Berlin's writings is Henry Hardy, 'A Bibliography of Isaiah Berlin', in his edition of Isaiah Berlin, *Against the Current: Essays in the History of Ideas* (London, 1979; 1997). I have adopted the following abbreviations for Berlin's work in the notes:

KM: *Karl Marx: His Life and Environment*, (London, 1939; reprinted with an introduction by Alan Ryan, and a guide to further reading by Terrell Carver 4th ed., Oxford 1978; 1995)

AE: *The Age of Enlightenment: The Eighteenth Century Philosophers*, (New York, 1956; Oxford, 1979)

4E: *Four Essays on Liberty* (London, 1969)

ZP: *Zionist Politics in Wartime Washington: A Fragment of Personal Reminiscences*, Yaachov Herzog Memorial Lecture (Jerusalem 1972, Hebrew University of Jerusalem)

VH: *Vico and Herder: Two Studies in the History of Ideas* (London, 1976)

RT: *Russian Thinkers*, ed. Henry Hardy and Aileen Kelly, introduction by Aileen Kelly (London, 1978)

CC: *Concepts and Categories: Philosophical Essays*, ed. Henry Hardy, introduction by Bernard Williams (London, 1978)

AC: *Against the Current: Essays in the History of Ideas*, ed. Henry Hardy, introduction by Roger Hausheer (London, 1979)

WD: *Washington Despatches, 1941-1945: Weekly Political Reports from the British Embassy*, ed. H.G. Nicholas, introduction by Isaiah Berlin (London, 1981)

PI: *Personal Impressions*, ed. Henry Hardy, introduction by Noel Annan (London 1980; 2nd ed. 1998): references are to the second edition.

CTH: *The Crooked Timber of Humanity: Chapters in the History of Ideas*, ed. Henry Hardy (London, 1990)

MN: *The Magus of the North: J.G. Hamann and the Origins of Modern Irrationalism*, ed. Henry Hardy (London, 1993)

SR: *The Sense of Reality: Studies in Ideas and their History*, ed. Henry Hardy, introduction by Patrick Gardiner (London, 1996)

PSM: *The Proper Study of Mankind: An Anthology of Essays*, ed. Henry Hardy and Roger Hausheer, foreword by Noel Annan, introduction by Roger Hausheer (London, 1997)

RR: 'The Roots of Romanticism', Mellon Lectures, National Gallery of Art, Washington, 1965, unpublished typescript, Berlin Archive, Wolfson College. [*The Roots of Romanticism*, ed. Henry Hardy (forthcoming, London, 1999)]

The following additional abbreviations are used in the notes:

DNB: Dictionary of National Biography

FO: Foreign Office Papers, PRO, Kew

NYRB: New York Review of Books

PRO: Public Record Office, Kew

THES: Times Higher Education Supplement

TLS: Times Literary Supplement

1. ALBANY

1 He was referring to Patricia de Bendern, née Douglas. See pages 111–112.

2 MI/IV Stephen Spender, 1992.

3 Joseph Brodsky, 'Isaiah Berlin: A Tribute', in A. and E. Margalit (eds), *Isaiah Berlin: A Celebration* (London, 1991), 208; see also Solomon Volkov, *Conversations with Joseph Brodsky* (New York, 1998), 230–1, 268.

4 Virginia Woolf, *Letters*, V (London, 1979), 410–11: 'argued with Isaiah, who is a very clever, much too clever, like Maynard in his youth, don: a violent Jew'.

5 Albert Einstein to Felix Frankfurter, 12.3.52.

Notes

2. RIGA, 1906–15

1 I journeyed to Riga in 1991 and wish to thank Marger Vesterman of the Latvian Society of Jewish Culture for his assistance in re-creating the world of Riga Jewry before the Holocaust. See also *Fragments of the Jewish History of Riga*, 1991, published by the Museum and Documentation Centre of the Latvian Society of Jewish Culture. The details of Berlin's family ancestry and his early life in Riga are largely taken from his own recollections. See MI/IV IB, 20.10.88, 11.10.89 and 27.9.90.

2 I Samuel 1–2.

3 S.M. Eisenstein *Immoral Memories: An Autobiography*, (London, 1986), 26; Marie Seton (ed.) *S.M. Eisenstein* (London, 1952), 17–30.

4 Mendel Bobe, *The Jews in Latvia* (Tel Aviv, 1971), 243–61.

5 'Riga', *Encyclopedia Judaica*, vol. 14; H.D. Löwe, *The Tsars and the Jews* (Chur, 1993), 85–101.

6 Mendel Berlin, 'Autobiographical Notes', 11.3.46, transcribed by Henry Hardy, Berlin Archive, Wolfson College.

7 L.B. Namier, 'Zionism', *New Statesman*, 5.11.27, 103–4; reprinted in *Skyscrapers and Other Essays* (London, 1931); see also IB, 'L.B. Namier', in **PI**, 91–111.

8 See 'Shneur Zalman of (Liozna) Lyady, 1745–1813', in *Encyclopedia Judaica*, vol. 14; Ada Rapoport-Albert (ed.), *Hasidism Reappraised* (London, 1997), 298–9, 433–4, 356, 436.

9 For a memorable description of the Jewish timber-workers of the Dvina, see Simon Schama, *Landscape and Memory* (London, 1995), 26–32.

10 IB to Anthony Storr, 29.9.78.

3. PETROGRAD, 1916–20

1 M. Berlin, 'Autobiographical Notes', 47–8. MI/IV IB, 27.9.90, 20.10.88 and 11.10.89.

2 IB to Roma Schapiro, 3.11.83. Also unpublished interview with IB by Harry Shukman, St Antony's College, 5.6.86.

3 Ramin Jahanbegloo, *Conversations with Isaiah Berlin* (London, 1992), 3–6; Steven Lukes, 'Interview with Isaiah Berlin', part 1, 1991.

4 IB, 'Yitzak Sadeh', in **PI**, 78–91; see further Chapter 12.

5 He was the grandfather of Aline de Gunzbourg, whom IB was to marry in 1956.

6 M. Berlin, 'Autobiographical Notes', 60.

7 M. Berlin, 'Autobiographical Notes', 61.

8 On the dating of IB's departure from Riga and arrival in England, see Mendel Berlin to Henry Snowman, 14.1.26.

4. LONDON, 1921–8

1 Vladimir Nabokov, *Speak, Memory*; Berlin quotations in this chapter are to be found in MI/IV IB, 27.10.88, tapes 1 and 2.
2 IB, 'The Three Strands in My Life', in **PI**, 257.
3 IB, "The Purpose Justifies the Ways", *NYRB*, 14.5.98, 53.
4 M. Berlin, 'Autobiographical Notes', 60.
5 M. Berlin, 'Autobiographical Notes', 64.
6 Mendel Berlin to Henry Snowman, 11.2.26; see also Mendel Berlin, 'Particulars Regarding Application for Naturalisation', typescript, 16.2.26; updated 11.2.30.
7 A.H. Mead, *A Miraculous Draught of Fishes: A History of St Paul's School, 1509–1900* (London, 1990), 115. See also IB to J. Donaldson, 28.10.71.
8 Christopher Dean, Archivist of St Paul's School, to Michael Ignatieff, 21.6.91.
9 Arthur Calder-Marshall to Henry Hardy, 3.4.91.
10 Berlin papers, St Paul's School Reports, autumn 1927.
11 Berlin's response to St Paul's can be compared to that of his contemporary Walter Ettinghausen, who, as Walter Eytan, was to become a distinguished Israeli diplomat. See Walter Eytan to Henry Hardy, 18.3.92.
12 IB to Edward Lowbury, 12.4.89.
13 **KM**, preface; see also S. Rachmilievitch to IB, 14.12.35.
14 Betty Spiro married the physician and psychiatrist Emanuel Miller in 1933 and became a novelist and scholar. See Sarah Miller's introduction to Betty Miller, *On the Side of the Angels* (London, 1985), esp. x, for IB's reminiscences of her. Their son is the doctor, theatre and opera director, Jonathan Miller.
15 IB to Ida Samunov, undated, 1928.
16 *The Debater*, no. 10, November 1928, St Paul's School.

5. OXFORD, 1928–32

1 IB interviewed by Brian Harrison in *Corpuscles* (Oxford, 1994).
2 MI IV Spender, 16.10.89.
3 See, for example, editorial, *Oxford Outlook*, 10 (1930), 561–5.
4 Diana Hopkinson, *The Incense Tree* (London, 1969), 82–4; see also her letter to Henry Hardy, 8.3.95.
5 Shiela Sokolov Grant to IB, 1983; MI/IV S. Sokolov Grant 1983, 1985, 1993.
6 G.E. Moore, *Principia Ethica*, 95.
7 IB, 'Maurice Bowra', in **PI**, 156; see also Hugh Lloyd-Jones (ed.), *Maurice Bowra* (London, 1974); Noel Annan, *Our Age* (London, 1990), 94–5.
8 For a contemporary description of Bowra in full spate, see IB to Mary Fisher, 23.3.36; Bowra's translations of Blok are to be found in C.M. Bowra, 'The Position of Alexander Blok', in *Criticism*, xi, 44, April 1932, 422–38.

9   IB to Jenifer Fischer Williams, undated.

10 IB to Bowra, undated, from the Reform Club, for IB's clearest expression of what he owed Bowra.

11 IB's interest in things Russian continued through his undergraduate days. See, for example, his translation of Alexander Blok's 'The Collapse of Humanism', in *Oxford Outlook*, 11 (1931), 89–112.

12 IB to Charles Henderson, 9.31.

13 Spender to IB, undated, from Berlin.

14 Stephen Spender, *World Within World* (London, 1951), 70.

15 MI/IV Spender, 9.89

16 Spender to IB, undated, 1932.

17 Spender, *World Within World*, 71–2; M.P. Steinberg, *The Meaning of the Salzburg Festival* (Ithaca, NY, 1990), 29, 37, 219, 324.

18 MI/IV Spender, 9.89.

19 Spender to IB, 19.5.35; see also IB, 'The Naïveté of Verdi', in **AC**, 287–96, and Bernard Williams' discussion of the 'naïve' and 'sentimental' distinction in A. and E. Margalit (eds), *Isaiah Berlin*, 180–93.

20 See IB's review of Sir Thomas Beecham's 'Eroica' in *Oxford Outlook*, 12 (1932), 57.

21 IB to Charles Henderson, 20.9.31.

22 On Berlin's viva, see M. Corley to IB, 24.7.32.

6. ALL SOULS

1   For All Souls in the 1930s, see MI/IV IB, 30.11.88, 13.12.88.

2   IB, 'John Petrov Plamenatz', in **PI**, 146.

3   IB and Stuart Hampshire, 'Reminiscences', All Souls, 6.3.92, unpublished typescript, Berlin Archive, Wolfson College.

4   IB to Mrs James de Rothschild, 8.5.57. IB, 'Mr James de Rothschild: "Grand Seigneur" ', *The Times*, 13.5.57.

5   A.L. Rowse, *All Souls and Appeasement* (London, 1961).

6   IB to H.A.L. Fisher, 1.2.37.

7   IB to Spender, undated 1935.

8   W.H. Auden and L. MacNeice, *Letters from Iceland* (London, 1937).

9   MI/IV Spender, 1989; Philip Toynbee, *Diaries*, vol. 11, 19.5.37. Toynbee Archive in the possession of Sally Toynbee.

10 IB to Elizabeth Bowen, undated, autumn 1937.

11 Victoria Glendinning, *Elizabeth Bowen* (London, 1977) (1988 ed.), 40–3, 114–22.

12 IB to Bowen, 30.11.33; see also Harrison, *Corpuscles*; IB to Mary Fisher, undated, 1933; Hermione Lee, *Virginia Woolf* (London, 1996), 647.

13 V. Woolf, *Letters*, V, 255.

14 IB, 'Virginia Woolf ', in **PI**.

15 IB to Spender, undated, 1935.

16 IB to Spender, undated, 2.35.

17 IB to Bowen, undated, 1937.

18 MI/IV Edward Mortimer, 13.6.95.

19 Rachel Walker to IB, 26.8.35.

20 Rachel Walker to IB, undated, 1935.

21 Mary Fisher to B.J. Lynd, 10.11.35.

22 IB to John Hilton, 13.10.35.

23 IB to Bowen, undated 10.35.

24 Bowen to IB, 27.9.35.

25 MI/IV IB, 4.1.89, 3.

26 MI IV Edward Mortimer, 13.6.95; Edward Mortimer to Henry Hardy, 21.5.94.

27 H.A.L. Fisher Papers, Bodleian Library, Oxford.

28 Christopher Hill to IB, 30.8.35; also 9.11.35, 26.11.35, 14.12.35.

29 **RT**, 82–113, 186–210.

30 IB to Shiela Grant Duff, undated 1936.

31 IB to John Hilton, 13.10.35.

32 Shiela Grant Duff, *The Parting of Ways* (London, 1982), 55.

33 **PI**, 112, 114; IB and Stuart Hampshire, 'Reminiscences', 7.

34 IB to Shiela Grant Duff, 18.8.36.

35 IB to Mary Fisher, undated, 12.36?

36 Moore Crossthwaite to IB, 11.38.

37 Shiela Grant Duff, *The Parting of Ways*, *passim*.

38 Shiela Grant Duff, *A Noble Combat: The Letters of Shiela Grant Duff and Adam von Trott zu Solz, 1932–9*, ed. K. von Klemperer (Oxford, 1988), *passim*.

39 Giles MacDonogh, *A Good German* (London, 1989), 33–60; Christopher Sykes, *Troubled Loyalty* (London, 1968); Christabel Bielenberg, *The Past is Myself* (London, 1968).

40 MI/IV IB, 13.12.88, 7.

41 Hopkinson, *The Incense Tree*, 148; *Manchester Guardian*, 22,23.1 34.; MacDonogh. *A Good German*, 60–1; Sykes, *Troubled Loyalty*, 104; see Trott's Letter in *Manchester Guardian*, 21.2.34.

42 IB to Adam von Trott, undated, 7.34?; also IB to Shiela Grant Duff, undated, 3.34; Sykes, *Troubled Loyalty*, 110–11.

43 Von Trott to IB, undated, 3.37?

44 Von Trott to IB, undated, 11.37?; MacDonogh, *A Good German*, 91, 96.

45 Sykes, *Troubled Loyalty*, 265.

46 IB, 'L.B. Namier', in **PI**, 100.

47 Maurice Bowra, *Memories* (London, 1966), 304–6.

48 IB to Shiela Grant Duff, 21.6.56; see his ' A Personal Tribute to Adam von Trott (Balliol 1931)', Balliol College Annual Record, 1986, 61–2; see also H.O. Malone,

Adam von Trott zu Solz: The Road to Conspiracy against Hitler, unpublished PhD thesis, University of Texas, Austin, 1980.

7. THE BRETHREN, 1934–40

1 On mandate Palestine, see A.J. Sherman, *Mandate Days: British Lives in Palestine, 1918–48* (London, 1997); Amos Elon, *The Israelis* (New York, 1983); Elie Kedourie and S.G. Haim (eds), *Zionism and Arabism in Palestine and Israel* (London, 1982); Bernard Wasserstein, *Herbert Samuel: A Political Life* (Oxford, 1992).
2 MI/IV IB, 13.12.88.
3 IB to Felix Frankfurter, 7.12.34.
4 IB to Frankfurter, 7.12.34; Sherman, *Mandate Days*, 92.
5 IB to M. Berlin, undated.
6 IB to Frankfurter, 7.12.34.
7 Thomas Hodgkin, *Letters from Palestine, 1932–6* (London, 1986).
8 IB to M. Berlin, undated.
9 See references to Berlin's visits to Palestinians in Bernard Wasserstein, 'Staying to Get Out', *TLS*, 24.4.98.
10 MI/IV IB, 13.12.88, 14.
11 IB to Marion Frankfurter, 20.3.35.
12 MI/IV IB, 13.12.88. On Stern, see H.M. Sachar, *A History of Israel* (New York, 1996), 246–9.
13 Ben Rogers, *A.J. Ayer: A Biography* (forthcoming, London, 1999); see also A.J. Ayer, *Part of My Life* (Oxford, 1978) 97-8; also his *More of My Life* (London, 1984).
14 A.J. Ayer to IB, undated, Vienna, 1932.
15 Bernard Williams, 'Introduction', in **CC**, xiii.
16 A.J. Ayer to IB, 26.2.33.
17 Ray Monk, *Ludwig Wittgenstein: The Duty of Genius* (New York, 1990), 241–5; A.J. Ayer, *Wittgenstein* (London, 1985); Allan Janik and Stephen Toulmin, *Wittgenstein's Vienna* (New York, 1973).
18 IB, 'Felix Frankfurter in Oxford', in **PI**, 117–18.
19 A.J. Ayer, *Language, Truth and Logic* (London, 1936), preface.
20 IB, 'I'm going to tamper with your beliefs a little', dialogue with Stuart Hampshire on the birth of Oxford analytical philosophy, one of six films by Michael Chanan, 1972, [H. Hardy transcript, 5]. On IB's official estimate of Ayer as philosopher, IB to Registrar, Oxford University, 9.1.59, in support of Ayer's candidature for the Wykeham Professorship of Logic.
21 IB, Review of Julius Weinberg, *An Examination of Logical Positivism*, *Criterion*, 17 (1937), 174–82.
22 Annan, *Our Age*, 303.
23 MI/IV Richard Wollheim.
24 **PI**, 143.
25 **PI**, 136. The observer was IB's friend Jasper Ridley. See Ridley Diaries, 1935, in the

possession of Cressida Ridley.

26 **PI**, 140; also MI/IV IB, 30.11.88.

27 MI/IV IB, 30.11.88, 11.

28 J.L. Austin to IB, 18.1.37.

29 Arthur MacIver to IB, 6.2.38.

30 **PI**, 144–5; see also IB to Benedict Nicolson, undated, 1935.

31 IB, 'Induction and Hypothesis', *Proceedings of the Aristotelian Society*, suppl. vol. 16 (1937), 63–102; 'Verification', *Proceedings of the Aristotelian Society*, 39 (1939), 225–48; **CC**, 12–32.

32 IB, 'Logical Translation', in **CC**, 78.

33 Bernard Williams, 'Introduction', in **CC**, xii.

34 MI/IV IB, 30.11.88, 1.

35 **CC**, 146–7.

36 See his unpublished undergraduate essay, undated, 'Can the divergence of ethical judgements be reconciled with the existence of an absolute standard of morality?', Berlin Archive, Wolfson College. Also **CC**, 146–7.

37 Stuart Hampshire to IB, undated, 1937.

38 IB to Elizabeth Bowen, 11.33.

39 MI/IV Stuart Hampshire, 1994; see also Stuart Hampshire, 'The Man of Feeling', *TLS*, 29.5.98.

40 Glendinning, *Elizabeth Bowen* 40–3, 114–22; see also MI/IV IB, 12.3.94, 10.

41 IB to Elizabeth Bowen, undated, 1938. IB to M. Berlin, 26.8.38, 28.8.38, 8.9.38, 10.11.38. Also MI/IV IB, 14.12.88, 6. **KM**, preface, xv.

42 MI/IV IB, 14.12.88.

43 MI/IV IB, 11.10.89, 6–7.

44 MI/IV IB, 23.3.89; see also **PI**, 34–65.

45 Sherman, *Mandate Days*, 125.

46 H.M. Murray to IB, 23.1.40.

47 IB to Elizabeth Bowen, undated, 1939.

48 MI/IV IB, 14.12.88, 7; **KM**, xviii; IB to A.D. Lindsay, 31.10.39.

49 Guy Branch to IB, undated, 1940.

50 **KM**, 7.

51 IB to Felix Frankfurter, 23.6.40.

52 MI/IV IB, 7.3.90.

53 Goronwy Rees, *A Chapter of Accidents* (London, 1972), 110–36.

54 MI/IV IB, 8.2.94; see also Andrew Boyle, *The Climate of Treason* (London, 1979), 195; A. Purdy and D. Sutherland, *Burgess and MacLean* (London, 1963), 46–55; Rees, *A Chapter of Accidents*, 134–9. B. Penrose and S. Freeman, *Conspiracy of Silence*, 230–2.

55 See V.W. Newton, *The Cambridge Spies*, 19; Andrew Boyle, *The Climate of Treason*, 195–8; Y. Modin, *My Five Cambridge Friends*, (London 1994), 84.

Notes

8. ISAIAH'S WAR: NEW YORK, 1940–1

1   IB to M. Berlin, 16.7.40.
2   IB to Mary Fisher, 30.7.40.
3   MI/IV IB, undated. See also MI/IV IB, 12.3.94, 6–7.
4   MI/IV IB, undated. J. Costello, *Mask of Treachery* (London, 1988), 378–9.
5   MI/IV IB, 8.2.94.
6   MI/IV IB, 8.2.94; IB to Marion Frankfurter, 5.8.40; PRO/FO 371/24847 – N 6064/40/38.
7   IB to Mary Fisher, 21.8.40; MI/IV IB, 30.1.89.
8   IB to Marion Frankfurter, 5.8.40; see also IB to Shiela Grant Duff, 22.8.40.
9   IB to Marion Frankfurter, 23.6.40; MI/IV IB; see also Humphrey Carpenter, *W.H. Auden: A Biography* (London, 1981), 292; IB to Marion Frankfurter, 23.8.40.
10 H. Nicolson to IB, 9.9.40; IB to M. Berlin, 5.10.40.
11 IB to Mary Fisher, 21.8.40; IB to M. Berlin, 31.7.40; IB to Mary Fisher, 30.7.40.
12 IB to M. Berlin, 31.7.40.
13 John Wheeler-Bennett, *Special Relationship* (London, 1975), 126.
14 MI/IV IB, 8.2.94.
15 IB to M. Berlin, 5.10.40.
16 Harold Nicolson, *Diaries and Letters*, II (1939–45) (London, 1967), 124.
17 IB to Maire Lynd, 3.1.41.
18 Nicholas Cull, *Selling War: The British Propaganda Campaign against American 'Neutrality' in World War II* (Oxford, 1995), 127–31, 163–8.
19 IB to Maire Lynd, 3.1.41.
20 MI/IV Daphne Straight, 15.11.95.
21 IB to Mary Fisher, 25.10.41.
22 Donald F. Drummond, *The Passing of American Neutrality, 1937–41* (London, 1955); T.A. Bailey, *The Man in the Street* (New York, 1948); MI/IV IB, 30.1.89.
23 Wheeler-Bennett, *Special Relationship*, 128; Cull, *Selling War*, ch. 6.
24 Sherman, *Mandate Days*, 154.
25 IB to M. Berlin, 27.2.41; see also Stephen Wise, *Challenging Years* (London, 1951).
26 MI/IV IB, 30.1.89; **ZP**, 12–13.
27 MI/IV IB, 30.1.89; 27.9.90; see also IB to Marion Frankfurter, 5.8.40; T. Michael Ruddy, *The Cautious Diplomat* (London, 1986).
28 MI/IV IB, 30.1.89, 10.
29 **PI**, 49; IB to M. Berlin, 17.5.41.
30 *Letters and Papers of Chaim Weizmann*, ed. Barnett Litvinoff (London, 1980), XX, 134, 339, 369, 373, 386.
31 See S. Teveth, *Ben-Gurion: The Burning Ground 1886–1948* (London, 1987); Norman Rose, *Chaim Weizmann: A Biography* (London, 1987).
32 PRO/FO 371/27128 – E 5649/60/31.
33 **ZP**, 28.

34   MI/IV Daphne Straight, 15.11.95.

9. ISAIAH'S WAR: WASHINGTON, 1942–5

1   While reporting to the Foreign Office, he continued to work out of the British Information Services in New York until the spring of 1942. See IB to M. Berlin, 14.2.42. PRO/FO 371/26162 A 4562/16/45.
2   IB to M. Berlin, 12.12.41, 2.1.42; see also **PI**, 11.
3   David Brinkley, *Washington Goes to War* (New York, 1988).
4   IB to Walter Bell, 8.4.81.
5   *Letters and Papers of Chaim Weizmann*, XX, 316.
6   Arthur Schlesinger, Jr., ' "Prich": A New Deal Memoir', *NYRB*, 28.3.85; Katharine Graham, *Personal History* (London, 1997), 106–8. MI/IV Mrs John Ferguson, 1995; MI/IV Katharine Graham, 1997.
7   IB to M. Berlin, 21.2.43.
8   MI/IV IB, 4.1.89, 6–8.
9   MI/IV Stuart Hampshire, 1994.
10 MI/IV IB, 4.1.89, 8. Isaiah's recollection is contradicted by his letter to the Manager of the St. Regis Hotel, 14.9.43, returning a key to Room 415. Since this letter is dated September and he recollected going to Oklahoma in December, it is possible that the letter refers to a previous visit.
11 IB to M. Berlin, 16.8.43, for his visit to Washington State; see also IB to M. Berlin, 26.9.43, for visits to San Francisco, Los Angeles, Chicago.
12 **WD**, vii–xiv.
13 MI/IV IB, 6.5.94.
14 William Hayter, *A Double Life* (London, 1974), 69; MI/IV Hayter, 1994.
15 H.G. Nicholas to IB, 21.5.43.
16 IB to H.G. Nicholas, 7.7.43.
17 PRO/FO 371/30378.6, 23.2.42.
18 PRO/FO 371/31379, 9.7.42.
19 *Letters and Papers of Chaim Weizmann*, XX, 321.
20 IB to Weizmann, 26.10.42.
21 IB to M. Berlin, 2.10.42, 5.10.42, 7.10.42, 17.10.42, 17.10.42.
22 M. Weisgal to C. Weizmann, 27.10.42, Weizmann Archives.
23 E.L. Woodward, *History of British Foreign Policy in the Second World War* (London, 1972), 386–9.
24 PRO/FO 371/35034, 22.5.43.
25 MI/IV IB, 5.4.89.
26 PRO/FO 371/35036 4212, 10.7.43.
27 MI/IV IB, 23.3.89; see also Peter Grose, *Israel in the Mind of America* (New York, 1983), 179–81.
28 **WD**, 43. PRO/FO 371/35037 5043, 28.8.43. See also IB to H.G. Nicholas, 4.8.43.
29 **ZP**, 26.

30 PRO/FO 371/45041, 15.11.43.

31 PRO/FO 371/4019 4745, 21.1.44.

32 PRO/FO 371/40131 4690, 6.6.44.

33 PRO/FO 371/30131 4690, 9.6.44.

34 **ZP**, 47–8; see also Blanche Dugdale, *Baffy: The Diaries of Blanche Dugdale* (London, 1988), 217.

35 H.L. Feingold, *The Politics of Rescue* (New York, 1980); A.D. Morse, *While Six Million Died* (London, 1968); Wise, *Challenging Years*, 190–4; Tony Kushner, *The Holocaust and the Liberal Imagination* (London, 1994), ch. 6; J.B. Schechtman, *The United States and the Jewish State Movement* (New York, 1966), 92–117, 134–7.

36 PRO/FO 371/350234, 22.5.43.

37 PRO/FO 371/35036 4674, 6.7.43; MI/IV IB, 23.3.89, 30.1.89.

38 MI/IV/IB, 30.1.84; see also W.D. Rubinstein, *The Myth of Rescue: Why the Democracies Could Not Have Saved More Jews From the Nazis* (London, 1997).

39 PRO FO 371/40129 4745, 9.2.44.

40 S. Volschonok to IB, 19.1.40.

41 MI/IV IB, BBC2, broadcast 18.11.97.

42 MI/IV David Daiches, 11.97.

43 **ZP**, 60.

44 **ZP**, 66.

45 **ZP**, 40.

46 PRO/FO 371/38537 9019, 19.1.44, 28.1.44.

47 IB to M. Berlin, 26.9.43; MI/IV IB, 30.1.89.

48 MI/IV IB, 30.1.89, 3–4; MI/IV IB, BBC2, 18.11.97; John Colville, *Footprints in Time* (London, 1984), 168–70; see also John Colville, *The Fringes of Power: Downing Street Diaries, 1939–1955* (London, 1985), 471–2; L. Bergreen, *As Thousands Cheer: The Life of Irving Berlin* (London, 1990), 430–2; IB to Ted Weeks, 13.12.79.

49 John Russell to IB, undated, April 1944.

50 A. Chisholm and D. Davie, *Beaverbrook: A Life* (London, 1992), 450, 472.

51 IB to M. Berlin, 12.12.44; Earl of Birkenhead, *Halifax: The Life of Lord Halifax* (London, 1965), 496–7.

52 R. Skidelsky, *J.M. Keynes* (London, 1992), II, 427, dates the meeting to 1930. IB's own recollection was that it was in 1935: MI/IV IB, 5.6.94, 6.

53 MI/IV IB, 5.6.94, 6–8. See also Milo Keynes (ed.) *Lydia Lopokova* (London, 1983), pp. 170–3.

54 **WD**, 535.

55 Graham, *Personal History*, 155–7; MI/IV IB, 8.2.94; Boyle, *The Climate of Treason*, 291–3.

56 MI/IV IB, n.d.

57 IB to David Scott, 23.3.45.

58 MI/IV IB, 11.10.89, 5.

59 IB to Anthony Rumbold, 11.1.45.

60 IB to Donald Hall, 11.12.44.

61 **CC**, vii–viii.

62 IB to Herbert Hart, 23.2.45.

63 IB to H.G. Nicholas, 4.4.45.

64 **WD**, 545–6.

65 IB to H.G. Nicholas, 8.5.45.

66 IB to Joe Alsop, 11.2.44. See also Charles Bohlen, *The Transformation of American Foreign Policy* (London, 1970); Charles Bohlen, *Witness to History: 1929–1969* (London, 1973), 126; T.M. Ruddy, *The Cautious Diplomat* (London, 1986), 48–51.

67 MI/IV IB, 9.12.95, 10.12.95.

68 MI/IV IB, 18.6.89.

69 J. Balfour to IB, 27.7.45.

70 IB to M. Berlin, 31.1.44.

71 IB to M. Crosthwaite, 12.5.45.

72 IB to H.G. Nicholas, 8.5.45.

73 IB to Warden Sumner, 6.6.45.

74 MI/IV IB, 12.3.94, 13.

75 MI/IV Noel Annan, 1992; see also Noel Annan, *Changing Enemies: The Defeat and Regeneration of Germany* (London, 1996).

76 IB to M. Berlin, 5.5.45.

10. MOSCOW, 1945

1 IB to M. Crosthwaite, 12.4.45.

2 IB to Charles Henderson, 20.9.31, re. visiting Moscow.

3 IB to Miriam Gross, 4.5.71; he said the same to Stephen Spender. MI/IV Spender.

4 **PI**, 206.

5 **PI**, 206; Marie Seton, *Eisenstein*, 442–48.

6 V. Shentalinsky, *The KGB's Literary Archive* (London, 1995), 25–6.

7 P.B. Maggs, *The Mandelstam and 'Der Nister' Files: An Introduction to Stalin-era Prison and Labour Camp Records* (London, 1996), 5; on Babel's fate, see Shentalinsky, *The KGB's Literary Archive*, ch. 2; Eugenia Ginzburg, *Within the Whirlwind* (London, 1981); Veronique Garros *et al.* (eds), *Intimacy and Terror: Soviet Diaries of the Thirties* (New York, 1995); Nadezhda Mandelstam, *Hope Against Hope* (London, 1971), *Hope Abandoned*, (London, 1974).

8 L. Fleishman, *Boris Pasternak* (London, 1990), 234–9.

9 PRO/FO 371/56725 N 1811/24/38, 'A Note on Literature and the Arts in the Russian Soviet Federated Socialist Republic in the Closing Months of 1945'.

10 **PI**, 208–10.

11 **PI**, 205.

12 IB to M. Berlin, 19.9.45.

13 IB to M. Berlin, 11.10.45.

14 IB to M. Berlin, 19.9.45; MI/IV IB, 5.1.94, 25.1.96.

15 IB to M. Berlin, 24.10.45.

16 IB to M. Berlin, 5.12.45: 'I saw Rosa Raskin the other day – still nice – longs to go back – her mama not well – her uncle says nobody left in Riga as far as he knows . . .'; see also IB, 'Extract from a book entitled "Imprisoned by the Red Pharaoh" ', unpublished typescript 21.3.96, for details of the life of Leo Berlin.

17 IB to Angus Malcolm, 20.2.46.

18 PRO/FO371/47925.

19 PI, 211–12.

20 PI, 213–26.

21 Fleishman, *Pasternak*, 191; see also J. Rubenstein, *Tangled Loyalties: The Life and Times of Ilya Ehrenburg* (New York, 1996), 125–9; **PI**, 214; Peter Levi, *Boris Pasternak* (London, 1990), 188–9.

22 Shentalinksy, *The KGB's Literary Archive*, 38–41.

23 Fleishman, *Pasternak*, 204.

24 E. Radzinsky, *Stalin* (London, 1996), 301–2; Mandelstam, *Hope Against Hope*, 172–8; Fleishman, *Pasternak*, 180–2; Shentalinsky, *The KGB's Literary Archive*, 183 **PI**, 223–4.

25 PI, 217.

26 L.P. Levi, *Boris Pasternak*, 64, 209, 241; G.G. de Mallac-Sauzier, *Boris Pasternak* (Norman, Oklahoma, 1981), 182–5.

27 PI, 216.

28 PI, 219; see also PRO/FO 371/56725, 28.

29 Leonid Pasternak, *Memoirs*, trans. Jennifer Bradshaw, intro. Josephine Pasternak (London, 1982), 125–78; **PI**, 221.

30 PI, 222.

11. LENINGRAD, 1945

1 Brenda Tripp, Diary, 12.11.45; **PI**, 232.

2 PRO/FO 371/56724, 21.

3 Joseph Brodsky, *Less Than One* (New York, 1986), 4; see also S. Volkov, *Conversations with Joseph Brodsky* (New York, 1998).

4 PRO/FO 371/56724, 22.

5 PRO/FO 371/56724, 24.

6 IB to Anna Kurt, 19.12.88; Mikhail Zoshchenko, *Scenes from the Bathhouse*, trans. Sidney Monas (Ann Arbor, 1962).

7 IB to M. Bowra, 7.6.45; C.M. Bowra, *A Book of Russian Verse* (London, 1943); see also his *A Second Book of Russian Verse* (London, 1948).

8 PI, 233.

9 Roberta Reeder, *Anna Akhmatova* (New York, 1995); see also Amanda Haight, *Anna Akhmatova: A Poetic Pilgrimage* (London, 1976).

10 See the 'chronology' in *The Complete Poems of Anna Akhmatova*, trans. Judith Hemschemeyer, ed. Roberta Reeder (Boston, 1989), 59–60.

11 Osip Mandelstam, *The Eyesight of Wasps*, trans. James Greene (London, 1989), 78. The beard-shaver is a reference to Peter the Great.

12 Mandelstam, *Hope Against Hope*, 8–12, 14–17, 20, 30.

13 Hemschemeyer, 388.

14 Hemschemeyer, 384.

15 Lydia Chukovskaya, *The Akhmatova Journals* I (1938–41), trans. M. Michalski, S. Rubashova (London, 1994), 6–7; see also Lydia Chukovskaya, *Sofia Petrovna*, trans. D. Floyd (London, 1989).

16 Mandelstam, *Hope Against Hope*.

17 György Dalos, *The Guest From the Future: Anna Akhmatova and Sir Isaiah Berlin*, trans. Antony Wood (London, 1998), 25–7.

18 **PI**, 233.

19 Hemschemeyer, 423.

20 **PI**, 233–4.

21 Jon Stallworthy, 'The guest from the future: a triptych, 1940–1988', *Oxford Magazine*, 48 (1989).

22 IB, 'Mrs Salome Halpern' (obituary), *The Times*, 17.5.82; Reeder, *Anna Akhmatova*, 38–42.

23 Stallworthy, 'The guest from the future'.

24 Stallworthy, 'The guest from the future'.

25 Reeder, *Anna Akhmatova*, 38.

26 Hemschemeyer, 393.

27 **PI**, 237.

28 PRO/FO 371/56724, 25.

29 Chukovskaya, *The Akhmatova Journals*, 19; **PI**, 238–9.

30 **PI**, 203.

31 Dalos, *The Guest From the Future*, 162–3.

32 MI/IV IB, 10.11.94, 5.6.94.

33 Stallworthy, 'The guest from the future': 'and his hand with a cigar/conducting Something by Mozart'.

34 **PI**, 242.

35 MI/IV Tripp.

36 PRO/FO 371/56725 N 1811/24/38.

37 Hemschemeyer, 770.

38 Haight, *Anna Akhmatova*, 143.

39 Hemschemeyer, 453.

40 MI/IV IB, 5.6.94, 21.2.89.

41 IB to Frank Roberts, 20.2.46.

42 Hemschemeyer, 454.

43 Heinrich Böll Stiftung, *Stasi, KGB und Literatur* (Cologne, 1993), 115–26; Dalos, *The Guest From the Future*, 11, 48–78.

44 Reeder, *Anna Akhmatova*, 289.
45 Boris Pasternak to IB, 26.7.46.
46 J. Livingstone to IB, 1.6.46.
47 Mandelstam, *Hope Abandoned*.
48 Haight, *Anna Akhmatova*, 144.
49 Hemschemeyer, 547.
50 Brenda Tripp to IB, 12.2.47.
51 Unsigned letter to IB, 19.2.47.
52 PRO/FO 371/66395.
53 Unsigned letter to IB, 12.4.48.
54 Heinrich Böll Stitung, *Stasi, KGB und Literatur*, 115–25.
55 MI/IV Harry Shukman; Dalos, *The Guest From the Future*, 102–7.
56 IB to Jean Floud, 31.7.75.
57 Gennadi Kostyrchenko, *Out of the Red Shadows: Anti-Semitism in Stalin's Russia* (Amherst, NY, 1995), 282–3.
58 IB notes on Russian edition of Kostyrchenko, 21.3.96; MI/IV IB, 26.1.96.

12. THE TRIBE, 1946–8

1 IB, Review of David Footman, *The Primrose Path*, Third Programme, BBC, 17.12.46; see also Humphrey Carpenter, interview with IB on Radio 3, 3.1.96.
2 Chisholm and Davie, *Beaverbrook*, 472.
3 MI/IV IB, 18.5.89, 13; IB to Marion Frankfurter, 29.11.53; IB to John Sparrow, 21.11.53; IB to Anna Kallin, 2.12.53; MI/IV IB, 18.5.89; see also **PI**, 126–7.
4 A.J. Ayer to IB, undated, 1951.
5 Martin Gilbert, *W.S. Churchill* VIII, (London, 1988), 383, 391, 393, 394.
6 IB to Winston Churchill, 14.2.48; see also W.S. Churchill, *The Gathering Storm* (London, 1948), 64–5, 225, 287.
7 IB, 'Political Ideas in the Twentieth Century', *Foreign Affairs*, 28 (1950), reprinted in **4E**; under the pseudonym O. Utis, 'Generalissimo Stalin and the Art of Government', *Foreign Affairs*, 30 (1952), 197–214. On the pseudonym, see IB to Hamilton Fish Armstrong, 16.8.51: 'as I have (I hope still) relations in the USSR and as I visited innocent litterateurs there, I have always followed the policy of publishing nothing about the Sov. Union directly under my own name, because that might easily lead to something frightful being done to people I talked to there'.
8 IB, 'Why the Soviet Union Chooses to Insulate Itself', transcript of a talk given at the Royal Institute of International Affairs, Chatham House, 27.6.46.
9 PRO/FO 371/66395, 'Philosophy in the Soviet Union', sent to IB, 24.11.47.
10 Antony Beevor and Artemis Cooper, *Paris After the Liberation, 1944–9* (London, 1994), 349; Alex Danchev, *Oliver Franks: Founding Father* (Oxford, 1993), 81.
11 IB to Chaim Weizmann, 15.9.47.

12 Ronald Hope to Henry Hardy, 19.1.98.

13 Isabel Roberts to MI, 24.11.97; see also Bernard Ely to MI, 7.12.97; Michael Goldman to MI, 1.1.98; Deborah Thornton to MI, 14.1.98; David Butler, 'Isaiah Berlin and Felix Frankfurter', undated, 1998, to MI.

14 IB to Sybil Colefax, 9.11.46.

15 MI/IV Stuart Hampshire.

16 MI/IV Clarissa Eden, 6.95; see also MI/IV Stuart Hampshire, Jenifer Hart.

17 RT, 22; Lord Oxford to H. Hardy, 5.2.92.

18 MI/IV IB, 10.11.94.

19 IB, 'The Trends of Culture', contribution to 'The Year 1949 in Historical Perspective', in 1950 Britannica Book of the Year, xxii–xxxi; see also IB to Anna Kallin, 27.7.51: 'Don't have anything to do with [Karl] Jaspers. He talks dim rubbish . . .'.

20 Karl Popper, The Open Society and its Enemies, 2 vols (London, 1945); Bryan Magee, Popper (London, 1973).

21 MI/IV IB, 12.3.94; Christopher Hill, Lenin and Revolution (London, 1947), 217.

22 RT, 155.

23 IB to Alice James, 3.9.50.

24 IB to Alice James, 14.8.51.

25 Stuart Hampshire to IB, 16.12.47.

26 Oliver Lyttelton to IB, 4.7.50. Lyttelton became Colonial Secretary in Churchill's second administration, 1951–4; DNB.

27 Speech to Zionist Congress, Basle, draft, 12.11.46, Weizmann Archive.

28 Chaim Weizmann to M. Weisgal, 18.11.46, Weizmann Archive.

29 Chaim Weizmann to Felix Frankfurter, 7.1.47; see also 18.3.47; Sachar, A History of Israel, 267–8.

30 MI/IV IB, 23.3.89.

31 IB to Patrick Reilly, 3.8.47; Sherman, Mandate Days, 206–7.

32 IB to M. Berlin, undated, 1947; M. Berlin to IB, 6.8.47.

33 IB to M. Berlin, undated, 8.47.

34 IB to Patrick Reilly, 3.8.47.

35 MI/IV IB, 5.4.89.

36 IB to Patrick Reilly, 3.8.47.

37 IB to Felix Frankfurter, 12.9.49.

38 MI/IV IB, 5.4.89.

39 MI/IV IB, 5.4.89.

40 PI, 78–84.

41 IB to Patrick Reilly, 3.8.47.

42 Sachar, A History of Israel, 295–325.

43 IB to Chaim Weizmann, 6.6.48; Weizmann to IB, 12.6.48.

44 MI/IV IB, 5.4.89.

45 IB to Chaim Weizmann, 16.9.48.

Notes

46 Abba Eban, *Personal Witness* (London, 1993), 38–9; George Weidenfeld, *Remembering My Good Friends* (London, 1995), 202–3, 211; see also IB to Walter Eytan, undated, 4–5.51.

47 Vera Weizmann to IB, 19.6.51.

48 MI/IV IB, 5.4.89.

49 IB to Marion Frankfurter, 17.8.50.

50 **PI**, 88.

51 IB to Felix Frankfurter, 10.1.51.

52 Avi Shlaim, *Collusion Across the Jordan* (Oxford, 1988), 611–12.

53 'Israel – A Survey', in *The State of Israel* (London, 1953), 42–55.

54 IB to Alice James, 9.12.52; IB, 'Dr Chaim Weizmann' (supplementary obituary), *The Times*, 17.11.52; IB, 'The Biographical Facts', in M.W. Weisgal and J. Carmichael (eds), *Chaim Weizmann* (London, 1962), 17–56; also **PI**, 34–66.

55 *Jewish Chronicle*, 5.5.50; see also Arthur Koestler, 'Judah at the Crossroads', in *The Trail of the Dinosaur and Other Essays* (London, 1955), 106–42; IB letter in Douglas Villiers (ed.), *Next Year in Jerusalem: Jews in the Twentieth Century* (London, 1976); IB to Arthur Koestler, 18.11.54; Koestler to Berlin, 16.11.54 (in Koestler Archive, Edinburgh University). References courtesy of Dr David Cesarani. See Koestler Diary/Notebook, 1944–9 (MS 2304), 29.4.44: 'Met Isaiah Berlin – rather unpleasant, oily … awkwardness …'; 29.12.54: Berlin – 'frivolous and superdonnish'.

56 IB, 'Jewish Slavery and Emancipation', *Jewish Chronicle*, 9.51; appears in Norman Bentwich (ed.), *Hebrew University Garland* (London, 1952), 18–42. See also F. Raphael, 'Berlin Revisited', *Jewish Quarterly*, Spring 1998, 11–17.

57 IB to Goronwy Rees, 23.12.52; Avishai Margalit, 'Address', Sheldonian Theatre, Oxford, 21.3.98.

58 IB, 'Jewish Slavery', 11.

59 MI/IV IB, undated.

60 K. Joseph to IB, undated, 10.51?

61 IB, 'Jewish Slavery', 21–2: all reference to Eliot was removed from the *Festschrift* version.

62 *Criterion*, 27 (1937), 174–82; T.S. Eliot to IB, 1.2.49.

63 Anthony Julius, *T.S. Eliot, anti-Semitism and Literary Form* (Cambridge, 1995), 37, 217; Dannie Abse, *A Poet in the Family* (London, 1974), 130–2; Peter Ackroyd, *T.S. Eliot* (London, 1984), 201; see also Christopher Ricks, *T.S. Eliot and Prejudice* (London, 1994), 63–76.

64 T.S. Eliot to IB, 28.11.51.

65 IB to Eliot, 30.1.52; see also T.S. Eliot, *After Strange Gods* (London, 1934); Julius, *T.S. Eliot*, 146–67.

66 T.S. Eliot to IB, 9.2.52.

67 See IB to Eliot, 7.11.52, thanking him for 'your most effective and fascinating letters about the Jews etc.'. In 1996 IB asked his editor Henry Hardy to reinstate the excised references to Eliot if he ever republished 'Jewish Slavery'.

68 T.S. Eliot, *Notes Towards the Definition of Culture* (London, 1948), 48, 70, 122.

13. COLD WAR, 1949–53

1 M. Bowra to IB, 1.10.49.

2 IB, 'Notes on the Way', *Time and Tide*, 30 (1949), 1133–4, 1157–8, 1187–8.

3 IB, 'Notes on the Way'; see also IB to Shirley Anglesey, 9.5.49: 'Cambridge itself is not self-confident but guilt-ridden: learning is seen as a luxury to be atoned for by very bogus forms of social work.'

4 IB to E.H. Carr, 14.5.49; IB to Alan Bullock, 23.2.49.

5 MI/IV IB, 10.11.94; see also 'The Divorce between the Sciences and the Humanities', in **AC**, 80–110.

6 IB to L. Fisher, 3.6.49.

7 A. Schlesinger, Jr, 'A Great Man in a Grim Time: In Memory of Isaiah Berlin', *New York Times*, 10.11.97; MI/IV IB, 29.4.89.

8 Robert W. Merry, *Taking on the World: Joseph and Stewart Alsop – Guardians of the American Century* (New York, 1996); see also E.W. Yoder, *Joe Alsop's Cold War* (Chapel Hill, N.C., 1995).

9 E. Prichard to IB, 31.10.49: 'I have no special feeling that I have been victimised, but rather that a long run of phenomenal good luck has deserted me. The affair has also made me acutely conscious of the dire possibilities of post-graduate prankishness. I grew up so early in some respects that I was late growing up in others; and the intense desire to kick over the shit-house at Hallow'en, while it has become less frequent in recent years, did not leave me in time to prevent disaster.' See also IB to Joe Alsop, 1.8.49, 21.10.49.

10 **PI**, 172.

11 Edmund Wilson to Mamaine Koestler, 6.6.49; Jeffrey Meyers, *Edmund Wilson: A Biography* (Boston, 1995), 157, 166, 324, 346–9.

12 IB to E. von Hoffmansthal, 10.6.49; IB to Clarissa Avon, 10.5.49.

13 IB, 'Democracy, Communism and the Individual', unpublished lecture, Mount Holyoke College, June 1949.

14 'Study of Marxism Backed at Parley', *New York Times*, 29.6.49. See Berlin's letter, 30.6.49: 'my actual lecture stressed the incompatibility between any form of democratic belief and Marxist doctrine'.

15 IB to George Kennan, 30.6.49; Kennan to Loach, 5.7.49.

16 IB to Alice James, 16.7.49; see also IB to Joe Alsop, 1.7.49: 'I feel that the rest of my life will be spent in dementis to people like the Provost of Harvard that I am an ambiguous snake of some sort . . . I don't want to blow it up unnecessarily but I feel absolutely berserk at the moment.'

17 IB to Marion Frankfurter, 5.1.50: 'I feel in a frivolous mood, suddenly, and that nothing very bad is happening anywhere, despite Hiss, Formosa, Communists in

China, Bevin etc., everything has suddenly lost its fateful and sinister significance.' See also IB to M. Frankfurter, 2.2.50; IB to Marietta Tree, 16.7.49.

18   Roy Harrod to IB, undated, 1953: 'Guy Burgess sends Isaiah his greetings, if he will accept them.' W. Hayter to IB, 6.51; N. Annan to IB, 6.51; Peter Wright, *Spycatcher* (London, 1987); MI/IV IB, 12.3.94, 6: the debriefing with Wright occurred in 1961–2, according to Berlin.

19   Rees, *A Chapter of Accidents*; see also J. Rees, *Looking for Mr Nobody: A Life of Goronwy Rees* (London, 1987).

20   *The People*, 4.56; IB to Goronwy Rees, 27.4.56; G. Rees to IB, undated, 4.56: 'Guy is now a terribly dangerous man . . . he is capable of doing a great deal of harm to a great many people, some of whom . . . are friends of yours and mine.' See also IB to J. Rees, 16.11.94: 'What upset some of Goronwy's friends was not the attack on Burgess in 1956 . . . it was the general tone and in particular the irresponsible attacks on the Foreign Office as a nest of homosexual communists . . .'.

21   Albert Einstein to Felix Frankfurter, 12.3.52.

22   IB to Vera Weizmann, 10.4.52; see also **PI**, 66–77.

23   'The Anglo-American Predicament', *Listener*, 42 (1949), 518–19, 538; see also 'Mr Berlin', *Evening Standard*, 3.10.49, 4; IB to Joe Alsop, 9.10.49: 'it is v. Hearstish, personal and below the belt. But does Lord B. know where the belt is?' See also IB to Joe Alsop, 21.10.49; IB to Felix Frankfurter, 12.9.49: 'It is a v. poor American 5th columny sort of talk and will I fear, if they see it, annoy Messrs Laski and Eccles equally . . .'.

24   IB, 'Mr Churchill', *Atlantic Monthly*, 184, 3 (September 1949); reprinted as 'Mr Churchill and F.D.R.', *Cornhill Magazine*, 981 (1950), 219–40; **PI**, 1–23.

25   **PI**, 4.

26   Harold Laski to IB, 26.2.50, 4.3.50; see also Isaac Kraunick and B. Sheerman, *Harold Laski: A Life on the Left* (London, 1993).

27   S. Rachmilievitch to IB, 30.3.50.

28   IB to Roland Burden-Muller, 29.12.49; see also 2.4.50.

29   MI/IV IB, undated. IB gave differing versions of his remark. Sometimes it was, 'Don't darken judgement.'

30   MI/IV IB William Deakin, 11.97; see also IB to Joe Alsop, 29.12.49: 'The article on Winston has drawn a telegram, also Xmas card with Mte Ste Victoire painted by him: brave after Cézanne and very very bad.' Winston Churchill to IB, 24.12.49: 'I have read with so much pleasure what you write in your American article. Best wishes for Christmas and New Year, Winston Churchill.'

31   IB on *Desert Island Discs*, BBC Radio 4, 19.4.92.

32   IB to Vera Weizmann, 30.12.49; see also IB to R. Burden-Muller, 30.12.49.

33   MI/IV IB, 10.11.94.

34   **4E**, 38. See also Daniel Bell, *The End of Ideology*; and his *The Cultural Contradictions of Capitalism* (London, 2nd ed., 1979), 257–61.

35   *The Times*, leader, 11.52; see also IB, 'The Fate of Liberty', *The Times*, 16.12.52, 9. Carr was actually commenting on the broadcast of 'Freedom and its Betrayal' in

11.52, but his remarks apply equally to the *Foreign Affairs* article.

36 H.R. Luce to IB, 26.4.50; IB to H.R. Luce, 4.5.50, 25.5.50, 1.6.50.

37 IB to Herbert Elliston, 30.12.50. On Elliston, see Graham, *Personal History*, 104, 148, 163, 169, 171–2, 196, 200, 208.

38 Neil Berry, 'Encounter', *Antioch Review* (1993), 194–211; N. Nabokov, *Bagazh: Memoirs of a Russian Cosmopolitan* (London, 1975), 178, 208–10, 214–16.

39 IB to J. Rees, 16.11.94. On IB's role when the CIA's role in *Encounter* became known, see M. Lasky to IB, 13.4.67; IB to S. Spender, 30.5.67; also Mel Lasky to Dwight MacDonald, 12.4.67; and IB to Melvin Lasky, 18.4.67, in Josselson Papers, Harry Ransom Center, Austin, Texas. I am grateful to Frances Stonor Saunders for this reference.

40 IB, 'The Birth of the Russian Intelligentsia', *Encounter*, 4, 6 (June 1955), 27–39; 'Belinsky: Moralist and Prophet', *Encounter*, 5, 12 (December 1955), 22–43; 'Herzen and the Grand Inquisitors', *Encounter*, 6, 5 (May 1956), 20–34.

41 IB to Hamilton Fish Armstrong, 27.5.50; IB to Marion Frankfurter, 17.8.50.

42 George Kennan to IB, 26.4.50.

43 IB to George Kennan, 13.2.51.

44 IB, 'Political Ideas in the Romantic Age: Their Rise and Influence on Modern Thought', Chapter 3: 'Two Concepts of Freedom: Romantic and Liberal', unpublished, Berlin Archive, Wolfson College.

45 IB, 'Freedom and its Betrayal', unpublished mss., Berlin Archive, Wolfson College, 171.

46 Popper, *The Open Society and its Enemies*; Jacob Talmon, *The Origins of Totalitarian Democracy* (London, 1952).

47 IB, 'Freedom and its Betrayal', 188–9.

48 Humphrey Carpenter, interview with IB, BBC Radio 3, 1.96; Asa Briggs, *The History of Broadcasting in the UK*, 5 (London, 1995); see also Humphrey Carpenter, *The Envy of the World: 50 Years of the BBC Third Programme and Radio 3, 1946–1986* (London, 1996).

49 IB to Alice James, 9.12.52; IB to R. Niebuhr, 30.10.52.

50 IB to Marion Frankfurter, 28.12.52.

51 MI/IV IB, 29.4.89.

52 IB, 'Historical Inevitability', August Comte Memorial Trust Lecture, 1 (London, 1954), in **PSM**, 119–90

53 **PSM**, 189.

14. LATE AWAKENING

1 IB to Shiela Grant Duff, then Shiela Newsome, 6.6.49.

2 IB, translation of Ivan Turgenev, *First Love*, with *Rudin*, trans. Alex Brown, and an introduction by Lord David Cecil (London, 1950); reissued as *First Love and Other Stories* (London, 1994).

Notes

3 MI/IV IB, 10.11.94. On Shirley Anglesey, see Weidenfeld, *Remembering My Good Friends*, 155–7; S. Angelsey to MI, 1.7.98.

4 IB to Shirley Anglesey, 9.5.49; see *First Love and Other Stories*, 8.

5 *First Love and Other Stories*, 68.

6 MI/IV IB, 10.11.94, 4.1.89.

7 MI/IV Aline Berlin, 11.10.89; Philippe de Gunzbourg, 'Les Origines Russes', unpublished typescript in the possession of Lady Berlin, Headington House.

8 MI/IV IB, 11.10.89.

9 MI/IV Peter Halban, 1997; Philippe Halban, 1998. See also David Shoenberg to MI, 14.1.99, re: Halban's arrival in Britain in 1940.

10 RT, 81; see also Weidenfeld, *Remembering My Good Friends*, 234. Published as 'Lev Tolstoy's Historical Scepticism', *Oxford Slavonic Papers*, 2 (1951), 17–54. Reprinted as *The Hedgehog and the Fox: An Essay on Tolstoy's View of History* (London, 1953); see also W.H. Auden's review, 'Holding up the Mirror to History', *The New Yorker*, 25.9.54; also R.D. Hines, *Auden* (London, 1995), 269.

11 MI/IV Aline Berlin, 11.10.89.

12 IB to R.B. Muller, 2.12.52.

13 IB to A. Kallin, 13.1.54; see also IB to Shirley Anglesey, 3.1.54: 'I was absolutely devoted to him and don't quite realise that I shall never see him again.' IB to Noel Annan, 13.1.54: '. . . he was an innocent, youthful, elegant, agreeable, civilised, mild and pure-hearted man whose society I loved and whom I loved as a kind of younger brother.' IB to Irving Singer, 4.1.54: 'it is a strange moment when one is suddenly promoted to the senior generation, one has to look after rather than be looked after'. IB to Mary Fisher, 13.1.54: 'He was so very innocent, young, elegant in habits of mind, fastidiously dressed, and knew neither what life nor dying was like.'

14 IB to R. B. Muller, 14.2.54.

15 IB to Alice James, 22.12.53.

16 IB to Aline Halban, 20.4.54; MI/IV IB, 4.1.89.

17 MI/IV IB, 4.1.89.

18 MI/IV Aline Berlin, 11.10.89.

19 M. Berlin to John Sparrow, 28.2.56.

20 MI/IV Aline Berlin, 11.10.89.

21 IB to Mrs Irving Singer, 9.8.55: 'I admire the French and am delighted to be in their country. I think every face is intelligent, full of life, individual, exactly what human beings are intended to be. In fact they are more like human beings as described both in works of philosophy and fiction than anyone else. And yet to live among them I think absolutely impossible. They are too unspontaneous, too buttoned up and ladle out their emotions by the thimble full.'

22 MI/IV Richard Wollheim; see also R. Wollheim to H. Hardy, 29.5.92.

23 IB to Arthur Schlesinger, 2.5.55: 'Picasso was quite funny about how it was that every time he was invited to Moscow he suggested that he might open an exhibition of his own works there and how this always brought the invitation to an abrupt end. He is perfectly independent, his communism is not really relevant to anything, and it is a pleasure to be in his society. He belongs ultimately to the same type of

humanity as Casals, Toscanini and, despite his silliness, Einstein. The head and face are very moving, but then as Edmund Wilson once severely informed me, I am a hero worshipper and my remarks about persons whom I choose to worship are not to be believed.'

24 IB to M. Berlin, 19.4.55.

25 IB to Hamilton Fish Armstrong, 23.12.54.

26 IB to M. Berlin, undated, 5.55; see also IB, 'Generalissimo Stalin and the Art of Government', 197–214.

27 See Leo Strauss, 'Relativism', in *The Rebirth of Classical Political Rationalism: An Introduction to the Thought of Leo Strauss*, essays and lectures by Leo Strauss, ed. Thomas L. Pangle (Chicago, 1989), 13–26, esp. 13–18.

28 IB to Arthur Schlesinger, undated, 1955?

29 IB to M. Berlin, 3.11.55, 20.11.55.

30 IB to Aline Berlin, undated, 10–11.55.

31 IB to Marion Frankfurter, 13.8.54.

15. FAME, 1957–63

1 IB to Marie Berlin, 8.58.

2 IB to Peter Halban, 8.6.61, 5.10.62, 25.10.62.

3 IB to T.S. Eliot, 21.6.57; Harold Macmillan to IB, 13.5.57; MI/IV IB, 13.4.89, for his mother's reaction.

4 IB to Mary Fisher, 20.6.57; M. Berlin to J. Sparrow, 18.7.57; IB to Morton White, 19.7.57: '. . . the Prime Minister was dispensing patronage to people who entertain or amuse him in one fashion or another. Which may indeed be true, for the reason for this "elevation" is genuinely obscure to me as to others.'

5 Patricia de Bendern to IB, undated, 6.57.

6 IB to Shirley Anglesey, 13.7.57.

7 Robert Kee, 'Eternal Oxford', *Picture Post*, 25.10.50: 'Fat, animated, forty, swollen with sedentary delight at the miracles and absurdities of this persisting world, he regarded us and our assignment with benevolent horror.'

8 IB to Ved Mehta, 17.1.63; IB to the Editor, *Sunday Times*, 7.11.66; Kenneth Rose to IB, 20.11.64; William Shawn to IB, 4.1.65; see also Robert Craft to IB, 24.1.64, agreeing to withdraw a published diary entry with derogatory remarks about IB; see also Ved Mehta, *Fly and the Fly-Bottle* (London, 1963).

9 See IB, 'Jewish Slavery and Emancipation', *Jewish Chronicle*, 21.9.51, 28.9.51, 5.10.51, 12.10.51.

10 MI/IV Robert Silvers, 1997.

11 MI/IV G. A. [Jerry] Cohen, 1998.

12 IB to Oxford University Registrar, 5.2.57; Richard Pares to Registrar, 14.2.57; Charles Webster to Registrar, 10.2.57; Gilbert Ryle to Registrar, 28.2.57; Registrar to IB, 12.3.57. Oxford University Archives.

13　Edmund Ions, 'Isaiah Berlin: Lectures and Graduate Classes at Oxford, c. 1957–1964', mss., Berlin Archive, Wolfson College, 2–3; Peter Jay to IB, 3.6.87.

14　IB to Marc Raeff, 12.3.58.

15　IB to Anna Kallin, 25.9.58: 'I am in my usual state of despair on the subject which will not be unfamiliar to you, this is re: the inaugural lecture. This time from far graver intellectual causes than before, i.e. that I no longer know the truth and think I shall utter not platitudes but confusions and falsehoods.'

16　IB to Richard Wollheim, 13.10.58.

17　**4E**, 166; Alsop, *To Marietta from Paris* (London, 1976), 331, for an account of listening to the lecture.

18　**PSM**, 202.

19　**PSM** 197.

20　**PSM**, 239.

21　M. White to IB, 17.3.58; IB to White, 6.5.58.

22　IB, 'From Hope and Fear Set Free', in **PSM**, 91–118.

23　**PSM**, 242.

24　IB to Stephen Spender, 18.11.58: 'To feed and clothe people may be more important than to liberate them, and to talk about freedom to the naked and the starving may be frivolous and heartless, but this doesn't seem to me to alter the fact that freedom, at least in one of its political senses, is freedom from interference; and the fact that other values may be more important, and incompatible with this – say love or equality or fraternity or friendly co-operation, or all the things that people like Rousseau and G.D.H. Cole believe in (for all their talk about liberty they prefer these warm-hearted and cosy things to liberty, which is not particularly warm and not at all cosy) – does not make liberty identical with them.'

25　Kennan to IB, 5.3.59.

26　Bloom to IB, 16.5.59.

27　IB to S. Lukes, 4.4.63; IB to Bernard Crick, undated, 1966; see also IB to Stephen Spender, 18.11.58.

28　Karl Popper to IB, 17.2.59.

29　IB to Karl Popper, 26.3.58; Popper to IB, 21.3.59.

30　Charles Taylor, 'What's Wrong with Negative Liberty', in Alan Ryan (ed.), *The Idea of Freedom* (Oxford, 1979), 75–195; see also IB, Introduction to James Tully (ed.), *Philosophy in an Age of Pluralism: The Philosophy of Charles Taylor in Question* (Cambridge, 1994), 1–3.

31　A. Blunt to IB, undated, 1956; for Guy Burgess' 'greeting' to Berlin, see Roy Harrod to IB, 1.4.58.

32　IB to unknown correspondent, 22.2.62.

33　IB to Violet Bonham Carter, 10.1.57.

34　IB, 'The Silence in Russian Culture', *Foreign Affairs*, 36 (1957), 1–24; 'Four Weeks in the Soviet Union', unpublished typrescript, Berlin Archive, Wolfson College.

35　**PI**, 184–7.

36　IB to Hamish Hamilton, 5.10.56; IB to Stephen Spender, 18.10.57.

37　IB to Edmund Wilson, 17.12.57; IB to Mark Bonham Carter, 15.11.57; IB to David

Astor, 27.10.58; IB to James Billington, 25.11.58; IB to A. Kallin, 13.10.58; IB to N. Nabokov, 2.4.59.

38 IB to R.B. Muller, 18.6.58; see also Lord Dacre to MI, 6.2.98.

39 MI/IV IB, 5.9.94, MI/IV Aline Berlin, 1996; Dalos, *The Guest From the Future*, ch. 6.

40 MI/IV Harry Shukman, 1995; Haight, *Anna Akhmatova*; Anatoly Nayman, *Remembering Anna Akhmatova* (London, 1989), 98.

41 IB to Jean Floud, 31.7.75.

42 IB to Philip Toynbee, 24.1.58.

43 IB to Stephen Spender, 11.11.60: 'I do not see how one can sign a document supporting a pro-FLN manifesto, if, in fact, one thinks that the consequences of their success, if carried out by methods which they are employing, would be worse than even the horrible present situation. I could not have signed the manifesto for Lenin, or Bela Kun or the Jewish terrorists either.'

44 IB to Stephen Spender, 11.11.60; IB to Ignazio Silone, 2.11.60; Silone to IB, 8.11.69; Silone and Chiaromonte to IB, 2.1.61.

45 MI/IV IB, undated.

46 IB to Kenneth Tynan, 1.5.61; Tynan to IB, 8.5.61.

47 Perry Anderson, 'Components of the National Culture', *New Left Review*, 50 (July–August 1968), 3–57, esp. 25–8; IB's reaction to Anderson is in IB to Anna Kallin, 1.4.69.

48 IB to J.S. Fulton, 4.4.63; *Black Dwarf*, 14.2.69; IB to Tamara Deutscher, 2.6.69; IB's opinion of Deutscher is in IB to David Astor, 13.5.58.

49 R.H. Crossman to IB, 5.2.63; IB to Crossman, 11.2.63 and 6.4.63. He cited Tawney with approval in 'Two Concepts', **PSM**, 240.

50 IB to E.H. Carr, 3.7.61: 'I know of no historians who do not in fact, either by commission or by omission, pass moral judgments: after all, you yourself identify some forces or persons as progressive, others as futile or troublesomely reactionary – your evaluation of Lenin ... I was really not trying to urge people to moralise, so much as telling them that they cannot help it in any case ...'.

51 IB, 'What is History?', *Listener*, 65 (1961), 877, 1048–9; E.H. Carr, *What is History?* (London, 1962); IB, 'Mr Carr's Big Battalions', review of E.H. Carr, *What is History?*, *New Statesman*, 63 (January–June 1962), 15–16. See also IB to E.H. Carr, 3.7.61, 31.1.62; IB to Hugh Trevor Roper, 6.3.62; IB to Morton White, 15.1.62.

52 IB to Clarissa Eden, 1.11.56; for his change of mind, see IB to Violet Bonham Carter, 10.1.57; see also IB to Michel Strauss, 8.11.56.

53 Robert Rhodes James, *Anthony Eden* (London, 1987), 552; MI/IV IB, undated.

54 IB to David Ben Gurion, 23.1.59; also IB, 'Memories of Brief Meetings with Ben Gurion', *Jewish Quarterly*, 333 (1986).

55 IB to David Ben Gurion, 23.1.59, Ben Gurion Archive, Beersheba, Israel.

56 Robert Craft to IB, 26.9.58, informing IB that Craft had given Stravinsky IB's 'Marx, Hedgehog and Fox and Historical Inevitability'. Craft to IB, 17.11.58; IB to Igor Stravinsky, 21.9.58.

57 IB to R.B. Muller, 17.11.58.

58 IB to Shirley Anglesey, 27.4.79.

59 IB to Robert Craft, 7.11.61, 28.12.61, 12.1.62.

60 IB to R.B. Muller, 20.10.61; Robert Craft, *Chronicle of a Friendship, 1948–1971* (London, 1972), 122–3, 223–5.

61 IB to Nicolas Nabokov, 7.9.63, 20.8.64; IB to Robert Craft, 10.9.64.

62 Edmund Wilson, *The Sixties: The Last Journal*, ed. L. Dabney (New York, 1993), 5.

63 Stephen Spender, *Journals, 1939–1983* (London 1985), 274.

64 Arthur Schlesinger, 'Oral History Interview with Sir Isaiah Berlin', 12.4.65, J.F. Kennedy Library; see also IB to Bertell Ollman, 3.12.62; IB to Aline Berlin, 17.10.62.

65 IB to Aline Berlin, 17.10.62.

66 IB to Aline Berlin, 17.10.62; see also S.M. Alsop, *To Marietta from Paris* for another view of the Kennedy-Bohlen dinner.

67 IB to Aline Berlin, 30.10.62.

68 IB to Noel Annan, 6.12.62.

69 MI/IV IB and Aline Berlin, 1995–6; IB to Aline Berlin, 30.10.62; see also IB to Maurice Bowra, 27.10.62. The talk at the White House is reprinted in revised form as 'Artistic Commitment: A Russian Legacy', in **SR**, 194–231.

70 IB to Robert Oppenheimer, 4.12.62.

71 MI/IV IB, 1989.

16. LIBERAL AT BAY, 1963–71

1 **RR**, Lecture 2, 28–30; delivered as 'Sources of Romantic Thought', since the hero of Saul Bellow's *Herzog* (1964) is struggling unsuccessfully with a course of lectures entitled 'The Roots of Romanticism'. Henry Hardy's publication of the lectures in 1999 will restore the original, more resonant title.

2 **RR**, 82.

3 **RR**, 182–7.

4 MI/IV Philippe Halban, 3.98.

5 Henry Hardy, 'Broadcasts by Isaiah Berlin', Berlin Archive, Wolfson College, item 33.

6 IB to R.H. Crossman, 31.1.63.

7 IB to Jean Floud, 5.7.68; see also IB to Jean Floud, undated (August 1967): '. . . I always want everybody to be satisfied: the wolf, as the Russian proverb says, to be satisfied and yet the sheep to remain uneaten: which, I daresay, cannot be done in this world . . .'

8 **CTH**, 191.

9 **CTH**, 193–4.

10 **CTH**, 179–80.

11 **CTH**, 121.

12 MI/IV IB, 1.1.90; see also IB to MI, 7.6.91: 'I do not regard the Nazis as, in my and

your sense, outside the pale; some of them, perhaps, but not Nazis as such, not moral idiots, not pathological murderers, pathological torturers as some of Stalin's and Hitler's people certainly either were or became. But – as you yourself say – I regard them as people trapped by emotions which are universal – namely, nationalism – driven to the point of pathological extreme; but still not inhuman; and fed by empirical nonsense, but intelligible nonsense, just false and false in a way that indicates a profound misunderstanding of life in general – but still not inhuman.' See Michael Ignatieff, 'Understanding Fascism', in A. and E. Margalit (eds), *Isaiah Berlin*, 135–46.

13 **CTH**, 203.
14 **CTH**, 204.
15 IB, 'The Pursuit of the Ideal', in **CTH**, 17.
16 MI/IV Larry Siedentop, 1994.
17 IB to Jean Floud, 16.8.68.
18 IB to Norman Birnbaum, 5.12.59.
19 IB to Richard Pipes, 13.9.67.
20 MI/IV IB, 1989.
21 IB to J.V. Stephenson, 21.1.63.
22 IB, 'Georges Sorel', in **AC**, 328.
23 **AC**, 330.
24 Maurice Cranston, 'Herbert Marcuse', *Encounter*, 32, March 1969, 38–50.
25 IB to Jean Floud, 8.3.69; see also IB to Gershom Scholem, 18.2.72.
26 IB to Bernard Crick, 4.11.63: 'for when I met her in 1942, her fanatical Jewish nationalism which has now turned into its opposite was I remember too much for me'.
27 IB, 'Between Philosophy and the History of Ideas, a conversation with Steven Lukes', Berlin Archive, Wolfson College, 43: 'In so extreme a situation, no act by the victims can (pace Miss Arendt) be condemned. Whatever is done must be regarded as fully justified. It is inexpressible arrogance on the part of those who have never been placed in so appalling a situation to pass judgment on the decisions and actions of those who have. Praise and blame are out of place – normal moral categories do not apply. All four choices – heroic martyrdom, and the saving of innocent lives at the expense of those of others, can only be applauded.'
28 See Jahanbegloo, *Conversations with Isaiah Berlin*, 81–5; see also 'IB in Conversation with Ramin Jahanbegloo', Oxford, 7.7.97, unpublished interview, Berlin Archive, Wolfson College; see also *Between Friends: The Correspondence of Mary McCarthy and Hannah Arendt, 1949–1975* (London, 1995), 4.10.53, 14; Elisabeth Young-Bruehl, *Hannah Arendt: For Love of the World* (New Haven, 1982), 343–7.
29 IB to Bernard Williams, 19.2.69; see also IB to Gerry Cohen, 10.2.69.
30 IB to Maurice Bowra, 2.4.69.
31 IB to Anna Kallin, 1.10.68.
32 IB to Jean Floud, 28.3.69.

33 IB in Cecil Woolf and John Bagguley (eds), *Authors Take Sides on Vietnam* (New York, 1967), 20–1.

34 IB to John Roberts, 21.4.70.

35 IB to McGeorge Bundy, 15.10.69.

36 IB to Franco Venturi, 28.11.69.

37 IB to A. Walicki, 26.6.70; see also A. Walicki's 'Commentary to a Selection of Isaiah Berlin's Letters', published in Polish in the journal *Res Publica* (1995).

38 IB to Noel Annan, 13.5.70: 'I propose to deal with Turgenev as a man who got many more kicks than ha'pence for walking a causeway between Scylla (Dostoyevsky and squires he liked best) and Charybdis (bearded students and London and Paris revolutionaries he admired and was privately and reasonably liked by) . . .'.

39 IB, 'Fathers and Children: Turgenev and the Liberal Predicament', in **RT**, 263.

40 Adam Smith, *The Theory of Moral Sentiments*, ed. D.D. Raphael and A.L. Macfie (Oxford, 1976); see also Istvan Hont and Michael Ignatieff (eds), *Wealth and Virtue: The Shaping of Political Economy in the Scottish Enlightenment* (Cambridge, 1983).

41 IB to Jean Floud, 27.8.69: 'I wish I had not inherited my father's timorous, rabbity nature! I can be brave, but oh after what appallingly superhuman struggles with cowardice!'

42 IB, 'Introduction' to Ivan Turgenev, 'A Fire at Sea', in *First Love and Other Stories*, 243.

17. WOLFSON, 1966–75

1 Kenneth Wheare to IB, 6.11.65.

2 *Wolfson College: The Early Years* (Oxford, 1979) (Wolfson College Website edition); MI/IV Michael Brock, 1997.

3 MI/IV IB, 18.5.89.

4 MI/IV Jean Floud, 1995.

5 MI/IV IB, 1989; see also IB to John Sparrow, 21.11.53.

6 MI/IV Raymond Hoffenberg, 19.7.91, Berlin Archive, Wolfson College.

7 IB to K. Wheare, 19.11.65; IB to Wheare, 30.11.65; Wheare to IB, 6.11.65.

8 Alan Bullock to IB, 1.12.65; Herbert Hart to IB, 18.12.65; MI/IV William Hayter, 1994; W. Hayter to IB, 1.7.66; Marcus Dick to IB, 14.12.65.

9 IB to Maurice Bowra, 3.12.65; see also IB to K. Wheare, 19.11.65; MI/IV IB, 1989.

10 IB to John Sparrow, 14.3.64; see also IB to Sparrow, 12.11.65; IB to H.G. Nicholas, 13.7.65; see also John Lowe, *The Warden: A Portrait of John Sparrow* (London, 1998), 193–212.

11 IB and Stuart Hampshire, 'Reminiscences'; see also IB to John Sparrow, 17.1.64 and 12.65, undated.

12 *Report of the Commission of Inquiry* (The Franks Report), 2 vols (Oxford, 1966), i. 49 (para. 96); MI/IV Jean Floud, 1994.

13 IB to Marcus Dick, 22.12.65.

14   IB to Pat Utechin, 6.2.66.
15   IB to J.V. Stephenson, 21.1.63.
16   Report of Iffley College, 1965–6 (Oxford, 1966); see also John Dancy, *Walter Oakeshott: A Diversity of Gifts* (London, 1995), 258–9.
17   *Wolfson College: The Early Years*, 'The New Buildings', 1.
18   IB to Joe Alsop, 13.3.66.
19   IB to Maurice Bowra, 20.1.63; by April 1966 he had been converted to Bundy's virtues. See IB to Joe Alsop, 20.4.66.
20   MI/IV IB, 1989; IB/IV Hoffenberg, 1991.
21   M. Bundy to L. Wolfson, 20.4.66.
22   M. Bundy to IB, 18.2.66.
23   MI/IV IB, 1989.
24   IB/IV Hoffenberg.
25   MI/IV IB, 18.5.89.
26   L. Wolfson to IB, 4.5.66; on Crosland's attitude, see also THES, 3.1.97.
27   IB to Joe Alsop, 20.4.66: 'Solly was like the villain of the piece: violently hostile to the scheme, pathologically opposed to Oxford and Cambridge, not very keen on me.'
28   MI/IV Michael Brock, 1998; Solly Zuckerman, 'From Apes to Warlords (1978), ch. 5. (London, 1988).
29   IB to R. von Hofmannsthal, 16.4.66.
30   IB to Oliver Franks, 9.5.66.
31   IB to Provost Florey, 19.4.66; MI/IV IB, 1989.
32   MI/IV IB, 18.5.89; IB/IV Hoffenberg, 1991.
33   IB to Joe Alsop, 20.4.66.
34   MI/IV IB, 18.5.89; IB/IV Hoffenberg, 1991.
35   Report of Iffley College, 1965–6; Hugh Trevor Roper to IB, 29.6.66; IB to Anthony Crosland, 13.6.66; Maurice Bowra to IB, 18.5.66; IB to H.G. Nicholas, 25.7.66.
36   I am grateful to Polly Friedhoff, St Antony's College, for this information, 20.5.98.
37   IB to Sylvester Gates, 25.7.66; *Wolfson College: The Early Years*.
38   IB to Philip Johnson, 7.6.67; Wolfson College Record, 1992–3, 'From the Archives: The Search for Architects for a New College, 1967,' 43–63.
39   Michael Brock, 'Nine Years with Isaiah Berlin', *Oxford Magazine*, Michaelmas 1997, 8th week, 13.
40   Wolfson College Record, 1992–3; IB, 'Memorandum of a Visit to Cambridge', 27.2.67.
41   Wolfson College Record, 1992–3, 56–8.
42   Wolfson College Record, 1992–3, 60.
43   *Wolfson College: The Early Years*.
44   IB, 'Notes on the Foundation of Wolfson College', *Lycidas* (Wolfson College magazine), 1 (1973), 2–4.
45   Roger Hausheer, 'Some Memories of Early Wolfson', Wolfson College Record, 1991–2, 36–44.

46 IV/IB in *THES*, 14.7.72.

47 IB to Leonard Wolfson, 3.5.71.

48 MI/IV Michael Brock, 12.97.

49 IB to unknown correspondent, 13.9.66.

50 MI/IV IB, 1989.

51 Brock, 'Nine Years with Isaiah Berlin', 13.

52 MI/IV Aline Berlin, 1995; MI/IV Michael Brock, 26.6.96. Also M. Argyle, 'Isaiah Berlin and the Creation of Wolfson College', unpublished talk, Wolfson College, 20.6.98.

53 IB to Shirley Anglesey, 6.6.71; IB to Noel Annan, 3.6.71: 'I am, I really am, perfectly clear that my attributes have been *wildly* overestimated . . .'; IB to Arthur Calder Marshall, 7.6.71.

54 See IB, 'Notes on the Foundation of Wolfson College', 2–4.

55 MI/IV Michael Brock, 1996.

56 IB to Hamilton Fish Armstrong, 13.6.72: 'she is in her ninety-third year, has had a kind of stroke, and is now in what doctors rather frigidly call the "pre-terminal stage". In short, she recognises only me, Aline, the doctor and one of the nurses.'

57 MI/IV IB, 1988–9; IB to John Sparrow, 16.2.74.

58 IB to Jean Floud, 16.2.74; IB to Herbert Hart, 15.2.74.

59 IB to Stuart Hampshire, 23.2.74; see also IB to Sheila Sokolov Grant, 19.2.74.

60 IB to Noel Annan, 21.2.74: 'But it is oneself one grieves over: the inability now to use certain words, allusions, jokes – something which no one now will understand (this is no doubt what loneliness is – that nobody understands what one wishes to say) – in my case a vast Russian-Jewish world has moved off – the bridge is destroyed – it is visible but not visible . . .'.

61 Martin Gilbert to IB, 13–14.2.74.

18. RETROSPECT, 1975–97

1 Speech of Harold Macmillan at the opening of Wolfson College, *Lycidas*, 3 (1974–5), 9–10.

2 See IB, Introduction to *Derek Hill: Portraits* (London, 1978).

3 IB, Presidential Address, *Proceedings of the British Academy*, 61 (1975), 78–9.

4 IB, Presidential Address, 77.

5 IB, Presidential Address, *Proceedings of the British Academy*, 64 (1978), 3.

6 IB, 'Performances memorable – and not so memorable', *Opera*, 26 (1975), 116–20. For an example of his involvement in Covent Garden, see IB to Clive Priestley, 10.7.83.

7 IB to unknown correspondent, 20.11.84.

8 IB to Jean Floud, 12.8.75.

9 IB to Richard Pipes, 24.11.70.

10 IB to Morton White, 16.3.77.

11 IB to James Billington, 20.12.88; Library of Congress *Information Bulletin*, 28.11.88, 13.2.89.

12 IB to Morton White, 1.10.86.

13 IB to Bernard Crick, 1.11.79; IB to J. Alsop, 2.2.81, 3.3.81.

14 IB to Joe Alsop, 2.2.81.

15 IB to unknown correspondent, 20.11.84.

16 'Headlines and Footnotes', *British Book News*, January 1978, 15.

17 Maurice Bowra to Noel Annan, 1971; see Noel Annan, 'A Man I Loved', in H. Lloyd-Jones (ed.), *Maurice Bowra: A Celebration* (London, 1974), 53.

18 See IB, *The Roots of Romanticism* (forthcoming, London, 1999), editor's preface.

19 Henry Hardy, 'Isaiah Berlin Papers Project: Summary of Progress, Sept. 1991–July 1992', 2.

20 Henry Hardy, 'Isaiah Berlin Papers Project: Summary of Progress, November 1990–August 1991', 3.

21 Alan Ryan (ed.), *The Idea of Freedom: Essays in Honour of Isaiah Berlin* (Oxford, 1979); A. and E. Margalit (eds), *Isaiah Berlin*.

22 MI/IV IB, 1989.

23 MI/IV IB, 1989.

24 IB to Joe Alsop, 18.4.88.

25 IB, 'The Pursuit of the Ideal', in **CTH**.

26 Arnoldo Momigliano, 'On the Pioneer Trail', *NYRB*, 11.11.76; see also IB, 'Note on Alleged Relativism in Eighteenth-Century European Thought', in **CTH**.

27 **CTH**, 11–12.

28 **CTH**, 12.

29 **CTH**, 13.

30 See the quotation from IB that begins Eric Hobsbawm, *The Age of Extremes* (London, 1994), preface. Also MI/IV IB, 'The Late Show', BBC2, 11.97.

31 See Henry Hardy, 'Writings about Isaiah Berlin', unpublished handlist, Berlin Archive, Wolfson College, 24.11.94.

32 See James Fitzjames Stephen, *Liberty, Equality, Fraternity* (1873) (Indianapolis, 1993), 93ff, 118, 169, 172, 174, 180, 206, 225. (Reference established by Henry Hardy.)

33 Gray, *Berlin*, ch. 6.

34 See Hardy, 'Writings about Isaiah Berlin', 24.11.94. See especially Claude Galipeau, *Isaiah Berlin's Liberalism* (Oxford, 1994); see also J. Steinberg, 'Post-Enlightenment Philosophy and Liberal Universalism in the Political Thought of Isaiah Berlin and Richard Rorty', unpublished D. Phil thesis, Oxford University, 1998.

35 MI/IV Pat Utechin; also IB to H.R. Hoetink, 15.6.83; IB to Beata Polanowska-Sygulska, 17.7.97, 24.2.86.

36 IB to Mary Bennett, 9.8.74.

37 Stephen Spender to IB, 14.7.93; the poem was reprinted in the *Sunday Telegraph*, 18.7.93.

38 IB to Natasha Spender, 1.8.95.

39 MI/IV Noel Annan, 1998.

40 IB to Morton White, 21.5.91.
41 On nationalism, see MI/IV IB, 'The Late Show', BBC2, 5.2.92; IB, 'Nationalism: Past Neglect and Present Power', in **AC**, 333–56.
42 MI/IV Alfred and Reni Brendel, 1998.

19. EPILOGUE

1 MI/IV IB, 1.11.90, 12
2 IB, 'The Three Strands in My Life', in **PI**, 255–61.
3 **CTH**, 2.
4 IB to Chimen Abramsky, 5.7.78; IB to Walter Eytan, 11.4.80: '. . . almost no Gentile (it seems to me) anywhere, and few Jews (at least in this country) can any longer offer unqualified support to Israel under its present government.'
5 MI/IV Jerry Cohen, 1998.
6 IB to I. Jakobovits, 27.7.96.
7 MI/IV Peter Oppenheimer, 1998.
8 MI/IV Claus Moser, 1997.
9 IB to Fred Worms, 24.2.92.
10 IB to Peter Oppenheimer, 13.10.81.
11 IB to Fred Worms, 3.12.92: 'I believe that Abraham fully believed that if need be he had to sacrifice his son, and that that is the whole point of the "trial" – that what the Lord commands has to be done no matter how deeply it offends against natural morality.' I am grateful to Leon Wieseltier for pointing out the connection between Berlin's aesthetic respect for *terribilità* in art and his respect for the nature of religious commands.
12 IB to Joe Alsop, 30.9.81; MI/IV IB, 1989–90.
13 Anna Howard, *Breaking the Taboo* (London, 1996), 31–7.
14 MI/IV Pat Utechin, 1997.
15 MI/IV IB, 11.10.89, 6; Freud's unfinished portrait of Berlin is now in the possession of Aline Berlin.
16 MI/IV Bernard Williams, 1998; Reni Brendel, 1998.
17 IB to Anatoly Nayman, 31.10.97; see also his *Remembering Anna Akhmatova*.
18 MI/IV Avishai and Edna Margalit, 1997. The statement, 'Israel and the Palestinians', dated 16.10.97, was approved for publication by IB on 5.11.97, and published in Israeli newspapers on 7.11.97.
19 See IB/IV with Steven Lukes in the *Sunday Telegraph*, 21.9.97; also *Prospect*, 10.97.
20 Tony Blair to IB, 23.10.97.
21 For a reaction from the right, see Paul Johnson, 'A Low Risk Philosopher', *New York Times*, 12.11.97; for a reaction from the left, see Christopher Hitchens, 'Farewell to Berlin', *The Nation*, 19.11.97.
22 *Daily Telegraph*, 10.11.97.
23 Katharine Graham at the British Embassy, Washington, 28.1.98.

24 Noel Annan, 'Address at Hampstead Synagogue', 14.1.98.
25 Bernard Williams, Avishai Margalit and Stuart Hampshire, Sheldonian Theatre, 21.3.98.
26 MI/IV IB, BBC2, 24.11.97.

Index

Index